MASTERING
REAL ESTATE
MATHEMATICS
A SELF-INSTRUCTIONAL TEXT

MASTERING
REAL ESTATE
MATHEMATICS
A SELF-INSTRUCTIONAL TEXT

William L. Ventolo, Jr. • Wellington J. Allaway • G. E. Irby

Fifth Edition

REAL ESTATE EDUCATION COMPANY
a division of Longman Financial Services Institute, Inc.

While a great deal of care has been taken to provide accurate and current information, the ideas, suggestions, general principles and conclusions presented in this book are subject to local, state and federal laws and regulations, court cases and any revisions of same. The reader is thus urged to consult legal counsel regarding any points of law—this publication should not be used as a substitute for competent legal advice.

© 1974, 1977, 1979, 1985, 1989 by Longman Group USA Inc.

Published by Real Estate Education Company
a division of Longman Financial Services Institute, Inc.

Printed in the United States of America

89 90 91 10 9 8 7 6 5 4 3 2 1

Library of Congress Cataloging-in-Publication Data

Ventolo, William L.
    Mastering real estate mathematics.

    Includes index.
    1. Business mathematics—Real estate business—
Programmed instruction.   I. Allaway, Wellington J.
II. Irby, G. E.   III. Title.
HF5716.R4V46   1989   333.33'01'5121   88–32383
ISBN 0–88462–813–2

Executive Editor: Richard A. Hagle
Sponsoring Editor: Cheryl D. Wilson
Project Editor: Jack L. Kiburz
Manager, Composition Services: Gayle Sperando

Contents

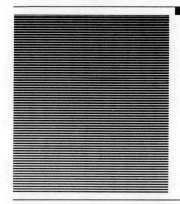

Preface

The people involved in the real estate business—brokers, salespeople, owners, managers, investors and others—all need a great deal of specialized knowledge. Basically, they need to know the ways in which real estate may be defined and the methods by which it may be owned or financed. But they also need to know how to compute the figures that underlie most real estate transactions: costs, values, income, expenses, profits, taxes, and many variations and innovations.

This book was written to assist the interested real estate person in learning to be at home with figures. Whether readers are new to or experienced in the applied use of mathematics, the following pages will serve to sharpen their skills by carefully explaining the kinds of problems encountered in real estate activity.

The authors are grateful for the time and personal resources contributed by: **Richard O. Bomhard,** Department Chairman, Real Estate Management/Marketing Technology, Columbus Technical Institute, Columbus, OH; **Charles P. Cartee,** PhD, CRA, Parham Bridges Chair of Real Estate, University of Southern Mississippi, Hattiesburg, MS; **Lu Mikeal Fischbeck,** Lecturer, Catonsville Community College, Catonsville, MD; **Ronald Hutchinson,** Coldwell Banker Russell T. Baker, Inc., Saverna Park, MD; **Joseph N. Irwin,** Houston Community College, Houston, TX; **Earl Jeter,** Parkland College, Champaign, IL; **Ronald W. Mahler,** Broker, ERA-First City Realtors, San Antonio, TX; **Edward P. Norris,** Director, Norris School of Real Estate, Albuquerque, NM; **Nancy Dagget White,** Mississippi County Community College, Blytheville, AR.

The following have given permission to use the forms reprinted in this book: Columbus Board of REALTORS®—Statement of Settlement and Worksheet (Ch.14); Stewart Title Company, a subsidiary of Commonwealth Land Title Insurance Company—Settlement Statement and Disbursements Sheet (Ch.14).

The authors wish to thank the staff of Real Estate Education Company for their exacting attention to the preparation of *Mastering Real Estate Mathematics*.

ABOUT THE AUTHORS

William L. Ventolo, Jr., received his master's degree in psychology from the University of Pittsburgh. He has written many textbooks and industrial training manuals, including *Fundamentals of Real Estate Appraisal, Residential Construction,* and *Principles of Accounting.* He resides in Sarasota, Florida.

Wellington J. Allaway was with the Northern Trust Company, Chicago, for 45 years, serving as real estate manager and residential loan officer. His experience also includes teaching various real estate courses, including mathematics for the Realtors' Institute of Illinois, and writing several textbooks, including *Modern Real Estate Practice.* In addition, Allaway was an item writer for Educational Testing Service and American College Testing Service. He resides in Oak Park, Illinois.

G. E. Irby is a Broker-Owner of the G. E. Irby Company, REALTORS®, of Hurst, Texas. He is the supervisor of the non-credit real estate program for the Tarrant County Junior College District and served as chairman of the REALTOR®–Lawyer Committee for the Texas Association of REALTORS®. Irby holds a BS degree in physics and math. He is the author of a handbook on the Texas promulgated real estate contract forms and a textbook on Texas earnest money contract law, both published by the Texas Association of REALTORS®. He is also the author of *Modern Real Estate Principles in Texas* and the co-author of *Texas Real Estate Law,* both published by Real Estate Education Company in Chicago. Since 1976, Irby has been a broker appointee of the Texas Real Estate Commission to Texas's Statutory Real Estate Broker–Lawyer Committee, which drafts the contract forms used in Texas. He is a frequent seminar speaker.

The term REALTOR® refers to a member of the National Association of REALTORS® who subscribes to its Code of Ethics.

Introduction:
How To Use This Book

BASIC MATH SKILLS

This textbook starts at a very basic math level. This is done deliberately in order to offer some relief to any persons who may experience anxiety in dealing with mathematical concepts. The early discussion of calculators in the Introduction is an effort to integrate a valuable math tool into the text, along with some basic math concepts. If calculators are new to you, these paragraphs should make their use easier.

This type of instructional book may be new to you. The subject matter has been broken down into a series of numbered exercises. By following the exercises, you can teach yourself the mathematics involved in real estate transactions. Additionally, it is designed to be augmented by classroom instruction.

The sequence of the exercises is important and designed to help you learn more efficiently. For that reason, you should not skip around in the book.

Almost every exercise presents a learning task that requires some response from you. You should have little difficulty arriving at each correct answer, provided you follow directions precisely, read the material, and work through the book with care.

This kind of book also provides you with immediate feedback by giving you the answers to the questions asked. These answers have been placed at the end of each chapter involved. The immediate feedback is an important part of the learning process and will enable you to determine readily how your learning is progressing.

Do not look at the correct answer until *after* you have recorded your own answer. If you look before answering, you will only impair your own learning. If you make an error, be sure you know *why* before continuing.

Finally, this text is designed to be used as a workbook. Work out each problem by writing your computations in the spaces provided. This helps both the student and the instructor when discussing the solutions.

Study Strategy

It seems appropriate to open our discussion of study strategy by a brief mention of a common experience among students of mathematics: math anxiety. Many people are intimidated by the anticipated difficulties of working mathematical problems, to the point that they become victims of stress, and needlessly so. This book does not provide a psychological analysis of this matter. Rather, we hope to set forth some principles that will help the students taking this course to feel more comfortable with math.

Anxiety about one's ability to perform mathematical calculations is very common. Even college mathematics majors often dread math examinations! If this is so, how can we effectively help people who have no special background in mathematics, who suddenly find that they need some basic math skills in order to pass a licensing examination or function more competently as a real estate licensee?

In their article, "Mastering Math Anxiety," Dr. William L. Boyd of Hardin Simmons University and Mrs. Elizabeth A. Cox of Howard Payne University offer several ideas:

1. Math anxiety is not an indication of inability. It may be more an indication of excessive concern over possible embarrassment in front of our peers, our instructors, our clients or our customers.
2. Aptitude in math is not necessarily something we are born with. Our aptitude may reflect our attitude rather than our genes. The old saw, "If you think you can or if you think you can't, you're right," certainly applies in this situation. Through practice and study, we can build our skills and our confidence.
3. Self-image can affect our performance in many areas, including math. Make a determined effort to develop your competency in math. If others expect you to fail, don't fall to the level of their expectations! Rather, rise to the level of your potential through a little extra effort.
4. Learn to congratulate yourself on your successes. When you arrive at a correct solution, make a point of giving yourself the credit for your success.[1]

The following are study strategies that will work to your benefit:

1. Take time to understand thoroughly just what is being asked. Consider the information given in the problem and decide how each portion relates to the solution. Careful and thoughtful reading will help you understand the problem.
2. Learn to discard those facts that have no bearing on the solution. You do this automatically in many areas of everyday life. Begin to practice this in math also, by evaluating each bit of information.
3. Make a special effort to be neat. Sloppy figures carelessly jotted down are an invitation to error.
4. Develop a systematic approach to problem solving. Consider each aspect of the problem in its proper place and do not jump to conclusions. It is better to write down each step in the solution, no matter how trivial it seems, than to rely on performing a calculation "in your head."
5. Learn to restate the problem in your own words. By doing this, you can remove many obstacles to a solution. In fact, once you state the problem correctly, you only need to perform the mechanics of the arithmetic accurately to arrive at the solution.
6. Form the habit of checking and double-checking your work. It is all too easy to make a mistake out of carelessness. If that error is not discovered, your solution will be flawed.
7. Request help when you need it. Don't hesitate to ask questions! Others who are puzzled by the same point as you are may be reluctant to say so. If you ask the question, you and the entire class benefit.
8. Learn to question the "reasonableness" of the solution. If the answer you have calculated seems unlikely, perhaps it is! Your common sense can often reveal an error due to carelessness.
9. Become proficient with your calculator. The calculator's accuracy helps ensure your good results. But never rely on the machine to do it all! Learn to make your own estimate and compare this with the results of the calculator. If the calculator's answer does not seem plausible, clear the display and work the problem again, making sure you enter the figures and operations correctly. The calculator does not replace you! But it is a wonderful tool to enhance your professionalism.

---

1. William L. Boyd and Elizabeth A. Cox, "Mastering Math Anxiety," *Real Estate Today* (March/April 1984): 41–43.

EXERCISES AND EXAMINATIONS

Each chapter concludes with a two-part Achievement Exercise. The first part consists of open-response questions that require you to work out calculations and supply an answer. The second section is a series of multiple-choice questions patterned after those found in state licensing examinations prepared by testing services and licensing commissions. Answers for the Achievement Exercise appear at the end of each chapter.

At the end of this book are two Final Examinations covering all of the material in the text. Again, the first is an open-response format and the second is multiple choice.

Answers to all examination questions are in the Answer Keys at the end of each exam. These solutions to the questions show the step-by-step mathematics.

LOCAL PRACTICES

Since this textbook is used nationally, some of the situations described may differ from practice in your local area. In these cases, your instructor may wish to skip certain portions of the textbook.

CALCULATORS

The popularity of hand-held calculators has increased as their cost has decreased. Their speed, accuracy and flexibility are distinct advantages to the real estate practitioner. They are highly recommended for use in the classroom, during examinations, and on the job. If you are not accustomed to using a calculator but want to learn how to do so, work out the text exercises on paper; then use the calculator to verify your answer. As you become more proficient in electronic calculations, you'll be able
to eliminate many longhand procedures, although you will still have to record your computations on paper as you proceed. In addition, a real estate licensee will appear more professional to both buyers and sellers as the use of a calculator is mastered. Most (if not all) states permit the use of a silent calculator on the licensing examination.

A calculator can be an invaluable aid in the practice of real estate, and there are many models by several manufacturers on the market. The least expensive are the so-called "four-function" calculators which merely add, subtract, multiply and divide. More sophisticated models have the ability to store and recall numbers in memory, which reduces the need to write down answers to be used in subsequent calculations. Still others compute percent directly, but the most sophisticated calculators have financial, statistical and engineering functions that easily can perform complex calculations. Even these are surprisingly inexpensive.

Logic Functions

Calculators can be divided into general types by the form of logic that they employ. Chain logic and algebraic logic are the most common types. The difference between these two types of logic is illustrated as follows.

Consider the calculation:

$$2 + 3 \times 4 = ?$$

If the numbers and arithmetic functions are entered into the calculator as shown above, the answer on the chain logic calculator will be 20, but on the algebraic logic calculator, the answer will be 14. The chain logic sees the data entered in the order that it is keyed in as:

$$2 + 3 = 5, \text{ then}$$
$$5 \times 4 = 20,$$

whereas the algebraic logic sees that data as *"My Dear Aunt Sally,"* for algebraic logic follows the order of *M*ultiplication, *D*ivision, *A*ddition and then *S*ubtraction:

$$3 \times 4 = 12, \text{ then}$$
$$12 + 2 = 14.$$

Some calculators use chain logic but employ something known as "reverse polish notation." One of these is the Hewlett-Packard, and there is no "=" key. In its place is an "ENTER" key. Certain Sharp calculator models also use reverse polish notation. Using the previous example of:

$$2 + 3 \times 4 = ?$$

the Hewlett-Packard keystrokes are:

$$\boxed{2}$$
$$\boxed{\text{ENTER}}$$
$$\boxed{3}$$
$$\boxed{+}$$
$$\boxed{4}$$
$$\boxed{\times}$$

with the answer being 20.

Data on other calculators are entered using chain logic, just as the user would write it, such as:

Press $\boxed{2}$
Press $\boxed{+}$
Press $\boxed{3}$
Press $\boxed{\times}$
Press $\boxed{4}$
Press $\boxed{=}$

Most calculators use chain logic, and all of the examples in this text are designed to fit that type. The user should also *thoroughly study the instructions furnished with the calculator.*

Four-Function versus Multi-Function Calculators

A basic four-function calculator will certainly be sufficient for this course, but if you plan to purchase a calculator, it is strongly recommended that you spend a few more dollars on one having the financial functions. This type of calculator can be easily identified by these additional keys:

$$\boxed{n}, \boxed{i}, \boxed{PMT}, \boxed{PV}, \boxed{FV}$$

where,

$\boxed{n}$ is the number of interest compounding periods;

$\boxed{i}$ is the amount of interest per compounding period;

$\boxed{PMT}$ is the payment;

$\boxed{PV}$ is the present value;

$\boxed{FV}$ is the future value.

The meanings of these terms and their uses are covered in the chapter on "Time Value of Money."

Rounds versus Truncates

Some calculators may display six, eight or ten digits, but regardless of the number, the calculator retains far more numbers than are displayed in a calculation. For example, if a calculator displays six digits, or single numbers, such as 123456, the calculator knows what follows the last digit, or single number, displayed. This last digit depends upon whether the calculator "rounds" or "truncates." Consider an answer of 123456.7. The answer displayed on a six-digit calculator will be 123457 for a calculator that "rounds" and 123456 for a calculator that "truncates."

"Rounds" means that if the next digit not displayed is *less than* 5, the last digit to be displayed remains the same. However, if the next digit not displayed is *greater than* 5, the last digit to be displayed will be *increased* or *rounded* up to the next larger digit.

"Truncates" means that regardless of the value of the next digit not displayed, the calculator merely *cuts off the display,* or "truncates," when its display capacity is full.

Whether your calculator rounds or truncates can make a difference in your answer when working with numbers having several digits. Therefore, if your answer in a complex calculation differs from your neighbor's by a few cents, do not worry about it. Furthermore, do not be concerned if your answers differ slightly from those in the book.

Greater calculator accuracy can be obtained if the answer is *left on the display* and the next calculation is performed by depressing keys rather than writing down the answer, clearing the calculator and re-entering that answer as the first step of the following calculation.

CALCULATOR PROBLEMS

At this point, try solving some simple problems with your calculator, to bolster your confidence. The keystrokes shown apply to any calculator except most models of the Hewlett-Packard and certain models of the Sharp line. Follow along with the steps shown for each if you need assistance.

1. Try adding 123 + 456.

    First, turn your calculator on. If your calculator has a "continuous memory," you may have to depress the "CLEAR" and the "CLEAR MEMORY" keys to be sure that no unwanted numbers are left in your calculator from a previous calculation.

Press	Display
1 then 2 then 3	123
+ (the plus, or addition, key)	123 (no change)
4 then 5 then 6	456
= (the equal sign key)	579 (the answer, or "sum")

2. Now, try this multiplication problem:

    123.45 times (or "×") 6.789

Press	Display
1 then 2 then 3 then . then 4 then 5	123.45

    Note: You *must* press the "period," or "decimal point," just as if it were a digit, or a single number, itself. Otherwise, the answer will not include the decimal point and will be *incorrect*.

Press	Display
× (the multiplication, or "times," key)	123.45 (no change)
6 then . then 7 then 8 then 9	6.789
= (equal sign)	838.1 (or 838.1020500)

3. Next, divide 56,789 by 1,234.

Press	Display
5 then 6 then 7 then 8 then 9	56,789 (Your calculator may not have the comma.)
÷ (the division key) (divided *by;* not into)	56,789
1 then 2 then 3 then 4	1,234
= (the equal sign key)	46.02
	(or 46.02025932)

4. Finally, subtract .0123 from 4.56.

Press	Display
4 then . then 5 then 6	4.56

Note: Because of the way the problem was stated, you must enter the last number, 4.56, first. This is because the calculator expects the number to be subtracted to be entered second.

Press	Display
— (the subtract, or "minus," key)	4.56
. then 0 then 1 then 2 then 3	.0123

Note: You *must* press the zero key. Disregard of it will result in the wrong answer. Zeros are digits and parts of numbers; do not skip them.

Press	Display
= (equal sign key)	4.55
	(or 4.547700000)

Remember the previous discussion of rounding or truncating.

Review of Basic Arithmetic Skills

INTRODUCTION

Many students using this text-workbook may find themselves in a math class after several years of doing other things, and it is to this group that this text is primarily addressed. Some students also have built up a fear of math over the years. It is hoped that the exercises in this text will eliminate those fears and give the student sufficient knowledge and self-confidence not only to pass a licensing examination, but also to function adequately in the field of real estate listing and sales.

ENTRY EVALUATION

Since readers will have varying amounts of knowledge and experience, the short test that follows will allow you to determine your familiarity with the material to be covered. Try all the problems before looking at the answers, which begin on page 17.

- What is the product of 1,234 times 5,678?

- How many acres are there in 4,356,000 square feet?

■   What is the answer to the following problem?

$$(5 \times 6) + (3 \times 4) - (6 \times 7) = ?$$

Perhaps a brief review of things you learned when you were first taught arithmetic will be helpful. One reason many people have trouble with number skills is that they do not practice neatness and legibility in working out the problems. For example, it is easier to make a mistake in adding these numbers

$12,345.67
89.10
5,432.08
76543

than it is to add the same numbers when care has been given to neatness and legibility:

$12,345.67
89.10
5,432.08
76,543.00

The importance here is to keep the decimal points in a straight vertical line and write each digit of each number directly beneath the one above it. This becomes even more important in multiplication and division. Imagine that your paper has vertical columns so that each number must be written in its proper place. (Note that the following number 1,234 uses the digits 1 and 2 and 3 and 4.)

```
                    4 . 6 0 1 2 9 6
      1,234 ) 5 , 6 7 8 . 0 0 0 0 0 0
              4 , 9 3 6
                  7 4 2 0
                  7 4 0 4
                      1 6 0 0
                      1 2 3 4
                        3 6 6 0
                        2 4 6 8
                          1 1 9 2 0
                          1 1 1 0 6
                              8 1 4 0
                              7 4 0 4
                                7 3 6
```

EXAMPLE: Now try a division problem as a way to refresh the skills you already have.

$$204\overline{)\,38{,}556}$$

$$
\begin{array}{r}
189 \\
204\overline{)\,38{,}556} \\
\underline{20\ 4} \\
18\ 15 \\
\underline{16\ 32} \\
1\ 836 \\
\underline{1\ 836} \\
0
\end{array}
$$

Next, check your answer of 189 in the foregoing problem. If you multiply 189 (called the "quotient") by the number 204 (called the "divisor"), you should obtain the number 38,556 (called the "dividend"), if the division answer is correct. Perform that multiplication in the following space:

$$
\begin{array}{r}
189 \\
\times\,204 \\
\hline
756 \\
3780 \\
\hline
38556
\end{array}
\qquad \text{OR} \qquad
\begin{array}{r}
189 \\
\times\,204 \\
\hline
756 \\
000 \\
378 \\
\hline
38556
\end{array}
$$

Remember that when adding figures (indicated by the "+" sign), always start with the right-hand column. When the sum of any vertical column is greater than 9, the extra 1, 2, etc. must be carried over to the top of the next column to the left and treated as if it were a part of that column, as in the following:

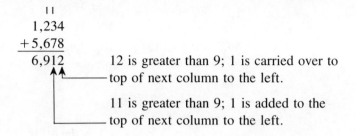

12 is greater than 9; 1 is carried over to top of next column to the left.

11 is greater than 9; 1 is added to the top of next column to the left.

In any large number, each digit represents some multiple of 1, 10, 100, 1,000, etc. To illustrate,

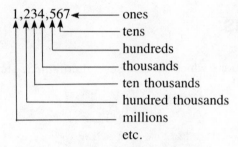

1,234,567 ── ones
── tens
── hundreds
── thousands
── ten thousands
── hundred thousands
── millions
etc.

When subtracting (indicated by the "−" sign), the opposite of the addition rule is true. When the digit in the lower number in the vertical column is greater than the one above it, a 1 must be "borrowed" from the top of the next column to the left. This has the effect of adding 10 to the original top number, but it only reduces the second top number by 1. To illustrate:

$$
\begin{array}{r}
\overset{1\,2}{1,2\cancel{3}\cancel{4}} \\
-567 \\
\hline
667
\end{array}
$$

You can "break down" this subtraction problem into its multiples of 1, 10, 100, and 1,000, as discussed. The problem 1,234 − 567 = ? may be written in at least two more formats:

1,000		1,000
+ 200		+ 100
+ 30		+ 120 ──100 was "borrowed"
+ 4	OR	+ 14 ──10 was "borrowed"
− 500		− 500
− 60		− 60
− 7		− 7
667		667

Multiplication presents a treatment similar to addition except that it is a multiple of 10 (such as 10, 20, 30 or 40) that is added to the product of the next multiplication step:

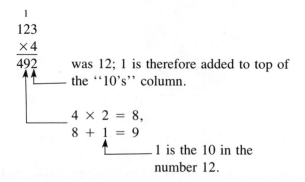

ORDER OF OPERATIONS

As we progress into multiple operations which involve several arithmetic steps, remember:

> Multiply or divide
> *before*
> adding or subtracting.
> (*My Dear Aunt Sally*)

> Parentheses are used to identify the part of an operation that is to be completed before any other calculations are performed.

Consider this problem:

$$2 + (3 \times 4) = ?$$

Since:

$$3 \times 4 = 12$$

the answer is:

$$2 + 12 = 14$$

Please recall that this is very similar to the example given in the comparison of chain vs. algebraic logic. In algebraic logic, the calculator presumes to rewrite the problem into a format that first clears up the function inside the parentheses (multiplication) before performing the addition function.

EXAMPLE: Now try this problem:

$$(1 \times 2) + (3 \times 4) + (5 \times 6) - (4 \times 11) = ?$$

That problem looks complicated, but it actually becomes simple once you try it. First you perform the arithmetic operations *inside* the parentheses. This gives you:

$$2 + 12 + 30 - 44$$

and $44 - 44 = 0$.

USING UNITS OF MEASUREMENT

Just as apples cannot be compared to oranges, numbers must be of the same kind or in the same form before you perform the arithmetic functions. If you try to add these unlike things:

$$1/2 + 1/3$$
or
4 inches + 5 feet
or
6 acres + 7,890 square feet

you must first put each into similar form such as

1/2 = 3/6, and 1/3 = 2/6
3/6 + 2/6 = 5/6
or
4 inches = 4/12 or 1/3 foot
1/3 foot + 5 feet = 5-1/3 feet
or
6 acres = 43,560 square feet $\times$ 6 = 261,360 square feet
261,360 square feet + 7,890 square feet = 269,250 square feet

EXAMPLE: Suppose that you measure your house for carpet and find that you need 1,125 square feet, but the carpet store's ad priced it at $18 per square *yard*. What will your carpet cost? Now try this problem:

First you must get the units of measurement to be alike. For simplicity, convert the 1,125 square feet to square yards. There are 9 square feet in each square yard, so:

$$\frac{1{,}125 \text{ square feet}}{9 \text{ square feet/square yard}} = 125 \text{ square yards}$$

Now the units agree, so you can compute the price:

$$125 \text{ square yards} \times \$18/\text{square yard} = \$2{,}250.00$$

BALANCING EQUATIONS

Later, when you progress into simple equations, remember that the "=" (equals) sign means *absolutely* that. You would not write

$$1 + 2 = 3 + 4$$

They are not equal since 3 is *not* equal to 7. That is *not* an equality or an equation. It is an inequality because it is out of *balance*. In order for it (the "equation") to balance, the numbers on the left-hand side of the "=" must actually be equal to the numbers on the right-hand side. If you think of an equation as a child's see-saw, or a balance scale, you recognize that both sides must have the same weight at the same point or the system will tilt and not balance. Therefore, if you wish to consider the preceding example as an equation (where both sides are equal), you must either add something to the left side or subtract something from the right side.

$$
\begin{array}{ll}
1 + 2 = 3 + 4 & \text{No} \\
3 = 7 & \text{No} \\
\text{but} & \\
3 + 4 = 7 & \text{Yes} \\
\text{or} & \\
3 = 7 - 3 - 1 & \text{Yes}
\end{array}
$$

If two numbers are related by addition ($+$), you can break that relationship by subtraction ($-$); if they are related by multiplication ($\times$), you can break that relationship by division ($\div$). To illustrate,

$$
\begin{aligned}
5 + 6 &= 7 + \text{what} \\
11 &= 7 + \text{what}
\end{aligned}
$$

The 7 is joined to "what" by addition; therefore, you must employ subtraction. In solving this problem you must separate the knowns from the unknowns. You know all but the "what." Recalling the illustration of the scales, if you subtract 7 from the right-hand side of the equal sign, the equation will be out of balance unless you also subtract the same 7 from the left-hand side:

$$
\begin{array}{rll}
11 = & 7 + \text{what} & \\
\underline{-7 \quad -7} & \leftarrow & \text{subtracted from both sides} \\
4 = & 0 + \text{what} & \\
4 = & \text{what} &
\end{array}
$$

Sometimes, it is the simplest things that we forget over the years. For instance, what is:

$$(7 - 7) \times 8 = ?$$

Here, you must first perform the operation indicated within the parentheses. In this case, that result is zero. Then, zero times any other number is zero.

Or, if you have a number divided by itself, the answer is always one. (Note that the "divided by" sign in the following examples is the slash.) So that,

$$1/1 = 1 \text{ or } 486/486 = 1$$

You can also treat units of measurement or algebraic letters the same way; for example:

$$feet/feet = 1$$
$$acres/acres = 1$$
$$x/x = 1$$
$$LW/LW = 1$$

Having obtained the answer of "one" from any of these operations, if you then multiply that one (1) by any other number, unit of measurement, etc., the answer is that same number, unit of measurement, or algebraic symbol:

$$1 \times 23 = 23$$
$$1 \times foot = foot$$
$$1 \times y = y$$

Also, it is important to recall that you cannot divide a number by zero. But, if you divide a number by one, you have not changed the value of the original number.

Please do not become anxious or nervous because each subject was treated so sparingly. Remember, this is merely a very basic review of things you already know. The purpose of this chapter is to stir your memory, as well as to introduce briefly some of the material to be covered in the following chapters.

Finally, in this text, you will encounter two basic types of exercises. These include number problems, which are already set up into the proper format, such as $123 + 456 = ?$, and word, or stated, problems. To gain proficiency in solving word problems, which are similar to "real world" situations, you should begin by analyzing the problem. Learn to recognize certain "function indicators" or key words which "indicate" to you whether to add, subtract, multiply or divide.

Addition indicators:	plus, more than, sum, increase, and
Subtraction indicators:	minus, less than, decrease, difference, take away
Multiplication indicators:	of, times, factor, product,
Division indicators:	quotient, fraction, reciprocal

ACHIEVEMENT EXERCISE

When you have finished both parts of this exercise, check your answers against those on page 17. If you miss any of the questions, review this chapter before going on to Chapter 2.

Part I—Open Response

1. Fill in the blanks.

    a. 12 feet = _____ yards

    b. 99 square yards = _____ square feet

    c. 1 acre = _____ square feet

2. What number is represented by the following?

    ```
      4,000
    +   300
    +    20
    +     1
    ```

3. Sam Seller owns two acres of commercially zoned property. If he sells it for $1.00 per square foot, what is the sales price?

4. Solve this problem:
    $(8 \times 9) - (6 \times 7) + (4 \div 2) \times (3 - 1) = ?$

Part II—Multiple Choice   Select the response from the choices supplied.

5. Which of the following should be done when working a math problem?

    a. Be very neat and legible.
    b. Be sure you understand what is being asked
    c. Be careful about decimal alignment.
    d. all of the above

6. Arithmetic operations inside parentheses are to be completed:

    a. after other calculations are performed.
    b. before other calculations are performed.
    c. at any time, whether before or after other calculations are performed.
    d. as the last step before the final answer.

7. Which of the following is (are) true?

    I. If two numbers are related by subtraction, the relationship can be broken by addition
    II. If two numbers are related by division, the relationship can be broken by multiplication.

    a. I only   c. both I and II
    b. II only   d. neither I nor II

8. Which of the following is (are) true?

  I. In order to maintain the balance, or equality, of an equation, the same thing must be done to both sides.
  II. If you divide a number by zero, the answer is one.

  a. I only   c. both I and II
  b. II only   d. neither I nor II

9. Which of the following is (are) true?

  I. Multiplication indicators are "of, times, factor, product."
  II. Division indicators are "quotient, fraction, reciprocal."

  a. I only   c. both I and II
  b. II only   d. neither I nor II

ANSWER KEY

Entry Evaluation

- $1{,}234 \times 5{,}678 = 7{,}006{,}652$

- $\dfrac{4{,}356{,}000 \text{ sq. ft.}}{43{,}560 \text{ sq. ft./acre}} = 100 \text{ acres}$

- Zero

Achievement Exercise

1. a. 1 yard = 3 feet
  12 feet ÷ 3 feet/yard = ? yards
  12 ÷ 3 = 4 yards

  b. 1 square yard = 9 square feet
  99 square yards × 9 square feet/square yard = 891 square feet

  c. 1 acre = 43,560 square feet

2. 4,321

3. 1 acre = 43,560 sq. ft.
  2 acres × 43,560 sq. ft./acre = 87,120 sq. ft.
  $1.00/sq. ft. × 87,120 sq. ft. = $87,120

4. 72 − 42 + (2 × 2) = 72 − 42 + 4 = 34
  (Remember to multiply or divide; then add or subtract)

5. d

6. b

7. c

8. a

9. c

Percentages, Fractions and Decimals

INTRODUCTION

Most of the mathematical problems you will encounter in the real estate field will require that you have a basic knowledge of percentages, fractions and decimals. Chapter 2 is designed to teach you these basic skills, or merely to refresh your memory.

ENTRY EVALUATION

Since readers will have varying amounts of knowledge and experience, the short test that follows will allow you to determine your familiarity with the material to be covered. Try both problems before looking at the answers, which are on page 45.

- Mr. Jones was one of five equal owners of an apartment building. The building was sold for $250,000, 2% of which was deducted for fees. How much money did Mr. Jones receive? What percent of the net did he receive? What fraction of the net did he receive?

- If Mr. Jones originally paid $40,000 for his share in this building, what percent was his profit?

At the outset of this chapter, a word about calculators is important. Some calculators have a "%" key, which requires fewer keystrokes to calculate percents. However, due to the several ways of entering data on different calculators, we will not discuss the use of the "%" key.

PERCENTAGES

> Percent (%) means per hundred or per hundred parts.
> "per" means "by the"
> "cent" means "100"

For example, 50% means 50 parts out of a total of 100 parts (100 parts equal 1 whole), and 100% means all 100 of the 100 total parts, or 1 whole unit.

50% means 50/100, or .50, or 1/2
100% means 100/100, or 1.00, or 1

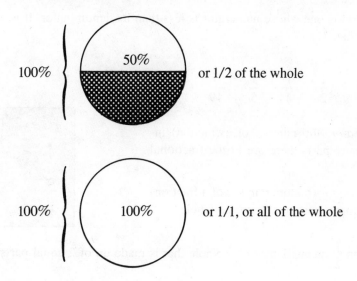

Therefore, you can change the number .50 to a percent by moving the decimal point (.) two places or two digits to the right and adding the percent symbol (%). By moving the decimal point two places to the right, you have actually *multiplied* .50 by 100, to equal 50. When you add the percent symbol, you have *divided* the 50 by 100 according to the definition of percent, so that .50 = 50%. Therefore, the actual value hasn't changed at all, or you are back where you started.

Any percentage that is less than 100% means a part or fraction of the whole unit.

EXAMPLE: Since 99% means 99 parts out of 100 parts, it is less than the whole.

EXAMPLE: Since 150% means 1 whole (100 parts) plus 50 parts of a second whole, it is more than the whole.

1. Which of the following means 35%? Circle your choice.

    a. 35 parts out of 1,000 parts

    b. 35 parts out of 100 parts

    c. 3,500 parts

    d. 35 parts

    e. none of the above

Answers for questions are at the end of each chapter.

FRACTIONS

Proper Fractions

A proper fraction is one whose numerator is less than its denominator. It is a part of a whole, and its value is *always* less than 1.

EXAMPLES: $\dfrac{1}{2}$ $\dfrac{1}{4}$ $\dfrac{1}{5}$ $\dfrac{5}{19}$ $\dfrac{7}{100}$

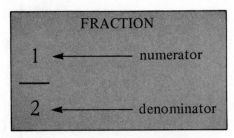

The *numerator* (top number of a fraction) indicates how many parts there are in the fractional amount.

The *denominator* (bottom number of a fraction) tells you how many parts make up the whole.

The fraction $\dfrac{1}{2}$ means 1 part of a whole that is made up of 2 equal parts.

The fraction $\dfrac{3}{4}$ means 3 parts of a whole that has 4 equal parts.

The figure 35% means 35 parts out of the 100 parts that make up a whole. It can also be written as the fraction 35/100 or as the decimal .35.

2. Write the following percentages as fractions (percent always means per hundred, or the whole is divided into 100 equal parts). Do not reduce the fractions.

    a. 20% =

    b. 50% =

    c. 5% =

    d. 97% =

Improper Fractions

An improper fraction is one whose numerator is equal to or greater than its denominator. The value of an improper fraction is *never* less than 1.

EXAMPLES: $\dfrac{4}{4}$ $\dfrac{5}{4}$ $\dfrac{10}{9}$ $\dfrac{81}{71}$

To change an improper fraction to a whole number (without any fraction) or mixed number (a whole number plus a fraction), divide the numerator by the denominator. Any part left over should be shown as a fraction having the original denominator.

EXAMPLE: Change $\dfrac{8}{5}$ to a mixed number.

$$\frac{8}{5} = 8 \div 5 = 1 \text{ whole unit of 5 parts with 3 more parts left over}$$

$$\frac{8}{5} = 1\frac{3}{5}$$

3. Change the following improper fractions to mixed numbers.

a. $\dfrac{5}{4} =$

c. $\dfrac{16}{5} =$

b. $\dfrac{9}{2} =$

d. $\dfrac{26}{9} =$

Mixed Numbers

A mixed number (a whole number and a fraction) such as $1\dfrac{3}{4}$ can be changed to an improper fraction by multiplying the whole number by the denominator:

$$1 \times 4 = 4$$

adding the numerator to that answer:

$$4 + 3 = 7 \text{ (This is called the sum.)}$$

and placing that sum over the denominator of the mixed number:

$$\frac{7}{4}$$

4. Change the following mixed numbers to improper fractions.

a. $2\dfrac{1}{4} =$

c. $8\dfrac{1}{4} =$

b. $3\dfrac{2}{3} =$

d. $1\dfrac{5}{6} =$

Simple Fractions

A simple fraction is one that cannot be *reduced*. That is, you cannot divide the numerator and denominator evenly by the same number.

EXAMPLES: $\dfrac{3}{5}$ $\dfrac{1}{3}$ $\dfrac{77}{78}$ $\dfrac{9}{10}$

Many fractions can be changed to simple fractions by dividing the same number into both the numerator and the denominator. You'll notice that this division does not change the value of the fraction.

EXAMPLES:

$$\frac{20}{100} = \frac{20 \div 20}{100 \div 20} = \frac{1}{5}$$

$$\frac{15}{25} = \frac{15 \div 5}{25 \div 5} = \frac{3}{5}$$

$$\frac{2}{4} = \frac{2 \div 2}{4 \div 2} = \frac{1}{2}$$

The following illustrates that $\dfrac{2}{4} = \dfrac{1}{2}$.

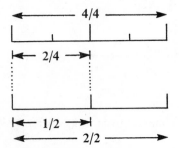

Two parts of a whole that is divided into four equal parts is $\dfrac{2}{4}$.

One part of the same whole divided into two equal parts is $\dfrac{1}{2}$.

The fraction $\dfrac{2}{4}$ covers the same distance as the fraction $\dfrac{1}{2}$.

When the top and bottom of a fraction can no longer be divided by the same number, the fraction has been reduced to its simplest form. For instance, if you divide the numerator and denominator by 2, you get:

$$\frac{8}{16} = \frac{4}{8} = \frac{2}{4} = \frac{1}{2}$$

5. Reduce (convert) the following fractions to simple fractions:

a. $\dfrac{25}{100}$ c. $\dfrac{60}{100}$ e. $\dfrac{34}{100}$

b. $\dfrac{75}{100}$ d. $\dfrac{52}{100}$

6. Reduce each of these fractions to its simplest form.

a. $\dfrac{4}{8} =$ d. $\dfrac{3}{12} =$

b. $\dfrac{8}{16} =$ e. $\dfrac{3}{8} =$

c. $\dfrac{3}{9} =$

MULTIPLYING FRACTIONS

Refer to the example at the right as you read.
To multiply fractions:

1) multiply the numerators, then multiply the denominators (the result of a multiplication step is called the "product"),

2) place the products of the numerators over the products of the denominators, and

3) reduce the fraction to its simplest form.

Problem: $\dfrac{3}{4} \times \dfrac{1}{6} =$

1) $\dfrac{3 \times 1}{4 \times 6} = \dfrac{3}{24}$

2) $\dfrac{3}{24} =$

3) $\dfrac{3 \div 3}{24 \div 3} = \dfrac{1}{8}$

Canceling

Some fractions can be reduced before multiplying.

EXAMPLES: In example A on the right, the numerator, 3, and the denominator, 6, have both been divided by 3.

A

$\dfrac{\overset{1}{\cancel{3}}}{4} \times \dfrac{1}{\underset{2}{\cancel{6}}} = \dfrac{1}{8}$

This type of reducing is called *canceling,* which is a division process, or the elimination of factors.

In example B, the numerator, 2, and the denominator, 10, have both been divided by 2. The numerator, 9, and the denominator, 3, have both been divided by 3.

B

$\dfrac{\overset{1}{\cancel{2}}}{\underset{1}{\cancel{3}}} \times \dfrac{\overset{3}{\cancel{9}}}{\underset{5}{\cancel{10}}} = \dfrac{3}{5}$

Improper Fractions

A whole number can be changed to an improper fraction by placing the whole number over 1.

$$4 = \dfrac{4}{1}$$

To multiply a fraction by a whole number, treat the whole number like a numerator, with a denominator of 1.

EXAMPLE: $4 \times \dfrac{1}{6} = \dfrac{4}{1} \times \dfrac{1}{6} = \dfrac{4}{6} = \dfrac{2}{3}$

7. Multiply the following fractions.

a. $\dfrac{2}{3} \times \dfrac{1}{8} =$

b. $\dfrac{5}{2} \times \dfrac{2}{3} =$

c. $\dfrac{3}{20} \times \dfrac{5}{6} =$

d. $5 \times \dfrac{3}{5} =$

e. $\dfrac{45}{100} \times 300 =$

f. $3\dfrac{2}{3} \times 2\dfrac{1}{2} =$

DIVIDING FRACTIONS

Refer to the example at the right as you read.

To divide one fraction by another, invert the fraction you are dividing by (the divisor), so that the numerator becomes the denominator and the denominator becomes the numerator.

Then complete the problem by following the steps for multiplication.

$$\dfrac{2}{3} \div \dfrac{5}{6} =$$

$$\dfrac{2}{3} \times \dfrac{6}{5} =$$

$$\dfrac{2 \times 6}{3 \times 5} =$$

$$\dfrac{12}{15} =$$

$$\dfrac{12 \div 3}{15 \div 3} = \dfrac{4}{5}$$

The same problem can be solved by canceling after the fraction used as the divisor is inverted:

$$\dfrac{2}{3} \div \dfrac{5}{6} = \dfrac{2}{\overset{}{\underset{1}{\cancel{3}}}} \times \dfrac{\overset{2}{\cancel{6}}}{5} = \dfrac{4}{5}$$

8. Divide the following fractions.

a. $\dfrac{4}{5} \div \dfrac{1}{10} =$

b. $\dfrac{5}{8} \div \dfrac{2}{3} =$

c. $\dfrac{5}{6} \div 5 =$

d. $\dfrac{9}{16} \div \dfrac{3}{8} =$

e. $\dfrac{2}{3} \div 1\dfrac{1}{2} =$

f. $1\dfrac{1}{4} \div \dfrac{1}{2} =$

CONVERTING FRACTIONS TO DECIMALS

To change a fraction to a decimal, divide the numerator of the fraction by the denominator.

EXAMPLE:

$$\frac{1}{4} = 4\overline{)\begin{array}{l} .25 \\ 1.00 \end{array}}$$
$$\begin{array}{r} \underline{8} \\ 20 \\ \underline{20} \end{array}$$

This decimal figure can be converted easily to a percentage. Move the decimal point two places to the right and add a % sign. Remember, this does not change the value of a number; it only changes its form.

EXAMPLE: $\frac{1}{4} = .25 = 25\%$

9. a. Find the decimal equivalent of the fraction:

$$\frac{1}{2} =$$

b. Find the percentage equivalent of the fraction:

$$\frac{1}{2} =$$

c. Find the percentage equivalent of the fraction:

$$\frac{7}{8} =$$

CONVERTING DECIMALS TO PERCENTAGES

This process is the reverse of the one you just completed. Move the decimal point two places to the *right* and add the % sign.

EXAMPLES:

$$\begin{array}{rcl} .10 &=& 10\% \\ 1.00 &=& 100\% \\ .98 &=& 98\% \\ .987 &=& 98.7\% \end{array}$$

10. Change the following decimals to percentages:

a. .37 =

b. .09 =

c. .080 =

d. .10000 =

e. .7095 =

f. .01010 =

CONVERTING PERCENTAGES TO SIMPLE FRACTIONS

By combining the processes covered thus far, you can convert percentages to simple fractions.

EXAMPLES:

Percentage	$\rightarrow$	Fraction	$\rightarrow$	Simple Fraction
$50\% =$		$\dfrac{50}{100} \div \dfrac{50}{50} =$		$\dfrac{1}{2}$
$25\% =$		$\dfrac{25}{100} \div \dfrac{25}{25} =$		$\dfrac{1}{4}$
$150\% =$		$\dfrac{150}{100} = 1\dfrac{50}{100} \div \dfrac{50}{50} =$		$1\dfrac{1}{2}$

11. Change the following percentages into simple fractions.

a. $40\% =$ d. $26\% =$

b. $20\% =$ e. $160\% =$

c. $10\% =$

CONVERTING PERCENTAGES TO DECIMALS

To change a percent to a decimal, move the decimal point two places to the left and drop the % sign.

All numbers have a decimal point although it is usually not shown when only zeros follow it.

EXAMPLES:
    99 is really 99.0
     6 is really 6.0
    $1 is the same as $1.00

So, percents can be readily converted to decimals.

EXAMPLES:
    $99\% = 99.0\% = .990 = .99$
    $6\% = 06.0\% = .060 = .06$
    $5\% = 05.0\% = .050 = .05$
    $70\% = 70.0\% = .700 = .70$

Note: Adding zeros to the *right* of a decimal point after the last figure does not change the value of the number.

12. Change the following percentages to decimals.

    a. 1% =   c. 75.5% =

    b. 65% =   d. 2.1% =

ADDING DECIMALS

Decimals are added like whole numbers, but decimal points *must* be lined up under each other as shown in the examples.

EXAMPLES:

```
     300          .3          .891
       5          .005        .05
    +590        + .59       + .063
    ────         ────        ─────
     895          .895       1.004
```

13. Add these decimals:

```
a.    .05          b.    .983
      .2                 .006
    + .695             + .32
    ─────              ─────
```

SUBTRACTING DECIMALS

Decimals are subtracted like whole numbers, and again, line up the decimal points.

```
     861          .861
   − 190        − .190
   ─────        ──────
     671          .671
```

Subtract .32 from .549.

Note the correct answer:

```
          .549
        − .32
        ──────
          .229
```

14. Practice adding and subtracting decimals.

    a. .23 + .051 + .6 =   c. .588 − .007 =

    b. .941 − .6 =   d. .741 + .005 + .72 =

MULTIPLYING DECIMALS

Decimals are multiplied like whole numbers, but the decimal point must be considered. Count the number of digits to the right of the decimal in each of the two numbers being multiplied to determine the number of decimal places in the product (answer). Study the examples below to note where to place the decimal point in the answer.

EXAMPLES:

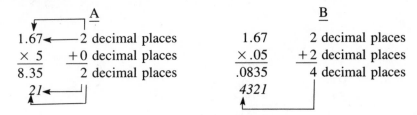

	A
1.67	← 2 decimal places
× 5	+ 0 decimal places
8.35	2 decimal places
21	

	B
1.67	2 decimal places
× .05	+ 2 decimal places
.0835	4 decimal places
4321	

In example B you have to add a zero to make four decimal places.

EXAMPLE: Place the decimal point in the proper place below:

$$
\begin{array}{r}
.265 \\
\times .85 \\
\hline
1325 \\
2120 \\
\hline
22525
\end{array}
$$

The product has five decimal places:

.265	3 decimal places
× .85	2 decimal places
1325	
2120	
.22525	5 decimal places

15. Practice multiplying.

a. .100
   × 3

b. 4.006
   × .51

c.   .035
   × .012

DIVIDING DECIMALS

Dividing by Whole Numbers

There are two different situations involved in dividing decimals, since you can divide by a *whole number* or by a *decimal number*.

When you divide a decimal by a whole number, place the decimal point in the answer *directly* above the decimal point in the dividend, as illustrated to the right.

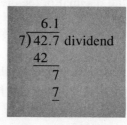

$$\begin{array}{r} 6.1 \\ 7\overline{)42.7} \text{ dividend} \\ \underline{42} \\ 7 \\ \underline{7} \end{array}$$

EXAMPLE: Divide the following:

$$9\overline{)27.36}$$

$$\begin{array}{r} 3.04 \\ 9\overline{)27.36} \\ \underline{27} \\ 36 \\ \underline{36} \end{array}$$

Note that 9 is a *whole number,* and, therefore, the decimal point is placed directly above the decimal point in the dividend.

If you are using a calculator to divide, please remember that you must first enter the number *to be divided,* then the divisor. For instance, if you wish to divide 30 by 600, write

$$30/600, \text{ or } 600\overline{)30}, \text{ or } 30 \div 600$$

The calculator key strokes are:

Press	Display
3 0	30
÷	(means divided *by,* not into)
6 0 0	600
=	.05

16. Practice dividing.

   a. $2\overline{).08}$ b. $3\overline{).36}$ c. $5\overline{).15}$

Dividing by Decimals

To divide by a decimal, you first need to change the decimal in the divisor to a whole number.

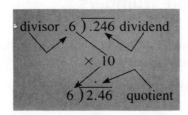

EXAMPLE: In the example at the right, the divisor, .6, is multiplied by 10 to make a new divisor, 6.

Remember to move the decimal in *both* the divisor and the dividend to the right a sufficient number of places so that the divisor is *always* greater than 1. In the example, the number "6" is greater than 1 but the number ".6," a decimal fraction, is the same as 6/10, which is less than 1. This operation *must* be performed in any division problem.

Study the chart below to find out how to convert decimals to whole numbers by multiplication.

Tenths	Hundredths	Thousandths
.6	.06	.006
× 10	× 100	× 1000
6.0	6.00	6.000

Notice that the number of places in the decimal tells you what number you have to multiply by.

17. What number would you multiply by to change each of the following decimals to whole numbers?

   a. .225

   b. .9

   c. .53

Again, if you multiply a decimal divisor by a number, you must also multiply the dividend by the same number.

In the example at the right, just as .6 must be multiplied by 10 to form a whole number, the dividend *must* also be multiplied by 10:

divisor .6)‾.246 dividend
× 10
6)‾2.46

$$\begin{array}{r} .246 \\ \times 10 \\ \hline 2.460 \end{array}$$

Multiplying the divisor and the dividend by the same number does not change the answer, and the answer to each of the problems at the right is 3.

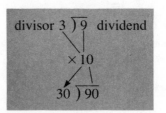

Shortcut for Dividing by Decimals

Here's a shortcut to use when dividing by a decimal.

1. Change the decimal to a whole number by moving the decimal point to the right.

2. Move the decimal point the same number of places in the dividend, and mark the place with a "caret" ($\wedge$).

3. Divide.

4. Place the decimal above the caret in the quotient (answer).

18. Divide the following.

a. $.04\overline{)\,.932}$ b. $.003\overline{)\,.3111}$ c. $4\overline{)\,.008}$

d. $.04\overline{)\,.168}$ e. $.007\overline{)\,.4928}$

Multiplying or Dividing by 100

Remember that "percent" means "by the hundred" or, divided by 100. If you divide by 100, merely move the decimal 2 places to the *left*. This corresponds to the number of zeros in 100. For example, we know that 99% = .99 because

$$100\overline{)\,99.00}\quad\,.99$$

To multiply a number by 100, just move the decimal 2 places to the right. Note that the value of the number is not changed if you multiply by 100 and then add the percent sign (%), which means divide by 100. Therefore, .10 is equal to 10%.

DECIMAL FRACTIONS

A fraction that has a power of 10 as its denominator is a decimal fraction.

A power is a multiple of the same number. The first power of 10 (10^1) is 10; the second power of 10 (10^2) is 100 (10 × 10); the third power of 10 (10^3) is 1,000 (10 × 10 × 10), and so on.

EXAMPLES: $\dfrac{1}{10}$ $\dfrac{50}{100,000}$ $\dfrac{79}{100}$

19. Using the definition given above, which of the following are decimal fractions?

a. $\dfrac{10}{50}$ b. $\dfrac{5}{10}$ c. $\dfrac{100}{200}$ d. $\dfrac{25}{1,000}$ e. $\dfrac{4}{25}$

20. Fill in the following chart.

	Simple Fraction	Decimal	Percent	Decimal Fraction
a.			75%	
b.				$\dfrac{20}{100}$
c.		.80		
d.	$\dfrac{1}{8}$			
e.	$\dfrac{3}{10}$			
f.			67%	
g.		.56		

PERCENTAGE PROBLEMS

Percentage problems usually involve three elements.

EXAMPLE: 5%   of 200 is   10

percent   total   part

Look at the example below. A problem involving percentages is really a multiplication problem. To solve this problem, you first convert the percentage to a decimal, then multiply.

EXAMPLE: What is 25% of 300?
$300 \times 25\% = ?$
$25\% = .25$
$300 \times .25 = 75$

Answer: 25% of 300 is 75.

Another way to solve this type of problem is to change the *percent to a decimal fraction* with a denominator of 100 and the *whole number to a fraction*.

EXAMPLE:

$$25\% = \frac{25}{100}$$

$$300 = \frac{300}{1}$$

$$\frac{\overset{3}{\cancel{300}}}{1} \times \frac{25}{\cancel{100}_{1}} = \frac{75}{1} = 75$$

A generalized formula for solving percent problems is:

$$\text{total} \times \text{percent} = \text{part}$$
(*or,* percent × total = part; the order of multiplication is not important.)

In order to solve a percent problem, you must know the value of two of the elements of this formula. The value that you must find is called the *unknown* (most often shown in the formula as x).

EXAMPLE: Mr. Jones has purchased a secondhand stereo unit at 45% of the original cost, which was $150. What did Mr. Jones pay for the unit?

$$\text{percent} \times \text{total} = \text{part}$$
$$45\% \times \$150 = x$$
$$.45 \times \$150 = \$67.50$$

This problem can also be solved by the decimal fraction method.

$$45\% \times \$150 = x \qquad\qquad\qquad \$150 \times 45\% = x$$

$$\frac{45}{100} \times \frac{150}{1} = \frac{45}{\cancel{100}_{2}} \times \frac{\cancel{150}^{3}}{1} = \frac{135}{2} = \$67.50 \quad \text{OR} \quad \frac{150}{1} \times \frac{45}{100} = \frac{\cancel{150}^{3}}{1} \times \frac{45}{\cancel{100}_{2}} = \frac{135}{2} = \$67.50$$

21. Now, you try a problem. Ms. Smith spent 60% of her total savings of $3,000. How much did she spend?

    a. What formula will you use?

    b. Solve the problem below.

FORMULAS

Just as many people seek shortcuts in their everyday tasks, there are some shortcuts in performing math functions that lead to a correct answer. Generally, if the method or concept is clearly understood, the solution to a problem is easy. In fact, the correct recognition or identification of a certain type of problem puts you rather close to the solution itself.

In working with problems involving percents, there are several ways of stating the same relationship. For example, we might say that:

$$P = B \times R$$

where, P is the percentage of the whole;
             B is the base, or whole;
             R is the rate.

Or,

$$I = RV$$

where, I is the amount of interest;
             R is the rate;
             V is the value or whole.

Or,

$$\text{Part} = \text{Whole} \times \text{Rate}$$

Actually, each of the foregoing examples has merely stated the *same relationship* in three ways, since the product is equal to one element times another.

If you want to find out how many square feet are in 20% of an acre, you must first know how many square feet there are in an acre. This number is 43,560 and you should memorize it. You can then solve the problem by employing any one of the three formulas above. For example,

$$\text{Part} = \text{Whole} \times \text{Rate}$$
$$\text{Part} = 43{,}560 \text{ sq. ft} \times 20\%$$
$$\text{Part} = 8{,}712 \text{ sq. ft.}$$

(Remember that 20% is the same as .20.)

But, what percent of an acre does 17,424 square feet represent? Remember that:

$$\text{Part} = \text{Whole} \times \text{Rate}$$

where the Rate expresses what portion the Part is of the Whole. In this problem, you know the "Part" and the "Whole," so you must rearrange the formula so that all the "knowns" are on one side of the "=" sign, and the unknown is alone on the other side. In Chapter 1, an equation was compared to a balanced see-saw, and whatever is done to one side of the see-saw must also be done to the other side to maintain the balance. If two numbers are joined by multiplication, the bond can be broken by division. Therefore, to find the percent or rate in the following formula:

$$\text{Part} = \text{Whole} \times \text{Rate}$$

Divide both sides by "Whole":

$$\frac{\text{Part}}{\text{Whole}} = \frac{\text{Whole}}{\text{Whole}} \times \text{Rate}$$

So that the $\dfrac{\text{Whole}}{\text{Whole}}$ is 1, and

$$\frac{\text{Part}}{\text{Whole}} = \text{Rate}$$

Therefore:

$$\frac{17{,}424}{43{,}560} = .40 \text{ or } 40\%$$

Again, remember that .40 is 40/100 or 40%.

You can employ a shortcut to this process by considering the relationship expressed by this figure, where, from our previous discussion:

$$\text{Part} = \text{Part}$$
$$\text{Total} = \text{Whole}$$
$$\% = \text{Rate}$$

This figure shows all three of the elements of the equation:

$$\text{Part} = \text{Whole} \times \text{Rate, or}$$
$$\text{Part} = \text{Total} \times \%$$

In order to apply this formula to the preceding figure, you must remember that:

1. you can find any one of the three elements if you know the other two;
2. the long horizontal line separates circle into division areas;
3. the short vertical line separates the circle into multiplication areas.

Knowing this, now merely cover up the portion of the circle that contains the unknown (or what you are looking for) and then perform the indicated multiplication or division.

Applying this to the previous example in which you found 20% of 43,560, the "Part" is the unknown. If you cover up the "Part" in the circle, you are left with "Total" and "%" separated by a multiplication function.

However, in the example of "What percent of 43,560 does 17,424 represent?" you are looking for the %. By covering up this word in the circle, you leave "Part" and "Total" separated by a division function. After performing the indicated division, the answer is .40 or 40%.

This shortcut can be used to solve many types of problems, including the following.

EXAMPLE: If 30% of the 1,500 houses in your area have 4 bedrooms, how many houses have 4 bedrooms?

We know:

$$\% = 30\%, \text{ or } .30$$
$$\text{Total} = 1,500$$

Cover up "Part."

$$\text{Total} \times \% = ?$$
$$1,500 \times .30 = 450$$

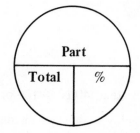

22. If 20% of the houses in your area are less than 5 years old and this amounts to 500 houses, how many houses are there in your area?

23. Which value is missing from this problem: 6 is 12% of what number?

   a. total   b. part   c. percent   d. none of these

In Exercise 23, the value missing from the problem is the total. We know the part is 6 and the percent is 12%, so we know to divide part by %, or $6 \div .12 = 50$. If you prefer to use the formula introduced on page 33, Part = Whole × Rate, or Part = Total × Percent, then write Total = $\dfrac{\text{Part}}{\text{Percent}}$, since you know the "Part" and the "Percent," and must solve for the "Total."

To divide, you must move the decimal point to make .12 a whole number. When you do this, of course, you must also move the decimal point inside the division sign.

$$\text{total} = .12\overline{)6.00.} = 12\overline{)600} = 50$$
$$\underline{60}$$

EXAMPLE: Here is another example: 30 is 50% of what number?

The suggested problem-solving sequence is:

Step 1.   Read the problem carefully.

Step 2.   Analyze the problem, pick out the important factors, and put those factors into a simplified question.

Step 3.   State the formula.   total   = $\dfrac{\text{part}}{\text{percent}}$

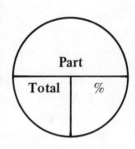

Step 4.   Substitute values.   total   = $\dfrac{30}{50\%}$

Step 5.   Solve the problem.   total   = $\dfrac{30}{.50}$ total = $.5\overline{)30}$

total   = $5\overline{)300}$ total = $5\overline{)300}$
$$\underline{30}$$

total = 60

24. Solve this problem: 1,500 is 300% of what number?

Step 1.

Step 2.

Step 3.

Step 4.

Step 5.

25. Try to solve this problem without looking back: $125 is 20% of what amount?

Note that the percent element is missing from the following problem.

What percent of 56 is 14?

By covering the % in the circle to your right, you know
to divide the part by the total, or in detail,

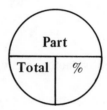

$$\frac{\text{Part}}{\text{Total}} = \%$$

Next, substitute the values from the problem for those elements in the new formula.

$$\text{percent} = \frac{14}{56}$$

Then, divide.

$$\begin{array}{r} .25 \\ 56 \overline{)\ 14.00} \\ \underline{11\ 2} \\ 2\ 80 \\ \underline{2\ 80} \end{array}$$

Finally, convert the decimal to a percent.

$$\text{percent} = .25 \times 100\%$$
$$100\% \times .25 = 25\%$$
$$\text{percent} = 25\%$$

Note: Follow these rules when dividing:

Carry all *percentage* calculations to *three* decimal places, if there is a remainder.

$$\frac{76}{85} = 89.4\%$$

$$\begin{array}{r} .894 \\ 85 \overline{)\ 76.000} \\ \underline{68\ 0} \\ 8\ 00 \\ \underline{7\ 65} \\ 350 \\ \underline{340} \\ 10 \end{array}$$

Carry all *dollars* and *cents* calculations with remainders to *three* decimal places and round off to *two* decimal places, unless stated otherwise. To round, increase the second decimal figure by one, if the third decimal figure is 5 or more. If the third decimal figure is less than 5, leave it as it is.

$$\frac{\$42}{29} = \$1.45$$

$$\begin{array}{r} 1.448 \\ 29 \overline{)\ 42.000} \\ \underline{29} \\ 13\ 0 \\ \underline{11\ 6} \\ 1\ 40 \\ \underline{1\ 16} \\ 240 \\ \underline{232} \\ 8 \end{array}$$

EXAMPLE: What percent of 87 is 17?

Step 1.   State the formula. $percent = \dfrac{part}{total}$

Step 2.   Substitute values. $percent = \dfrac{17}{87}$

Step 3.   Divide.

$$percent = 87\overline{)17.000}$$

$$\begin{array}{r} .195 \\ \underline{8\ 7} \\ 8\ 30 \\ \underline{7\ 83} \\ 470 \\ \underline{435} \\ 35 \end{array}$$

Step 4.   Convert the decimal to a percent. $percent = .195 \times 100\% = 19.5\%$

26. Solve this problem: What percent of 95 is 18? Include all the necessary steps.

Remember: This diagram will help you remember the formulas for part, total and percent.

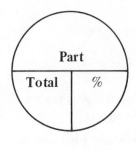

Since *part* is over *percent*, you make a fraction of these two elements when looking for a *total*.

$$total = \dfrac{part}{percent}$$

Since *part* is over *total*, you make a fraction of these two elements when looking for a *percent*.

$$percent = \dfrac{part}{total}$$

Since *percent* and *total* are both in the lower part of the diagram, multiply these two to get the *part*.

$$percent \times total = part$$

Now you will try some problems related to the real estate field, using what you've learned about percentages, fractions and decimals.

27. A house is assessed at 42% of market value, which is $50,000. What is its assessed value?

   a. What element must you solve for?

   b. What is the formula?

   c. Solve the problem.

28. A house sold for $81,000, which was 90% of the original price. What was the original list price?

   a. First, state the problem in formula form.

   b. What is the unknown value?

   c. Solve the problem, showing all your calculations.

29. A property has an assessed value of $15,000. If the assessment is 34% of market value, what is the market value?

   a. State the problem in formula form.

   b. What is the unknown value?

   c. Solve the problem. Round off your answer to the nearest hundred dollars.

PERCENT OF CHANGE

If you hear that houses in your area have increased in value 8% during the past year, and you know that the average price of houses sold last year was $60,000, what is the average price of houses sold today?

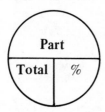

This is a two-step problem. First you must find the part; you know the total and percent. So,

$$\$60,000 \times .08 = \$4,800$$

Add the $4,800 increase to last year's average price of $60,000, giving this year's average price of $64,800.

Consider a similar problem from a different starting point: If the average price of houses today is $70,000 compared to $60,000 one year ago, what is the percent of change?

First, you must find the *amount* of change: $70,000 − $60,000 = $10,000. Next, use the circle aid to find the *percent* of change:

Part = $10,000
Total = $60,000
    % = $10,000 ÷ $60,000
      = .167 × 100%
      = 16.7%

Or, remember this general formula:

$$\text{percent change} = \frac{\text{new value} - \text{old value}}{\text{old value}}$$

30. If there were 800 foreclosures this year and 700 last year, what is the percent of change?

Suppose that this year's foreclosures numbered 700 and last year's equaled 800. What is the percent of change?

new value = 700
old value = 800
difference − 100 (negative number)

$$\text{percent change} = \frac{\text{new value} - \text{old value}}{\text{old value}}$$

$$\text{percent change} = \frac{700 - 800}{800}$$

$$\text{percent change} = \frac{-100}{800}$$

$$\text{percent change} = -.125 \text{ or } -12.5\%$$

This means the change occurred in a "downward" direction.

In summary, remember that fractions, decimals, and percents are all interrelated. For example, each of the following represents the same relationship:

$$\frac{1}{2} = .5 = 50\% = \frac{5}{10} = \frac{50}{100}$$

$$\frac{1}{2} = \frac{123}{246}$$

$$\frac{3 \text{ acres}}{6 \text{ acres}} = \frac{1}{2} \text{ or } 50\% \text{ or } .5 \text{ of the whole.}$$

Therefore, if you know any one of them (the fraction $\frac{1}{2}$), you can easily convert to the other two (decimal or percent).

31. An individual buys property for $20,000. Its value goes up, and he sells it for $25,000. What percentage of profit did he make on his investment? (Remember that the original cost is the "whole.")

   a. What is the unknown?

   b. What is his profit in dollars?

   c. State the actual problems in words.

   d. Give the formula to be used.

   e. Solve the problem.

You have now completed Chapter 2. If you feel you have understood the material in this chapter, you should now work the Achievement Exercise. If you feel you would like to review the material first, you may do so. The Achievement Exercise will serve both to test your comprehension and to review the highlights of Chapter 2. After working the Achievement Exercise, you may find that you are unsure about certain points the test raises. You should review those points before continuing with the next chapter.

ACHIEVEMENT EXERCISE

When you have finished both parts of this exercise, check your answers against those on page 51. If you miss any of the questions, review this chapter before going on to Chapter 3.

Part I—Open Response   Complete the following problems.

1. Complete the chart.

Simple Fraction	Decimal	Percent	Decimal Fraction
		15%	
			$\dfrac{20}{100}$
1/6			
	.25		
	.05		

2. A house listed for $55,000 and sold for 90% of the list price. What was the sale price of the house?

3. Mr. Tomas's house sold for $40,000, which was 92% of the list price. What did the house list for? Round off your answer to the nearest hundred dollars.

4. Mrs. Burns purchased her house for $80,000. She sold it for $90,000. What percent profit did she make on her investment?

Part II—Multiple Choice   Select the correct response from the choices supplied.

5. Salesperson Rose Accetta is computing her share of the commission on a $46,500 sale. The full commission rate is 7%, and the salesperson's share is 60%, which is:

    a. $1,974.   c. $1,935.
    b. $1,953.   d. $1,997.

6. The assessed value of a residence is 22% of the market value of $39,000, which is:

    a. $7,800.   c. $8,580.
    b. $8,700.   d. $8,850.

7. The office in which you work sold 128 homes last year. You sold 29 of these. Your sales are what fraction of the total sales and what percentage?

    a. $\dfrac{28}{129} = .217 = 21.7\%$

    b. $\dfrac{128}{29} = 4.412 = 44.13\%$

    c. $\dfrac{129}{28} = 4.607 = 46.07\%$

    d. $\dfrac{29}{128} = .227 = 22.7\%$

8. What percent of $800 is $420?

    a. 1.90%   c. 19%
    b. 52.5%   d. 5.25%

9. By selecting from a, b, c, or d, indicate which of the following statements is (are) true.

    I. When dividing decimals by a whole number, place the decimal point in the answer directly above the decimal point in the dividend.
    II. When converting decimals to percentages, move the decimal point two places to the right and add the % sign.

    a. I only
    b. II only
    c. both I and II
    d. neither I nor II

10. Which of the following statements is true?

    a. When adding decimals, the decimal points are lined up under each other.
    b. When dividing decimals, subtract the number of decimal places in the dividend from the number in the divisor.
    c. When adding decimals, the decimal points must be eliminated.
    d. When adding decimals, all numbers must be converted to fractions.

11. By selecting from a, b, c or d, indicate the order in which the formula for solving math problems is followed.

    I. Change percent to decimal.
    II. Substitute values.
    III. State or determine the formula.
    IV. Solve.

    a. I, II, III, IV
    b. IV, II, III, I
    c. III, I, II, IV
    d. III, II, I, IV

12. Which of the following formulas is incorrect?

    a. total = part × percent
    b. part = percent × total
    c. percent = part ÷ total
    d. total = part ÷ percent

13. Carolyn Grisho bought a lot for $10,000 and sold it several years later for $18,000. Her percentage of profit is:

    a. 180%.   c. 44%.
    b. 80%.   d. 100%.

14. One-sixth is equal to what percent?

    a. 8.25%   c. 1.65%
    b. 12.5%   d. 16.67%

ANSWER KEY

Entry Evaluation

- Mr. Jones received \$49,000, which was 20% or $\frac{1}{5}$ of the proceeds.

- He made a 22.5% profit.

Pages 20–42

1. The correct answer is b.

2. a. $\dfrac{20}{100}$ c. $\dfrac{5}{100}$

    b. $\dfrac{50}{100}$ d. $\dfrac{97}{100}$

3. a. $\dfrac{5}{4} = 5 \div 4 = 1\dfrac{1}{4}$ c. $\dfrac{16}{5} = 16 \div 5 = 3\dfrac{1}{5}$

    b. $\dfrac{9}{2} = 9 \div 2 = 4\dfrac{1}{2}$ d. $\dfrac{26}{9} = 26 \div 9 = 2\dfrac{8}{9}$

4. a. $2\dfrac{1}{4} = \dfrac{(2 \times 4) + 1}{4} = \dfrac{9}{4}$ c. $8\dfrac{1}{4} = \dfrac{(8 \times 4) + 1}{4} = \dfrac{33}{4}$

    b. $3\dfrac{2}{3} = \dfrac{(3 \times 3) + 2}{3} = \dfrac{11}{3}$ d. $1\dfrac{5}{6} = \dfrac{(1 \times 6) + 5}{6} = \dfrac{11}{6}$

5. a. $\dfrac{25 \div 25}{100 \div 25} = \dfrac{1}{4}$ d. $\dfrac{52 \div 4}{100 \div 4} = \dfrac{13}{25}$

    b. $\dfrac{75 \div 25}{100 \div 25} = \dfrac{3}{4}$ or $\dfrac{52 \div 2}{100 \div 2} = \dfrac{26 \div 2}{50 \div 2} = \dfrac{13}{25}$

    c. $\dfrac{60 \div 20}{100 \div 20} = \dfrac{3}{5}$ e. $\dfrac{34 \div 2}{100 \div 2} = \dfrac{17}{50}$

6. a. $\dfrac{4 \div 4}{8 \div 4} = \dfrac{1}{2}$ d. $\dfrac{3 \div 3}{12 \div 3} = \dfrac{1}{4}$

    b. $\dfrac{8 \div 8}{16 \div 8} = \dfrac{1}{2}$ e. The fraction $\dfrac{3}{8}$ is already in its simplest form.

    c. $\dfrac{3 \div 3}{9 \div 3} = \dfrac{1}{3}$

Pages 20–42 continued

7. a. $\dfrac{\overset{1}{\cancel{2}}}{3} \times \dfrac{1}{\underset{4}{\cancel{8}}} = \dfrac{1}{12}$

   d. $5 \times \dfrac{3}{5} = \dfrac{\cancel{5}^{1}}{1} \times \dfrac{3}{\cancel{5}} = \dfrac{3}{1} = 3$

   b. $\dfrac{5}{\underset{1}{\cancel{2}}} \times \dfrac{\overset{1}{\cancel{2}}}{3} = \dfrac{5}{3} = 1\dfrac{2}{3}$

   e. $\dfrac{45}{100} \times 300 = \dfrac{45}{\underset{1}{\cancel{100}}} \times \dfrac{\overset{3}{\cancel{300}}}{1} = \dfrac{135}{1} = 135$

   c. $\dfrac{\overset{1}{\cancel{3}}}{\underset{4}{\cancel{20}}} \times \dfrac{\overset{1}{\cancel{5}}}{\underset{2}{\cancel{6}}} = \dfrac{1}{8}$

   f. $3\dfrac{2}{3} \times 2\dfrac{1}{2} = \dfrac{11}{3} \times \dfrac{5}{2} = \dfrac{55}{6} = 9\dfrac{1}{6}$

8. a. $\dfrac{4}{5} \div \dfrac{1}{10} = \dfrac{4}{\underset{1}{\cancel{5}}} \times \dfrac{\overset{2}{\cancel{10}}}{1} = \dfrac{8}{1} = 8$

   d. $\dfrac{9}{16} \div \dfrac{3}{8} = \dfrac{\overset{3}{\cancel{9}}}{\underset{2}{\cancel{16}}} \times \dfrac{\overset{1}{\cancel{8}}}{\cancel{3}} = \dfrac{3}{2} = 1\dfrac{1}{2}$

   b. $\dfrac{5}{8} \div \dfrac{2}{3} = \dfrac{5}{8} \times \dfrac{3}{2} = \dfrac{15}{16}$

   e. $\dfrac{2}{3} \div 1\dfrac{1}{2} = \dfrac{2}{3} \div \dfrac{3}{2} =$

   c. $\dfrac{5}{6} \div 5 = \dfrac{5}{6} \div \dfrac{5}{1} =$

   $\dfrac{2}{3} \times \dfrac{2}{3} = \dfrac{4}{9}$

   $\dfrac{\overset{1}{\cancel{5}}}{6} \times \dfrac{1}{\cancel{5}} = \dfrac{1}{6}$

   f. $1\dfrac{1}{4} \div \dfrac{1}{2} = \dfrac{5}{4} \div \dfrac{1}{2} =$

   $\dfrac{5}{\underset{2}{\cancel{4}}} \times \dfrac{\overset{1}{\cancel{2}}}{1} = \dfrac{5}{2} = 2\dfrac{1}{2}$

9. a. $\dfrac{1}{2} = 2 \overline{)\, 1.00}^{\;.50}$
      $\phantom{= 2 \overline{)}}\underline{1\,0}$

   c. $\dfrac{7}{8} = 8 \overline{)\, 7.000}^{\;.875}$
      $\phantom{= 8 \overline{)}}\underline{6\,4}$
      $\phantom{= 8 \overline{)}\,}60$
      $\phantom{= 8 \overline{)}\,}\underline{56}$
      $\phantom{= 8 \overline{)}\,}40$
      $\phantom{= 8 \overline{)}\,}\underline{40}$

   b. $.50 = 50\%$

10. a. $.37 = 37\%$

    b. $.09 = 9\%$

    c. $.080 = 8\% \ (8.0\% = 8\%)$

    d. $.10000 = 10\% \ (10.000\% = 10\%)$

    e. $.7095 = 70.95\%$

    f. $.01010 = 1.01\% \ (01.010\% = 1.01\%)$

11. a. $40\% = \dfrac{40}{100} \div \dfrac{20}{20} = \dfrac{2}{5}$

b. $20\% = \dfrac{20}{100} \div \dfrac{20}{20} = \dfrac{1}{5}$

c. $10\% = \dfrac{10}{100} \div \dfrac{10}{10} = \dfrac{1}{10}$

d. $26\% = \dfrac{26}{100} \div \dfrac{2}{2} = \dfrac{13}{50}$

e. $160\% = \dfrac{160}{100} = 1\dfrac{60}{100} \div \dfrac{20}{20} = 1\dfrac{3}{5}$

12. a. $1\% = 01.0\% = .010 = .01$

b. $65\% = 65.0\% = .650 = .65$

c. $75.5\% = .755$

d. $2.1\% = 02.1\% = .021$

13. a.
```
  .05
  .2
+ .695
─────
  .945
```

b.
```
  .983
  .006
+ .32
─────
 1.309
```

14. a.
```
  .23
  .051
+ .6
─────
  .881
```

b.
```
  .941
− .6
─────
  .341
```

c.
```
  .588
− .007
─────
  .581
```

d.
```
  .741
  .005
+ .72
─────
 1.466
```

15. a.
```
  .100
×   3
─────
  .300
```

b.
```
   4.006
 ×  .51
 ──────
   4006
  20030
 ──────
 2.04306
```

c.
```
   .035
 × .012
 ──────
    70
    35
 ──────
 .000420
```

16. a.
```
     .04
 2) .08
     8
```

b.
```
     .12
 3) .36
     3
     6
     6
```

c.
```
     .03
 5) .15
     15
```

17. a. 1000

b. 10

c. 100

Pages 20–42 continued

18. a.
$$\begin{array}{r} 23.3 \\ .04\overline{\smash{)}93.2} \\ \underline{8} \\ 13 \\ \underline{12} \\ 1\ 2 \\ \underline{1\ 2} \end{array}$$

c.
$$\begin{array}{r} .002 \\ 4\overline{\smash{)}.008} \\ \underline{8} \end{array}$$

d.
$$\begin{array}{r} 4.2 \\ .04\overline{\smash{)}16.8} \\ \underline{16} \\ 8 \\ \underline{8} \end{array}$$

b.
$$\begin{array}{r} 103.7 \\ .003\overline{\smash{)}311.1} \\ \underline{3} \\ 11 \\ \underline{9} \\ 2\ 1 \\ \underline{2\ 1} \end{array}$$

e.
$$\begin{array}{r} 70.4 \\ .007\overline{\smash{)}492.8} \\ \underline{49} \\ 2\ 8 \\ \underline{2\ 8} \end{array}$$

19. b and d (If you included c: 200 is a multiple of 10 (10 × 20) but *not* a power of 10 and is not, therefore, a decimal fraction.)

20. a. $75\% = \dfrac{75}{100} = \dfrac{3}{4} = .75$

e. $30\% = \dfrac{30}{100} = \dfrac{3}{10} = .30$

b. $20\% = \dfrac{20}{100} = \dfrac{1}{5} = .20$

f. $67\% = \dfrac{67}{100} = \dfrac{67}{100} = .67$

c. $80\% = \dfrac{80}{100} = \dfrac{4}{5} = .80$

g. $56\% = \dfrac{56}{100} = \dfrac{14}{25} = .56$

d. $12.5\% = \dfrac{125}{1,000} = \dfrac{1}{8} = .125$

21. a. percent × total = part

b. 60% × $3,000 = x   .60 × $3,000 = $1,800

or 60% × $3,000 = x

$$60\% = \dfrac{60}{100} \quad \dfrac{60}{\cancel{100}} \times \dfrac{\overset{30}{\cancel{3,000}}}{1} = \dfrac{1,800}{1} = \$1,800$$

22. We know:

Percent = 20% or .20

Part = 500

Total = $\dfrac{500}{.20}$

Total = 2,500

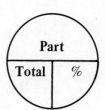

23. a. total

24. Step 1. Read the problem.

Step 2. Analyze the problem.

Step 3. total = $\dfrac{\text{part}}{\text{percent}}$

Step 4. total = $\dfrac{1,500}{300\%}$

Step 5.
$$3)\overline{\,1,500\,} \quad \begin{array}{r} 500 \\ \hline \end{array}$$
$$\underline{1\ 5}$$

25. total = $\dfrac{\text{part}}{\text{percent}}$

total = $\dfrac{125}{20\%}$

total = $\dfrac{125}{20}$

total = $.20)\overline{\,125.00\,}$

total = $20)\overline{\,12500\,}$

total = $20)\overline{\,12500\,}$
$$\begin{array}{r} 625 \\ \underline{120} \\ 50 \\ \underline{40} \\ 100 \\ \underline{100} \end{array}$$

total = $625

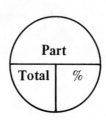

26. percent = $\dfrac{\text{part}}{\text{total}}$

percent = $\dfrac{18}{95}$ = $95)\overline{\,18.000\,}$ = .189 × 100% = 18.9% (or 19% if you were rounding to a whole number)
$$\begin{array}{r} .189 \\ \underline{9\ 5} \\ 8\ 50 \\ \underline{7\ 60} \\ 900 \\ \underline{855} \\ 45 \end{array}$$

27. a. part

b. percent × total = part

c. 42% × $50,000 =
$$\begin{array}{r} \$50,000 \\ \times\ .42 \\ \hline 1\ 000\ 00 \\ 20\ 000\ 0 \\ \hline \$21,000.00 \end{array}$$

Pages 20–42 continued

28. a. $\dfrac{\text{part}}{\text{percent}} = \text{total}$ or $\dfrac{\$81,000}{90\%} = \text{total}$

 b. total

 c. $\dfrac{81,000}{90\%} = \dfrac{81,000}{.90} = {.90)\overline{81000.00}} = 90)\overline{8100000} = \$90,000$
$$\underline{810}$$

90000 = \$90,000

29. a. $\dfrac{\text{part}}{\text{percent}} = \text{total}$ or $\dfrac{\$15,000}{34\%} = \text{total}$

 b. The total is the unknown.

 c. $\dfrac{\$15,000}{34\%} = \dfrac{\$15,000}{.34} = .34)\overline{15000} = 34)\overline{1500000.000}$ ... 44117.647

$$
\begin{array}{r}
44117.647 \\
34)\overline{1500000.000} \\
\underline{136} \\
140 \\
\underline{136} \\
40 \\
\underline{34} \\
60 \\
\underline{34} \\
260 \\
\underline{238} \\
22\,0 \\
\underline{20\,4} \\
1\,60 \\
\underline{1\,36} \\
240 \\
\underline{238} \\
2
\end{array}
$$

 total = \$44,117.65 rounded off to \$44,100

30. new value = 800
 old value = 700
 difference = $\overline{100}$

 percent change = $\dfrac{\text{new value} - \text{old value}}{\text{old value}}$ 　　percent change = $\dfrac{100}{700}$

 percent change = $\dfrac{800 - 700}{700}$ 　　percent change = .143 or 14.3%

31. a. The percent is the unknown.

 b. $\begin{array}{r} \$\,25,000 \\ -20,000 \\ \hline \$\ \ \ 5,000\ \text{profit} \end{array}$

 d. $\dfrac{\text{part}}{\text{total}} = \text{percent}$

 c. What percent of \$20,000 (investment) is \$5,000 (profit)?

 e. percent = $\dfrac{5,000}{20,000} = 20,000)\overline{5,000.00} = 25\%$

$$
\begin{array}{r}
.25 \\
20,000)\overline{5,000.00} \\
\underline{4\,000\,00} \\
1\,000\,00 \\
\underline{1\,000\,00}
\end{array}
$$

Note: The percent of profit is based upon the *original purchase price,* the cost.

Achievement Exercise

1.

Simple Fraction	Decimal	Percent	Decimal Fraction
$\frac{3}{20}$	.15	15%	$\frac{15}{100}$
$\frac{1}{5}$	.20	20%	$\frac{20}{100}$
$\frac{1}{6}$	.167	16.7%	$\frac{16.7}{100}$
$\frac{1}{4}$	.25	25%	$\frac{25}{100}$
$\frac{1}{20}$	.05	5%	$\frac{5}{100}$

2. $90\% \times \$55,000 = \$49,500$

3. $\frac{\$40,000}{92\%} = \$43,478.26$ rounded to $\$43,500$

4. $\$90,000 - \$80,000 = \$10,000$

$\frac{\$10,000}{\$80,000} = .125 = 12.5\%$

5. b. $\$46,500 \times 7\% \times 60\% = \$1,953$ salesperson's share

6. c. $\$39,000 \times 22\% = \$8,580$ assessed value

7. d. $29 \div 128 = 22.7\%$ of sales

8. b. $\$420 \div \$800 = 52.5\%$

9. c.

10. a.

11. d.

12. a.

13. b. $\$18,000 - \$10,000 = \$8,000 \div \$10,000 = 80\%$ profit

14. d. $6 \div 1 = 16.7\%$

Commission

INTRODUCTION

This chapter will help you apply what you have learned about percentages to the specific problem of calculating real estate commissions. If you have difficulty with any of these problems, review Chapter 2.

ENTRY EVALUATION

Since readers will have varying amounts of knowledge and experience, the short test that follows will allow you to determine your familiarity with the material to be covered. Try both problems before looking at the answers, which are on page 62.

■ A house sold for $75,000. The total commission received by the broker was $5,000. What was the rate of commission?

■ The listing broker negotiated a 7½% commission with Mr. & Mrs. Watts. If the house is sold by another broker for $120,000, what amount of commission does the selling salesperson receive if the listing broker pays 60% to the selling broker who then pays 70% to the salesperson?

PROBLEM-SOLVING STRATEGY

This chapter begins with a look at how to solve *word* problems. Here's strategy you should use:

Step 1.   Read the problem carefully.

Step 2.   Analyze the problem, pick out the important factors and put those factors into a simplified question, disregarding unimportant factors.

Step 3.   Choose the proper formula for the problem.

Step 4.   Substitute the figures for the elements of the formula.

Step 5.   Solve the problem.

If you use this strategy throughout this chapter and wherever it applies in this book, you'll have an easier time with word problems. Remember, word problems are simply everyday situations reduced to writing. Do not become fearful.

EXAMPLE: Consider an example that applies the step-by-step strategy to a problem involving a broker's commission.

Step 1.   Read the following problem carefully.

A house sold for $62,300. The selling broker received a 7% commission on the sale. What amount did the broker receive?

Step 2.   Analyze the problem, pick out the important factors and put those factors into a question.

What is 7% of $62,300?

Step 3.   Choose the proper formula for the problem from the following.

percent $\times$ total $=$ part

$$\frac{\text{part}}{\text{percent}} = \text{total}$$

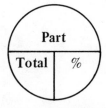

$$\frac{\text{part}}{\text{total}} = \text{percent}$$

The correct formula for this problem is: percent $\times$ total $=$ part (cover the element sought).

Step 4.   Substitute the figures for the elements of the formula.

7% $\times$ $62,300 $=$ part

Step 5.   Solve the problem.

7% $\times$ $62,300 $=$

$$\begin{array}{r} \$62,300 \\ \times\,.07 \\ \hline \$4,361.00 \end{array}$$

Note: The steps and the solution would be the same if irrelevant factors such as the date of sale, amount of closing costs, type of financing, etc. had been included. Learn to sift out these unimportant factors, and do not be confused by them.

Now you will apply this strategy to another commission problem. Be careful—this one's a bit different. When you are finished, check your answer below.

Step 1.   Read the problem carefully.

The selling broker received the entire commission of $1,662 on a real estate transaction. What was the selling price of the property, if his rate of commission was 6%?

Step 2.   Analyze the problem, pick out the important factors and put those factors into a simplified question.

Step 3.   Choose the proper formula for the problem. (If you need to, refer to the formulas shown on the preceding page.)

Steps 4.   Substitute the figures for the elements of the formula and solve.
and 5.

The answers are as follows:

Step 2. $1,662 is 6% of what?

Step 3.   total $= \dfrac{\text{part}}{\text{percent}}$

Step 4.   total $= \dfrac{\$1,662}{6\%}$

Step 5.   total $= \dfrac{\$1,662}{.06}$ $= .06.)\overline{1,662.00.}$

```
           277 00      ←  divisor
      _____          quotient
.06.)  1,662.00.     ←  dividend
       1 2
       ___
        46
        42
        __
         42
         42
         __
```

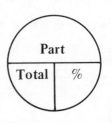

The selling price is $27,700.

This problem can also be solved as follows. This is called the *decimal fraction method*. It does not matter which method you use; either will work. Use the method you find easier.

$$\frac{\$1,662}{6\%} = total$$

$$\frac{\$1,662}{1} \div \frac{6}{100} = total$$

$$\$1,662 \times \frac{100}{6} = total$$

$$\frac{\overset{277}{\cancel{\$1,662}}}{1} \times \frac{100}{\underset{1}{\cancel{6}}} = total$$

$$\$277 \times 100 = \$27,000$$

1. Complete the following formulas. Try not to look back in the book.

part = _____ × _____

total =

percent =

2. Apply the problem-solving strategy to this problem.

Miss Martin received $9,080 for a parcel of real estate after the broker deducted a 5% commission and an allowance of $40 for advertising expenses. How much did the real estate sell for?

a. Step 2.   Analyze the problem and state it in simplified terms.

b. What value are you looking for (what is the unknown)?

c. What formula will you use?

Let's take a further look at the last problem. First of all, you know that the real estate sold for:

$$\$9,080 + \$40 + 5\% \text{ commission (5\% of the total)}$$

Therefore, you must add:

$$\begin{array}{r} \$9,080 \\ +\ \ \ 40 \\ \hline \$9,120 \end{array}$$

Then, $9,120 plus the 5% commission is equal to the total.

What percent of the total is $9,120? The total, or the sales price, must equal 100%, so:

$$
\begin{array}{r}
100\% \\
-\ \ 5\% \\
\hline
95\%
\end{array}
$$

Therefore, you can say that $9,120 is 95% of the total sales price. Or, in question form:

$9,120 is 95% of what?

Since you must solve for the total, the correct formula is:

$$\text{total} = \frac{\text{part}}{\text{percent}}$$

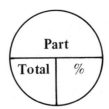

3. Now, substitute the figures for the elements of the formula and solve the problem.

4. Using the figures in Exercise 3, and the problem-solving strategy, find the amount of the broker's commission. Fill in the missing steps below and complete the problem.

a. Step 1.

b. Step 2. Analyze, pick out the important parts, and restate the problem.

c. Step 3. Choose the proper formula. (Try not to look back.)

d. Step 4.

e. Step 5.

5. Apply the problem-solving strategy to the following problem. List the steps as you work them.

A house sold for $75,000. The total commission received by Dave Weiner, the broker, was $4,500. What was the rate of commission?

a. Step 1.

b. Step 2.

c. Step 3.

d. Step 4.

e. Step 5.

SPLITTING COMMISSIONS

Broker and Salesperson

When commissions are divided between a broker and his or her salesperson, the total commission is calculated first, and then the broker's and/or the salesperson's shares are determined.

The next problem deals with splitting commissions. Apply your problem-solving strategy. Think the steps as you go along. If you feel you need to, write each step down in the space provided.

6. Property was sold for $5,800. The salesperson involved in the transaction received 40% of the 6% broker's commission. How much money did the salesperson receive?

7. Analyze and restate this problem.

Mr. Johnson's house sold for $55,000, and the total commission was 6% of that amount. The broker received three-fourths of the commission and the salesman received one-fourth. How much was the salesperson's commission?

Here's another type of commission problem. Follow the steps you've learned to solve it.

8. What was the selling price of a house if the salesperson received $3,000 as his or her half of the 6% commission charged by the broker?

9. The 6% commission charged by a broker for selling a house was divided as follows: 10% to the salesperson getting the listing, and one-half of the balance to the salesperson making the sale. What was the selling salesperson's commission, if the sale price was $40,000?

10. List the five steps involved in the problem-solving strategy and the three equations you've used in solving commission problems.

More than One Broker

Frequently, a real estate transaction involves more than one broker. Broker A's salesperson might list the property, and Broker B's salesperson might sell it. The amount of commission that Broker A charges the seller is a matter of negotiation between those two parties, and the division of the commission between the two brokers is subject to negotiation by the two brokers. The manner in which each listing broker shares his or her portion of the commission with each salesperson is decided by each broker.

11. Consider the sale of a $100,000 house that involved two brokers. The listing broker negotiated a 6½% commission with the seller, and then agreed to pay the selling broker 55% of the total commission. The listing salesperson received 25% of his broker's commission, and the selling salesperson received 30% of his broker's commission. How much did each receive?

12. A house sold for $85,000, and the commission was 7.25%. The broker paid a franchise fee of 5.5% of the total commission plus a multiple-listing service transaction fee of ¼ of 1% of the total commission. Of the remainder, the agent received 55% of the office net commission and paid a $20 computer use fee to the broker on the transaction. How much did the office and the salesperson receive?

Your problem analysis should reveal seven steps to obtain the solution. Work in an orderly fashion.

ACHIEVEMENT EXERCISE

When you have finished both parts of this exercise, check your answers against those on page 64. If you miss any of the questions, review this chapter before going on to Chapter 4.

Part I—Open Response   Complete the following problems.

1. A 6% commission was charged by the broker for the sale of a house which sold for $50,000. The commission was divided as follows: 10% to the salesperson getting the listing, one-half of the balance to the salesperson making the sale and the remainder to the broker. What was the amount of each commission?

2. What was the selling price of a house, if the salesperson received $1,000 as his or her half of the 5% commission charged by the broker?

3. Mr. Brinner's house sold for $85,000 and the total commission was 6.5% of that amount. The broker received three-fourths of that amount and the salesperson received one-fourth. How much was the broker's commission? The salesperson's commission?

Part II—Multiple Choice   Select the correct response from the choices supplied.

4. Salesperson Mike Scherer received $787.50 as his half of his broker's 7% commission on a sale. The sale price was:

   a. $45,000.   c. $22,000.
   b. $22,500.   d. $25,000.

5. Two cooperating brokers split equally the 6% commission on a sale. Broker A paid her salesperson $1,620 as his 60% of broker A's share. The sale price of the property was:

   a. $27,000.   c. $63,000.
   b. $54,000.   d. $90,000.

6. A broker paid his salesperson $3,600, the agreed three-fifths share of the 6% commission. By selecting from a, b, c, or d, indicate which of the following statements is (are) true.

    I. The broker's full commission was $6,000.

    II. The sale price was $100,000.

        a. I only
        b. II only
        c. both I and II
        d. neither I nor II

7. A salesperson received $2,250 as his 50% of the commission on a $75,000 sale. The full commission was computed at the rate of:

        a. 5%.
        c. 6%.
        b. 5.5%.
        d. 6.5%.

8. When the dollar amount and percentage rate of the commission are known, what is the correct procedure for finding the sale price? Indicate your choice of a, b, c, or d.

    I. The sale price is determined by dividing the amount of commission by the rate of commission.

    II. The sale price is determined by dividing the amount of commission by 100% minus the rate of commission.

        a. I only
        b. II only
        c. both I and II
        d. neither I nor II

9. On the sale of a house, broker Audrey Kirch earns 7% of the first $50,000 and 3% of any amount over $50,000. What was the selling price of a house if her total commission was $4,475?

        a. $44,750
        c. $32,500
        b. $89,500
        d. $82,500

10. A broker was paid 6% commission on the first $100,000 of a house that sold for $150,000. If the total commission was $8,500, what was the percent of commission paid on the balance?

        a. 5%
        c. 1.7%
        b. 5.7%
        d. 2.5%

11. John Bellows earns an 8% commission on the first $75,000 of sales for the month and 3% for all sales over that amount. If Mr. Bellows sold houses totaling $162,100 for the month, how much more would he have earned at a straight 6% commission?

        a. $1,113
        c. $9,726
        b. $810.50
        d. $2,613

12. The brokerage fee on a house that listed for $90,000 is 6%. What is the commission loss to the broker if the actual sale price of the house was 10% less than the list price?

        a. $4,860
        c. $5,400
        b. $3,600
        d. $540

13. Salesperson George Sutter sells a house for $84,500. The listing broker receives 50% of the 6% commission. How much does the salesperson receive if he gets 40% of the commission due the selling broker?

        a. $2,028
        c. $2,535
        b. $1,014
        d. $5,070

14. Alice Listor took a listing for her company, ABC Realty, which sold for $82,500. Betty Bought, who works for First Realty, produced the purchasers. The brokers have agreed to divide the 7% commission equally and Alice will receive 55% of her broker's share, which is:

        a. $2,887.50.
        c. $1,588.13.
        b. $5,775.00.
        d. $1,229.38.

ANSWER KEY

Entry Evaluation

- 6.67%

- \$120,000 sale price $\times$ $7\frac{1}{2}\%$ = \$9,000 commission

    \$ 9,000 $\times$ 60% = \$5,400 to selling broker
    \$ 5,400 $\times$ 70% = \$3,780 to selling salesperson

Pages 55–61

1. part = total $\times$ percent (part = percent $\times$ total)

    total = $\dfrac{\text{part}}{\text{percent}}$

    percent = $\dfrac{\text{part}}{\text{total}}$

2. a. Step 2.   \$9,080 + \$40 is 95% of what?

    b. You are looking for the total.

    c. total = $\dfrac{\text{part}}{\text{percent}}$

3. $\dfrac{\$9,120}{95\%}$ = total $\dfrac{\$9,120}{.95}$ = $.95\overline{)9120.00}$ = $95\overline{)912000}$ = \$9,600 total

    $$\begin{array}{r} 9600 \\ 95\overline{)912000} \\ 855 \\ \hline 570 \\ 570 \\ \hline \end{array}$$

Note: Remember to move the decimal point in the divisor and dividend when dividing by longhand. If you are using a calculator, you must enter the decimal in the proper place.

4. Step 1.   Read the problem carefully.

    Step 2.   What is 5% of \$9,600?

    Step 3.   percent $\times$ total = part

    Step 4.   Substitute the figures for the elements of the formula.

         5% $\times$ \$9,600 = part

    Step 5.   Solve the problem.

         .05 $\times$ \$9,600 = part

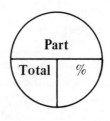

$$\begin{array}{r} \$9,600 \longleftarrow \text{multiplicand} \\ \times\,.05 \longleftarrow \text{multiplier} \\ \hline \$480.00 \text{ broker's commission} \longleftarrow \text{product} \end{array}$$

Note: Remember to count the number of decimal places in both the multiplicand and the multiplier; then, begin at the right hand of the product and count left the same number of places to insert the decimal.

You could also solve this problem by substituting the dollar amounts.

$$
\begin{array}{rr}
100\% & \$9,600 \\
-95\% & -9,120 \\
\hline
5\% & \$\;\;480 \quad \text{broker's commission} \\
\end{array}
$$

5. Step 1. Read the problem carefully.

Step 2. Analyze, pick out the important parts and restate the problem.

$4,500 is what percent of $75,000?

Step 3. Choose the correct formula.

$$
\text{percent} = \frac{\text{part}}{\text{total}}
$$

Step 4. Substitute.

$$
\text{percent} = \frac{\$4,500}{\$75,000}
$$

Step 5. Solve.

$$
\frac{\$4,500}{\$75,000} = 75,000 \overline{)4,500.00}^{.06} = 6\% \text{ broker's commission rate}
$$
$$
\underline{4\;500\;00}
$$

6. Analysis: What is 6% of $5,800? (Part 1)
What is 40% of that figure? (Part 2)

Formula: Part 1. percent × total = part
Part 2. percent × total = part

Substitution: Part 1. 6% × $5,800 = part
.06 × $5,800 = part

$$
\begin{array}{r}
\$\;5,800 \\
\times\;.06 \\
\hline
\$348.00 \quad \text{total commission} \\
\end{array}
$$

Part 2. 40% × $348 = part
.40 × $348 = part

$$
\begin{array}{r}
\$348 \\
\times\;.40 \\
\hline
\$139.20 \quad \text{salesperson's share of the commission} \\
\end{array}
$$

7. This problem also has two parts:

Part 1: What is 6% of $55,000?

Part 2: one-fourth = $\dfrac{1}{4}$ = 25%

What is 25% of the figure found in Part 1?

Formula: Part 1: percent × total = part
Part 2: percent × total = part

Pages 55–61 continued

Substitution: Part 1. 6% × $55,000 = part

Solution: Part 1. .06 × $55,000 = $3,300 total commission

Substitution: Part 2. 25% × $3,300 = part

Solution: Part 2. .25 × $3,300 = part = $825 salesperson's commission

8. Analysis and restatement of problem: $3,000 is one-half of the total commission, so $3,000 plus $3,000 equals $6,000, which is the total commission. $6,000 is 6% of what?

If you missed this step, correct your solution before you read the rest of the answer.

Formula: total $= \dfrac{\text{part}}{\text{percent}}$

Substitution: total $= \dfrac{\$6,000}{6\%}$

Solution: total $= \dfrac{\$6,000}{.06} = .06\overline{)6000.00} = 6\overline{)600000.00}^{100000.00} = \$100,000$ selling price of the house

9. Analysis and restatement of problem: This problem has three parts:

Part 1.   What is 6% of $40,000?
Part 2.   What is the selling salesperson's percentage of the total commission?
Part 3.   What is the selling salesperson's commission?

Part 1.   part = percent × total
          part = 6% × $40,000
          part = $2,400 total broker's commission

Part 2. $2,400 is 100% of the commission. The salesperson getting the listing receives 10%. This leaves 90% (100% − 10% = 90%) to be split evenly $\left(\dfrac{1}{2} \text{ and } \dfrac{1}{2}\right)$ between the broker and the selling person. One-half of 90% is 45%, which is the selling salesperson's percentage of the total commission.

Part 3.   What is 45% of $2,400?

Part = percent × total = 45% × $2,400 = $1,080 selling salesperson's commission

Or, you could solve this problem as follows:

part = total × percent

total commission = $40,000 × 6% = $40,000
                                   × .06
                                  $2,400.00

listing salesperson's share = $2,400 × 10% = $2,400
                                              × .10
                                             $240.00

remaining balance = $2,400 − $240 = $2,400
                                     − 240
                                    $2,160

The selling salesperson gets one-half (50%) of the remaining balance.

selling salesperson's commission = $2,160 × 50% = $2,160 or $2,160 × $\frac{1}{2}$ = $1,080

$$\begin{array}{r} \times\ .50 \\ \hline \$1,080.00 \end{array}$$

10. a. Read the problem carefully.

b. Analyze the problem, pick out the important factors and put those factors into a simplified question.

c. Choose the proper formula for the problem.

d. Substitute the figures for the elements of the formula.

e. Solve the problem.

percent × total = part

$\dfrac{\text{part}}{\text{percent}}$ = total

$\dfrac{\text{part}}{\text{total}}$ = percent

11. Step 1. First, calculate the total commission:

$$\begin{array}{r} \$100{,}000 \text{ sale price} \\ \times\ .065 \qquad \text{change percent to decimal form} \\ \hline 500000 \\ 600000 \\ \hline \$6{,}500.00 \quad \text{Total Commission} \end{array}$$

Step 2. <u>Listing Broker</u>
$6,500.00 × .45 = $2,925

Step 3. <u>Selling Broker</u>
$6,500 × .55 = $3,575

Students should develop the habit of checking for errors in calculations. For example,

$$\begin{array}{r} \$2{,}925 \\ +3{,}575 \\ \hline \$6{,}500 \end{array}$$

so that it is safe to proceed to the next step.

Step 4. <u>Listing Salesperson</u>
$2,925 × .25 = $731.25

Step 5. <u>Selling Salesperson</u>
$3,575 × .30 = $1,072.50

If you had difficulty here, do not forget the problem-solving roadmap that was discussed earlier, that is:

Step 1.   Read the problem.   Step 4.   Make substitutions.
Step 2.   Analyze the problem.   Step 5.   Solve the problem.
Step 3.   Choose the formula.

Pages 55–61 continued

12. Calculate the total commission:

Step 1.
$85,000 sale price
× .0725 commission rate
$6,162.50 Total Commission

Step 2.
$6,162.50 total commission
× .055 franchise rate
$ 338.94 Franchise Fee

Step 3.
$6,162.50 total commission
× .0025 MLS rate
$ 15.41 MLS Fee

Step 4.
$6,162.50 total commission
− 338.94 franchise fee
− 15.41 MLS fee
$5,808.15 Office Net Commission

Step 5.
$5,808.15 office net commission
× .55 salesperson's share
$3,194.48 Salesperson's Gross Commission

Step 6.
$3,194.48 salesperson's gross commission
− 20.00 computer use fee
$3,174.48 Salesperson's Net Commission

Step 7.
$5,808.15 office net commission
− 3,194.48 salesperson's gross commission
+ 20.00 computer use fee
$2,633.67 Amount Office Received
From This Transaction

Achievement Exercise

1. 6% × $50,000 = $3,000 total commission
10% × $3,000 = $300 listing salesperson's commission
50% × (3,000 − $300) = 50% × $2,700 = $1,350 selling salesperson's commission
$3,000 − $300 − $1,350 = $1,350 broker's commission

2. $1,000 × 2 = $2,000 $\dfrac{\$2,000}{5\%}$ = $40,000 selling price

3. 6.5% × $85,000 = $5,525 total commission
75% × $5,525 = $4,143.75 broker's commission
$5,525 − $4,143.75 = $1,381.25 salesperson's commission

4. b. $787.50 × 2 = $1,575.00
$1,575 ÷ 7% = $22,500 sale price

5. d. $1,620 ÷ 60% = $2,700
$2,700 × 2 = $5,400
$5,400 ÷ 6% = $90,000 sale price

6. c. $3,600 ÷ 3/5 = $6,000 commission
$6,000 ÷ 6% = $100,000 sale price

7. c. $2,250 × 2 = $4,500
$4,500 ÷ $75,000 = .06 = 6% commission

8. a.

9. d. $50,000 $\times$ 7% = $3,500
$4,475 $-$ $3,500 = $975
$975 $\div$ 3% = $32,500
$50,000 + $32,500 = $82,500 selling price

10. a. $100,000 $\times$ 6% = $6,000
$8,500 $-$ $6,000 = $2,500
$150,000 $-$ $100,000 = $50,000
$2,500 $\div$ $50,000 = .05 = 5% commission

11. a. $75,000 $\times$ 8% = $6,000
$162,100 $-$ $75,000 = $87,100
$87,100 $\times$ 3% = $2,613
$6,000 + $2,613 = $8,613
$162,100 $\times$ 6% = $9,726
$9,726 $-$ $8,613 = $1,113 difference

12. d. $90,000 $\times$ 6% = $5,400
$5,400 $\times$ 10% = $540 loss

13. b. $84,500 $\times$ 6% = $5,070
$5,070 $\times$ 50% = $2,535
$2,535 $\times$ 40% = $1,014 selling agent's share

14. c. $82,500 $\times$ 7% = $5,775
$5,775 $\div$ 2 = $2,887.50
$2,887.50 $\times$ 55% = $1,588.13 Alice's share

Sale Price, List Price and Net Price Problems

INTRODUCTION

In this chapter, you will apply what you have learned about percentages in solving list price and net listing problems. If you have difficulty with any of the problems, review Chapter 2.

ENTRY EVALUATION

Since readers will have varying amounts of knowledge and experience, the test question below will allow you to determine your familiarity with the material to be covered. Try the problem that follows before looking at the answer, which is on page 79.

- A house sold for $54,000, which was 90% of the list price. What did the house list for? If the broker deducted a 6% commission, and the house was originally purchased for $38,070, what percent was the seller's profit?

Here is the basic equation you've been working with:

$$\text{part} = \text{total} \times \text{percent}$$

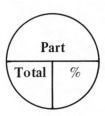

In Chapter 3, total, part, and percent *usually* meant:

Total	Total sale price
Part	Commission amount
Percent	Commission percentage

However, in this chapter, which deals with list, gross sale, and net sale prices, the three components of this basic equation will *generally* mean:

Total	Gross selling price (what the buyer pays for the real estate)
Part	Net amount (what the seller receives for the house— gross price minus expenses, commission, etc.)
Percent	100% minus deductions (expenses, commission, etc.)

The same equations and mathematics apply. If you have any difficulty with the problems in this chapter, review Chapter 2.

1. What are the equations for solving for total and percent if:

$$\text{total} \times \text{percent} = \text{part}$$

You will use the same problem-solving strategy presented in Chapter 3, as well as the same basic formulas. In case you did not complete Chapter 3, review the following strategy.

Step 1. Read the problem carefully.

Step 2. Analyze the problem, pick out the important factors and put those factors into a simplified question, disregarding unimportant factors.

Step 3. Choose the proper formula for the problem.

Step 4. Substitute the figures for the elements of the formula.

Step 5. Solve the problem.

If you use this strategy throughout this chapter, and wherever it applies in this book, you'll have an easier time with word problems.

Now, apply the problem-solving strategy to a typical real estate problem.

Step 1. Read the problem carefully.

A house sold for $61,625, which was 85% of the original list price. At what price was the house originally listed?

Step 2. Analyze the problem, pick out the important factors and put those factors into a simplified question.

$61,625 is 85% of what?

Step 3. Choose the proper formula for the problem.

$$\text{total} = \frac{\text{part}}{\text{percent}}$$

Step 4. Substitute.

$$\text{total} = \frac{\$61,625}{85\%}$$

Step 5. Solve the problem.

$$\text{total} = \frac{\$61,625}{.85} = .85\overline{)\,61,625.00} = 85\overline{)\,61,625.00} = \$72,500 \text{ list price}$$

$$\begin{array}{r} 72,500 \\ \hline 59\ 5 \\ \hline 2\ 12 \\ 1\ 70 \\ \hline 425 \\ \underline{425} \end{array}$$

2. To prove the answer for the preceding example, you must ask if $61,625 is really 85% of $72,500, or, What is 85% of $72,500?

Complete the proof of this problem.

3. Now, apply the problem-solving strategy to the following problem.

The net amount received by Kenneth Plummer for his house after the broker had deducted a sales commission of 6% was $55,648. What was the selling price? (Since net sale proceeds and commission rates are known, find the gross sales price.)

Analyze and restate the problem.

Choose the proper formula.

Substitute.

Solve the problem.

Remember: The selling price, or *gross* selling price, is the agreed total price to be paid by the purchaser. After the broker deducts the sales commission and expenses from this amount, the seller will be entitled to the *net* amount of the selling proceeds.

4. Prove your answer for Exercise 3.

5. Solve this problem. Work it out step by step, as you've learned.

Ms. Cornelius paid $75,500 for a house. She now wants to sell it at a 20% profit after paying the broker's commission. She gave the broker the listing at 5%. What would the list price have to be?

6. In the preceding problem, Ms. Cornelius wanted 20% profit on the original cost of her home. She did not want 20% of the list price. The broker, on the other hand, received 5% of the list price.

This is why you had to compute 20% of $75,500 to get the seller's profit. How would you compute the broker's commission in dollars?

Figure the amount of the broker's commission. Round the list price in Exercise 5 to the nearest hundred.

7. If you bought a home for $64,000, which was 20% less than the list price, what percentage of profit would you make on your investment if you sold the house for 10% more than the original list price? What would your profit in dollars amount to?

8. Try solving another problem.

A house listed for $54,000. The seller received $48,450 net after the broker deducted $2,550 for her 5% commission.

a. What was the sale price of this house?

b. What percent of the list price did the house sell for?

NET PRICE

Frequently, a seller will tell the broker or salesperson that he or she wants to net a certain amount from the sale of his or her property. The broker or agent must then estimate the total costs to be paid by the seller and determine if the resulting list price is within the market value range. (**Note:** Net listings are prohibited in some states and discouraged in others.)

EXAMPLE: If a seller wants to net $80,000 from a property without a mortgage, what will the list price be if the commission is 7% and the seller's closing costs on a new loan are 4% of the loan amount?

First, you must total the expenses:

$$\begin{array}{r} 7\% \text{ commission} \\ +4\% \text{ closing costs} \\ \hline 11\% \text{ Total Sales Expenses} \end{array}$$

If the seller is to net $80,000, then that amount must be equal to the list price less the sales expenses, or:

$$\text{Net} = \text{List Price} - \text{Sales Expenses}$$

The list price equals 100%, the sales expenses equal 11%, so that means that the $80,000 net price must equal 89% (100% − 11%) of the list price. To express this mathematically,

$$\$80,000 = 89\% \text{ of list price}$$

Apply this formula:

$$\text{Total} = \frac{\text{Part}}{\text{Percent}}$$

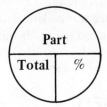

Substitute figures:

$$\text{Total} = \frac{\$80,000}{.89} = \$89,887.64$$

Proof: Step 1.
$$\begin{array}{rl} \$89,887.64 & \text{list price} \\ \times \quad\quad .07 & \text{commission rate} \\ \hline \$\ 6,292.13 & \text{Commission} \end{array}$$

Step 2.
$$\begin{array}{rl} \$89,887.64 & \text{list price} \\ \times \quad\quad .04 & \text{other closing costs rate} \\ \hline \$\ 3,595.51 & \text{Other Closing Costs} \end{array}$$

Step 3.
$$\begin{array}{rl} \$\ 6,292.13 & \text{commission} \\ +3,595.51 & \text{other closing costs} \\ \hline \$\ 9,887.64 & \text{Total Sales Expenses} \end{array}$$

Step 4.
$$\begin{array}{rl} \$89,887.64 & \text{list price} \\ -9,887.64 & \text{total sales expenses} \\ \hline \$80,000.00 & \text{Seller's Net} \end{array}$$

The most common error made in this type of problem is for the salesperson to multiply the seller's net times the total sales expense rate, add this amount to the seller's net, and call this figure the "list price." Let's see what happens:

Step 1. $80,000   seller's net
          ×   .11   total sales expense rate
          $ 8,800   Total Sales Expenses

Step 2. $80,000   seller's net
          + 8,800   total sales expenses
          $88,800   "List Price"

Now, for the proof of error:

Step 1. $88,800   "list price"
          ×   .11   total sales expense rate
          $ 9,768   Total Sales Expenses

Step 2. $88,800   "list price"
          − 9,768   total sales expenses
          $79,032   Seller's Net

Notice that the seller's net indicated in the proof is $79,032 and $968 *less* than what the seller wants. Understandably, the seller will be distressed. Who do you suppose the seller might expect to pay for this error?

PERCENT OF PROFIT

Another arithmetic exercise encountered in the field by an agent in this situation:

EXAMPLE: If a person buys a house for 20% less than the list price and then sells it for the original list price, what percent of profit was made?

First, let's examine two diagrams and visualize them as two rulers, one five inches long and one four inches long:

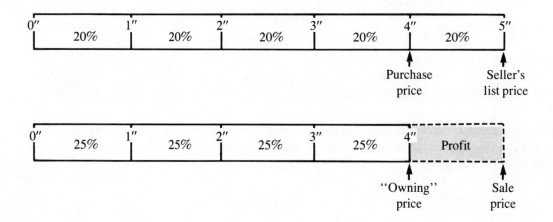

In the 5-inch ruler example, each of the 1-inch increments, or divisions, represents 20% of the entire length of 5 inches to total 100% of the list price. Since the buyer bought the house for 20% less than the seller's list price, the purchase price can be represented graphically as being at the 4-inch mark on the 5-inch ruler:

$$100\% - 20\% = 80\%, \text{ or the 4-inch mark}$$

The buyer now owns the house, so his 80% price now represents 100% of his "owning" price or cost. This can be represented graphically as a 4-inch ruler. His percent of profit upon resale is calculated upon his cost or his purchase price. When the house is resold for the original list price, this has the effect of lengthening the 4-inch ruler by an amount sufficient to make it the original length of 5 inches. Therefore, this graphically displays the original list price for:

1. Each inch on the 5-inch ruler represents 1/5 (20%) of the total length of this ruler, yet
2. Each inch is the same absolute length regardless of which of the two rulers is used, but
3. Each inch on the 4-inch ruler represents 1/4 (25%) of the total length of this ruler.

By examining both diagrams, you can deduce the answer to the problem to be 25%. In percentages, it depends upon where you *start,* and that starting point is called the "base." Therefore, the percent of *profit must be "based" upon what the person paid for the house,* not the list price.

However, the percent of *reduction must be based upon the list price.* It all depends on the starting point, the "base." If you are still not clear at this point, you may wish to refer back to Chapter 2 and re-read "Percent of Change."

Now, let's presume that the list price was $100,000, and the buyer paid 20% less and resold at list price. What was the percent of profit? First, find the buyer's cost or price:

Step 1.	$100,000	list price	Step 2.	$100,000	list price
	× .20	reduction rate		− 20,000	reduction (based on list price)
	$ 20,000	Reduction		$ 80,000	Purchase Price or Cost

Next, we find that the resale price is $100,000, which is the original list price.

Step 3.	$ 80,000	purchase price
	+ 20,000	profit
	$100,000	Resale Price

Finally, find the *percent of profit*. Remember, this is based or figured on the purchase price or cost, so:

Step 4: $$\frac{\$20{,}000 \text{ profit (part)}}{\$80{,}000 \text{ purchase price or cost (total)}} = .25 \text{ (percent)}$$

A rather clever way of recalling how to apply this concept is to remember this little formula:

$$\frac{\text{Saved}}{\text{Paid}} = \text{Made}$$

where:

Saved = percent of reduction
Paid = percent of list price
Made = percent of profit

9. Now, try another problem similar to the one just illustrated. If Beryl Stewart bought a house for 25% less than the list price and resold it for the list price, what percent of profit was realized?

PERCENT OF LOSS

The percent of loss is calculated in exactly the same way as for profit except that the order of the numbers is reversed. In each case, the percent of profit *or* loss is figured in relation to the *original* number or amount.

ACHIEVEMENT EXERCISE

When you have finished both parts of this exercise, check your answers against those on page 82. If you miss any of the questions, review this chapter before going on to Chapter 5.

Part I—Open Response   Complete the following problems.

1. Jay's house sold for $62,250, which was 75% of the list price. What did the house list for?

   Mr. Barker bought this house and resold it at 5% less than list price (it was listed at the same price it was when Jay sold the house). What percent profit did Mr. Barker make on this sale? What was his profit in dollars?

2. Mrs. Tomas received a net of $73,320 for her house after the broker deducted a 6% commission. What was the gross sale price of this house?

3. The Harrington family wishes to sell their house at a 14% profit, net. They purchased the house for $37,000. What would the sale price have to be to give the Harringtons a 14% profit after paying the selling broker a 6.5% commission on the sale price? Round off your answer to the nearest hundred dollars.

Part II—Multiple Choice Select the correct response from the choices supplied.

4. A seller received $51,700 after her broker deducted the agreed 6% commission. The sale price was:

    a. $50,000.   c. $55,000.
    b. $60,000.   d. $57,000.

5. When the sale on the Morgan house was closed, the broker paid the seller's title expense of $250, after deducting his 6½% commission of $5,200, and delivered to the seller a net check for:

    a. $74,550.   c. $84,350.
    b. $75,000.   d. $71,750.

6. A house sold for $75,200, which was 94% of the listing price of:

    a. $78,875.   c. $79,712.
    b. $78,125.   d. $80,000.

7. The owners want to make a 15% profit on the sale of their house after payment of a 6% broker's fee. Their cost was $40,000. What will their listing or sale price have to be?

    a. $46,000   c. $48,936
    b. $42,936   d. $49,836

8. Indicate the net amount received by the seller from a sale in which the broker received a 6% commission of $3,480, and the seller's other expenses were $175 for the title insurance fee and $95 for the transfer tax and recording fee.

    a. $54,520   c. $54,250
    b. $55,250   d. $57,730

9. Jenny Banks bought a house for $48,000, with the intention of remodeling it and then selling it in 2 years for $78,000. How much can Jenny spend on remodeling if taxes are $1,200 per year, the commission rate is 6% of the intended selling price and the profit required is $12,000?

    a. $12,120   c. $10,920
    b. $13,320   d. $12,720

10. Joan and Bob Thatcher bought an 80-acre tract for $1,980 per acre. Taxes, insurance, and other expenses amounted to $12,400 per year. At the end of 4 years, the property was sold for a net price of 1-3/4 times its original cost. What was the net profit on the sale of the property?

    a. $118,800   c. $227,600
    b. $69,200   d. $32,000

11. Five years ago, an investor bought four lots for $10,000 each. A house was built on one of the lots at a cost of $60,000. The lot with the house recently sold for $100,000, and the remaining vacant lots sold for 2-1/2 times their original cost. The percent of gross profit was:

    a. 42.8%.   c. 175%.
    b. 57.1%.   d. 75%.

12. If you bought a house for the list price less 20% and sold it for the list price, what percent of profit would you make?

    a. 25%   c. 80%
    b. 20%   d. 125%

13. A house listed for $60,000. The seller received $50,760 net after the broker deducted $3,240 for his commission. By selecting from a, b, c or d, indicate which of the following equations can be used to find the sale price of the house.

    I. $\text{total} = \dfrac{\text{part}}{\text{percent}}$

    II. sale price = net price + commission

    a. I only   c. both I and II
    b. II only   d. neither I nor II

14. You bought a home for $50,000, which was 20% less than the list price, and you sold the house for 10% more than the original list price. By selecting from a, b, c or d, indicate which of the following statements is (are) true.

  I. The list price was $62,500.
  II. The profit was 37-1/2%.

    a. I only   c. both I and II
    b. II only   d. neither I nor II

15. You bought a house for 15% less than list price and sold it for list price one month later. Your percent of profit was:

    a. 85%.   c. 15%.
    b. 82.4%.   d. 17.6%.

ANSWER KEY

Entry Evaluation

■ $60,000 list price   33.3% profit

Pages 69–76

1. total $= \dfrac{\text{part}}{\text{percent}}$ percent $= \dfrac{\text{part}}{\text{total}}$

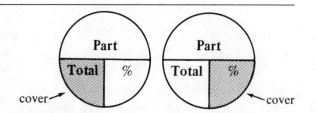

2. part $=$ total $\times$ percent $=$ $72,500 $\times$ 85% $=$

$72,500
$\times$ .85 ← 2 decimal places here means answer must
3 625 00   also have 2 decimal places.
58 000 0
$61,625.00   Yes, $61,625 is 85% of $72,500.
↑

3. Analysis and restatement: $55,648 is 94% of what? (Since the price is the total less 6%, 100% $-$ 6% $=$ 94%)

Formula: The total is missing, so total $= \dfrac{\text{part}}{\text{percent}}$ is the formula.

Substitution: total $= \dfrac{\$55,648}{94\%}$

Pages 69–76 continued

Solution: total = $\dfrac{\$55,648}{100\% - 6\%} = \dfrac{55,648}{94\%}$ = $.94\overline{)55648.00}$ = $94\overline{)5564800}$ = \$59,200

$$94\overline{)5564800}\quad 59200$$
$$\underline{470}$$
$$864$$
$$\underline{846}$$
$$188$$
$$\underline{188}$$

4. Is \$55,648 really 94% of \$59,200? or
What is 94% of \$59,200?

$$\$59,200$$
$$\underline{\times\ .94}$$
$$236800$$
$$\underline{532800}$$
$$\$55,648.00$$

5. Analysis and restatement: list price or total = cost + profit + 5% commission

Part 1.　Compute profit.　What is 20% of \$75,500?

part = percent × total = .20 × \$75,500 = \$15,100

Part 2.　Now compute the seller's price or the net sale price.

cost + profit = seller's net price　\$75,500 + \$15,100 = \$90,600

Part 3.　What percent of the total is the seller's net price?

total list price = seller's net + 5% commission　100% − 5% = 95%

Part 4.　\$90,600 is 95% of what?

total = $\dfrac{\text{part}}{\text{percent}} = \dfrac{\$90,600}{.95}$ = $95\overline{)9060000.000}$ = \$95,368.42 list price

$$95368.421$$
$$\underline{855}$$
$$510$$
$$\underline{475}$$
$$350$$
$$\underline{285}$$
$$650$$
$$\underline{570}$$
$$800$$
$$\underline{760}$$
$$40\ 0$$
$$\underline{38\ 0}$$
$$2\ 00$$
$$\underline{1\ 90}$$
$$100$$
$$\underline{95}$$
$$5$$

Total or list price must equal at least \$95,368.42. This could be rounded to \$95,350, but if rounded to \$95,400, both the broker and seller would be assured of their full amounts.

6. 5% of the list price of $95,400 is the broker's commission.

part = total × percent = $95,400 × 5% = $95,400

$$\begin{array}{r} \times\ .05 \\ \hline \$4,770.00 \text{ broker's commission} \end{array}$$

7. Part 1.　　What percent of the list price is $64,000?

list price % − 20% = sale price %　　100% − 20% = 80%

Part 2.　　$64,000 is 80% of what?

$$\text{total} = \frac{\text{part}}{\text{percent}} = \frac{\$64,000}{80\%} = 80\overline{)6400000}^{\,80000} = \$80,000$$
$$\underline{640}$$

Part 3.　　What is 10% of $80,000?

part = percent × total = 10% × $80,000 = $8,000

Part 4.　　What will the sale price be?

original list price + 10% = new sale price

$80,000 + $8,000 = $88,000

Part 5.　　What is the amount of the profit?

sale price − purchase price = profit

$88,000 − $64,000 = $24,000 profit

Part 6.　　What percent of $64,000 is $24,000?

$$\text{percent} = \frac{\text{part}}{\text{total}} = \frac{\$24,000}{64,000} = 64,000\overline{)24000.000}^{\,.375}$$
$$\begin{array}{r} \underline{19200\ 0} \\ 4800\ 00 \\ \underline{4480\ 00} \\ 320\ 000 \\ \underline{320\ 000} \end{array}$$

Had you made this investment, you would have made a 37.5% profit, or a dollar amount of $24,000.

8. a. The sale price can be computed in two ways.

A	B
$2,550 is 5% of what?	sale price = net price + commission
	sale price = $48,450 + $2,550

A:

$$\text{total} = \frac{\text{part}}{\text{percent}} = \frac{\$2,550}{5\%}$$

$$5\overline{)255000}^{\,51000} = \$51,000 \text{ sale price}$$
$$\begin{array}{r}\underline{25}\\5\\\underline{5}\end{array}$$

B:

$$\begin{array}{r} \$48,450 \\ +2,550 \\ \hline \$51,000 \text{ sale price} \end{array}$$

b. Compute the percent of the list price that the sale price is. That is, what percent of $54,000 is $51,000?

Pages 69–76 continued

$$\text{percent} = \frac{\text{part}}{\text{total}} = \frac{\$51,000}{\$54,000} = 54000\overline{)51000.000} = 94.4\%$$

$$\begin{array}{r}
.944 \\
54000\overline{)51000.000} \\
\underline{48600\ 0} \\
2400\ 00 \\
\underline{2160\ 00} \\
240\ 000 \\
\underline{216\ 000} \\
24\ 000
\end{array}$$

The sale price of the house was 94.4% of the list price.

9. A shortcut that uses the illustrated visual demonstration is:

$$\begin{array}{r}
100\% \text{ list price} \\
\underline{-25\% \text{ reduction}} \\
75\% \text{ purchase price}
\end{array}$$

Since the reduction is the same dollar amount as the profit, we can write:

$$\frac{\text{Seller's profit } 25\% \text{ (Part)}}{\text{Seller's cost } 75\% \text{ (Total)}} = .333$$

or, 33-1/3%

Achievement Exercise

1. $\dfrac{\$62,250}{75\%} = \$83,000$ list price

$\$83,000 - (5\% \times \$83,000) = \$83,000 - \$4,150 = \$78,850$

$\$78,850 - \$62,250 = \$16,600$ profit $\dfrac{\$16,600}{\$62,250} = 26.7\%$ profit

2. $100\% - 6\% = 94\%$ $\dfrac{\$73,320}{94\%} = \$78,000$

3. $14\% \times \$37,000 = \$5,180$ profit
$\$37,000 + \$5,180 = \$42,180$
$\$42,180 = 100\% - 6.5\%$ commission $= 93.5\%$ of sale price.

$\dfrac{\$42,180}{93.5\%} = \$45,112.299$ rounded to $\$45,100$ sale price

4. c. $\$51,700 \div .94 = \$55,000$ sale price

5. a. $\$5,200 \div .065 = \$80,000$
$\$80,000 - \$5,200 = \$74,800$
$\$74,800 - \$250 = \$74,550$ net

6. d. $\$75,200 \div 94\% = \$80,000$ list price

7. c. $40,000 × 15% = $6,000
$40,000 + $6,000 = $46,000
$46,000 ÷ .94 = $48,936.17 sale price

8. c. $3,480 ÷ 6% = $58,000
$58,000 − $3,480 − $175 − $95 = $54,250 net

9. c. $1,200 × 2 = $2,400
$78,000 × 6% = $4,680
$78,000 − $2,400 − $4,680 − $12,000 − $48,000 = $10,920 remodel

10. b. 80 × $1,980 = $158,400
$12,400 × 4 = $49,600
$158,400 × 1.75 = $277,200
$277,200 − $158,400 − $49,600 = $69,200 net profit

11. d. $10,000 × 4 = $40,000
$40,000 + $60,000 = $100,000
$30,000 × 2.5 = $75,000
$100,000 + $75,000 = $175,000
$175,000 − $100,000 = $75,000
$75,000 ÷ $100,000 = 75% gross profit

12. a. 20% ÷ 80% = 25% profit

13. c.

14. c. $50,000 ÷ 80% = $62,500 list price
$62,500 × 110% = $68,750
$68,750 − $50,000 = $18,750
$18,750 ÷ $50,000 = 37.5% profit

15. d. 15% ÷ 85% = 17.6% profit

Area and Volume

INTRODUCTION

You should know how to compute the area of any shape, since land and buildings may not be regularly shaped. Also, you may have to compute the cubic feet of space in a building, or the volume of a building such as a warehouse to determine its value. In this chapter, you will learn how to find the area of lots as well as area and volume of common building shapes. Sometimes the problem states only the dimensions without providing a picture. Sketch the picture yourself before working the problem.

ENTRY EVALUATION

Since readers will have varying amounts of knowledge and experience, the short test that follows will allow you to determine your familiarity with the material to be covered. Try all of the problems before looking at the answers, which begin on page 111.

■ Compute the area of each lettered division of the following figure.

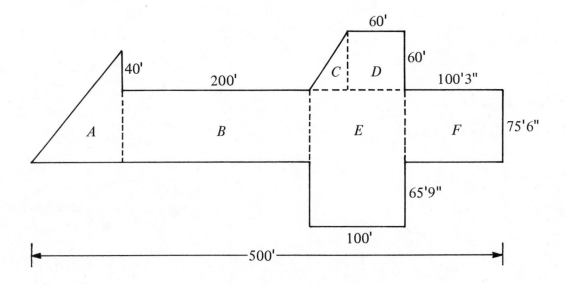

■ Each lettered division of the figure in the first question represents a lot that is for sale. Mr. Jorgenson is considering buying all of them. At $1.20 per square foot, how much would all six lots cost him?

■ Mr. Bower is the broker for the foregoing property. Mr. Simmons would like to buy lot E, which sells by itself for $1.50 per square foot. Mr. Bower receives 6% commission. If this sale goes through, how much will Mr. Bower's commission be?

■ The owner of Lot F proposes to build an office-showroom building that is 40 feet high, 30 feet wide and 45 feet long. If the bid is $70,000, what is the cost of this building per cubic foot?

AREA

Anyone in the field of real estate must be able to compute such measurements as the area of a lot and the area of floor space in a building.

Before you start working area problems, let's review some basics about shapes and measurements. This review will help you in computing areas in later problems.

> The space inside a two-dimensional shape is called its *area*.

A *right angle* is the angle formed by one-fourth of a circle. Since a full circle is 360 degrees, and one-fourth of 360 degrees is 90 degrees, a right angle is a 90-degree angle.

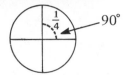

A *rectangle* is a closed figure with four sides that are at right angles to one another. In other words, each angle in a rectangle is 90 degrees.

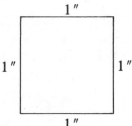

1. A *square* is a special type of rectangle. Circle the statement below that best describes a square (illustrated at the right).

   a. All sides of a square are of equal length.
   b. Only the opposite sides of a square are of equal length.
   c. Squares are rectangles with four sides of equal length.
   d. Rectangles are squares.
   e. Squares are rectangles with equal angles.

Note: The symbol for *inch* is ''. The symbol for *foot* is '. The abbreviations are *in.* and *ft.*, respectively. When the symbols or abbreviations are used in this fashion, they refer to *linear* units, or the distance between two points.

2. Which of the following figures are squares? _____ Which are rectangles? _____

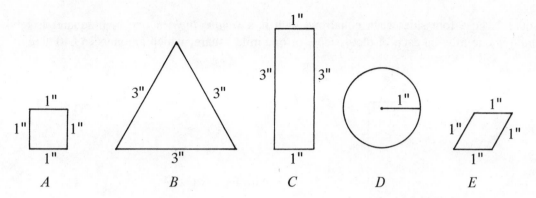

In math, the word *square* may be defined as:

- a shape whose four sides are of equal length and each angle is 90 degrees;

- a unit for measuring the area of various shapes; or

- a multiple of a number by, or times, itself.

EXAMPLES: The number 9 is the "square" of 3 because if you multiply 3×3, the answer is 9.

Units of measurement can be treated in the same manner that numbers are handled, and a clear understanding of this fact greatly simplifies math. For example, if $3 \times 3 = 9$, which is the square of 3, then yards $\times$ yards = square yards. Or, to illustrate this example further,

$$3 \text{ yards} \times 3 \text{ yards} = ?$$

Step 1.   Multiply the numbers together:

$$3 \times 3 = 9$$

Step 2.   Multiply the units of measurement together:

$$\text{yards} \times \text{yards} = \text{square yards or yards}^2$$

The *superscript* ^{2} indicates how many times the number, or unit of measurement, is multiplied by itself. This is called *power* of the number or unit of measurement. The superscript is written a half-space above the line.

Now let's look at some *square units*.

A square whose four sides each equal one inch is a *square inch* or one inch square. Likewise, one square mile is one mile on each of the 4 sides, or one mile square, which amounts to 640 acres.

EXAMPLE:

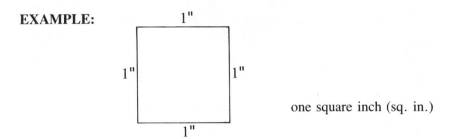

one square inch (sq. in.)

A square whose four sides each equal one foot is a *square foot*.

EXAMPLE:

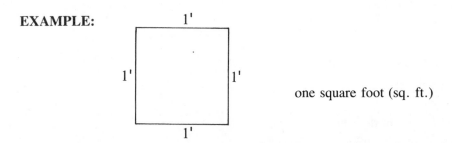

one square foot (sq. ft.)

To measure the area inside a shape, measure the number of *square units* inside the shape. One way to find the number of square units in a shape is to place the shape on a larger number of square units and count the number of square units inside the shape.

3. Count the number of square inches inside this square to find its area.

What is the area of this square?

4. What is the area of the rectangle below? (Count the number of square inches in the rectangle.)

Front Foot versus Area

In certain situations, the price of a tract of land may be priced at $x per "front foot." Typically, this occurs where the tract "fronts" onto or faces something quite desirable so that the frontage is the major element of value. This is true because it is the *frontage* of a tract that provides access to something of value such as a main street, a river or a lake. This avenue of access then becomes quite valuable, so much so that it assumes the pricing burden of the entire tract.

For example, consider a tract of land facing (or fronting on) a lake:

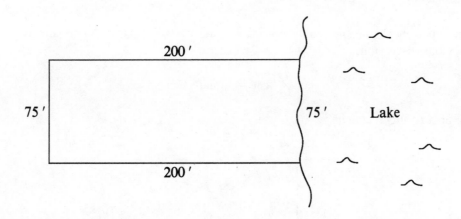

The area of the lot is 15,000 square feet (75′ × 200′ = 15,000 sq. ft.). If this lot sells for $30,000, this is equivalent to a price of $2 per square foot ($30,000 ÷ 15,000 sq. ft. = $2/sq. ft.). The price also could be shown as $400 per *front foot* ($30,000 ÷ 75 front feet = $400/front foot).

Let's try a practical application. Eagle Mountain Lake has a regulation to control the length of piers. The pier length cannot exceed 150% of the water frontage of the lot. If a lot sold for $600 per front foot and the total price was $60,000, what is the maximum pier length permitted?

$$\$60,000 \div \$600/\text{front foot} = 100 \text{ front feet}$$

$$100 \text{ front feet} \times 150\% = 150' \text{ pier length}$$

Area of Squares and Rectangles

Since counting squares is a cumbersome method, use the following formula to compute the area of any rectangle.

$$A \text{ (area)} = L \text{ (length)} \times W \text{ (width)}$$

Check your figures in Exercises 3 and 4, applying this formula. The formula should give you the same answer that counting squares did.

$$2'' \times 2'' = 4 \text{ sq. in.} \qquad 1'' \times 3'' = 3 \text{ sq. in.}$$

5. Compute the area of the following rectangle, using the formula $A = L \times W$.

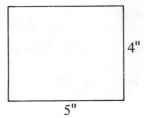

Your answer to Exercise 5 should have been 20 *square* inches. The term 20 inches refers to a straight line 20 inches long, which is a *linear* unit of measurement. Your answer should have referred to a specific *area* of 20 square inches.

Remember: When inches are multiplied by inches, the answer must be in square inches. Likewise, recalling our previous discussion,

feet $\times$ feet $=$ square feet

6. What is the area of this rectangle?

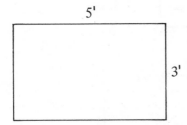

7. What is the area of this square?

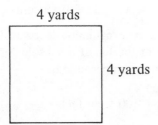

Now, you can apply what you have learned about the area of a rectangle to a practical real estate problem.

8. Mr. Gingham leases a parking lot that measures 80 feet by 150 feet. How much rent must he pay per year if the lot rents for $.30 per square foot per year?

What must be done first?

What is the formula?

What is the answer?

Conversion—Using Like Measures for Area

When an area is computed, all of the dimensions used must be given in the *same kind of units*. When you found areas in Exercises 3 and 4, by counting square units, all of the units you counted were of the same kind—inches. When you use a formula to find an area, you must also use units of the same kind for each element of the formula, with the answer as square units of that kind. So inches must be multiplied by inches to arrive at square inches, feet must be multiplied by feet to arrive at square feet and yards must be multiplied by yards to arrive at square yards.

If the two dimensions you want to multiply are in different units of measure, you must convert one to the other. The following chart shows how to convert one unit of measure to another.

> 12 inches = 1 foot
> 36 inches = 1 yard
> 3 feet = 1 yard
>
> To convert *feet* to *inches*, multiply the number of feet by 12.   (ft. × 12 = in.)
>
> To convert *inches* to *feet*, divide the number of inches by 12.   (in. ÷ 12 = ft.)
>
> To convert *yards* to *feet*, multiply the number of yards by 3.   (yd. × 3 = ft.)
>
> To convert *feet* to *yards*, divide the number of feet by 3.   (ft. ÷ 3 = yd.)
>
> To convert *yards* to *inches*, multiply the number of yards by 36.   (yd. × 36 = in.)
>
> To convert *inches* to *yards*, divide the number of inches by 36.   (in. ÷ 36 = yd.)

9. Solve the following problems.

   a. 36″ × 3′ = _____ square feet *or* _____ square inches

   b. 15″ × 1.5′ = _____ square feet *or* _____ square inches

   c. 72″ × 7′ = _____ square feet *or* _____ square inches

   d. What is the area of the square at the right in square inches?

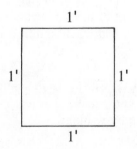

Look at your answer to problem a in Exercise 9.

$$36″ × 3′ = 9 \text{ sq. ft.} = 1,296 \text{ sq. in.}$$

Are all of these equivalent? You can find out easily.

To convert 9 square feet to square inches, multiply 9 by the square-inch equivalent of 1 square foot, which is 144 square inches (12″ × 12″).

> 144 sq. in. per sq. ft.
> × 9 sq. ft.
> ――――――――
> 1,296 sq. in.

To convert 1,296 square inches to square feet, divide by the square-inch equivalent of 1 square foot, again, 144 square inches.

$$144\overline{)\,1{,}296}^{\textstyle 9}$$
$$\underline{1\ 296}$$

Thus, 9 square feet are equivalent to 1,296 square inches.

To convert square inches, square feet and square yards, use the following chart.

To convert *square feet* to *square inches*, multiply the number of square feet by 144 (12 × 12).	(sq. ft. × 144 = sq. in.)
To convert *square inches* to *square feet*, divide the number of square inches by 144.	(sq. in. ÷ 144 = sq. ft.)
To convert *square yards* to *square feet*, multiply the number of square yards by 9 (3 × 3).	(sq. yd. × 9 = sq. ft.)
To convert *square feet* to *square yards*, divide the number of square feet by 9.	(sq. ft. ÷ 9 = sq. yd.)
To convert *square yards* to *square inches*, multiply the number of square yards by 1,296 (12 × 12 × 9).	(sq. yd. × 1,296 = sq. in.)
To convert *square inches* to *square yards*, divide the number of square inches by 1,296.	(sq. in. ÷ 1,296 = sq. yd.)

Sometimes, you may have difficulty in remembering whether to multiply or divide when converting one unit of measurement to another. Remember that units of measurement have to be of the *same kind,* and just as you would multiply oranges × oranges, you have to multiply feet × feet.

EXAMPLES: To determine how many yards there are in a mile, if you know that 5,280 feet = 1 mile, and 1 yard = 3 feet, you can begin by writing:

$$\frac{5{,}280\text{ feet}}{1\text{ mile}} \times \frac{1\text{ yard}}{\text{feet}} =$$

In the example, the unit of measurement "feet" is in the numerator (top figure) of one fraction and in the denominator (bottom figure) of the other fraction, and therefore, they *cancel* each other. Or, if the numerator is divided by the denominator, considering "feet" divided by "feet," the answer is 1:

$$\frac{5,280 \cancel{\text{feet}}}{1 \text{ mile}} \times \frac{1 \text{ yard}}{3 \cancel{\text{feet}}} =$$

$$\frac{5,280 \times 1}{1 \text{ mile}} \times \frac{1 \text{ yard}}{3 \times 1} =$$

When you multiply the numerators across, and the denominators across, the product is $\frac{5,280}{3}$ for the numbers and $\frac{\text{yards}}{\text{mile}}$ for the unit of measurement. By dividing:

$$\frac{5,280 \text{ yards}}{3 \text{ miles}}$$

your answer is:

$$1,760 \text{ yards per mile.}$$

Because miles were converted into yards, *yards had to be written in the numerator* (because that is where it will be in the answer). The conversion unit in the denominator will always cancel the unwanted unit in the numerator—feet in this example. It is very important to include the units of measurement in each step of a calculation. Otherwise, errors are likely to creep in, because we may forget which units those numbers describe.

A more complicated example is as follows. If a rancher has two sections of grassland to lease out, and his lease provides that there will not be more than one cow per ten acres, how much money does he receive for a 1-year lease if the land leases for $60 per cow per year? One section = 640 acres.

With practice, you can learn to express the relationships in a way that enables you to cancel the units you want to eliminate:

$$\frac{640 \text{ acres}}{1 \text{ section}} \times \frac{2 \text{ sections}}{1} \times \frac{1 \text{ cow}}{10 \text{ acres}} \times \frac{\$60}{1 \text{ cow}}$$

or:

$$\frac{640 \text{ acres} \times 2 \text{ sections} \times 1 \text{ cow} \times \$60}{1 \text{ section} \times 10 \text{ acres} \times 1 \text{ cow}}$$

Cancelling, we now have:

$$\frac{640 \cancel{\text{acres}} \times 2 \cancel{\text{sections}} \times 1 \cancel{\text{cow}} \times \$60}{1 \cancel{\text{section}} \times 10 \cancel{\text{acres}} \times 1 \cancel{\text{cow}}}$$

$$\frac{640 \times 2 \times 1 \times \$60}{1 \times 10}$$

This leaves only numbers in the problem, plus the dollar sign in the numerator.

Work this on your calculator:

Press: 6 then 4 then 0
Press: ✕ (multiplication)
Press: 2
Press: ✕ (multiplication)
Press: 6 then 0
Press: ÷ (division)
Press: 1 then 0
Press: = (equal sign)
Display: 7,680 ($7,680.00)

10. Now, try a problem. There are 16.5 feet in a rod and 5,280 feet in a mile. How many rods are there in one mile?

Now, solve the next problem.

11. Mr. Milgren's house is on a lot which is 90 feet by 720 inches. What is the area of his lot?

Note: In the real estate business, lot sizes are generally referred to in feet rather than inches.

12. Compute the area of the lot below in square feet.

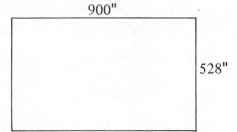

13. You have sold a lot with 66 feet and 9 inches of street frontage, and a depth of 150 feet to an alley. The sale price was $2.56 per square foot. Compute the amount you received from this sale, if your commission rate was 6%. What was the total sale price?

14. You have contracted to build a sidewalk in front of your house. It is to be 5 feet wide by $27\frac{1}{2}$ feet long. If the contractor charges $35 per square yard, how much will the sidewalk cost you?

Area of Triangles

 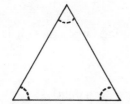 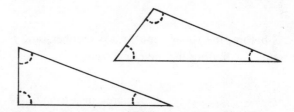

A *triangle* is a closed figure with three straight sides and three angles. *Tri* means three.

The square-inch figure at the right has been cut in half by a straight line drawn through the opposite corners, to make two equal triangles.

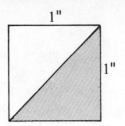

15. How many square inches are in the shaded part of the square?

a. $\frac{1}{2}$ sq. in.

b. $\frac{1}{4}$ sq. in.

c. 1 sq. in.

d. 2 sq. in.

16. How many square inches are contained in this triangle, when it is placed on a square-inch grid?

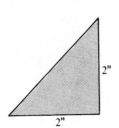 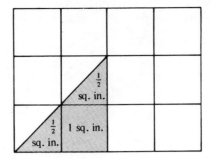

17. What is the area of the triangle below?

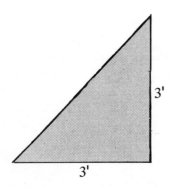 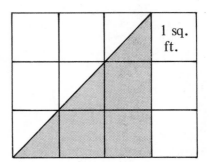

As before, the square-unit grid is cumbersome for computing large areas. It is more convenient to use a formula for finding the area of a triangle.

$$\text{area of a triangle} = \frac{1}{2} \ (\text{base} \times \text{height})$$

$$A \ \Delta = \frac{1}{2} \ (bh)$$

or

$$\text{area of a triangle} = \frac{b \times h}{2}$$

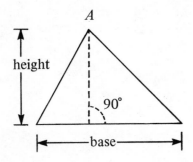 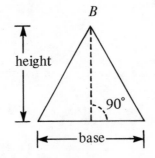 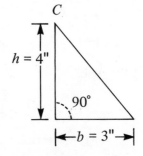

The *base* is the side on which the triangle sits.

The *height* is the straight line distance from the top of the uppermost angle to the base. The height line must form a 90 degree angle to the base.

18. Compute the area of triangle *C*.

19. The diagram below shows a lakefront lot. Compute its area.

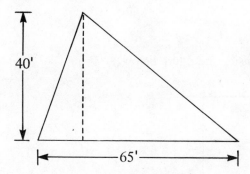

20. Mr. Wier has purchased the following lot at $.95 a square foot. His broker received a 10% commission on the sale. How much was the broker's commission?

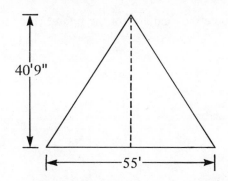

Area of Irregular Closed Figures

21. Here is a drawing of two neighboring lots. Find the area of each rectangle and add them.

    a. What is the area of lot *A*?

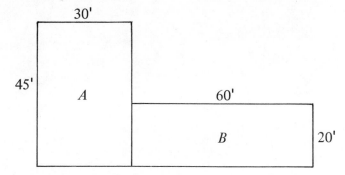

b. What is the area of lot *B*?

c. What is the total area of both lots?

22. Make two rectangles by drawing one straight line inside the figure below.

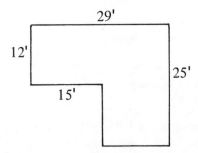

23. Now, using the measurements given in Exercise 22, compute the total area of the figure. (Find the area of each rectangle and add them.)

The area of an irregular figure can be found by dividing it into regular figures, computing the area of each regular figure and adding all the areas together to obtain the total area.

24. Divide this figure into rectangles.

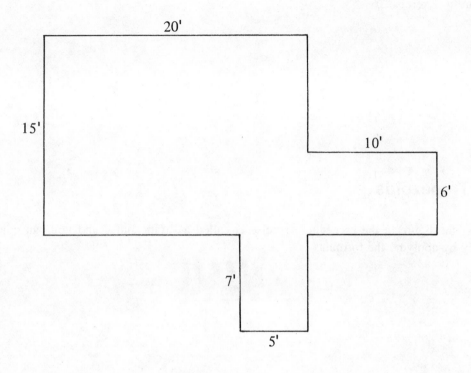

25. What is the total area of the figure in Exercise 24?

26. Make a rectangle and a triangle by drawing a single line through the figure below.

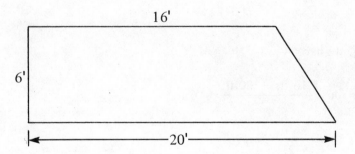

27. Since you know how to compute the areas of both rectangles and triangles, compute the total area of the figure in Exercise 26.

Area of Trapezoids

The shape of the figure in the preceding exercise is called a "trapezoid," and you can compute its area more directly by applying the formula:

$$A = \frac{a + b}{2} \times h$$

where,

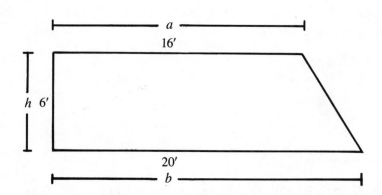

Now, substituting, we have:

Step 1.　　$A = \dfrac{16 \text{ ft.} + 20 \text{ ft.}}{2} \times 6 \text{ ft.}$

Step 2.　　$A = \dfrac{36 \text{ ft.}}{2} \times 6 \text{ ft.}$

Step 3.　　$A = 18 \text{ ft.} \times 6 \text{ ft.}$

Step 4.　　$A = 108 \text{ sq. ft.}$

Notice that this is exactly the same answer that you obtained when you broke up the irregular shape into a rectangle and a triangle.

28. Compute the area of each section of the figure below. Then, compute the total area.

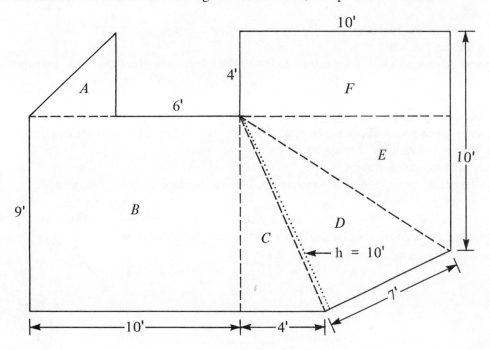

29. Mr. Rigby has purchased the following lot at $2.11 per square foot. His real estate broker received a 9% commission on the sale. What was the broker's total commission?

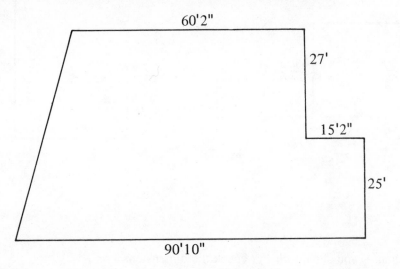

Living Area Calculations

Real estate salespersons frequently must compute the amount of living area in a house.

> The living area of a house is the area enclosed by the outside dimensions of the heated and air-conditioned portions of the house. This excludes open porches, garages, etc.

When measuring a house in preparation for calculating the living area, these steps should be followed:

1. Draw a sketch of the foundation.
2. Measure *all* outside walls.
3. If the house has an attached garage, treat the inside walls that are common to the house as outside walls of the house.
4. Measure garage.
5. Convert inches to tenths of foot (so that the same units of measurement are used in the calculations).
6. Before leaving the house, check to see that net dimensions of opposite sides are equal. If not, remeasure.
7. Section off your sketch into rectangles.
8. Calculate area of each rectangle.
9. Add up the areas, being careful to *subtract* the area of the garage, *if necessary.*

30. What is the living area of the house shown in the sketch? Follow the directions listed, and remember to compute each area separately. You do *not* have to complete step 6.

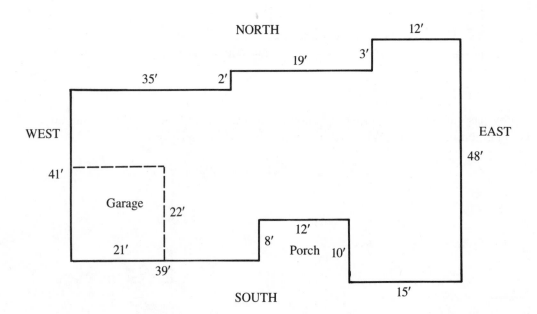

Before leaving the house, you should *always* check the dimensions:

> South side $= 39' + 12' + 15' = 66'$
> North side $= 35' + 19' + 12' = 66'$

> East side $= 48'$ O.K. (If this step is omitted
> West side $= 41' + 2' + 3' - 8' + 10' = 48'$ and a measurement
> error occurs, the an-
> swer will be wrong.)

Note the $-8'$ in the West side check. This is because we need the net difference in the $8'$ and $10'$ dimensions.

31. How many acres of land are in a tract having the dimensions shown? One acre is equal to 43,560 square feet.

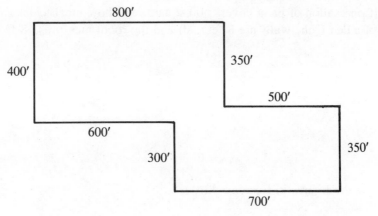

VOLUME

When a shape has more than one side and encloses a space, the shape has *volume*.

The space that a 3-dimensional object occupies is called its *volume*.

Technically speaking, each shape with 3 dimensions can also be measured in terms of its surface area. For example, a bedroom has volume because it has 3 dimensions—length, width, and height; however, *one wall* can be measured as a *surface area,* or: area = length × width.

32. a. Which of the following shapes have volume?

b. Which have only area?

A. Cube   *B.* Square   *C.* Box

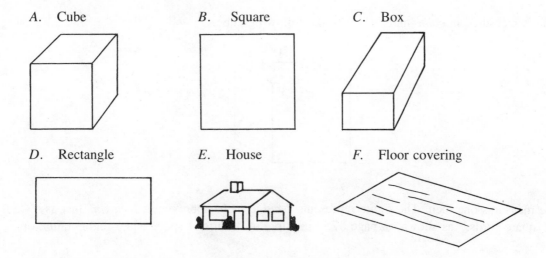

D. Rectangle   *E.* House   *F.* Floor covering

Flat shapes—squares, rectangles, triangles, and so on—do *not* have volume. Flat shapes have two dimensions (length and width or height), and shapes with volume have three dimensions (length, width and height).

33. Even though a room has volume, a salesperson might have to calculate its surface area to determine how many gallons of paint are required to repaint a den, in order to satisfy a loan requirement made by the appraiser. If one gallon of paint covers 500 square feet, how much paint is needed to paint the walls and ceiling of a den if the walls are 8 feet tall and the room measures 18 feet by 24 feet?

Now, take another look at the figures in Exercise 32.

34. A box is to a rectangle as a cube is to a _____ .

Cubic Units

A *cube* is made up of six squares. Look at the six sides of the following cube.

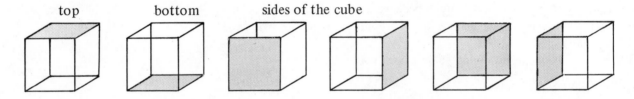

top   bottom   sides of the cube

Volume is measured in *cubic* units. Look at the following cube.

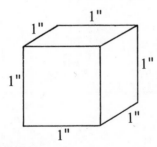

Each side measures one inch. The figure represents *1 cubic inch,* abbreviated *1 cu. in.* Just as "yards × yards = square yards," as shown on page 87, a multiple of 3 units of space equals cubic units, or:

$$\text{inches} \times \text{inches} \times \text{inches} = \text{cubic inches}$$

Cubic inches can also be indicated as inches^3, and the superscript ^{3} means to multiply *inches* by itself 3 times.

35. How many cubic inches are there in the following figure?

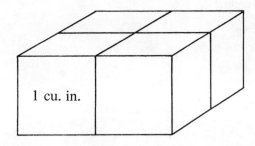

1 cu. in.

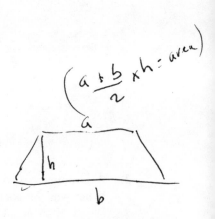

The following figure represents 1 cubic foot, abbreviated 1 cu. ft.

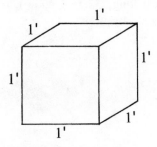

36. How many cubic feet are represented by the following figure?

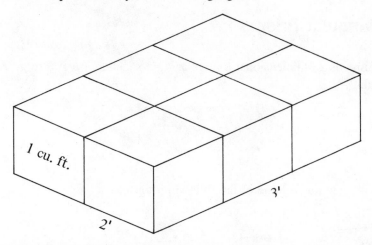

1 cu. ft.

2'   3'

Volume of Box Shapes

37. Find the volume of each of the boxes below, using the formula for computing volume.

V (volume) $= L$ (length) $\times W$ (width) $\times H$ (height)

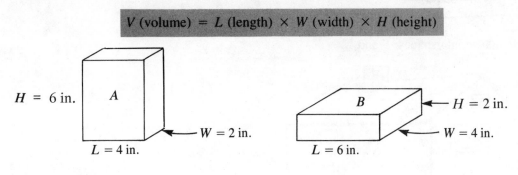

$H = 6$ in. A

$W = 2$ in.

$L = 4$ in.

B $H = 2$ in.

$W = 4$ in.

$L = 6$ in.

a. volume of box $A =$

b. volume of box $B =$

38. How many cubic feet of dirt must be excavated to dig a hole 5 feet long, 4 feet wide and 4 feet deep? (Depth is the equivalent of height.)

39. A building cost $90,000. It is 50 feet long, 35 feet wide and 40 feet high, including the basement. What was the cost of this building per cubic foot?

Volume of Triangular Prisms

To compute the volume of a 3-dimensional triangular figure, called a *prism* (e.g., an A-frame house), use the following formula:

$$\text{volume} = \frac{1}{2}(b \times h \times w)$$

EXAMPLE: To compute the volume of the following house:

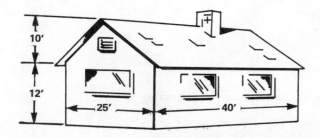

1. Divide the house into shapes, *S* and *T*.

2. Find the volume of S.

$$V = \frac{1}{2}(b \times h \times w) = \frac{1}{2}(25' \times 10' \times 40')$$

$$= \frac{1}{2}(10{,}000 \text{ cu. ft.}) = 5{,}000 \text{ cu. ft.}$$

3. Find the volume of T.
   $V = L \times W \times H = 25' \times 40' \times 12' = 12{,}000$ cu. ft.

4. Total volumes S and T.
   5,000 cu. ft. + 12,000 cu. ft. = 17,000 cu. ft.

40. The Farrity family has purchased a two-story house for $58,000. The house is 35 feet long, 20 feet wide and the first story is 10 feet high. The second story is A-shaped, with an 8 foot high roof at the highest point. How much did the house cost per cubic foot?

Conversion—Using Like Measures for Volume

To convert cubic inches, feet and yards, use the following chart.

To convert *cubic feet* to *cubic inches*, multiply the number of feet by 1,728 (12 × 12 × 12).	(cu. ft. × 1,728 = cu. in.)
To convert *cubic inches* to *cubic feet*, divide the number of cubic inches by 1,728.	(cu. in. ÷ 1,728 = cu. ft.)
To convert *cubic yards* to *cubic feet*, multiply the number of cubic yards by 27 (3 × 3 × 3).	(cu. yd. × 27 = cu. ft.)
To convert *cubic feet* to *cubic yards*, divide the number of cubic feet by 27.	(cu. ft. ÷ 27 = cu. yd.)
To convert *cubic yards* to *cubic inches*, multiply the number of cubic yards by 46,656 (12 × 12 × 12 × 27).	(cu. yd. × 46,656 = cu. in.)
To convert *cubic inches* to *cubic yards*, divide the number of cubic inches by 46,656.	(cu in. ÷ 46,656 = cu. yd.)

41. How many cubic yards of space are there in a flat-roofed house 27 feet long, 18 feet wide and 9 feet high?

42. What is the cost of pouring a concrete driveway 20 feet wide, 80 feet long and 4 inches thick if concrete costs $60 per cubic yard and the finishing costs $.28 per square foot including setting the forms and furnishing the steel?

ACHIEVEMENT EXERCISE

When you have finished both parts of this exercise, check your answers against those on pages 119–120. If you miss any of the questions, review this chapter before going on to Chapter 6.

Part I—Open Response   Complete the following problems.

1. Find the total area of this figure.

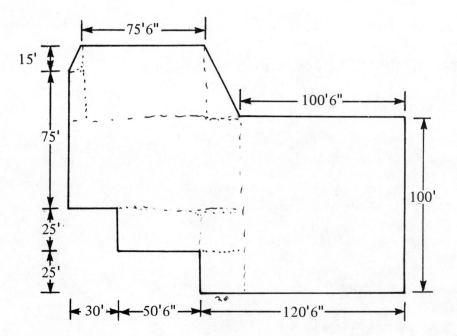

2. 12′ × 4′ = _____ sq. ft. = _____ sq. in. = _____ sq yd.

   3′ × 3′ × 3′ = _____ cu. ft. = _____ cu. in. = _____ cu. yd.

3. The following building costs $48 per cubic yard. What is the total cost of this building?

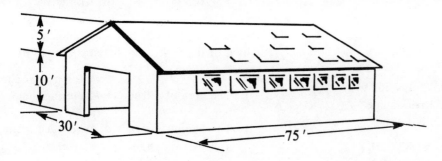

Part II—Multiple Choice   Select the correct response from the choices supplied.

4. By selecting from a, b, c or d, indicate which of the following statements is (are) true.

   I. The width of a rectangle is twice its height.
   II. A rectangle is a closed figure with four sides that are at right angles to one another.

      a. I only
      b. II only
      c. both I and II
      d. neither I nor II

5. The area of a rectangle that is 5 feet by 17 feet is:

      a. 22 feet.
      b. 85 square feet.
      c. 44 square feet.
      d. 44 lineal feet.

6. John Bowers owned a tract of land 150 feet wide and 700 feet long, with the 150 feet fronting on an east-west road. Bowers sold the northern 300 feet of this tract. The remaining land was leased to a neighbor at the annual rate of $500 an acre (an acre is 43,560 square feet). The neighbor's approximate yearly rent is:

      a. $666.   c. $690.
      b. $515.   d. $650.

7. You as broker sold a triangular tract of land for $750 an acre. What is the amount of your commission at 8% if the land had a base length of 1,200 feet and the height of the triangle measured 700 feet?

      a. $1,156.80.   c. $550.00
      b. $578.40   d. $976.00

8. A seller owned a rectangular 10-acre tract of land with a frontage of 726 feet along the south side of a paved road. After selling the southern half of this tract, the owner fenced the remaining land at a cost of $1 a running, or lineal, foot. The fence cost:

      a. $2,652.   c. $2,052.
      b. $1,326.   d. $2,126.

9. A U-shaped barn consists of two rectangles 30 feet by 75 feet and a connecting section 20 feet by 50 feet. The approximate cost of a concrete floor 4 inches thick, at the rate of $36 a cubic yard, is:

      a. $44,000.   c. $2,442.
      b. $2,222.   d. $1,444.

10. A building has been razed to make parking spaces, and the basement area must be filled with earth and solid fill. The hold is 35 feet wide by 79 feet long and is 6 feet deep. What is the approximate amount of cubic yards of fill required?

    a. 614   c. 5,530
    b. 2,765   d. 18,590

11. An L-shaped lot 85′ by 190′, plus 55′ 9″ by 120′, has been sold at $2 per square foot. The broker's 8% commission is:

    a. $3,490.60.   c. $1,827.20.
    b. $3,654.40.   d. $1,820.00

12. What is the cost of 2/5 of 174,240 square feet of land if the price per acre is $1,500?

    a. $2,400   c. $1,500
    b. $6,000   d. $1,200

13. A 60′ by 175′ lot has a 35′ by 70′ right triangle alley easement on one corner. The square feet of usable area is:

    a. 8,050.   c. 9,275.
    b. 10,395.   d. 10,500.

14. By selecting from a, b, c or d, indicate which of the following statements is (are) true.

    I. The area of a triangle = base × height.
    II. The height line of a triangle must form a 90 degree angle to the base.

    a. I only
    b. II only
    c. both I and II
    d. neither I nor II

15. What is the square footage of the living area of the house shown in the following illustration?

    a. 2,750   c. 3,486
    b. 3,531   d. 3,738

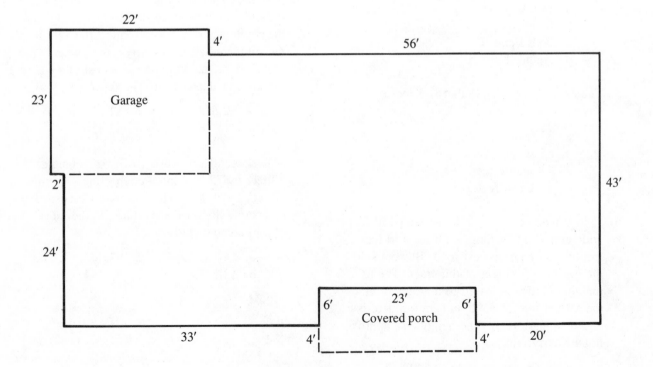

ANSWER KEY

Entry Evaluation

- A = 5,760.56 sq. ft.   B = 15,100 sq. ft.   C = 1,200 sq. ft.
  D = 3,600 sq. ft.   E = 14,125 sq. ft.   F = 7,568.88 sq. ft.

- $56,825.33

- $1,271.25

- $1.30

Pages 86–108

1. The correct answer is c. Alternatives a and e may be true, but they are incomplete. You would not be able to recognize a square given only the information in either a or e.

2. Figure A is a square. Figures A and C are rectangles.

3. 4 square inches (You must include word *square* to be correct.)

4. 3 square inches

5. A (area) = L (length) $\times$ W (width) = $4'' \times 5'' = 20$ sq. in.

6. $A = L \times W = 3' \times 5' = 15$ sq. ft.

7. $A = L \times W = 4$ yd. $\times 4$ yd. $= 16$ sq. yd.

8. First, the area must be computed.
Formula: $A = L \times W = 150' \times 80' = 12,000$ sq. ft.

Multiply the number of square feet by the price per square foot to get the total rent.
number of square feet $\times$ price per square foot = total price
$12,000 \times \$.30 = \$3,600$

9. a. $36'' \times 3' = 3' \times 3' = 9$ sq. ft. *or* $36'' \times 3' = 36'' \times 36'' = 1,296$ sq. in.

b. $15'' \times 1.5' = 1.25' \times 1.5' = 1.875$ sq. ft. *or* $15'' \times 1.5' = 15'' \times 18'' = 270$ sq. in.

c. $72'' \times 7' = 6' \times 7' = 42$ sq. ft. *or* $72'' \times 7' = 72'' \times 84'' = 6,048$ sq. in.

d. $A = L \times W = 1' \times 1' = 12'' \times 12'' = 144$ sq. in.

10. $\dfrac{5,280 \text{ feet}}{1 \text{ mile}} \times \dfrac{1 \text{ rod}}{16.5 \text{ feet}} = ?$

Step 1. Cancel "feet" in both fractions.
Step 2. Perform the division.
Step 3. Write the answer.

$$\frac{5,280 \text{ feet}}{1 \text{ mile}} = \frac{1 \text{ rod}}{16.5 \text{ feet}} = \frac{5,280}{16.5} = \frac{320 \text{ rods}}{1 \text{ mile}}$$

Pages 86–108 continued

11. $720 \text{ inches} \times \dfrac{1 \text{ foot}}{12 \text{ inches}} = \dfrac{720}{12} = 60 \text{ feet}$

$720'' = 60' \ A = L \times W = 90' \times 60' = 5,400 \text{ sq. ft.}$

12. $900'' = 75' \quad 528'' = 44'$
$A = L \times W = 75' \times 44' = 3,300 \text{ sq. ft.}$
or
$900'' \times 528'' = 475,200 \text{ sq. in.} \qquad \dfrac{475,200}{144} = 3,300 \text{ sq. ft.}$

13. Compute area.
$9'' \div 12 = .75'$ (Convert inches to feet for consistency.)
$A = L \times W = 66.75' \times 150' = 10,012.5 \text{ sq. ft.}$

Find total cost of lot.
total = price per square foot × area = $2.56 × 10,012.5 = $25,632

Compute commission.
part = total × percent = $25,632 × 6% = $1,537.92 commission

14. Compute area.
$A = 27.5' \times 5' = 137.5 \text{ sq. ft.}$

Convert square feet to square yards.
137.5 sq. ft. ÷ 9 =

$$
\begin{array}{r}
15.277 = 15.28 \text{ sq. yd.} \\
9\overline{)137.500} \\
\underline{9} \\
47 \\
\underline{45} \\
2\,5 \\
\underline{1\,8} \\
70 \\
\underline{63} \\
70 \\
\underline{63} \\
7 \\
\end{array}
$$

Compute cost.
cost = price per sq. yd. × number of sq. yd. = $35.00 × 15.28 = $534.80

15. a

16. $\dfrac{1}{2} \text{ sq. in.} + \dfrac{1}{2} \text{ sq. in.} + 1 \text{ sq. in.} = 2 \text{ sq. in.}$

17. 4.5 sq. ft.

18. $A = \dfrac{1}{2}\,(bh) = \dfrac{1}{2}\,(3'' \times 4'') = \dfrac{1}{2}\,(12 \text{ sq. in.}) = 6 \text{ sq. in.}$

19. $A = \dfrac{1}{2}\,(bh) = \dfrac{1}{2}\,(40' \times 65') = \dfrac{1}{2}\,(2,600 \text{ sq. ft.}) = 1,300 \text{ sq. ft.}$

20. Find the area.

$$A = \frac{1}{2}(bh) = \frac{1}{2}(55' \times 40.75') = \frac{1}{2}(2,241.25 \text{ sq. ft.}) = 1,120.625 \text{ sq. ft.} = 1,120.63 \text{ sq. ft.}$$

Find the cost.
cost = price per sq. ft. × number of sq. ft. = $.95 × 1,120.63 sq. ft. = $1,064.598 = $1,064.60

Compute the commission.
part = total × percent = $1,064.60 × 10% = $106.46.

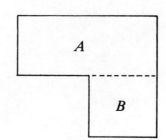

21. a. lot A = 30′ × 45′ = 1,350 sq. ft.

b. lot B = 60′ × 20′ = 1,200 sq. ft.

c. both lots = 1,350 sq. ft. + 1,200 sq. ft. = 2,550 sq. ft.

22. There are two possible answers.

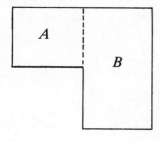

23. There are two ways to compute the answer.

area of A = 15′ × 12′ = 180 sq. ft.
area of B = 25′ × (29′ − 15″) = 25′ × 14′ = 350 sq. ft.
total area = 180 sq. ft. + 350 sq. ft. = 530 sq. ft.

area of A = 29′ × 12′ = 348 sq. ft.
area of B = (29′ − 15′) × (25′ − 12′) = 14′ × 13′ = 182 sq. ft.
total area = 348 sq. ft. + 182 sq. ft. = 530 sq. ft.

24. Here are three possible variations.

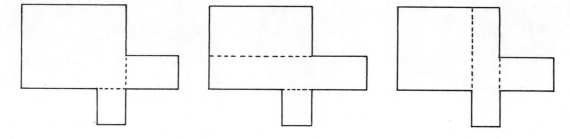

Pages 86–108 continued

25. This solution applies to the first possible division given in the answer to Exercise 24.

area of $A = 20' \times 15' = 300$ sq. ft.
area of $B = 10' \times 6' = 60$ sq. ft.
area of $C = 7' \times 5' = 35$ sq. ft.
total area $= 395$ sq. ft.

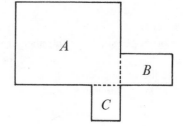

26.

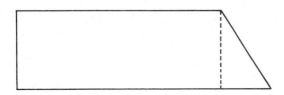

27. Compute area of rectangle.
$A = L \times W = 16' \times 6' = 96$ sq. ft.

Compute area of triangle.

$A = \frac{1}{2} (bh) = \frac{1}{2} (20' - 16') \times 6' = \frac{1}{2} (4' \times 6') = \frac{1}{2} (24 \text{ sq. ft.}) = 12$ sq. ft.

Total the two areas.
total area $= 96$ sq. ft. $+ 12$ sq. ft. $= 108$ sq. ft.

28. area of $A = \frac{1}{2} (10' - 6') \times 4' = 8$ sq. ft.

area of $B = 10' \times 9' = 90$ sq. ft.

area of $C = \frac{1}{2} (4' \times 9') = 18$ sq. ft.

area of $D = \frac{1}{2} (7' \times 10') = 35$ sq. ft.

area of $E = \frac{1}{2} (10' - 4') + 10' = 30$ sq. ft.

area of $F = 10' \times 4' = 40$ sq. ft.
total area $= (8 + 90 + 18 + 35 + 30 + 40)$ sq. ft. $= 221$ sq. ft.

29. a. Divide figure into regular shapes:

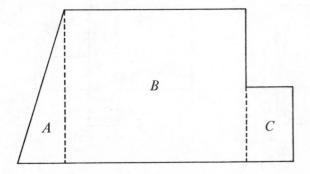

b. Find area of A.

area of $A = \frac{1}{2} (bh)$

$h = 27' + 25' = 52'$

$b = 90'10'' - (60'2'' + 15'2'') = 90'10'' - 75'4'' = 15'6'' = 15.5'$

area of $A = \frac{1}{2} (15.5' \times 52') = \frac{1}{2} (806.0) = 403$ sq. ft.

c. Find area of B.

(You may need to refer to problem 5 on page 90.)

area of $B = L \times W = 60'2'' \times (27' + 25') = 60.17' \times 52' = 3,128.84$ sq. ft.

d. Find area of C.

area of $C = L \times W = 15'2'' \times 25' = 15.17' \times 25' = 379.25$ sq. ft.

e. Total areas.

403.00 sq. ft. + 3,128.84 sq. ft. + 379.25 sq. ft. = 3,911.09 sq. ft. or 3,911 sq. ft.

f. Compute total cost of land.

total cost = number of sq. ft. × cost per sq. ft. = 3,911 sq. ft. × \$2.11 = \$8,252.21

g. Compute commission.

part = total × percent = \$8,252.21 × 9% = \$742.698 = \$742.70

The broker received a \$742.70 commission on this sale.

B and C may also be shown, and their areas computed, in this way:

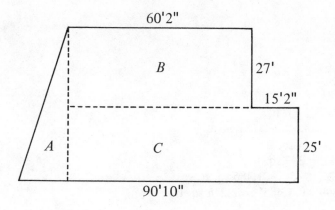

a. area of A = 403 sq. ft. as before

b. area of $B = L \times W = 60'2'' \times 27' = (60' + 2/12') \times 27' = 1,624.50$ sq. ft.

c. area of $C = L \times W \qquad L = 60'2'' + 15'2'' = 75'4'' = 75.33$

area of $C = 75.33' \times 25' = 1,883.25$ sq. ft.

d. Total: 403 sq. ft. + 1,624.50 sq. ft. + 1,883.25 sq. ft. = 3,910.75 = 3,911 sq. ft.

The rest of the solution is the same as the first method.

Pages 86–108 continued

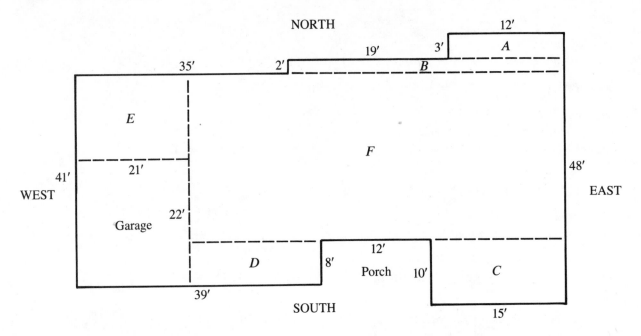

30. Compute each area separately. If you are having difficulty, see the solution under (b), which follows.

    a. area of A = 3′ × 12′ =   36 sq. ft.
       area of B = 2′ × 31′ =   62
       area of C = 10′ × 15′ =   150
       area of D = 8′ × 18′ =   144
       area of E = 19′ × 21′ =   399
       area of F = 33′ × 45′ = 1,485
                        Total = 2,276 sq. ft.

    b. area of A = 3′ × 12′ = 36 sq. ft.
       area of B = 2′ × (19′ + 12′) = 2′ × 31′ = 62 sq. ft.
       area of C = 10′ × 15′ = 150 sq. ft.
       area of D = 8′ × (39′ − 21′) = 8′ × 18′ = 144 sq. ft.
       area of E = (41′ − 22′) × 21′ = 19′ × 21′ = 399 sq. ft.
       area of F = (41′ − 8′) × (66′ − 21′) = 33′ × 45′ = 1,485 sq. ft.
       Total   = 36′ + 62′ + 150′ + 144′ + 399′ + 1,485′ = 2,276 sq. ft.

    Note that the area of the garage was *not* calculated or included in the total.

31. Divide into rectangles, such as:

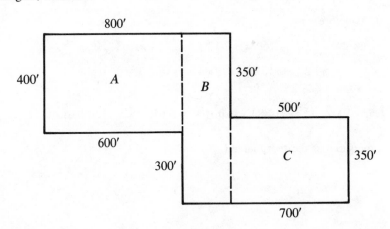

area of $A = 400' \times 600' = 240,000$ sq. ft.
area of $B = 200' \times 700' = 140,000$ sq. ft.
area of $C = 350' \times 500' = \underline{175,000}$ sq. ft.
$555,000$ sq. ft.

Convert square feet to acres:

$$555,000 \text{ sq. ft. } \times \frac{1 \text{ acre}}{43,560 \text{ sq. ft.}} = \frac{555,000}{43,560} = 12.74 \text{ (Square feet cancel.)}$$

32. a. *A, C* and *E* have volume.

b. *B, D* and *F* have area. (Technically, each side of *A, C* and *E* also has area; it is called *surface area.*)

33. First, count the flat areas in the room, and then calculate the number of square feet in each of these surface areas.

West wall:	8' tall × 18' wide	= 144 sq. ft.
East wall:	8' tall × 18' wide	= 144
North wall:	8' tall × 24' long	= 192
South wall:	8' tall × 24' long	= 192
Ceiling:	18' wide × 24' long	= 432
		1,104 sq. ft.

Recalling the earlier discussion on units of measurement treated as numbers, multiply the number of square feet by a fraction showing the amount of paint over the square feet it will cover, or:

$$1,104 \text{ square feet } \times \frac{1 \text{ gallon}}{500 \text{ square feet}}$$

Because "square feet" cancel, you can then divide 1,104 by 500. The answer is 2.21 gallons, since *gallons* is the only unit of measurement left. Obviously, you can't buy .21 of a gallon, but the area of the doors and windows in the den has not been subtracted. Therefore, only 2 gallons would probably be enough to cover the old paint.

34. square

35. You can put 4 cubic inches inside the box, so the volume of the box is 4 cubic inches.

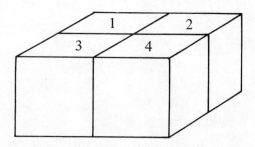

36. The volume of this figure is 6 cubic feet (6 cu. ft.).

37. a. volume of box $A = L \times W \times H = 4'' \times 2'' \times 6'' = 48$ cu. in.

b. volume of box $B = L \times W \times H = 6'' \times 4'' \times 2'' = 48$ cu. in.

38. $V = L \times W \times H = 5' \times 4' \times 4' = 80$ cu. ft.

Pages 86–108 continued

39. $V = L \times W \times H = 50' \times 35' \times 40' = 70{,}000$ cu. ft.

$$\text{cost per cubic foot} = \frac{\text{total cost}}{\text{volume}} = 70{,}000 \overline{)\,90{,}000.000\,}^{1.285} = \$1.29 \text{ or, } \frac{\$90{,}000}{70{,}000 \text{ cu. ft.}} = \frac{\$1.29}{\text{cu. ft.}}$$

$$
\begin{array}{r}
1.285 \\
70{,}000\overline{)90{,}000.000} \\
\underline{70\ 000} \\
20\ 000\ 0 \\
\underline{14\ 000\ 0} \\
6\ 000\ 00 \\
\underline{5\ 600\ 00} \\
400\ 000 \\
\underline{350\ 000} \\
50\ 000
\end{array}
$$

40. a. Compute volume of first story.
   $V = 35' \times 20' \times 10' = 7{,}000$ cu. ft.

   b. Compute volume of second story.

   $V = \frac{1}{2}(35' \times 20' \times 8') = \frac{1}{2}(5{,}600 \text{ cu. ft.}) = 2{,}800$ cu. ft.

   c. Total.
   $7{,}000$ cu. ft. $+ 2{,}800$ cu. ft. $= 9{,}800$ cu. ft.

   d. Find cost per cu. ft.

   $\text{cost} = \dfrac{\text{price}}{\text{number of cubic feet}} = \dfrac{\$58{,}000}{9{,}800 \text{ cu. ft.}} = \$5.92$ per cu. ft.

41. $V = L \times W \times H = 27' \times 18' \times 9' = 4{,}374$ cu. ft.
   cu. yd. = cu. ft. ÷ 27 so 4,374 cu. ft. ÷ 27 = 162 cu. yd.

42. Step 1: Determine the volume of concrete:

$$20 \text{ ft.} \times 80 \text{ ft.} \times \left(4 \text{ in.} \times \frac{1 \text{ ft.}}{12 \text{ in.}}\right) =$$

$$20 \text{ ft.} \times 80 \text{ ft.} \times \left(4 \text{ in.} \times \frac{1 \text{ ft.}}{12 \text{ in.}}\right) = 20 \text{ ft.} \times 80 \text{ ft.} \times \frac{4}{12} \text{ ft.} =$$

$\dfrac{6{,}400}{12} = 533.33$ cu. ft.

Convert 533.33 cu. ft. to cubic yards:

$533.33 \text{ cu. ft.} \times \dfrac{1 \text{ cu. yd.}}{27 \text{ cu. ft.}} \times 19.75$ cu. yd.

Step 2: Determine the cost of the concrete:

$19.75 \text{ cu. yds.} \times \dfrac{\$60}{1 \text{ cu. yd.}} \times \$1{,}185.00$

Note that if you have left all of the numbers in your calculator and performed the chain operations indicated, your answer at this point is $1,185.19. This is another example of how to obtain greater calculator accuracy.

Step 3: Determine the surface area of the driveway:

$20 \text{ ft.} \times 80 \text{ ft.} = 1{,}600$ sq. ft.

Step 4: Determine the cost of the finishing labor:

$$1,600 \text{ sq. ft.} \times \frac{\$.28}{1 \text{ sq. ft.}} = \$448.00$$

Step 5: Add the cost of concrete and labor:

$1,185.00 concrete
$\underline{+\ \ 448.00}$ labor
$1,633.00 Total Cost of Driveway

Achievement Exercise

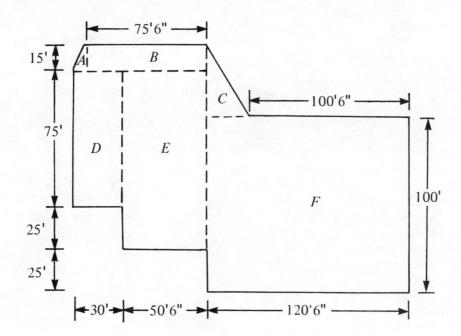

1. A. $b \times (30' + 50.5') - 75.5' = 5'$ $\frac{1}{2}(5' \times 15') = 37.5$ sq. ft.

    B. $75.5' \times 15' = 1,132.5$ sq. ft.

    C. $b = 120.5' - 100.5' = 20'$ $h = (15' + 75' + 25' + 25') - 100' = 40'$
       $\frac{1}{2}(20' \times 40') = 400$ sq. ft.

    D. $75' \times 30' = 2,250$ sq. ft.

    E. $50.5' \times (75' + 25') = 50.5' \times 100' = 5,050$ sq. ft.

    F. $120.5' \times 100' = 12,050$ sq. ft.
       37.5 sq. ft. + 1,132.5 sq. ft. + 400 sq. ft. + 2,250 sq. ft. + 5,050 sq. ft. +
       12,050 sq. ft. = 20,920 sq. ft.

2. $12' \times 4' = 48$ sq. ft.   48 sq. ft. $\times$ 144 = 6,912 sq. in.
    48 sq. ft. $\div$ 9 = 5.333 sq. yd.
    $3' \times 3' \times 3' = 27$ cu. ft.   27 cu. ft. $\times$ 1,728 = 46,656 cu. in.
    27 cu. ft. $\div$ 27 = 1 cu. yd.

Achievement Exercise continued

3. $75' \times 30' \times 10' = 22,500$ cu. ft.
$1/2(30' \times 5' \times 75') = 5,625$ cu. ft.
$22,500$ cu. ft. $+ 5,625$ cu. ft. $= 28,125$ cu. ft.
$28,125$ cu. ft. $\div 27$ cu. ft./cu. yd. $= 1,041.667$ cu. yd.
$1,041.667$ cu. yd. $\times \$48$/cu. yd. $= \$50,000$

4. b.

5. b. $5 \times 17 = 85$ sq. ft.

6. c. $150 \times 700 = 105,000$
$150 \times 300 = 45,000$
$105,000 - 45,000 = 60,000$ sq. ft.
$60,000 \div 43,560 = 1.38$ acre
$1.38 \times \$500 = \$690$ rent

7. b. $1,200 \times 700 \times 1/2 = 420,000$ sq. ft.
$420,000 \div 43,560 = 9.64$ acres
$9.64 \times 750 = \$7,231.40$
$\$7,231.41 \times 8\% = \$578.40$ commission

8. c. $10 \times 43,560 = 435,600$ sq. ft.
$435,600 \div 726 = 600$ ft.
$600 \div 2 = 300$ ft.
$(300 + 726) \times 2 = 2,052$ ft.
$2,052 \times \$1 = \$2,052$ cost to fence

9. c. $(30 \times 75) \times 2 = 4,500$ sq. ft.
$20 \times 50 = 1,000$ sq. ft.
$4,500 + 1,000 = 5,500$ sq. ft.
$5,500 \times .333 = 1,831.5$ cu. ft.
$1,831.5 \div 27 = 67.83$ cu. yds.
$67.83 \times \$36 = \$2,442$

10. a. $35 \times 79 \times 6 = 16,590$ cu. ft.
$16,590 \div 27 = 614.44$ cu yds.

11. b. $85 \times 190 = 16,150$ sq. ft.
$55.75 \times 120 = 6,690$ sq. ft.
$16,150 + 6,690 = 22,840$ sq. ft.
$22,840 \times \$2 = \$45,680$ sale price
$\$45,680 \times 8\% = 43,654.40$

12. a. $174,240 \times 2/5$ (or .4) $= 69,696$ sq. ft.
$69,696 \div 43,560 = 1.6$ acres
$1.6 \times \$1,500 = \$2,400$

13. c. $60 \times 175 = 10,500$ sq. ft.
$35 \times 70 \times 1/2 = 1,225$ sq. ft.
$10,500 - 1,225 = 9,275$ sq. ft. usable

14. b.

15. a. $19 \times 56 = 1,064$ sq. ft.
$24 \times 76 = 1,824$ sq. ft.
$6 \times 23 = 138$ sq. ft.
$1,064 + 1,824 - 138 = 2,750$ sq. ft.

6

Depreciation

INTRODUCTION

This chapter covers some of the more basic uses of depreciation. Since the use and the definition of depreciation are subject to federal and state laws, Internal Revenue Service regulations and Tax Court rulings, the reader is urged to consult legal counsel regarding any points of law. Any careless discussion of ''depreciation'' can lead an unsuspecting seller or buyer into tax consequences that may be unfavorable. The material presented in this chapter is intentionally very general in content. This is because of frequent and sometimes major changes in the tax laws. Do not be concerned about the generalizations. Instead, learn the concepts and methods so that you can apply them to whatever tax laws may be in effect. Remember that this textbook is an introduction to real estate math and not a text on taxation.

ENTRY EVALUATION

Since readers will have varying amounts of knowledge and experience, the short test that follows will allow you to determine your familiarity with the material to be covered. Try all the problems before looking at the answers, which begin on page 127.

- If Bobbye paid $75,000 for a rental property and if the house has a 30-year life, how much straight-line depreciation can she take each year if the lot is worth $15,000?

- How much depreciation has Bobbye used in 5 years?

■ How much depreciation does Bobbye have left after 5 years?

■ Jeny bought new printing equipment for $70,000, paying $10,000 cash and obtaining a loan for the remainder. If she depreciates the equipment over a 12-year term, how much depreciation can Jeny take the first year if she elects to use the straight-line recovery?

USES OF DEPRECIATION

The term *depreciation* has several shades of meaning, according to its application. The real estate salesperson is likely to encounter all of these uses. Generally, depreciation is used in appraising, tax reporting and accounting.

Depreciation in Appraisal

Depreciation is used in the cost approach method for appraising real property. Basically, it measures the amount by which the value of property diminishes owing to physical wasting away. This use of depreciation will not be discussed further here, because it is covered more completely in Chapter 7.

Depreciation for Income Tax Purposes

Depreciation may be used as a deduction on federal or state individual or corporate income taxes. As is the case for appraisal, depreciation for tax purposes applies only to buildings and improvements—such as parking lot surfaces, fences, utility lines and orchards—and *not* to land. Certain qualifying items of personal property used in a trade or business also may be depreciated. Some examples include furniture, equipment and vehicles. The length or term of depreciation is determined by tax law and IRS regulations.

Depreciation in Accounting—Bookkeeping Function

In accounting practices, depreciation may be calculated as a bookkeeping function. It is used in determining the profit and loss of a business establishment. Depreciation is listed as an expense, even though no *actual* expense for that item was incurred. If a business is still making payments on the item being depreciated, those payments and the amount of depreciation have no relationship to one another. The payment depends upon the amount and length of a loan or note, and its interest rate, while depreciation depends upon the economic, or useful, life of the item for bookkeeping purposes.

Note that the purpose of depreciation, when used in tax calculation or bookkeeping, is to allow an owner to recover the initial cost of the item being depreciated. The *depreciated value,* or *book value,* has no bearing on the *market value* (the price a willing buyer would pay) of the item being depreciated. For example, through inflation, the typical building has a market value considerably higher than its depreciated value. (If a building is sold for more than its depreciated value, the excess is taxable under various laws and regulations.)

STRAIGHT-LINE METHOD

The straight-line method of depreciation will be used in the following calculations. This method involves an equal amount of depreciation to be deducted on an annual basis. Note: the term *economic life,* which is used in the following example, refers to that period of time during which the article can be expected to provide an economic benefit.

EXAMPLE: Under the straight-line method, an air conditioner that cost $10,000 and has an economic life of 10 years can be depreciated at $1,000 per year for 10 years. By the end of the 10-year period, the entire $10,000 would have been recovered. To determine the annual depreciation amount, divide the initial cost of an item by its economic life, or:

   initial cost ÷ economic life = annual depreciation amount

   Now, you try it by working the following exercise.

1. Jean bought new display counters and furniture for her craft shop. The entire cost was $4,000. If she depreciates it over a period of 7 years, how much depreciation can Jean take, or use, each year?

   Using the same information, you can prepare a depreciation chart for the 7-year term, showing how the annual depreciation affects the book value of Jean's shop furnishings.

Year	Annual depreciation	Book value
New		$4,000.00
1	$571.43	3,428.57
2	571.43	2,857.14
3	571.43	2,285.71
4	571.43	1,714.28
5	571.43	1,142.85
6	571.43	571.43
7	571.42	-0-

EXAMPLES: Many real-world transactions are more complex than the preceding problem. The two examples that follow illustrate situations commonly encountered.

Lisa bought a new computer system for her office two years ago. At that time, she traded in her old system, which had a depreciated book value of $2,000. For the old system, she received a $2,000 credit toward the purchase of the new one. If the new system cost $16,000 and Lisa is depreciating it over 7 years, what is its depreciated value at the end of the second year?

This is a multi-step problem. First, you must determine Lisa's starting point for depreciation purposes (the time at which she bought the new system). There was $2,000 of unused depreciation on the old computer, and she had no gain or loss in the trade-in. Thus, the trade-in amount must be subtracted from the cost of the new computer:

$$\$16,000 - \$2,000 = \$14,000$$

Lisa's depreciation schedule must be based upon this $14,000 figure, and that amount is to be spread (or the cost is to be recovered) over a period of 7 years. With this information, you can calculate the annual depreciation amount:

$$\text{initial cost} \div \text{economic life} = \text{annual depreciation amount}$$

$$\$14,000 \div 7 = \$2,000 \text{ annual depreciation}$$

Lisa's present system is now 2 years old. To find its current depreciated value, first find out how much depreciation has been taken so far:

$$\$2,000 \times 2 \text{ years} = \$4,000$$

Subtracting the depreciation taken from the initial net cost gives you:

$$\$14,000 - \$4,000 = \$10,000 \text{ book value, or current depreciated}$$
$$\text{value}$$

The second example concerns Susan, who bought a rental house for $55,000 by paying $5,000 cash and obtaining a mortgage loan for $50,000 to be repaid over a 30-year term. The tax assessor values the lot at $10,000. If Susan depreciates the house over a 30-year period, how much depreciation can she take, or use, each year?

First, you must sort out the unessentials and disregard them. For example, the cash invested, the loan amount, and the length of the loan have no bearing on this problem. Also, remember that the lot, or the land, cannot be depreciated since, theoretically, it does not deteriorate in value. So, the value of the lot must be subtracted from the total cost of the property.

$55,000 total cost of property
− 10,000 value of lot
$45,000 Value of Building To Be Depreciated

Next, the depreciation period is 15 years, which is not related in any way to the length of the loan. Therefore, the value of the building must be divided by the number of years that the depreciation is to be taken.

$45,000 ÷ 30 = $1,500 annual depreciation

2. Your local multiple-listing service decides to buy its own printing press so that it can produce its own MLS book. If the press costs $40,000 and the multiple-listing service plans to depreciate it over 10 years, how much depreciation will the MLS have left (the book value) at the end of 4 years, when they plan to trade it in on a new laser press?

The following chart, or graph, shows the relationship of dollars to time in Exercise 2.

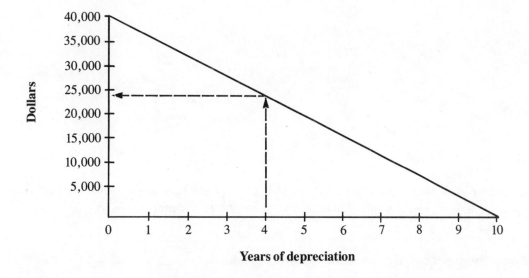

To determine the amount of depreciation left after 4 years, locate 4 years on the time line, or horizontal axis, then move straight up until you touch, or intersect, the diagonal line. At this point, move straight left to the dollar line, or vertical axis. The book value is $24,000, the same answer obtained in Exercise 2.

3. Now, you try it. From the graph illustrated, determine how much depreciation will be taken, or used up, at the end of 7 years.

Accumulated Depreciation

The initial figure used in Exercise 3 was $40,000, and $28,000 was "used up" in 7 years. The $28,000 is called *accumulated depreciation,* or

$40,000 initial cost
− 12,000 depreciation still allowable
$28,000 Accumulated Depreciation

Application of Depreciation

4. Elaine bought a 4-unit apartment house near the local community college. Her cost of the property was $120,000. The lot value was $22,500, and she paid $4,000 cash and signed a note to the seller for the balance of $104,000 bearing 10% interest to be paid in monthly installments for 25 years. If Elaine's first-year total operating costs including taxes and insurance were $2,000, the total rent income was $15,000, and the total payments on the mortgage loan were $11,340 (of which $985 was for principal), how much taxable income from this property does she have available at the end if that first year if she uses a 30-year depreciation schedule? (This is assuming that the tax laws permit her to use all of the depreciation.) How much depreciation per year is to be taken?

ACHIEVEMENT EXERCISE

When you have finished both parts of this exercise, check your answers against those on page 128. If you miss any of the questions, review this chapter before going on to Chapter 7.

Part I—Open Response   Complete the following problems.

1. You want to buy a new $12,000 car for use in your real estate business. If you plan to use it 100% in business and depreciate it over 5 years, how much depreciation can be taken each year?

2. A house and lot are valued at $80,000. If the lot is worth $20,000 and the property is to be depreciated over 30 years, how much depreciation has been taken in 3 years?

Part II—Multiple Choice   Select the correct response from the choices supplied.

3. Depreciation is:

    I. the physical wearing out of a building.
    II. used as an accounting procedure.

      a. I only
      b. II only
      c. both I and II
      d. neither I nor II

4. Even though real estate may appreciate in value:

    I. the owner may use depreciation techniques for a tax savings.
    II. the property is not really worth as much to a buyer as a newer one.

      a. I only
      b. II only
      c. both I and II
      d. neither I nor II

5. Property is depreciated over the:

    I. term of the note.
    II. life of the asset.

      a. I only
      b. II only
      c. both I and II
      d. neither I nor II

6. If $20,000 cash is paid down on a $125,000 property having a land value of $25,000, how much can be depreciated?

      a. $105,000
      b. $80,000
      c. $125,000
      d. $100,000

7. Bob bought a new central air-conditioning system for his building. It cost $9,000 and is to be depreciated over 9 years. How much depreciation has been taken after 3 years?

      a. $1,000   c. $3,000
      b. $9,000   d. $6,000

ANSWER KEY

Entry Evaluation

- $75,000 − $15,000 = $60,000
  $60,000 ÷ 30 = $2,000 per year
- 5 × $2,000 = $10,000
- $60,000 − $10,000 = $50,000
- $70,000 ÷ 12 = $5,833.33 first year

Pages 123–126

1. Divide the original cost by its economic life in years, or

    $40,000 ÷ 7 = $571.43 annual depreciation

Pages 123–126 continued

2. Step 1. $\dfrac{\$40,000 \text{ cost}}{10 \text{ years}}$ = \$4,000 annual depreciation

Step 2.
$$
\begin{array}{rl}
\$ 4,000 & \text{annual depreciation} \\
\underline{\times\ \ \ 4} & \text{years} \\
\$16,000 & \text{Total Depreciation Taken}
\end{array}
$$

Step 3.
$$
\begin{array}{rl}
\$40,000 & \text{original cost} \\
\underline{-16,000} & \text{total depreciation taken} \\
\$24,000 & \text{Depreciation Left (book value)}
\end{array}
$$

or,
$$
\begin{array}{rl}
\$ 4,000 & \text{annual depreciation} \\
\underline{\times\ \ \ 6} & \text{years remaining on schedule} \\
\$24,000 & \text{Depreciation Left (book value)}
\end{array}
$$

3. Starting at 7 years, going up to the depreciation line and over to the left, only \$12,000 is left, so \$28,000 has been taken or used.

4. Again, you must disregard the unessential figures in the calculations you are asked to perform. After sorting these out, figure the amount of cash available:

$$
\begin{array}{rl}
\$15,000 & \text{annual rent income} \\
-\ 2,000 & \text{operating expenses} \\
\underline{-11,340} & \text{principal and interest paid} \\
\$ 1,660 & \text{Cash Available to Owner}
\end{array}
$$

Then, compute the first year's depreciation.

$$
\begin{array}{rl}
\$120,000 & \text{total cost} \\
\underline{-22,500} & \text{lot cost} \\
\$ 97,500 & \text{Building Cost}
\end{array}
$$

Spread the \$97,500 building cost over the term of 30 years.

$$\dfrac{\$97,500}{30} = \$3,250 \text{ annual depreciation}$$

Achievement Exercise

1. \$12,000 ÷ 5 years = \$2,400 per year

2. \$80,000 − \$20,000 = \$60,000
\$60,000 ÷ 30 years = \$2,000
\$2,000 × 3 years = \$6,000

3. c.

4. a.

5. b.

6. d. \$125,000 − \$25,000 = \$100,000 building value

7. c. \$9,000 ÷ 9 = \$1,000
\$1,000 × 3 = \$3,000 depreciation taken

Appraisal Methods

INTRODUCTION

This chapter presents methods and formulas used in estimating property value. First, you will be given a general description of the most commonly used methods of appraising property, including a(n):

- direct sales comparison approach;

- cost approach; and

- income approach.

Then, you will analyze each method in detail. Appraisal is *not* a science. An appraisal is an *estimate* of value, which is dependent upon the experience and common sense of an appraiser who must evaluate the data involved.

ENTRY EVALUATION

Since readers will have varying amounts of knowledge and experience, the short test that follows will allow you to determine your familiarity with the material to be covered. Try all the problems before looking at the answers, which begin on page 152.

- What is the estimated replacement cost of the following building, if the cost is estimated to be $28.50 per square foot? Round off your answer to the nearest hundred dollars.

  If the land value estimate is $25,000 and the depreciation has been calculated to be $6,250, what is the value of the real estate?

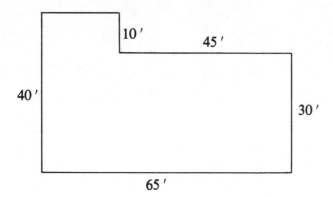

■ A building has a useful life of 50 years. How much will it depreciate in 20 years, if its original value was $50,000? What is the annual depreciation rate under the straight-line method of depreciation?

How much would the above building depreciate the first year under the double-declining-balance method? Under the sum-of-the-years'-digits method?

■ An apartment building earns a net income of $25,000 per year. If the property sold for $175,000, what is the percentage of income (income rate) for this property?

If Mr. Johnson is looking for property to yield an income rate of 20%, and he is interested in the foregoing property, what must the purchase price of the building be for him to make this rate?

■ If you were investing $265,000 in an apartment building and wished a 24% overall return on your investment, what income would a property have to produce to meet your required return?

VALUE

"Value" is not a finite number, but rather a concept involving the *benefits* the item returns to its owner or prospective owner. If you agree with this, then it is easier to understand the use of the term "value" not only in real estate practice but in other areas, as well. For example, how much would you be willing to pay for five gallons of gasoline if your car ran out of fuel as it rolled into the service station driveway? Then, how much would you be willing to pay for that same five gallons of gasoline if your car ran out of fuel fifty miles from a service station at midnight on a cold February night? Did the "value" of the fuel change for the service station owner? Did it change for you?

Or, how about the value of a 2,500-square-foot 4-bedroom house bought when energy was cheap and the children were all at home as compared to that same house today when all of the children are married, both spouses are in poor health and retired, and energy is expensive. Are the values still similar to the owners? Are the owners still receiving the same benefits of ownership that they once did?

Usually, exact property values are not possible to obtain. In the field of real estate, varying methods of estimating property value are used. Real estate is traditionally appraised by one of three methods: the *direct sales comparison approach* (also called the *market data approach*), the *cost approach* and the *income approach* (also called the *capitalization method*).

The *direct sales comparison approach* is used to estimate the value of a parcel of real estate by:

■ comparing the given real estate to comparable (or similar) properties in the current market, and

■ adding or subtracting the amount of any differences between the properties to or from the value of the comparable property so as to arrive at a more accurate comparison.

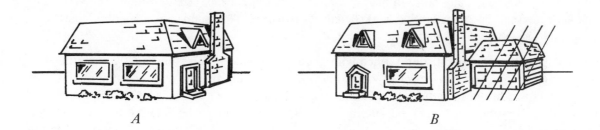

A   *B*

If House *A* is being appraised via the direct sales comparison approach to value, a comparable house is found, for example, House *B*, which sold for $56,000. In comparing the two houses, the only major difference between the houses may be that House *B* has a garage valued at $4,000, but House *A* has no garage. Therefore, $4,000 must be subtracted from the sale price of House *B* to arrive at the direct sales comparison approach appraisal of House *A*, which is $52,000.

In developing an estimate of value by the *cost approach*, the appraiser will:

■ estimate the value of the land,

■ estimate the cost of replacing the buildings on the land at current prices,

■ subtract the estimated amount of depreciation from the cost of the buildings, and

■ add these figures (algebraically) together for a composite value.

The *income approach* is used to estimate the value of a property on the basis of the income it produces. It is calculated by:

- subtracting the expenses from the total income of the property to determine the net income, and

- dividing the net income by an appropriate *capitalization rate*—a rate which is estimated to represent the proper relationship between the value of that property and the net income it produces.

Market Value

Even though value may be an abstract term, frequently it is necessary to determine the "market value" of a particular piece of real estate. Some examples of such uses are settlement of an estate, divorce or division of a partnership, establishment of a value for loan or tax assessment purposes, and so forth. In these situations, the appraiser must determine market value of the subject property. Market value is defined as the most probable price a property should bring in a competitive and open market under all conditions requisite to a fair sale. This presumes that the buyer and seller are knowledgable and are acting prudently and that the price is not affected by any undue stimulus. It further presumes that the property has been on the market for a reasonable length of time and that the purchase payment is made in cash.

DIRECT SALES COMPARISON APPROACH

The direct sales comparison, or market data, approach to value is the method most frequently used in estimating the value of residential properties. Many salespeople will never use the other two approaches to value because they typically perform market *estimates,* not appraisals. These estimates are typically called "market analyses" or "comparative market analyses (CMA)." An appraisal is a lengthy report which goes far beyond the scope of this textbook.

Belonging to a multiple-listing service with good, up-to-date information greatly simplifies the use of the direct sales comparison approach to value. For instance, if you can find only *one* similar, or comparable, house, as shown in the foregoing illustration, your estimate of the value of House *A* is totally dependent on the information obtained from the sale of House *B* and the similarities between the two. However, if a list of several similar properties is scanned and three or four of those most similar to the subject house are selected, the estimate of value will be much more accurate. Because the data base is larger, you have better statistics.

In selecting similar or comparable houses, a salesperson must be careful to consider the:

- size

- age

- physical condition

- location

- neighborhood

- "extras," such as pool or fireplace

- date of sale (Are sales prices increasing or decreasing?)

- type of financing in the sale (If the seller paid certain loan costs for the buyer, these must be subtracted from the sales price in order to obtain a "cash equivalent" sales price.)

- lot size

- style or type of house, and

- any unusual features such as a converted garage now used as a bedroom or the large size of a particular model when compared to the rest of the neighborhood.

Without printed data furnished by an appraisal file or a multiple-listing service, a direct sales comparison approach would be almost overwhelming, and subjective rather than objective. Most real estate offices also have forms or computer programs that are used to accumulate data on current listings and similar houses that have sold. Similar houses that are currently on the market tend to establish the maximum value of the property being appraised. Furthermore, these comparisons will allow owners to recognize their competition before they list or market their property.

The date of sale of similar houses and how they were financed also greatly influence the adjusted values of houses. Because the market changes, it is more accurate to use the most recent sales. For example, during a period of rapid economic expansion, house values may increase, or appreciate, by large amounts. Inflation certainly enters into this, and prices sometimes increase dramatically. By considering the date of sale, you can determine a comparative sales price by using the current rate of appreciation within a particular market.

Older sales figures particularly must be adjusted to allow for the lapse of time since the sale. When adjustments are made for the date of sale, a method similar to computing simple interest is used. For example, if you choose 6% per year as your appreciation adjustment factor (i.e., the amount you estimate real estate has gained in value due to inflation and other causes), you can reduce that to a monthly factor of 0.5% (.06 ÷ 12 = .005 = 0.5%). The monthly factor can then be multiplied by the number of months elapsed since the sale you are evaluating. This method of appreciation is used because it is similar to the straight-line method of depreciation, wherein a certain amount is *deducted* each year.

1. If housing prices are appreciating at a rate of 8% per year, what would be the adjusted sales price of a house that sold for $53,000 three years ago? (Round to the nearest dollar.)

The type of financing used in each sale affects the net amount received by the seller, and this has an indirect bearing on the true value of the house. For example, one seller might own a house free of any loan and sell for cash. This type of sale tends to be the most reliable, since financing plays no part at all. Another seller with an assumable loan at a below-market interest rate might obtain a higher price for his or her house. Still another seller might have had to pay very large loan costs in order to sell, which results in a much lower net price received by the seller. In this case, some of the high loan costs could be included in the sales price. Therefore, these costs must be subtracted from the sales price in order to remove this effect of financing from the sales price. Still another seller might have such a compelling reason to sell that he or she is willing to carry a large second lien note at a below-market interest rate. If each of the foregoing sales involved similar models in the same subdivision within a short period of time, the sales prices could vary considerably depending upon the type of financing. Appraisers obtain this data from various sources, including MLS membership, verification from the seller or buyer or from a broker involved in the sale. (The broker should obtain the buyer's written permission first.)

Table 7.1 is a useful format for gathering data concerning the sale of houses that are similar to and located near the subject house. It permits the user to adjust the sale prices for differences in extras, date of sale and method of financing. For this exercise, use an appreciation rate of 6% per year or 0.5% per month. (**Note:** The use of a factor for appreciation or depreciation depends upon a great many variables, such as the prevailing economic conditions, geographic location of the property, etc. Therefore, *careful* use should be made of such a factor.) After reading the explanation of the chart, you will fill in the missing amounts, considering appreciation and financing.

TABLE 7.1

House	Age	Rooms	Extras	Sale price	Sale date	Adjusted price	How financed	Final adjustment	Size	$ per sq. ft.
1	5 yrs.	3–2–2	Fireplace Pool ($10,000)	$70,000 (10,000) $60,000	1–1–89	$63,300	Cash	$63,300	1,500 sq. ft.	$42.20
2	4 yrs.	3–2–2	No fireplace + 1,000	$63,000 +1,000 $64,000	12–1–89	$64,000	Equity ($1,000)	$63,000	1,480 sq. ft.	$42.57
3	5 yrs.	3–2–2	Fireplace	$62,000	6–1–89		FHA ($1,800)		1,460 sq. ft.	
4*	5 yrs.	3–2–2	Fireplace	$61,000	8–1–89		Equity +2nd + $1,000		1,500 sq. ft.	
Subject	4 yrs.	3–2–2	Fireplace		Current Date 12–1–89				1,490 sq. ft.	

*This house involved a distress sale, and the seller agreed to carry back a large second lien note.

In Table 7.1, the first adjustment is for "extras." For House 1, subtract $10,000 for the pool, because the subject house does not have one. This gives you an estimate of the sale price for a house that, like the subject house, has no pool.

$$\begin{array}{ll} \$70,000 & \text{actual sales price for House 1} \\ -\,10,000 & \text{estimated value of pool} \\ \hline \$60,000 & \text{price of House 1 adjusted for pool} \end{array}$$

Next, adjust House 1's price for the sale date. Use an appreciation factor of 6% per year (or 0.5% per month) to account for elapsed time between sale dates:

$$\$60,000 \times 0.5\% = \$300 \text{ monthly appreciation}$$
$$\$300 \times 11 \text{ months} = \$3,300 \text{ total appreciation}$$
$$\$60,000 + \$3,300 = \$63,300 \text{ adjusted price}$$

Since this was a cash sale, no adjustment is made for financing, so the final adjustment leaves the price at $63,300.

This house has 1,500 square feet of living area (excluding garages and open porches), so:

$$\$63,300 \div 1,500 \text{ sq. ft.} = \$42.20 \text{ per sq. ft.}$$

The procedure is the same for House 2. First add $1,000 for a fireplace because all of the similar houses, including the subject house, have one. This results in an adjusted sale price of $64,000. The sale date is current, so no adjustment for date of sale is necessary. However, the house may have sold for about $1,000 more because of the attractive low-interest assumable loan. Therefore, adjust downward by this $1,000, to $63,300. The house has 1,480 square feet of living area, which yields a rate of $42.57 per square foot:

$$\$63,000 \div 1,480 \text{ sq. ft.} = \$42.57 \text{ per sq. ft.}$$

2. Now, you fill in the missing data for Houses 3 and 4 in Table 7.1.

Check your answers against the completed table in the answer key on page 153. These numbers can help you estimate a value for the subject house. One way of doing so that is in practice among many real estate licensees is to calculate a numerical average of the adjusted sales price per square foot for the comparables and use that average as the value per square foot of the subject property. The average value is multiplied by the square footage to estimate the value of the subject house. This method is acceptable because this represents an *estimate* of value, not an appraisal.

To compute an average, add the individual values together, then divide by the number of values you have added.

EXAMPLE: To compute the average of a set of numbers such as 12, 17, 23 and 14.2, first add those numbers:

$$12 + 17 + 23 + 14.2 = 66.2$$

Four values are being averaged, so divide by 4:

$$66.2 \div 4 = 16.55$$

Thus, the average of the 4 values is 16.55.

The next step in estimating the value of the subject house would be to take the average value per square foot and multiply it by the number of square feet in the subject house, to arrive at the total estimated value or price. Please note that a professional appraiser would probably use a more sophisticated method of arriving at the value per square foot of the subject house. Multiplying this different value per square foot by the square footage of the subject house would give the appraiser a different estimate of the value of the subject house.

3. Look again at the answers in the table on page 153. Using this information, compute an estimate of the value of the subject house, assuming that all of the eleven considerations listed on pages 132–133 have been accounted for, resulting in a favorable comparison.

Forms

The simple form that you used for accumulating data illustrates how the dates of sale and the financing affect the accuracy of the data. In times when appreciation or inflation is great, the sales price *must* be adjusted to reflect the date of sale of each comparable property.

Another form used nationwide is the appraisal form used by the Federal National Mortgage Association (FNMA), illustrated on pages 137 and 138. Notice that this is an *appraisal* form and not one just for an estimation of value. Therefore, it provides for adjustments to account for date of each sale, differences in amenities, or desirabilities, and the effects of financing on each property. Because this form is so detailed and elicits data that are not customarily used in a simple estimate of value (as in the solicitation of a listing), most brokers have devised forms similar to the one used in the example.

Please note that this chapter describes estimation of market value by a salesperson rather than a statistical appraisal of a property. There is a distinct difference.

COST APPROACH

The *cost approach* can be expressed as a formula.

$$\text{land value} + \text{building replacement cost} - \text{depreciation} = \text{estimated value}$$

Land value represents the present market value of the land alone. It does not include the value of improvements. It is arrived at through an analysis of current sales of comparable land in the general area. *It is computed separately because land is not depreciable.*

Building replacement (or *reproduction*) *cost* is the dollar amount that would be required to build a comparable building today. Note that this would result in a new building. If the subject building is not new, depreciation must be considered.

Depreciation represents the difference (loss) in value between a new building of this type (the replacement) and one in the present condition of the structure being appraised. This has *nothing* to do with IRS (Internal Revenue Service) depreciation or accelerated cost recovery. When depreciation is used in calculating an appraisal, it involves the actual wearing out of an improvement based on its actual age and compared to its projected remaining economic life. There are three types of depreciation that apply here—physical deterioration, functional obsolescence and economic obsolescence.

Property Description & Analysis   UNIFORM RESIDENTIAL APPRAISAL REPORT   File No.

SUBJECT

Property Address		Census Tract	LENDER DISCRETIONARY USE

Property Address _____ Census Tract _____ LENDER DISCRETIONARY USE
City _____ County _____ State _____ Zip Code _____ Sale Price $ _____
Legal Description _____ Date _____
Owner/Occupant _____ Map Reference _____ Mortgage Amount $ _____
Sale Price $ _____ Date of Sale _____ PROPERTY RIGHTS APPRAISED — Mortgage Type _____
Loan charges/concessions to be paid by seller $ _____ Fee Simple — Discount Points and Other Concessions
R.E. Taxes $ _____ Tax Year _____ HOA $/Mo. _____ Leasehold — Paid by Seller $ _____
Lender/Client _____ Condominium (HUD/VA) — De Minimis PUD — Source _____

NEIGHBORHOOD

LOCATION: Urban / Suburban / Rural
BUILT UP: Over 75% / 25-75% / Under 25%
GROWTH RATE: Rapid / Stable / Slow
PROPERTY VALUES: Increasing / Stable / Declining
DEMAND/SUPPLY: Shortage / In Balance / Over Supply
MARKETING TIME: Under 3 Mos. / 3-6 Mos. / Over 6 Mos.

PRESENT LAND USE %: Single Family, 2-4 Family, Multi-family, Commercial, Industrial, Vacant
LAND USE CHANGE: Not Likely / Likely / In process / To:
PREDOMINANT OCCUPANCY: Owner / Tenant / Vacant (0-5%) / Vacant (over 5%)
SINGLE FAMILY HOUSING PRICE $(000) AGE (yrs): Low / High / Predominant

NEIGHBORHOOD ANALYSIS (Good Avg. Fair Poor): Employment Stability, Convenience to Employment, Convenience to Shopping, Convenience to Schools, Adequacy of Public Transportation, Recreation Facilities, Adequacy of Utilities, Property Compatibility, Protection from Detrimental Cond., Police & Fire Protection, General Appearance of Properties, Appeal to Market

Note: Race or the racial composition of the neighborhood are not considered reliable appraisal factors.
COMMENTS: _____

SITE

Dimensions _____ Topography _____
Site Area _____ Corner Lot _____ Size _____
Zoning Classification _____ Zoning Compliance _____ Shape _____
HIGHEST & BEST USE: Present Use _____ Other Use _____ Drainage _____
UTILITIES Public Other / SITE IMPROVEMENTS Type Public Private / View _____
Electricity — Street — Landscaping _____
Gas — Curb/Gutter — Driveway _____
Water — Sidewalk — Apparent Easements _____
Sanitary Sewer — Street Lights — FEMA Flood Hazard Yes* ___ No ___
Storm Sewer — Alley — FEMA* Map/Zone _____
COMMENTS (Apparent adverse easements, encroachments, special assessments, slide areas, etc.): _____

IMPROVEMENTS

GENERAL DESCRIPTION: Units, Stories, Type (Det./Att.), Design (Style), Existing, Proposed, Under Construction, Age (Yrs.), Effective Age (Yrs.)
EXTERIOR DESCRIPTION: Foundation, Exterior Walls, Roof Surface, Gutters & Dwnspts., Window Type, Storm Sash, Screens, Manufactured House
FOUNDATION: Slab, Crawl Space, Basement, Sump Pump, Dampness, Settlement, Infestation
BASEMENT: Area Sq. Ft., % Finished, Ceiling, Walls, Floor, Outside Entry
INSULATION: Roof, Ceiling, Walls, Floor, None, Adequacy, Energy Efficient Items:

ROOM LIST

ROOMS	Foyer	Living	Dining	Kitchen	Den	Family Rm.	Rec. Rm.	Bedrooms	# Baths	Laundry	Other	Area Sq. Ft.
Basement												
Level 1												
Level 2												

Finished area **above** grade contains: ___ Rooms; ___ Bedroom(s); ___ Bath(s); ___ Square Feet of Gross Living Area

INTERIOR

SURFACES Materials/Condition: Floors, Walls, Trim/Finish, Bath Floor, Bath Wainscot, Doors, Fireplace(s) #
HEATING: Type, Fuel, Condition, Adequacy; COOLING: Central, Other, Condition, Adequacy
KITCHEN EQUIP.: Refrigerator, Range/Oven, Disposal, Dishwasher, Fan/Hood, Compactor, Washer/Dryer, Microwave, Intercom
ATTIC: None, Stairs, Drop Stair, Scuttle, Floor, Heated, Finished
IMPROVEMENT ANALYSIS (Good Avg. Fair Poor): Quality of Construction, Condition of Improvements, Room Sizes/Layout, Closets and Storage, Energy Efficiency, Plumbing-Adequacy & Condition, Electrical-Adequacy & Condition, Kitchen Cabinets-Adequacy & Cond., Compatibility to Neighborhood, Appeal & Marketability, Estimated Remaining Economic Life ___ Yrs., Estimated Remaining Physical Life ___ Yrs.

CAR STORAGE: Garage, Carport, None / Attached, Detached, Built-In / Adequate, Inadequate, Electric Door / House Entry, Outside Entry, Basement Entry
No. Cars ___ Condition ___
Additional features: _____

COMMENTS

Depreciation (Physical, functional and external inadequacies, repairs needed, modernization, etc.): _____

General market conditions and prevalence and impact in subject/market area regarding loan discounts, interest buydowns and concessions: _____

Freddie Mac Form 70 10/86 12Ch.   AH   Forms and Worms Inc.,® 315 Whitney Ave., New Haven, CT 06511 1(800) 243-4545   Item #111710   Fannie Mae Form 1004 10/86

Valuation Section   **UNIFORM RESIDENTIAL APPRAISAL REPORT**   File No. _____

Purpose of Appraisal is to estimate Market Value as defined in the Certification & Statement of Limiting Conditions.

COST APPROACH

BUILDING SKETCH (SHOW GROSS LIVING AREA ABOVE GRADE)
If for Freddie Mac or Fannie Mae, show only square foot calculations and cost approach comments in this space.

ESTIMATED REPRODUCTION COST - NEW - OF IMPROVEMENTS:

Dwelling _____	Sq. Ft. @ $ _____	= $ _____
	Sq. Ft. @ $ _____	= _____
Extras _____		= _____
		= _____
Special Energy Efficient Items _____		= _____
Porches, Patios, etc. _____		= _____
Garage/Carport _____	Sq. Ft. @ $ _____	= _____
Total Estimated Cost New		= $ _____

	Physical	Functional	External
Less Depreciation	_____	_____	_____	= $ _____

Depreciated Value of Improvements .... = $ _____
Site Imp. "as is" (driveway, landscaping, etc.) = $ _____
ESTIMATED SITE VALUE .... = $ _____
(If leasehold, show only leasehold value.)
INDICATED VALUE BY COST APPROACH .... = $ _____

(Not Required by Freddie Mac and Fannie Mae)
Does property conform to applicable HUD/VA property standards? ☐ Yes ☐ No
If No, explain: _____

Construction Warranty ☐ Yes ☐ No
Name of Warranty Program _____
Warranty Coverage Expires _____

The undersigned has recited three recent sales of properties most similar and proximate to subject and has considered these in the market analysis. The description includes a dollar adjustment, reflecting market reaction to those items of significant variation between the subject and comparable properties. If a significant item in the comparable property is superior to, or more favorable than, the subject property, a minus (−) adjustment is made, thus reducing the indicated value of subject; if a significant item in the comparable is inferior to, or less favorable than, the subject property, a plus (+) adjustment is made, thus increasing the indicated value of the subject.

SALES COMPARISON ANALYSIS

ITEM	SUBJECT	COMPARABLE NO. 1		COMPARABLE NO. 2		COMPARABLE NO. 3	
Address							
Proximity to Subject							
Sales Price	$	$		$		$	
Price/Gross Liv. Area	$	☑ $		$		$	
Data Source							
VALUE ADJUSTMENTS	DESCRIPTION	DESCRIPTION	+ (−) $ Adjustment	DESCRIPTION	+ (−) $ Adjustment	DESCRIPTION	+ (−) $ Adjustment
Sales or Financing Concessions							
Date of Sale/Time							
Location							
Site/View							
Design and Appeal							
Quality of Construction							
Age							
Condition							
Above Grade Room Count	Total : Bdrms : Baths	Total : Bdrms : Baths		Total : Bdrms : Baths		Total : Bdrms : Baths	
Gross Living Area	Sq. Ft.	Sq. Ft.		Sq. Ft.		Sq. Ft.	
Basement & Finished Rooms Below Grade							
Functional Utility							
Heating/Cooling							
Garage/Carport							
Porches, Patio, Pools, etc.							
Special Energy Efficient Items							
Fireplace(s)							
Other (e.g. kitchen equip., remodeling)							
Net Adj. (total)		☐ + ☐ − $		☐ + ☐ − $		☐ + ☐ − $	
Indicated Value of Subject		$		$		$	

Comments on Sales Comparison: _____

INDICATED VALUE BY SALES COMPARISON APPROACH .... $ _____
INDICATED VALUE BY INCOME APPROACH (If Applicable) Estimated Market Rent $ _____ /Mo. x Gross Rent Multiplier _____ = $ _____
This appraisal is made ☐ "as is" ☐ subject to the repairs, alterations, inspections or conditions listed below ☐ completion per plans and specifications.
Comments and Conditions of Appraisal: _____

Final Reconciliation: _____

RECONCILIATION

This appraisal is based upon the above requirements, the certification, contingent and limiting conditions, and Market Value definition that are stated in

☐ FmHA, HUD &/or VA instructions.
☐ Freddie Mac Form 439 (Rev. 7/86)/Fannie Mae Form 1004B (Rev. 7/86) filed with client _____ 19 ____ ☐ attached.
I (WE) ESTIMATE THE MARKET VALUE, AS DEFINED, OF THE SUBJECT PROPERTY AS OF _____ 19 ____ to be $ _____

I (We) certify: that to the best of my (our) knowledge and belief the facts and data used herein are true and correct; that I (we) personally inspected the subject property, both inside and out, and have made an exterior inspection of all comparable sales cited in this report; and that I (we) have no undisclosed interest, present or prospective therein.

Appraiser(s) SIGNATURE _____   Review Appraiser SIGNATURE _____   ☐ Did ☐ Did Not
NAME _____   (if applicable) NAME _____   Inspect Property

Freddie Mac Form 70 10/86 **12Ch.**   Forms and Worms Inc.,® 315 Whitney Ave., New Haven, CT 06511 1(800) 243-4545   Fannie Mae Form 1004 10/86

Physical deterioration may be defined as the physical wearing out of a structure.

EXAMPLES: Building that needs a new roof.

Obsolete wiring. No 220 wiring in an area in which it
is in great demand.

Functional obsolescence occurs as a result of an undesirable layout or an outdated design.

EXAMPLES: A two-story, five-bedroom house with one bathroom
on the first floor.

A house with a coal furnace.

A house with space heaters, rather than central
heating.

A house facing the rear of the lot, to take advantage
of a view that is no longer beautiful.

Economic obsolescence involves a loss of value from causes outside the property itself.

EXAMPLES: Loss of value due to a new highway constructed adja-
cent to property (dirt and noise).

Machine shop, elementary school, or drive-in restau-
rant built across from an apartment hotel designed for
retirees.

Excessive taxes, zoning changes, proximity of nuis-
ances, changes in land use can all be causes of economic obsolescence.

Now, use the cost approach formula to arrive at an estimate of value for the real estate in the following problems.

4. An appraiser estimates the value of a piece of land at $20,000 and the replacement cost of the building on that land at $90,000. The depreciation has been calculated to be $10,000. What is the estimated value of the real estate?

The estimated replacement cost of a building is often given as an amount per square or cubic foot.

5. A house has a total finished floor area of 1,450 square feet. Mr. Jorgenson has appraised the building and estimated its replacement cost at $36 per square foot.

   a. What is the estimated replacement cost of the building?

   b. If the value of the land is $18,500 and the depreciation is $5,200, what is the estimated value of the real estate, using the cost approach?

6. Mr. Robinson's house is 24 feet by 37 feet, with a finished family room addition, 15 feet by 20 feet. The appraiser has estimated the replacement cost at $35.25 per square foot, the land value at $14,000 and the depreciation at $8,400. What is the estimated value of the real estate?

7. What is the estimated replacement cost of the following building, if the cost estimate is $38.75 per square foot? What is the value of the real estate, if the land is estimated at $11,000 and depreciation at $5,500? Round off your answer to the nearest hundred dollars.

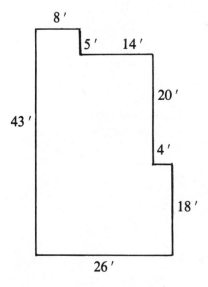

8. Compute the estimated value of the following real estate. The appraiser has told you that the replacement cost is $2.25 per cubic foot, the depreciation is $10,800 and the land value is $15,500. Round off your answer to the nearest hundred dollars.

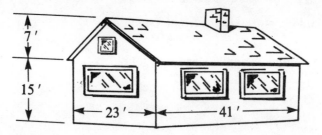

Calculating Depreciation

> *Depreciation* is the loss of value suffered by a building. It is the difference between an existing building and a brand new building of like specifications.

Straight-Line Method   The *straight-line method* of depreciation spreads the total depreciation over the useful life of a building in equal annual amounts, using the following formula. Remember that this "useful life" has nothing at all to do with the life used for IRS depreciation.

$$\frac{\text{replacement cost}}{\text{years of useful life}} = \text{annual depreciation charge}$$

A building most frequently becomes useless through economic or functional obsolescence rather than physical deterioration. For this reason, appraisers often refer to the useful life of real estate as the "estimated economic life." Note that the "useful life," "economic life" and "actual life" of a building are rarely the same. They are *not* synonymous, nor do they have anything to do with the depreciable life as assigned by the Congress in the IRS Code.

An appraiser estimates the remaining economic life of a property after considering the physical, functional and economic factors.

EXAMPLE: The appraiser has estimated the replacement cost of a building at $100,000. The building is 10 years old and has an estimated useful life of 50 years. What is the annual depreciation charge? What is the total depreciation for 10 years? What is the current value of the building?

Step 1.   Compute annual depreciation charge.

$$\frac{\text{replacement cost}}{\text{years of useful life}} = \text{annual depreciation charge}$$

$$\frac{\$100,000}{50} = \$2,000 \text{ annual depreciation charge}$$

Step 2.   Find amount of depreciation over 10 years.

$$\frac{\text{annual depreciation}}{\text{charge}} \times \frac{\text{number of}}{\text{years}} = \text{total depreciation}$$

$$\$2,000 \text{ per year} \times 10 \text{ years} = \$20,000$$

Step 3.   Find current value.

replacement cost − depreciation = current value

$100,000 − $20,000 = $80,000 current value

9. If the building in the preceding example was 30 years old, what would its current value be?

10. If the building in the example was on a piece of land worth $25,000, what would be the estimated value of the property after 30 years of use (computed in Exercise 9)?

11. If the building in Exercises 9 and 10 originally cost $75,000, what would be the current estimated value of the property?

Depreciation can also be expressed as a *percentage* or *rate*. To find the depreciation rate by the straight-line method, divide the total depreciation (100%) by the building's estimated useful years of life.

$$\frac{100\%}{\text{years of useful life}} = \text{annual depreciation rate}$$

EXAMPLE: If a building has a useful life of 25 years, $\frac{1}{25}$ of the building's value is depreciated in one year. That is, the building depreciates at a rate of 4% per year.

$$\frac{100\%}{\text{years of useful life}} = \text{depreciation rate}$$

$$\frac{100\%}{25 \text{ years}} = 4\% \text{ annual depreciation rate}$$

12. a. If a building has an estimated useful life of 40 years, what is its annual rate of depreciation?

b. What percentage will that building depreciate in 15 years?

c. If the building is 15 years old, and has a current replacement value of $180,000, what is the total amount that it has depreciated?

d. If the land that the building is on is valued at $40,000, what is the estimated value of the total real estate?

13. The replacement cost of a building has been estimated at $115,000, and the building has an estimated useful life of 50 years. The building is 9 years old.

   a. What is the annual depreciation rate?

   b. What is the total amount of depreciation that the appraiser will deduct?

Declining Balance Method   **Note:** The material in this section and the following section is optional for use by the instructor, since tax laws change. The following concepts and methods are valid numerically, but they may not be in practical use.

   In the *declining balance method* of computing depreciation, a fixed percentage is applied to the declining balance of the building. An acceptable fixed rate is double the straight-line rate of depreciation. This rate is then applied each year to the undepreciated cost of the building.

14. An appraiser estimates that the useful life of a building that cost $100,000 is 40 years. What is the annual depreciation rate under the *straight-line* method?

   To compute the depreciation on the building in Exercise 14 by the *double-declining-balance method*, double the straight-line rate of 2.5%, and apply this doubled rate to the cost of the building.

15. How much depreciation will be deducted the first year?

   The following chart shows the allocation of cost for the first 4 years, under the double-declining-balance method of depreciation.

Year	Computation	Yearly depreciation rounded to nearest dollar	Building value rounded to nearest dollar
1	$100,000 × 5%	$5,000	$95,000
2	95,000 × 5%	4,750	90,250
3	90,250 × 5%	4,513	85,737
4	85,737 × 5%	4,287	81,450
5			

16. Complete the chart for the fifth year.

Sum-of-the-Years'-Digits Method   The *sum-of-the-years'-digits method* of computing depreciation may also be used.

$$\frac{\text{remaining years of economic life}}{\text{sum of the years' digits}} \times \text{initial value} = \text{depreciation}$$

The denominator of the fraction of depreciation is the sum of all of the years in the economic life of the property.

EXAMPLE: To see how the sum-of-the-years'-digits method works, look at the following calculation of the depreciation on a $5,000 mobile home with an estimated remaining economic life of 4 years.

Step 1.   Add the number of years to find the sum of the years' digits.

$$1 + 2 + 3 + 4 = 10 \text{ (sum of the years' digits)}$$

Step 2.   Substitute values for first year's depreciation.

$$\frac{\text{remaining years of economic life}}{\text{sum of the years' digits}} \times \text{initial value} = \text{depreciation}$$

$$\frac{4}{10} \times \$5,000 = \text{depreciation}$$

Step 3.   Solve the problem.

$$\frac{4}{10} \times \$5,000 = \$2,000 \text{ depreciation}$$

The same steps can be followed for each succeeding year, using the new fraction of depreciation times value. The following chart carries through the mobile home example.

Year	Fraction of depreciation	Amount of depreciation	Remaining value
1	$\frac{4}{10}$	$2,000	$3,000
2	$\frac{3}{10}$	1,500	1,500
3	$\frac{2}{10}$	1,000	500
4			

17. Fill in the chart for the fourth year.

There is a mathematical formula you can use to find the sum of the digits for any given number of years.

$$S = \frac{n}{2}(a + l)$$

S is the sum of the digits, n is the number of years, a is the first year and l is the last year.

EXAMPLE: The sum of the years' digits for 10 years is:

$$S = \frac{10}{2}(1 + 10) = 5 \times 11 = 55$$

18. Find the sum of the years' digits for 20 years.

19. A company bought a building for $260,000 and estimated its useful life at 25 years. Under which of the following methods would the first year's depreciation be greatest? (Compute the amount of depreciation under each method.)

a. straight line   b. double declining balance   c. sum of the years' digits

20. Select the method or methods by which depreciation is greatest in the early years of a building's life and correspondingly less in the later years.

   a. straight line
   b. declining balance
   c. sum of the years' digits
   d. both b and c
   e. all three methods

INCOME APPROACH

The *income approach* (also called the *capitalization method*) is a technique used in appraising income-producing real estate. It is a method of estimating the value of a property by dividing the annual net rental income (gross income minus expenses) expected from the property by the investment rate of return (the capitalization or "cap" rate) for that property.

$$\frac{\text{net income}}{\text{rate of return}} = \text{value} \quad \text{or} \quad \frac{I}{R} = V \quad \text{or} \quad I \div R = V \quad \text{or} \quad I = RV$$

Does the formula look familiar? It's really the same as the formula you've used in previous chapters:

$$\frac{\text{part}}{\text{percent}} = \text{total}$$

EXAMPLE: What is the estimated value of an apartment building that is expected to produce a net annual income of $14,000? The appraiser estimates that the owner should receive a return of 10% on his investment. This percentage is the capitalization rate. It is the rate of return demanded by an investor, but it is subject to limitations beyond the scope of this text. (For example, it ignores fluctuations in the projected income.)

By substituting the appropriate figures into the formula, you get:

$$I \div R = V$$
$$\$14,000 \div 10\% =$$
$$\$14,000 \div .10 = \$140,000$$

21. Fill in the equations for the following. Remember, total is the same as value, part is the same as income, and percent is the same as rate (or capitalization rate).

$I =$

$R =$

$V =$

INCOME

RATE | VALUE

22. If you had $120,000 to invest and you wanted a 10% return on your investment, what net income would a property have to produce to meet your required return?

    a. First, fill in the known parts of the equation.

    value =   rate =   income =

    b. Restate the problem.

    c. What formula will you use?

    d. Solve the problem.

23. Assume that a property earns a net income of $26,250 per year. What percentage of net income (rate) is this, if the property is valued at $210,000?

    a. Restate the problem.

    b. Solve the problem.

24. An apartment building earns a net income of $10,000 per year. What price would a buyer pay for the property to show a minimum return of 10% on his or her investment?

25. A purchaser paid $175,000 for an apartment building that produced annual net rents of $16,850. Find the rate of return on the cost.

26. A purchaser bought a parcel of commercial real estate for $320,000, expecting a return of 12% on his investment. What annual net income does he expect?

27. The gross income from an apartment building is $27,500 and annual expenses total $14,000. If the owner expects to get a 9% return on his investment, what is the value of the property? Remember that gross income − expenses = net income.

As you can see, a small change in the rate of return, or capitalization rate, makes a big change in the value. So, again, be aware of the importance of estimates in *all* of the methods used in the appraisal, or estimation of value of real estate.

Be careful to observe that in the income approach, expenses do not include payments of principal and interest on any note. To do so would distort the data because some properties are debt free. Therefore, the net remaining after expenses are subtracted ought to be sufficient to service any debt (make the payments). If it is not, "negative cash flow" occurs. Finally, note that the terms "net annual income," "cash flow," "net spendable income" and "taxable income" are not synonymous. Detailed discussion of each is beyond the scope of this textbook.

Correlation of Data

After the appraiser has completed the tasks of gathering the data and calculating values based upon the three methods (or approaches to value), a determination must be made as to which method is most valid for each specific appraisal. This involves the correlation of data and a comparison of the various values. It is quite important to note that the correlation of data is *not* the averaging of data. These correlation operations are beyond the scope of this textbook.

SUMMARY

In summary, the three approaches to value must be used on the proper type of property. Following is a general list of types of property lending themselves to the various approaches or methods:

- Direct Sales Comparison Approach

  a. Single-family, owner-occupied houses, including condominiums
  b. Vacant lots
  c. Resort or recreation property

- Cost Approach—All types of property with buildings and other improvements constructed thereon; especially well-suited to newer buildings

- Income Approach—Only properties producing rent or income

There are, of course, many appraisals made by professionals who may employ two or all three of these methods. In the FNMA appraisal form shown on pages 137 and 138, all three approaches are used. In these appraisals, the appraiser must correlate and reconcile all of the data from all of the methods employed and write a report supporting the appraisal presented.

ACHIEVEMENT EXERCISE

When you have finished both parts of this exercise, check your answers against those on pages 156–157. If you miss any of the questions, review this chapter before going on to Chapter 8.

Part I—Open Response   Complete the following problems.

1. A building, 100 feet by 250 feet by 20 feet, is valued at $1.50 per cubic foot. The land is valued at $150,000 and the depreciation has been estimated at $75,000. What is the value of this property via the cost approach to value?

2. The replacement cost of a building has been estimated at $150,000. The building was estimated to have a useful life of 50 years; it is now 2 years old. The land is valued at $50,000. What is the estimated value of this real estate via the cost approach to value? Compute depreciation under each of these methods; straight line, double-declining-balance, sum of the years' digits.

3. A property valued at $100,000 produces a net income of $12,000 per year. What percentage of income (rate) does this property earn?

4. If the owner is selling the above property and a prospective buyer wishes a 15% income rate, what amount will the buyer be willing to pay for this property?

Part II—Multiple Choice   Select the correct response from the choices supplied.

5. In computing value by the cost approach, the appraiser estimated the economic life, or years of useful life, of a building to be 40 years. The replacement cost of the building is estimated as $170,000, and the age of the building is 8 years. The current value of the building is:

   a. $136,000.   c. $127,000.
   b. $164,687.   d. $170,000.

6. In the appraisal of a seven-story commercial building, the appraiser estimated the replacement cost per square foot to be $27. If the building is 92 feet wide and 117 feet deep, the replacement cost is estimated as:

   a. $1,729,483.   c. $2,034,396.
   b. $1,979,845.   d. $290,628.

7. By selecting from a, b, c or d, indicate which of the following statements is (are) true.

   I. The annual rate of depreciation is computed by the formula:

$$\frac{replacement\ cost}{years\ of\ useful\ life}$$

   II. The total depreciation is computed by the formula:

   annual depreciation charge × years of age

   a. I only   c. both I and II
   b. II only   d. neither I nor II

8. The appraiser has estimated the annual net income from a commercial building to be $142,700. When capitalized at a rate of 10.5%, the estimated property value is:

   a. $1,498,350.   c. $1,392,195.
   b. $1,427,000.   d. $1,359,048.

9. An apartment property has been appraised for $175,000, using a capitalization rate of 9.5%. The estimated annual net income is:

   a. $17,500.   c. $17,927.
   b. $16,625.   d. $18,421.

10. If the gross annual income from a property is $112,000, and the total expenses for the year are $53,700, what capitalization rate was used to obtain a valuation of $542,325?

   a. 10.75%   c. 10.25%
   b. 10.50%   d. 9.75%

11. What is the current appraisal value of a house originally costing $35,000 if the house has appreciated 112%?

    a. $66,250   c. $78,400
    b. $39,200   d. $74,200

12. If the rate of appreciation each year is 10% of the previous year's value, what is the current value of a house that was appraised at $40,000 4 years ago?

    a. $56,000   c. $66,667
    b. $53,240   d. $58,564

13. Charles Wilson bought a condominium for $60,000. Six months later he was transferred and had to sell the property for $54,600. Which of the following calculations would you use to find his percent of loss?

    a. $5,400 ÷ $60,000
    b. $5,400 ÷ $54,600
    c. $54,600 ÷ $60,000
    d. $60,000 ÷ $54,600

14. If similar houses are appraised, the estimate of value can vary tremendously because of an owner's:

    I. assumable mortgage.
    II. reason for moving.
    III. financing methods.
    IV. initial cost of the house.

    a. II only   c. I, II and III
    b. I and II   d. IV only

15. The "useful life," "economic life" and "actual life" of a building are:

    I. not synonymous.
    II. synonymous.
    III. different methods of appraisal.
    IV. used to calculate depreciation.

    a. I only   c. I and III
    b. II only   d. II, III and IV

ANSWER KEY

Entry Evaluation

- $61,300 building replacement cost $80,050 estimated value

- $20,000 depreciation in 20 years
  $1,000 annual depreciation by straight-line method
  $2,000 first year's depreciation by double-declining-balance method
  $1,961 first year's depreciation by sum-of-the-years'-digits method

- 14.3% income $125,000 purchase price

- $63,600

Pages 133–150

1. 8%/year ÷ 12 months/year = 0.67%/month
   3 years × 12 months/year = 36 months
   36 × 0.67% = 36 × .0067 = .24 appreciation factor
   $53,000 × .24 = $12,720 appreciation of house
   $53,000 + $12,720 = $65,720 adjusted sales price

2.

House	Age	Rooms	Extras	Sale price	Sale date	Adjusted price	How financed	Final adjustment	Size	$ per sq. ft.
1	5 yrs.	3–2–2	Fireplace Pool ($10,000)	$70,000 (10,000) $60,000	1–1–89	$63,300	Cash	$63,300	1,500 sq. ft.	$42.20
2	4 yrs.	3–2–2	No fireplace +1,000	$63,000 +1,000 $64,000	12–1–89	$64,000	Equity ($1,000)	$63,000	1,480 sq. ft.	$42.57
3	5 yrs.	3–2–2	Fireplace	$62,000	6–1–89	$63,860	FHA ($1,800)	$62,060	1,460 sq. ft.	$42.51
4	5 yrs.	3–2–2	Fireplace	$61,000	8–1–89	$62,220	Equity +2nd +$1,000	$63,220	1,500 sq. ft.	$42.15
Subject	4 yrs.	3–2–2	Fireplace		Current Date 12–1–89				1,490 sq. ft.	

House 3:

No adjustment for extras, since House 3 is similar to the subject house, but update the sales price at 0.5% per month resulting in $63,860. Since this was a new FHA loan, estimate that the seller had to pay $1,800 in loan costs. Thus, after subtracting this amount in order to arrive at a cash equivalent price, the final adjusted price is $62,060. This house has 1,460 square feet of heated and cooled space (excluding garage and covered porches), so its price per square foot is $42.51.

House 4:

Again, no adjustment need be made for extras, because House 4 is similar to the subject house, but you must account for the lapse of time since it sold. At 0.5% per month, this adjusts the sale price to $62,220. This was a "distress sale" and the seller agreed to carry back a portion of the equity in the form of a second lien note. This might affect the sale price, so add $1,000 for a final adjusted price of $63,220. The house has 1,500 square feet of living area. This yields $42.15 as the price per square foot.

Please notice that several estimates were made in this problem. They must be made based upon experience and judgment. Recall the earlier statement that appraising is not a science. These are some of the reasons that seem to make it more of an art.

3. First, compute the average value per square foot of the comparables:

$42.20
42.57
42.51
+42.15
$169.43

$169.43 ÷ 4 = $42.36 average value per sq. ft.

Next multiply the average value per sq. ft. by the total square footage of the subject house:

$42.36 × 1,490 = $63,116 (rounded) probable sales price

4. land value + building replacement cost − depreciation = estimated value
$20,000 + $90,000 − $10,000 = $100,000

Pages 133–150 continued

5. a. Compute cost of total area.

1,450 sq. ft. × $36 per sq. ft. = $52,200 replacement cost

b. Compute value using the cost approach formula.

land value + building replacement cost − depreciation = estimated value
$18,500 + $52,200 − $5,200 = $65,500

6. Compute the area.

$L \times W = A$ 24' × 37' = 888 sq. ft.   15' × 20' = 300 sq. ft.
888 sq. ft. + 300 sq. ft. = 1,188 sq. ft. total

Compute building replacement cost.
1,188 sq. ft. × $35.25 = $41,877

Compute estimated value.
$14,000 + $41,877 − $8,400 = $47,477

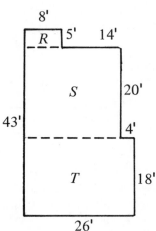

7. a. Compute total area.

$R = 8' \times 5' = 40$ sq. ft.
$S = 20' \times (14' + 8') = 440$ sq. ft.
$T = 18' \times 26' = 468$ sq. ft.
total area = 948 sq. ft.

Compute total cost of building.
948 sq. ft. × $38.75 = $36,735 (replacement cost)

b. Compute total real estate value via cost approach.
$11,000 land + $36,735 building − $5,500 depreciation = $42,235 rounded to $42,200

8. Compute volume of house.

$\text{volume}_1 = L \times W \times H = 41' \times 23' \times 15' = 14,145$ cu. ft. first story

$\text{volume}_2 = \frac{1}{2} (b \times h \times w) = \frac{1}{2} (23' \times 7' \times 41') = 3,300.5$ cu. ft. second story

total volume = 14,145 cu. ft. + 3,300.5 cu. ft. = 17,445.5 cu. ft.

Compute building replacement cost.
17,445.5 cu. ft. × $2.25 = $39,252.38

Use cost approach formula to compute value.
$15,500 + $39,252.38 − $10,800 = $43,952.38 rounded to $44,000

9. $2,000 annual depreciation charge × 30 years = $60,000 total depreciation
$100,000 replacement cost − $60,000 depreciation = $40,000 current value

10. land value + building replacement cost − depreciation = value estimate
$25,000 + $100,000 − $60,000 = $65,000

11. The current value would remain the same − $65,000. The original value of the building is not considered in this formula—only the appraiser's estimate of its replacement cost.

12. a. Calculate depreciation rate.
100% ÷ 40 = 2.5% rate of depreciation

b. Calculate depreciation rate for 15 years.
2.5% × 15 = 37.5% depreciation rate for 15 years, or .375

c. Calculate depreciation value for 15 years.
.375 × $180,000 = $67,500

d. Calculate estimated value.
land value + building replacement cost − depreciation = estimated value
$40,000 + $180,000 − $67,500 = $152,500 estimated value

13. a. 100% ÷ 50 = 2% annual depreciation rate

b. 2% × 9 years = 18% depreciation for 9 years, or .18
.18 × $115,000 building replacement cost = $20,700 total depreciation for 9 years

14. 100% ÷ 40 = 2.5%

15. 2.5% × 2 = 5%
$100,000 × .05 = $5,000

16. $81,450 × 5% $4,073 $77,377

17. 1/10   500   0

18. $S = \dfrac{20}{2}(1 + 20) = 10 \times 21 = 210$

19. First year's depreciation is the greatest by the double-declining-balance method.

a. Depreciation by the straight-line method:
$260,000 ÷ 25 = $10,400 depreciation or
100% ÷ 25 = 4%
.04 × $260,000 = $10,400

b. Depreciation by the declining-balance method:
100% ÷ 25 = 4% depreciation rate   4% × 2 = 8% depreciation
.08 × $260,000 = $20,800 depreciation

c. Depreciation by the sum-of-the-years'-digits method:

$$S = \frac{25}{2}(1 + 25) = 12.5 \times 26 = 325$$

$$\frac{25}{\overset{}{\underset{1}{\cancel{325}}}} \times \frac{\overset{800}{\cancel{260,000}}}{1} = \$20,000 \text{ depreciation}$$

20. d

21. $I = V \times R \qquad R = \dfrac{I}{V} \qquad V = \dfrac{I}{R}$

Pages 133–150 continued

22. a. value = $120,000   rate = 10%   income = unknown (annual income needed)

b. What is 10% of $120,000?

c. Formula: $I = R \times V$ (just remember the name "IRV")

d. $I = \$120,000 \times 10\% = \$120,000 \times .10 = \$12,000$ annual income needed

23. a. What percent of $210,000 is $26,250?

b. Formula: $R = \dfrac{I}{V} = \dfrac{\$26,250}{\$210,000} = .125$ or 12.5%

Answer: $26,250 per year net income is a 12.5% return on a value of $210,000.

24. $10,000 is 10% of what?

Formula: $V = \dfrac{I}{R} = \dfrac{\$10,000}{10\%} = \$100,000$ purchase price

25. $16,850 is what percent of $175,000?

$R = \dfrac{I}{V} = \dfrac{\$16,850}{\$175,000} = .096 = 9.6\%$ return

26. What is 12% or $320,000?

$I = V \times R = \$320,000 \times .12 = \$38,400$ annual income expected

27. What is the net income?

$27,500 gross income − $14,000 expenses = $13,500 net income

$13,500 is 9% of what value?

$V = \dfrac{I}{R} = \dfrac{\$13,500}{9\%} = \$150,000$ value

Achievement Exercise

1. $100' \times 250' \times 20' = 500,000$ cu.ft.
500,000 cu. ft. × $1.50 = $750,000
$150,000 + $750,000 − $75,000 = $825,000 estimated value

2. Straight-line method:

$150,000 ÷ 50 = $3,000 $3,000 × 2 years = $6,000 depreciation
$50,000 + $150,000 − $6,000 = $194,000 estimated vale

Double-declining-balance method:

100% ÷ 50 = 2% 2% × 2 = 4%
Year 1: $150,000 × 4% = $6,000 $150,000 − $6,000 = $144,000
Year 2: $144,000 × 4% = $5,760
$6,000 + $5,760 = $11,760 depreciation
$50,000 + $150,000 − $11,760 = $188,240 estimated value

Sum-of-the-years'-digits method:

$$S = \frac{50}{2}(1 + 50) = 25 \times 51 = 1,275 \text{ sum of the years' digits}$$

Year 1: 50 ÷ 1,275 × $150,000 = $5,882 depreciation (rounded to nearest $1)
Year 2: 49 ÷ 1,275 × $150,000 = $5,765 depreciation (rounded to nearest $1)
$5,882 + $5,765 = $11,647 total depreciation
$50,000 + $150,000 − $11,647 = $188,353 estimated value

3. $12,000 ÷ $100,000 = 12% rate of net income

4. $12,000 ÷ .15 = $80,000 price prospective buyer will pay

5. a. $170,000 ÷ 40 = $4,250 annual depreciation
$4,250 × 8 years = $34,000 depreciation taken
$170,000 − $34,000 = $136,000 current value

6. c. 92 × 117 = 10,764 sq. ft.
10,764 × $27 = 290,628
$290,628 × 7 = $2,034,396 replacement cost

7. b.

8. d. $142,700 ÷ 10.5% = $1,359,047.62 value

9. b. $175,000 × 9.5% = $16,625 annual net income

10. a. $112,000 − $53,700 = $58,300 net income ,
$58,300 ÷ $542,325 = 10.75% cap rate

11. d. $35,000 × 112% = $39,200 increase
$35,000 + $39,200 = $74,200 current value

12. d. $40,000 × 10% = $4,000 + $40,000 = $44,000 year 1 value
$44,000 × 10% = $4,400 + $44,000 = $48,400 year 2 value
$48,400 × 10% = $4,840 + $48,400 = $53,240 year 3 value
$53,240 × 10% = $5,324 + $53,240 = $58,564 year 4 value

13. a.

14. c.

15. a.

Interest

INTRODUCTION

Interest is the cost of using someone else's money. In this chapter, you will apply the formula for calculating interest to loan and mortgage problems, and manipulate the formula to solve for any one of the four variables (principal, time, rate and interest). You will also learn to calculate annual, semiannual, quarterly and monthly interest payments.

ENTRY EVALUATION

Since readers will have varying amounts of knowledge and experience, the short test that follows will allow you to determine your familiarity with the material to be covered. Try both problems before looking at the answers, which begin on page 168.

- A bank issued a loan of $21,000 at 11% interest for 2-1/2 years. If the loan was paid in full at the end of 2-1/2 years, how much money was paid to the bank?

- If the bank wished to earn $6,300 on a loan of the same amount over the same period of time, what interest rate would have to be charged?

Interest, as was stated in the Introduction to this chapter, is the cost of using someone else's money. A person who borrows money is required to repay the loan *plus* a charge for interest. This charge will depend upon the amount borrowed (*principal*), the length of time the money is used (*time*) and the percent of interest agreed upon (*rate*). Repayment, then, involves the return of the principal plus a *return* on the principal, which is called *interest*.

A person who signs a 10% interest-bearing note for $500, which will mature in one year, will be required to pay interest for one year (time) at 10% (rate) on the $500 (principal), as well as the face value of the note itself ($500).

Interest is usually *charged* monthly. When other periods are used, such as quarterly (3 months) or semiannually (6 months), this will be specified. However, interest rates are usually *calculated* on a yearly basis, that is, they are normally annual rates. For example, 10% means 10% of the principal, per year (per annum).

There are two types of interest, simple interest and compound interest. The first part of this chapter will deal with simple interest, and the latter section with compound interest. A further discussion of compound interest appears in Chapter 15. Most real estate loans involve interest paid *in arrears,* or *after* the use of the money has occurred.

SIMPLE INTEREST

The basic formula for computing simple interest is:

$$\text{principal} \times \text{rate} \times \text{time} = \text{interest}$$

The formula is commonly abbreviated as $PRT = I$.

EXAMPLE: To illustrate the formula, assume a note for $5,000, payable 2 years from date of loan, with interest at 12%. The amount of interest would be computed as follows.

$$\$5,000 \times .12 \times 2 = \$1,200 \text{ interest}$$

or

$$\overset{50}{\cancel{\$5,000}} \times \frac{12}{\cancel{100}} \times 2 = \$1,200$$
$$1$$

Using the formula $I = PRT$, solve the following problem. Work all dollar amounts to three decimal places, where necessary, and round off to two places only in the last step of a problem.

1. Find the interest on $1,000 at 10% for 3 years.

When the time of a loan is in months, T can be written as a fraction or a decimal fraction of a year.

EXAMPLE: 6 months $= \dfrac{6}{12} = \dfrac{1}{2} = 0.5$ year

2. Following the example, give the fractional and decimal equivalents of 4 months.

    4 months $=$

3. Find the amount of interest on a loan of $6,000 at 11% for 9 months.

4. Mrs. Broch borrowed $1,000 to paint her house, and the lender charged 13-3/4% interest. The loan was repaid in 3 months. What amount was repaid (the loan in full plus interest)?

When any three elements in the interest formula are known, the fourth can always be calculated.

Basic formula: $PRT = I$

Variations of formula: $\dfrac{I}{RT} = P$ $\dfrac{I}{PT} = R$ $\dfrac{I}{PR} = T$

5. If the interest rate is 10% per year, how much money will you have to lend in order to get $75 interest for 6 months?

    a. Which element in the equation is unknown?

    b. Write the equation you need to use to solve for the unknown.

EXAMPLE: Here is an example of how the principal is found when
I is $75, R is 10% and T is 6 months (1/2 year).

$$\frac{I}{RT} = P$$

$$\frac{\$75}{.10 \times \frac{1}{2}} = \frac{75}{.05} = \$1,500$$

6. Now, you try a problem, in which I is $24, R is 8% and T is 3 months.

7. How long will it take for $800 to yield $95 in interest at a rate of 9.5%?

8. John Millner received $75 interest on a loan of $1,200 for 6 months. What interest rate did he charge?

Interest payments may be made annually (once a year), semiannually (twice a year), quarterly (4 times a year), or monthly (12 times a year). To calculate the interest payment amount, compute the annual interest amount, then divide by the number of payments per year.

EXAMPLE: What will the quarterly payments be on a loan of
$5,000 at 10-1/2% per annum?

Step 1.   Compute the annual interest.
$5,000 \times .105 = \$525$

Step 2.   Divide by the number of payments per year.
$525 \div 4 = \$131.25$

The quarterly interest payments will be $131.25 each.

9. What will the quarterly interest payments be for a $60,000 loan with an interest rate of 13-3/4%, if the sales price is $70,000?

10. A loan for $15,000, with an interest rate of 9-3/4%, requires quarterly interest payments. How much will the quarterly interest payments be?

11. If the appraised value of a house is $56,000, how much will semiannual interest payments be on a $55,000 loan at 12-1/2% interest?

12. A loan has an interest rate of 12% and requires quarterly interest payments of $750. What is the principal of the loan?

13. A loan has an interest rate of 8.5% and requires semiannual payments of $637.50. What is the principal of the loan?

14. A $10,000 loan requires quarterly interest payments of $250. What is the interest rate on the loan?

15. A loan requires semiannual interest payments amounting to $2,152.50, and the principal of the loan is $42,000. What is the interest rate?

16. A $9,000 loan is to be paid in equal quarterly installments over one year. If the interest rate is 14%, what will the first quarterly payment be, including both principal and interest?

17. If a loan requires annual interest payments amounting to $2,975 and the principal amount is $34,000, what is the interest rate on the loan?

COMPOUND INTEREST

The term *compound interest* means that the interest is periodically added to the principal, and, in effect, the new balance (principal plus interest) draws interest. The annual interest rate may be calculated at different intervals, such as annually, semi-annually, quarterly, monthly, or daily. When the interest comes due during the compounding period (for instance, at the end of the month), the interest is calculated and accrues, or is added to the principal. The calculation of compound interest involves such a complex formula that either a compound interest table or a financial calculator is generally used. Compound interest is generally paid on deposits in savings banks and is also used to calculate amortization of a loan.

EXAMPLE: Consider a savings account with a starting balance of $1,000, earning compound interest at 12% per year, compounded annually. To determine how much money will be in the account at the end of 2 years, you would use the formula, $I = PRT$, where:

$$P = \$1,000$$
$$R = 12\%$$
$$T = 1 \text{ year}$$

Step 1. $1,000.00   starting balance, first year
           ×   .12   annual interest rate
           $ 120.00   first year's interest

Step 2. $1,000.00   previous balance
           + 120.00   first year's interest
           $1,120.00   balance at end of first year

Step 3. $1,120.00   starting balance, second year
           ×   .12   annual interest rate
              134.40   second year's interest

The *total compound interest* earned during the period of two years would be $254.40:

$$\$120.00 + \$134.40 = \$254.40$$

The $254.40 is added to the starting balance of $1,000 to give a total of $1,254.40 in the account at the end of the second year.

If this account were earning only *simple* interest, the interest would be calculated as follows:

Step 1. $1,000.00   starting balance, first year
           $\times$ .12   annual interest rate
           $ 120.00   first year's interest

Step 2. $ 120.00   interest per year
           $\times$ 2   years
           $ 240.00   *total simple interest* earned in 2 years

Compound interest made a difference of:

$$\$254.40 - \$240.00 = \$14.40$$

18. Now, you try a problem. If you have a $10,000 certificate of deposit earning interest at the rate of 12% annually, but the interest is compounded monthly, what will be your account balance at the end of 3 months?

Remember that the compounding period and the interest rate per year (called the "nominal" rate) do not have to be the same. When they are not, you must first compute the interest rate *per compounding period*. In our problem, this is:

$$\frac{12\% \text{ annual rate}}{12 \text{ months (compounding period)}} = \frac{1\%}{\text{month}}$$

Now, the calculation proceeds as in the previous example.

Chapter 15 will examine compound interest in more detail as it relates to real estate problems.

ACHIEVEMENT EXERCISE

When you have finished both parts of this exercise, check your answers against those on page 170. If you miss any of the questions, review this chapter before going on to Chapter 9.

Part I—Open Response   Complete the following problems.

1. Carl Bach has borrowed $2,000 at 10.5% interest. The loan will be repaid in 9 months. What amount will be repaid when the 9 months have elapsed?

2. The interest on a 10% loan was $72 for 6 months. What was the principal of the loan?

3. How long will it take for $15,000 to yield $1,125 at 10% interest?

4. Mrs. Ranty was charged $1,295 on a $14,000 loan for one year. What was the rate of interest?

5. What will quarterly interest payments be on a $16,500 loan at 11.5% interest for one year?

Part II—Multiple Choice   Select the correct response from the choices supplied.

6. By selecting from a, b, c or d, indicate which of the following statements is (are) true.

    I. Interest is the cost of using someone else's money.
    II. Interest rates are normally annual rates.

    a. I only
    b. II only
    c. both I and II
    d. neither I nor II

7. In applying the formula for computing interest, $PRT = I$, T could be:

    a. a fraction of a year.
    b. a multiple of a year.
    c. a year.
    d. all of the above

8. A homeowner borrows $1,500 from a lender at 11% interest. When this loan is paid off at the end of 7 months, the total paid will be:

    a. $1,500.00.   c. $1,596.25.
    b. $83.13.   d. $1,642.50.

9. A couple spent $1,200 on furnishings at a department store, charging it on their credit card. They were out of town and did not pay their bill when due. The following month's bill showed a finance charge of $18 added to the $1,200. What was the rate of interest used to compute the finance charge?

    a. 6%   c. 18%
    b. 12%   d. 24%

10. Mary Cavanaugh took her $5,000 bond to the bank as collateral for a loan of $2,300 which she wanted in order to buy furniture and equipment for her new office. The bank gave her the loan and had her sign a 6-month note at 13% interest. The amount of interest Mary will owe when the note matures is:

    a. $207.00.   c. $149.50.
    b. $225.00.   d. $127.00.

11. A bank issued a loan of $20,000 at 11% simple interest for 4-1/2 years. If the loan was paid in full at the end of 4-1/2 years, how much money did the bank receive?

    a. $8,550   c. $21,900
    b. $29,900   d. $11,450

12. If a bank wished to earn $9,000 on a loan of $20,000 over 4-1/2 years, what simple interest rate would have to be charged?

    a. 9%   c. 10%
    b. 45%   d. 12.2%

13. Which of the following short-term loans will yield the greatest amount of interest?

    a. $2,000 at 20% for 2-1/2 years
    b. $10,000 at 5% for 2 years
    c. $60,000 at 10% for 2 months
    d. All of the above are the same.

14. If an interest payment of $150 is made every 3 months on a $5,000 loan, what is the interest rate?

    a. 6%   c. 3%
    b. 12%   d. 9%

15. A loan is given for 80% of the appraised value of a house. If the interest on the loan is $2,500 semi-annually at an annual rate of 10%, what is the appraised value of the house?

    a. $50,000   c. $40,000
    b. $62,500   d. $31,250

16. If you place $10,000 in an account with interest compounded annually at 10% and a like amount bearing simple interest at 10%:

    I. the compound interest account will be larger in 1 year.
    II. the 2 accounts will have the same amounts in 1 year.

    a. I only
    b. II only
    c. both I and II
    d. neither I nor II

ANSWER KEY

Entry Evaluation

- $26,775 paid to bank
- 12% interest

Pages 159–165

1. $\begin{array}{cccc} P & \times R & \times T= & I \\ \$1{,}000 & \times .10 & \times 3= & \$300 \end{array}$

    or $\$\cancel{1{,}000} \overset{10}{} \times \dfrac{\cancel{10}}{\cancel{100}\,1} \times 3 = \$300$

2. 4 months $= \dfrac{4}{12} = \dfrac{1}{3}$ year *or* .333 year

3. 9 months $= \dfrac{9}{12} = \dfrac{3}{4} = .75$ $\$\cancel{6{,}000}^{\,60} \times \dfrac{11}{\cancel{100}\,1} \times \dfrac{3}{4} = \dfrac{1{,}980}{4} = \$495$

    or $\$6{,}000 \times .11 = \$660$ interest for 1 year $\$660 \times .75 = \$495$

    or $\$6{,}000 \times .11 \times .75 = \$495$ for 9 months.

4. $PRT = I$ $\dfrac{\$1{,}000}{1} \times \dfrac{13.75}{100} \times \dfrac{1}{4} = \$34.375$ interest for 3 months

    or $\$1{,}000 \times .1375 = \$137.50$ interest for year
    $\$137.50 \div 12 = \$11.458$ interest for 1 month
    $\$11.458 \times 3 = \$34.375$ interest for 3 months

    loan amount (principal) + interest = total due
    $\$1{,}000 + \$34.375 = \$1{,}034.375$ rounded to $\$1{,}034.38$

5. a. P (principal)   b. $\dfrac{I}{RT} = P$

6. $\dfrac{I}{RT} = P$ $\dfrac{\$24}{.08 \times \dfrac{1}{4}} = \dfrac{24}{.02} = \$1{,}200$

7. $\dfrac{I}{PR} = T$ $\dfrac{\$95}{800 \times .095} = \dfrac{96}{76} = 1.25 = 1\text{-}1/4$ years

8. $\dfrac{I}{PT} = R$ $\dfrac{\$75}{1{,}200 \times \dfrac{1}{2}} = \dfrac{75}{600} = 12.5\%$

9. Compute the annual amount of interest. (Disregard sales price.)
$60,000 × .1375 = $8,250

Divide by the number of payments per year.
$8,250 ÷ 4 = $2,062.50

10. $15,000 × .0975 = $1,462.50 $1,462.50 ÷ 4 = $365.625 = $365.63

11. $55,000 × .125 = $6,875 $6,875 ÷ 2 = $3,437.50 (Disregard appraised value.)

12. Compute the annual interest. $750 × 4 = $3,000

$$\frac{I}{RT} = P = \frac{\$3,000}{.12 \times 1} = \$25,000$$

13. $637.50 × 2 = $1,275 annual interest

$$\frac{I}{RT} = P = \frac{\$1,275}{.085} = \$15,000$$

14. $250 × 4 = $1,000 annual interest

$$\frac{I}{PT} = R = \frac{\$1,000}{\$10,000} = 10\%$$

15. $2,152.50 × 2 = $4,305 annual interest

$$\frac{I}{PT} = R = \frac{\$4,305}{\$42,000} = .1025 = 10\text{-}1/4\%$$

16. $9,000 ÷ 4 = $2,250 quarterly principal

$9,000 × .14 = $1,260 annual interest $1,260 ÷ 4 = $315.00 quarterly interest

$2,250 + $315 = $2,565 first quarterly payment

17. $\dfrac{I}{PT} = R$ $\dfrac{\$2,975}{\$34,000} = .0875 = 8.75\% \; or \; 8\text{-}3/4\%$

18. Step 1.

$$\begin{array}{r} \$10,000.00 \\ \times \quad .01 \\ \hline \$\;\;\;100.00 \end{array} \text{ first month}$$

Step 2. $10,000.00 + $100.00 = $10,100.00

$$\begin{array}{r} \times \quad .01 \\ \hline \$\;\;\;101.00 \end{array} \text{ second month}$$

Step 3. $10,100.00 + $101.00 = $10,201.00

$$\begin{array}{r} \times \quad .01 \\ \hline \$\;\;\;102.01 \end{array} \text{ third month}$$

Now, add this last monthly interest to the amount in the account at the start of the third month.

Step 4.

$$\begin{array}{r} \$10,201.00 \\ +\quad 102.01 \\ \hline \$10,303.01 \end{array}$$

Achievement Exercise

1. $2,000 × 10.5% × .75 = $157.50
   $157.50 + $2,000 = $2,157.50

2. $\dfrac{\$72}{10\% \times .5} = \dfrac{\$72}{5\%} = \$1,440$

3. $\dfrac{\$1,125}{\$15,000 \times 10\%} = .75$ (three-fourths of a year, or 9 months)

4. $\dfrac{\$1295}{\$14,000} \times 1 = .0925 = 9\frac{1}{4}\%$

5. $16,500 × .115 = $1,897.50 $1,897.50 ÷ 4 = $474.375 rounded to $474.38

6. c.

7. d.

8. c. $1,500 × 11% = $165 annual interest
   $165 ÷ 12 × 7 = $96.25 + $1,500 = $1,596.25 total due

9. c. $18 × 12 = $216 annual interest
   $216 ÷ $1,200 = 18% interest rate

10. c. $2,300 × 13% ÷ 2 = $149.50 interest due

11. b. $20,000 × 11% × 4.5 = $9,900 interest
    $20,000 + $9,900 = $29,900 total due

12. c. $9,000 ÷ 4.5 = $2,000 annual interest
    $2,000 ÷ $20,000 = 10% interest rate

13. d. $2,000 × 20% × 2.5 = $1,000
    $10,000 × 5% × 2 = $1,000
    $60,000 × 10% ÷ 12 × 2 = $1,000

14. b. $150 × 4 = $600 annual interest
    $600 ÷ $5,000 = 12% interest rate

15. b. $2,500 × 2 = $5,000 annual interest
    $5,000 ÷ 10% = $50,000 principal
    $50,000 ÷ 80% = $62,500 appraised value

16. b.

9

Real Estate Finance

INTRODUCTION

Real estate finance is such a critical area of the real estate business that entire courses and textbooks are devoted to it. The purpose of this chapter is to introduce the student to some of the most common and elementary calculations involved in the area of finance.

In this chapter, you will be introduced to the calculation of the buyer's loan qualification ratios, loan-to-value ratio, down payments, mortgage amounts, loan discount points, mortgage insurance premiums, amortization, funding fees and commitment fees.

ENTRY EVALUATION

Since readers will have varying amounts of knowledge and experience, the short test that follows will allow you to determine your familiarity with the material to be covered. Try all three problems before looking at the answers, which are on page 201.

- Ms. Ambrose has obtained a 70% mortgage on her home, which is valued at $60,000. She pays an interest rate of 10% annually. The monthly payment has been calculated to be $470.65, including interest and principal plus an annual tax and insurance reserve of $1,200. What will the balance of the principal of the mortgage be after the first payment is made?

- What will the principal of the mortgage be after the second month's payment?

■ Jan Walter is selling a home to a buyer who has obtained a VA loan. The loan is for $15,000 at 9% interest. The current market rate of interest is 9-3/4%. How many points will the lender require on this transaction? What is the amount of the discount that Jan will pay?

LOAN-TO-VALUE RATIO

In the financing of real estate, the lender will typically lend a certain percentage of the sale price, or appraised value, *whichever is less*. The relationship between the value (sale price) and the loan amount is known as the *loan-to-value ratio* (L/V ratio). The interest, then, is charged only on the amount of the loan, not the sales price. (Repayment of loans is discussed in the next chapter.)

EXAMPLE:

$80,000 sales price (value)
$72,000 loan

describes a 90% loan-to-value ratio. Here is how it works:

$$\frac{\$72,000 \text{ loan}}{\$80,000 \text{ value}} = .90 = 90\%$$

1. If a buyer obtains an 80% loan on a $90,000 sale, what is the loan amount?

2. If the loan in Problem 1 bears 12% simple interest and the loan is to be repaid in 1 year, with interest to be paid monthly, what is the amount of each interest payment?

The amount of interest charged and the total amount of money to be repaid relate *only* to the loan amount (the loan principal), and not to the sale price or value. (A VA loan, however, can have a 100% loan-to-value ratio.)

LOAN PAYMENT FACTORS

In Chapter 15, you will learn how to calculate the payments necessary to amortize a loan through the use of factors known as the Ellwood Tables. This is a very accurate method to calculate loan payments. However, it is sometimes acceptable to use simpler methods to calculate a loan payment. For example, Table 9.1 shows a family of numbers known as "loan payment factors." These factors are based upon a $1,000 loan. Therefore, it is necessary to divide the loan amount by 1,000. To use these factors, just locate the appropriate interest rate in the left-hand column and relate this to the appropriate loan term or length of repayment period. For simplicity, we show only 30-, 25-, 20- and 15-year terms. After choosing the correct factor, multiply the factor times the amount of the loan, divided by 1,000, as we discussed above.

To illustrate, suppose that we wish to know the payment required to amortize a $100,000 loan at 11% interest over a 30-year term. First, divide the loan amount of $100,000 by 1,000 ($100,000 ÷ 1,000 = $100). Then, locate 11.000% in the left-hand column. Next, find the factor that corresponds to the 30-year repayment term. We see that this factor is 9.52. Now, multiply this factor times the 100, which is the number of thousands of the loan amount. We then have $100 × 9.52 = $952 monthly payment.

We can simplify this process by combining the steps this way:

$$\frac{\$100,000 \times 9.52}{1,000} = \$952$$

Now you calculate the loan payment if the term is shortened to 25 years.

That's right!

$$\frac{\$100,000 \times 9.80}{1,000} = \$980.$$

TABLE 9.1
LOAN PAYMENT FACTORS
Principal and Interest Factors Per $1,000 of Loan Amount
Based upon Monthly Payments

RATE	TERM 30 Yrs.	25 Yrs.	20 Yrs.	15 Yrs.	RATE	TERM 30 Yrs.	25 Yrs.	20 Yrs.	15 Yrs.
7.000%	6.65	7.07	7.75	8.99	12.125%	10.38	10.62	11.10	12.08
7.125	6.74	7.15	7.83	9.06	12.250	10.48	10.72	11.19	12.16
7.250	6.82	7.23	7.90	9.13	12.375	10.58	10.81	11.27	12.24
7.375	6.91	7.31	7.98	9.20	12.500	10.67	10.90	11.36	12.33
7.500	6.99	7.39	8.06	9.27	12.625	10.77	11.00	11.45	12.41
7.625	7.08	7.47	8.13	9.34	12.750	10.87	11.09	11.54	12.49
7.750	7.16	7.55	8.21	9.41	12.875	10.96	11.18	11.63	12.57
7.875	7.25	7.64	8.29	9.48	13.000	11.06	11.28	11.72	12.65
8.000	7.34	7.72	8.36	9.56	13.125	11.16	11.37	11.80	12.73
8.125	7.42	7.80	8.44	9.63	13.250	11.26	11.47	11.89	12.82
8.250	7.51	7.83	8.52	9.70	13.375	11.36	11.56	11.98	12.90
8.375	7.60	7.97	8.60	9.77	13.500	11.45	11.66	12.07	12.98
8.500	7.69	8.05	8.68	9.85	13.625	11.55	11.75	12.16	13.07
8.625	7.78	8.14	8.76	9.92	13.750	11.65	11.85	12.25	13.15
8.750	7.87	8.22	8.84	9.99	13.875	11.75	11.94	12.34	13.23
8.875	7.96	8.31	8.92	10.07	14.000	11.85	12.04	12.44	13.32
9.000	8.05	8.39	9.00	10.14	14.125	11.95	12.13	12.53	13.40
9.125	8.14	8.48	9.08	10.22	14.250	12.05	12.23	12.62	13.49
9.250	8.23	8.56	9.16	10.29	14.375	12.15	12.33	12.71	13.57
9.375	8.32	8.65	9.24	10.37	14.500	12.25	12.42	12.80	13.66
9.500	8.41	8.74	9.32	10.44	14.625	12.35	12.52	12.89	13.74
9.625	8.50	8.82	9.40	10.52	14.750	12.44	12.61	12.98	13.83
9.750	8.59	8.91	9.49	10.59	14.875	12.54	12.71	13.08	13.91
9.875	8.68	9.00	9.57	10.67	15.000	12.64	12.81	13.17	14.00
10.000	8.78	9.09	9.65	10.75	15.125	12.74	12.91	13.26	14.08
10.125	8.87	9.18	9.73	10.82	15.250	12.84	13.00	13.35	14.17
10.250	8.96	9.26	9.81	10.90	15.375	12.94	13.10	13.45	14.25
10.375	9.05	9.35	9.90	10.98	15.500	13.05	13.20	13.54	14.34
10.500	9.15	9.44	9.98	11.05	15.625	13.15	13.30	13.63	14.43
10.625	9.24	9.53	10.07	11.13	15.750	13.25	13.39	13.73	14.51
10.750	9.33	9.62	10.15	11.18	15.875	13.35	13.49	13.82	14.60
10.875	9.43	9.71	10.24	11.29	16.000	13.45	13.59	13.91	14.69
11.000	9.52	9.80	10.32	11.37	16.125	13.55	13.69	14.01	14.77
11.125	9.62	9.89	10.41	11.44	16.250	13.65	13.79	14.10	14.86
11.250	9.71	9.98	10.49	11.52	16.375	13.75	13.88	14.19	14.95
11.375	9.81	10.07	10.58	11.60	16.500	13.85	13.98	14.29	15.04
11.500	9.90	10.16	10.66	11.68	16.625	13.95	14.08	14.38	15.13
11.625	10.00	10.26	10.75	11.76	16.750	14.05	14.18	14.48	15.21
11.750	10.09	10.35	10.84	11.84	16.875	14.16	14.28	14.57	15.30
11.875	10.19	10.44	10.92	11.92	17.000	14.26	14.38	14.67	15.39
12.000	10.29	10.53	11.01	12.00					

MORTGAGE INSURANCE PREMIUMS

Because of the increased risk to the lender that results from making a loan with a high loan-to-value ratio, lenders demand additional protection. This has come to be known as mortgage insurance. Do not confuse this with mortgage cancellation insurance that is designed to pay off a mortgage loan if the borrower dies. Mortgage insurance is designed to protect the lender in the event of default by the buyer and if the property will not sell for a sufficient amount at foreclosure to pay off the defaulted loan.

FHA was the originator of this concept, which has undergone a number of changes over the years. FHA currently permits the mortgage insurance premium (MIP) to be paid in cash in an amount of 3.661% of the loan amount, or it can be financed, in which case the rate is 3.8% of the loan amount. Since VA is a loan guaranty program rather than an insured loan program, there is no mortgage insurance required on VA loans. Conventional loans must have private mortgage insurance (PMI) if the loan-to-value ratio exceeds 80%. The premium for this can be paid in cash or added to the amount of the loan, as with an FHA loan. The amount of the premium depends upon the loan-to-value ratio and the type of loan (fixed-rate, buydown, ARM, etc.). Let us now calculate some mortgage insurance premiums.

FHA Mortgage Insurance Premium (MIP)

EXAMPLE: Suppose that Billy Bob Bennett has been approved for an $80,000 FHA-insured loan. He has the option of paying the MIP in cash or adding it to the amount of the note. What is the difference?

Cash MIP	$80,000 × 3.661% = $2,928.80
Financed MIP	$80,000 × 3.8% = $3,040.00. For a 30-year loan at 10.5%, this amounts to an additional $27.81 in each monthly payment. (Use chart in Table 9.1 to calculate the payment.)

Conventional Private Mortgage Insurance Premium (PMI)

What would be the cost of PMI if Billy Bob had obtained a 90% conventional loan? Assume that the insurer requires a cash premium of .5% plus .35% monthly renewal.

Cash PMI	$90,000 × .5% = $450.00 which is the prepaid premium for the first year. In addition, a renewal premium of .35 of the loan amount is added to the monthly payment. (This factor may change depending upon the company providing the mortgage insurance, loan-to-value ratio, type of loan, etc.)
	$90,000 × .35% = $315.00 ÷ 12 months = $26.25. Each year the monthly amount decreases because the amount of the loan decreases. The premium remains in effect until the

premium remains in effect until the loan balance has been reduced to 80% of the original purchase price of the house. (Remember that if Billy Bob had obtained an 80% loan instead of a 90% one, there would not have been any PMI at all.)

Financed PMI $90,000 × 2.85% = $2,565.00 amount of financed PMI (No cash payment required at closing.) $2,565 at 10.5% (for example) for 30 years = $23.63 additional monthly payment required to pay for PMI

VA FUNDING FEE

In an effort to make the VA-guaranteed loan program more self-supporting, the VA now charges a "funding fee" which currently amounts to 1% of the loan and can be paid by either the seller or the buyer. Typically, it is the buyer who pays the fee. There have been efforts in Congress to increase this funding fee to as much as 5% of the loan amount. The funding fee can be paid in cash or added to the amount of the note just as we discussed under FHA and conventional mortgage insurance premiums. There is a major difference, however, aside from the relative costs. There is no reduction in the amount for paying the VA funding fee in cash.

What funding fee costs would Billy Bob have had if he had obtained a $90,000 VA loan?

Funding fee paid in cash $90,000 × 1% = $900

Funding fee financed $90,000 × 1% = $900 At 10.5% on a 30-year loan, this amounts to an additional $8.23 per month. Or, $900 can be added to the $90,000 loan and the payment can be calculated on the $90,900 amount.

LOAN COMMITMENT FEE

If a builder desires to finance the construction of a new house, a short-term construction loan (also called an "interim" loan) is required. However, before the short-term lender funds the loan, they will require a loan commitment from a long-term lender to pay off their short-term loan and take them out of that property. Hence, the term "take-out" or "stand-by"commitment. The long-term lenders charge a "commitment fee" for this service of committing funds for a permanent loan. A typical commitment fee is 1% of the amount of the new long-term loan. This fee is generally nonrefundable. However, in some cases it is credited against the total loan discount charged to the seller. If such is the case, it is greatly to the builder's benefit to require the buyer to obtain the loan from the same lender who provided the builder's commitment.

If the proposed long-term or permanent loan is $150,000 and if the commitment fee is 1%, how much must the builder pay to the lender?

$150,000 × 1% = $1,500 commitment fee.

Loan commitment fees are not restricted to new construction loans. They frequently are charged on nonresidential loans and may be charged on certain residential loans, particularly the larger ones.

BUYER'S LOAN QUALIFICATION RATIOS

Prior to approving a buyer's loan application, the lenders want to be as sure as possible that the applicant has the financial ability to repay the requested loan and that the applicant has a history of paying off other debts satisfactorily. Before a real estate licensee invests a great deal of time and expense into working with the buyer, the licensee should perform a ''pre-qualification'' of the buyer. Of course this is not directly related to the actual loan qualification to be done by the lender.

Lenders verify the buyer-applicant's income and relate this to (1) the amount of the payments on the requested loan and (2) the total amount of all other payments now owed by the buyer. To accomplish this, lenders utilize arbitrary ratios. In the case of FHA and VA loans, the U.S. government sets these ratios. In the case of the secondary market such as FNMA and FHLMC, these agencies set the ratios. Or, if a lender plans to retain the loan in its own portfolio, the ratios are set individually. It is important to remember that each agency or lender is free to change the numbers in each ratio as well as which items are included in that ratio. These ratios also may vary depending upon the loan-to-value ratio and whether the interest is fixed or is subject to adjustment. Therefore, our discussion is intended to be general in its nature.

Qualification ratios are usually described as ''front'' and ''back'' ratios. The ''front'' ratio is a percentage of the buyer's income to be applied to the mortgage loan payment (including principal, interest, taxes, insurance and any mortgage insurance premiums or homeowner's association fees) and the ''back'' ratio is a percentage of the buyer's income to be applied to all of the buyer's present debts plus the mortgage loan payment as described above. Buyers must satisfy both ratios in order to obtain loan approval.

Conventional Loan Qualification

Let us now explore the calculation of these loan qualification ratios. Suppose that the front and back ratios for a 90% loan are 28% and 36% (expressed as 28/36) respectively. This means that the buyer's mortgage loan payment should not exceed 28% of the gross monthly income and that the mortgage loan payment plus all other debts should not exceed 36% of gross monthly income. (If the buyer is able to obtain a 95% loan, the lender may require ratios of 25/33 due to the fact that the loan has more risk because of the buyer's smaller cash investment.)

EXAMPLES: Mr. and Mrs. Rudy Ramirez have a combined gross monthly income of $3,600. They have selected a $100,000 house and plan to obtain a $90,000 loan at 10.5% for 30 years. The monthly principal and interest payment on this house is $823.27, the hazard insurance is $41, the taxes are $95 and the financed private mortgage insurance (PMI) premium is $26.25. Their only long-term debt is a $300 car payment. Can they qualify for the loan? (We are ignoring good credit, job history, etc.)

$823.27 principal and interest + $41 insurance + $95 taxes + $26.25 PMI = $985.52 total house payment ÷ $3,600 income = 27.4% (must not exceed 28%)

$985.52 total house payment + $300 car payment = $1,285.52

$1,285.52 total debt payment ÷ $3,600 income = 35.7% (must not exceed 36%)

Does the Ramirez family qualify for the loan? Yes, because their ratios are less than those required.

Could they qualify if they had a $100 monthly boat payment?

No, because their second or "back" ratio would be too high even though their first or "front" ratio is satisfactory. However, if they can pay off the boat out of funds currently on hand (not borrowed), the loan can be approved.

Now you try a few simple loan qualification problems.

Roy and Rita wish to obtain a new loan. If their combined income is $4,200 per month, what amount of conventional loan can they qualify for if the lender is using the 28/36 ratios and if they have no other debts?

$4,200 × 28% = $1,176 maximum amount of principal, interest, taxes and insurance (PITI)

John and Debbie Keating have been told that the monthly payment for PITI on the house they have selected is $1,234.56. If area conventional lenders are qualifying prospective buyers at 28/36, what is the required monthly income for the Keatings?

$$\frac{\$1,234.56}{.28} = \$4,409.14 \text{ minimum monthly income required}$$

Kit and Charlotte's combined monthly income is $5,000. What monthly PITI can they qualify for if area conventional lenders are qualifying at 28/36.

$5,000 × .28 = $1,400 maximum monthly PITI

Now, what is the maximum monthly debt they can have and still qualify for the loan?

$$\$5,000 \times .36 = \$1,800 \text{ maximum PITI plus debts}$$

Therefore: $1,800   total maximum monthly payments
            − 1,400   PITI
            $ 400   maximum allowable monthly debts to qualify

FHA Loan Qualification

When the FHA insures a loan, the buyer must meet its loan underwriting guidelines. For example, the current FHA ratios are 38/53 but the FHA uses the gross monthly income LESS income tax as the number for income comparison and they use the mortgage loan payment as described above PLUS their estimates for utilities, maintenance and repair costs as the buyer's total housing expense. These factors are used in calculating the front ratio. Calculation of the back ratio includes the total of the buyer's long-term debts (those with 10 months or more remaining) PLUS payments made to social security, child support, alimony and child care.

EXAMPLE: The Ling family's combined monthly income is $3,600. They have one child. Their monthly obligations are as follows: income tax withheld is $485, social security withheld is $270, car payment is $200 and school loan payment is $50. Can they qualify for a FHA-insured mortgage loan of $80,000 at 10.5% for 30 years, the monthly payment on which is $731.79 principal and interest, $41 insurance, $95 taxes and $27.81 FHA mortgage insurance premium (MIP) if FHA's estimates for the subject house are $200 for utilities and $80 for repairs and maintenance?

$3,600 gross income − $485 income tax = $3,115 net effective income

$731.79 principal and interest + $27.81 MIP + $95 taxes + $41 insurance + $200 utilities + $80 repairs = $1,175.60 total housing expense

$1,175.60 total housing expense ÷ $3,115 net effective income = 37.7% (must not exceed 38%)

$1,175.60 total housing expense + $270 social security + $200 car payment + $50 school loan payment = $1,695.60 total fixed payments

$1,695.60 total fixed payments ÷ $3,115 net effective income = 54.4% (must not exceed 53%)

Using these figures, the Lings technically cannot qualify for this loan. They can either pay off sufficient debts to reduce the back ratio to an acceptable level or they must start looking at less expensive houses.

Note: In addition to the qualifying ratios, FHA requires the buyer to meet other loan underwriting guidelines related to the amount of "residual income" the family will have after meeting the debt obligations discussed above. The residual income in our example is $3,115 net effective income − $1,695.6 = $1,419.40. The amount of required residual income is based upon the number of people in the family. In the Lings' case, their residual income is satisfactory (3 people requires only $790). This excess is considered to be a "compensating factor" along with other verifiable facts such as job stability, money in the bank, etc. Therefore, even though we stated above that the Lings technically could not qualify for the loan based strictly upon the ratios, it is quite possible that they actually can qualify because the back ratio is so close to the maximum permitted and their compensating factors are favorable.

VA Loan Qualification

VA requires that eligible veterans who wish to acquire VA-guaranteed loans meet only one qualifying ratio: the named expenses cannot exceed 41% of the buyer's gross income. Like FHA, VA also requires the buyer to meet certain "residual income" guidelines which are based upon family size.

EXAMPLE: Hermann and Hilda Homberg have a combined monthly income of $3,600. They have one child and have applied for a VA-guaranteed loan of $110,000 at 10.5% for 30 years on which the payments are $1,006.21 principal and interest, $10.06 financed VA funding fee, $120 taxes and $55 insurance. Can they qualify for this loan if their income tax withheld is $485, social security withheld is $270, their car payment is $250 and the VA's estimate for utilities is $200 and $80 for maintenance?

Ratio Calculation:

$3,600 gross income

$1,006.21 principal and interest + $10.06 financed VA funding fee + $120 taxes + $55 insurance + $250 car payment = $1,441.27 total monthly debt.

$1,441.27 total monthly debt ÷ $3,600 gross income = 40.0% (cannot exceed 41%) This ratio is satisfactory for loan qualification.

Residual income calculation:

$3,600 gross income − $485 income tax − $270 social security − $250 car payment − $1,006.21 principal and interest − $10.06 VA funding fee − $120 taxes − $55 insurance − $80 maintenance − $200 utilities = $1,123.73 residual income.

The amount required for loan qualification varies with respect to the area of the United States. Generally, this amount of residual income is sufficient for a family of 5. Therefore, they can qualify if their family size is 5 or less.

CALCULATION OF LOAN AMOUNTS AND DOWN PAYMENTS

The amount of money that the lender requires the buyer to pay toward the purchase price is called the down payment. The difference between the sales price and this down payment is the amount of the loan that the lender is willing to make on the subject property. This loan amount must be substantiated by an appraisal prepared by an appraiser of the lender's choice. The amount of the down payment and the loan amount (the loan-to-value ratio) is determined by the type of loan to be obtained.

VA Loans

A VA-guaranteed loan requires no down payment at all up to the maximum allowable loan amount, which is based upon the amount of the veteran's entitlement. Of course, the buyer may make a down payment in order to keep the payments lower.

FHA Loans

FHA-insured loans have a variety of down payments and loan amounts. We will not attempt to address but one type since this is not a finance textbook. Most FHA buyers prefer to make a minimum down payment and therefore obtain the maximum loan amount. In order for a buyer to obtain the maximum loan for FHA mortgage insurance purposes, FHA permits the buyer to add the amount of the buyer's closing costs (not including the pre-paid items) to the sales price. This amount is called the FHA "acquisition cost." This amount is then the basis upon which the loan amount is calculated.

Let's say that the sales price is $70,000. The FHA provides a table of allowable buyer's closing costs, which varies by geographic area. Suppose that these amount to $1,350. Acquisition cost is then $70,000 + $1,350 = $71,350. If the sales price is more than $50,000, the FHA uses a two-tiered loan-to-value ratio. It will insure 97% of the first $25,000 and 95% of the excess up to the maximum loan amount, which varies from one part of the United States to another.

In order to calculate the maximum mortgage amount:

$71,350 acquisition cost − $25,000 = $46,350

$46,350 × 95% = $44,032.50

Then $25,000 × 97% = $24,250

$44,032.50 + $24,250 = $68,282.50. FHA rounds this amount down to the next lowest $50 which amounts to $68,250.

This $68,250 is the maximum loan for FHA mortgage insurance purposes. We must now subtract this amount from the sales price (*not* the acquisition cost) so that:

$70,000 − $68,250 = $1,750 cash down payment required

Note: In addition to this amount, the buyer is required to pay $1,350 at closing as the FHA allowable closing costs plus the amount of the prepaid items.

Let us look at another FHA requirement known as the "buyer's minimum cash investment." This is calculated by:

$70,000 sales price − $25,000 = $45,000 × 5% = $2,250

$25,000 × 3% = $750

$2,250 + $750 = $3,000 minimum cash required.

In our example above, have we satisfied this requirement? Looking back, we see that the buyer's down payment was $1,750 and the buyer's closing costs were $1,350. The sum of these is $3,100 so that this buyer has paid $100 more (plus the pre-paid items which FHA does not consider to be closing costs) than FHA requires.

Now you try a simple problem.

If the FHA buyer's allowable closing costs are $1,450 on a house priced at $80,000, calculate the maximum loan for FHA mortgage insurance purposes.

```
    $80,000 sales price
 +   1,450 buyer's FHA closing costs (not including prepaid items)
     81,450
 − 25,000 × 97% =    $24,250
   $56,450 × 95% =  + $53,627.50
                     $77,877.50 (Round down to next $50 increment)
                     $77,850.   maximum FHA insurable loan
```

What is the amount of down payment on the transaction shown above?

```
      $80,000 sales price
    − 77,850 maximum FHA insurable loan
    $  2,150 down payment required by FHA
```

What is the amount of cash investment FHA requires the buyer to make?

$$
\begin{array}{r}
\$80,000 \text{ sales price} \\
\underline{-25,000} \times 3\% = \$\ \ 750 \\
\$55,000 \times 5\% = \underline{2,750} \\
\$3,500 \text{ FHA required minimum cash investment}
\end{array}
$$

Does the buyer in our example meet this requirement?

$$
\begin{array}{r}
\$2,150 \text{ FHA required down payment} \\
\underline{+1,450} \text{ FHA allowable closing costs for buyer} \\
\$3,600 \text{ cash investment by buyer}
\end{array}
$$

Yes, our buyer meets the FHA requirement and exceeds it by $100.

Conventional Loans

The maximum conventional loan available is generally 95% and there are usually stringent underwriting requirements for such a high loan to value ratio. Typically, a 90% loan is customary. However, private mortgage insurance (PMI) is required by the lender on any loan greater than 80% of the value (or sales price, whichever is less). The amount of the premium for this PMI varies among insurers and also varies with the type of loan. For example, a fixed-rate loan will have a smaller PMI premium than an adjustable-rate loan.

If the sales price is $100,000 and the buyer requests a 90% loan, how much cash down payment must the buyer make if the property appraises for $97,000? Remember that the loan amount is based upon the *lesser* of the sales price *or* the appraised value. In this case, the seller may not be willing to reduce the sales price to an amount equal to the appraised value. In this case, the buyer may either terminate the contract (which is a typical contract provision) or pay a larger down payment. Let's look at the figures:

$97,000 appraised value $\times$ 90% = $87,300 maximum loan amount which results in a $12,700 down payment ($100,000 − $87,300) unless the seller will reduce the sales price to the appraised value of $97,000 in which case the down payment will amount to $9,700.

LOAN DISCOUNT POINTS

Points are percentage points, more accurately described as a percent of the loan amount (1 "point" = 1% of the loan). This section will cover two types of points: mortgage loan discount points and origination fee points, which are sometimes referred to as "service fee" points. Origination fee points are charged by the lending institution to cover the costs of issuing a loan. This fee is generally 1 percent of the loan amount and generally is paid by the buyer.

The loan discount may vary from 1 to 6 percent or more of the loan amount and, therefore, can account for a large portion of the closing costs. Briefly, the loan discount is charged by an investor, (or lender) who also makes other investments such as commercial loans or purchases of annuities and bonds. Historically, the interest rates (or yields) on these other investments have been higher than on FHA-insured and VA-guaranteed loans because an artificial ceiling was imposed by the government. However, FHA loan rates have been deregulated, and VA rates also *may* be. Loan discounts may be charged on a conventional, FHA or VA loan. The VA still requires the seller to pay these points, but FHA and conventional programs permit the parties to negotiate the matter of which party pays the points.

The Purpose of Points

Interest rates on mortgage loans are set by two factors:

- supply and demand of available loan funds, which determines the current market rate of interest, and

- governmental regulation (a VA-guaranteed loan, for example) that sets a maximum, or ceiling, rate on interest for specific loans. FHA-insured loans *formerly* had regulated maximum interest rates. The FHA now permits sellers and buyers to share the payment of loan discounts but the VA will not permit the buyer to pay any loan discount.

Suppose the current market rate of interest quoted by a savings and loan association for mortgage loans is 14% and an individual is negotiating a loan at 13-1/2% interest for a mortgage loan regulated by the government. Compared to the current market rate, the savings and loan association would lose 1/2% interest by granting the government-regulated mortgage loan.

Loan discounts are used to equalize the interest on these loans. Lenders have calculated that a sum equal to approximately 1% (one percentage point, called simply a *point*) of the total loan amount is required to make up for each 1/8% interest rate loss. This ratio of 1% discount = 1/8% is mathematically correct for only a narrow band of interest rates, yet it continues to be a popular "rule of thumb." Chapter 15 includes a discussion of an accurate way to calculate loan discount points. The loan discount points are paid to the lender to make up for the difference in interest rates. This payment, in effect, prepays the interest that the lending institution will not be receiving over the life of the loan.

The collection of a loan discount actually increases the rate of return, or yield, to the lender or investor. Suppose that a borrower signed a note for $75,000, and an investor sends a check for this amount to the person closing the loan. The closer also collects a check in the amount of $3,000, known as the loan discount, from some party—usually the seller. The closer now sends the $3,000 check to the investor, along with the borrower's note for $75,000. The *net* amount that the investor loaned was $72,000. However, the borrower's loan payments will be based upon $75,000. By repeating this procedure 24 more times, the investor will collect enough cash to make another $75,000 loan using *none* of his or her own funds. Or, if the borrower's loan payments had been based upon the $72,000 net figure, they would be considerably lower than they are on the $75,000 loan. Thus, the loan discount fee is a way for the investor to increase the income on a loan. This is the "return," or "yield" on the loan.

To illustrate:

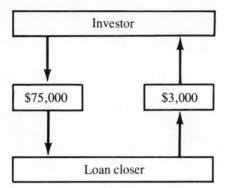

As discussed earlier, the 1/8% yield = 1% discount is a popular rule of thumb. In Chapter 16, this ratio will be further discussed, and its limitations will be illustrated.

EXAMPLE: The Rudolph Loan Company is negotiating a VA loan with Mr. Berg for $80,000 at the maximum rate of 10% interest. The current market rate of interest on mortgage loans is 10-1/2%. If the Rudolph Loan Company makes the VA loan, it will suffer a 1/2% interest rate loss. Therefore, a mortgage discount is required, and one point per 1/8% interest loss is needed to make up the loan company's loss.

Since 1/2% is the same as 4/8%, 4 points are required. As indicated, each point is equal to 1% of the total amount of the loan ($80,000). Four points, then, equal 4% of the total. The amount of the discount can be computed by simple multiplication.

$$4\% \times \$80,000 = \$3,200$$

The amount of the mortgage discount (or prepaid interest) in this case is $3,200.

The Rudolph Loan Company will probably sell this loan to an investor, who will be the actual lender, and will probably have to give the mortgage discount amount to the third party. So, the loan company will not make any money from issuing the loan, but will spend money in time, paper and personnel. As compensation, the loan company will charge an origination fee that will be expressed in points. A 1-point origination fee means that the loan company will take 1% of the amount of the loan to pay for the service of originating the loan.

Using the example, a 1-point origination fee on an $80,000 loan is 1% of $80,000, or $800. The loan company will collect $800 from the person who is taking out the loan.

The $3,200 discount, however, must be paid by the *seller,* since federal regulations prohibit charging the discount on VA loans to the buyer. However, some changes may be occurring in this practice.

Calculating Points

Here is the same example in a step-by-step explanation.

Step 1. Compute the difference in interest rates.

current market rate − government-regulated rate = difference

10-1/2% − 10% = 1/2%

Step 2. Convert the difference to eighths.

1/2% = 4/8%

Step 3. Determine number of points (one-eighth = 1 point).

4/8 = 4 points

Step 4. Compute discount rate (1 point = 1%).

4 × 1% = 4%

Step 5. Compute amount of discount, based upon the amount of the loan.

discount rate × total loan amount = discount amount

4% × $80,000 = $3,200

Note: This is the same as a 1/2% interest loss on $40,000 for 8 years.
1/2% × $80,000 = $400 $400 × 8 = $3,200

Step 6. Compute the origination fee (1 point = 1%).

total loan amount × points = origination fee

$80,000 × 1% = $800 origination fee

3. The Schwartz family is negotiating a mortgage loan with the United Savings and Loan Association. The interest on the loan is government-regulated and is less than the current market rate of interest. The amount of the loan is $72,000. The savings and loan has calculated that it needs a 4-point discount and a 1.5-point origination fee in order to extend this loan without losing interest. What is the dollar amount of the discount? What is the dollar amount of the origination fee?

4. The Robinsons are buying a residence with a VA mortgage loan for $88,000 at 12% interest, which is the maximum rate of interest permitted for this loan. If the market rate of interest for such a loan is 12-3/4%, what is the dollar amount of discount the seller will have to pay to help the buyer obtain the loan? If the loan company charges an origination fee of 1 point, what will be the amount of the origination fee? Who will pay it?

5. Ms. Brown is selling her house for $81,000 to a buyer who is obtaining a loan for $50,000 at 13% interest. The current market rate of interest is 13-1/4%. The seller has agreed to pay the discount asked by the bank. What is the amount she will have to pay to help the buyer obtain the loan?

6. The Ursa family had to pay a 4-point discount to help buyers obtain a $76,000 VA loan. The market rate of interest at the time was 13-1/4%. What was the VA loan interest rate, and what was the amount of the discount that the Ursas paid? Who received this discount?

7. Mr. Johns is trying to obtain a $68,000 VA loan in order to purchase the Bradburys' house. The present rate of interest is 13-3/4% and the present VA interest rate is 13-1/4%. The Bradburys have agreed to pay the mortgage discount to help Mr. Johns obtain the VA loan. What amount will the Bradburys pay and to whom will this money be paid? What is another name for a mortgage discount?

8. The Power family paid a $2,160 mortgage discount to help the buyer obtain a $72,000 loan. What were the number of points required for this loan? What was the interest difference between the VA interest rate and the open market interest rate at that time? If the VA rate was 14% what was the open market interest rate? The buyer paid a $720 origination fee. How many origination fee points did the mortgage company charge?

Bear in mind that even though VA loans have been used in the preceding examples, the loan discount is not limited to VA loans. In any other type of loan, the loan discount may be paid by either the seller or the buyer or shared by both. The loan discount is used on *any* loan for which the face amount of interest on the note is less than the market interest rate. The loan discount makes up for that difference. As long as the VA continues to impose an artificial interest rate ceiling on the loans that it guarantees, a loan discount will be charged. On other types of loans, however, there may not be a requirement by the lender to charge a loan discount, depending upon the relationship of the note rate to the market rate.

For example, if the borrower agrees to pay the market interest rate, no discount is required. If, however, the borrower wants a lower interest rate, a discount is required. The interest rate on the loan and the loan discount work in opposition to each other. As the interest rate is increased, the discount is decreased, (and vice versa) provided that the lender's yield remains the same.

MORTGAGE LOANS—OVERVIEW

Mortgage loans are usually made for definite periods of time, ranging from 5 to 30 years or more. Payments of both principal (face value of the mortgage) and interest are required during the term of the loan. A mortgage debt divided into equal, regular payments (usually monthly) over a period of time is called an *amortized mortgage*.

Under the terms of an amortized mortgage, the borrower makes a fixed monthly payment that includes one month's interest on the unpaid principal, plus a payment of part of the principal. The beginning monthly installments primarily pay interest, and only a small portion of each payment is applied to the reduction of the principal. As the principal is gradually reduced, also reducing the interest to be paid, an increasing percentage of the monthly payment can be applied to repayment of the principal, until the loan is repaid entirely.

A chart of typical amortized loan payments is shown in Figure 9.1. Notice how the amount of principal paid in each installment *increases*, while the amount of interest paid *decreases*. The reason for this is that interest is charged only on the outstanding balance of the loan. The last payment—in this example, number 300—is not shown. Please note that the percentages in each payment add up to 100%. This is because each payment on such a loan involves only principal reduction and interest on the balance, although the percentage changes with each payment.

Many mortgage lenders require the borrower to pay a monthly amount, in addition to the monthly amortization payment, to establish a reserve to pay real estate taxes and insurance premiums when they become due. The amount of this reserve will be indicated when it is to be included in a problem. It is not a part of the *loan* payment, however.

FIGURE 9.1
Amortized Mortgage for $80,000 at 13.5% Interest for 25 Years

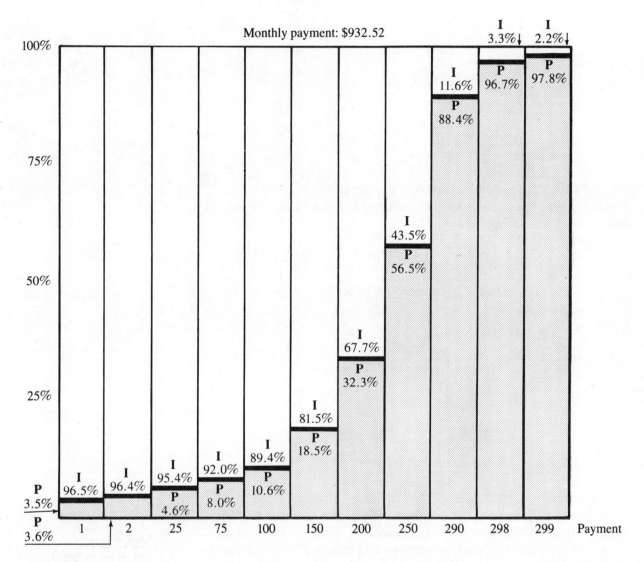

AMORTIZATION CALCULATIONS

You should be able to handle all the problems in this chapter by applying what you have learned about percentages, principal and interest. Work all dollar amounts out to three decimal places, and round off to two places only in the last step of a problem. Work carefully. If your answer does not agree with the one given, review until you understand why you were wrong. Then, correct your work before going on to the next problem.

9. Mrs. Walsh owns a residence valued at $77,000 and has been granted a mortgage loan equal to 75% of the value of the property. If the interest rate is 12-1/2%, compute the amount of interest charged for the first month of the loan. (Remember the loan-to-value ratio; in this example, it is 75%.)

EXAMPLE: Using the information in the last problem, if Mrs. Walsh's monthly payment is $616.34, what will be the balance of the principal of her loan next month?

Step 1.   Compute monthly interest on full principal (already worked out in the last problem). The answer is $601.56.

Step 2.   Find amount of payment that will be applied to reducing the principal.

    $616.34   total payment
    − 601.56   monthly interest
    $ 14.78   Amount Applied to Principal

Step 3.   Compute new principal balance.

    $57,750.00   old principal balance
    −   14.78   reduction
    $57,735.22   New Principal Balance

Please note again that there will be a few cents difference in the answer if you leave the numbers in the calculator and perform the chain functions as opposed to writing down each answer, clearing the calculator, and then reentering the numbers for the next step in the problem. Greater accuracy with a calculator is obtained if the numbers are left in the calculator, and the next calculation is then performed. In lieu of that, carry each answer to 3 or 4 decimal places and round *only* in the *final* answer to the problem.

10. Now calculate the balance of the principal of Mrs. Walsh's loan when the interest for the third payment is computed.

Accrued Interest and Loan Reduction

Typically, interest on a real estate loan is paid *after* it has been earned by the lender, or "accrued." For this reason, interest is paid "in arrears," which means that the June payment on a loan includes the interest earned during May and a remainder, which reduces the June principal.

Occasionally, interest may be paid in advance, but changes in the tax laws no longer invite this method of payment. A limited exception to this is found in nearly every new loan, however. Since a loan may be finalized, or "closed" on any day of the month, the buyer at closing usually pays interest from that day of closing through the end of the month. This is called "pre-paid" interest. Then, the first regular monthly payment will be on the first of the *following* month. That payment will include the interest for the intervening first full month of the loan. The buyer is not getting a "free ride," as some think. Examine the diagram below for a better understanding of this.

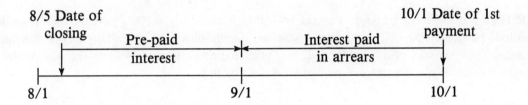

11. On May 1, Thomas Carter borrowed $45,000 at 11% interest. The loan was amortized over a 20-year period at $464.48 per month. How much of the June 1 payment was applied to interest, and how much was applied to principal?

12. Using the information given in the previous exercise, divide the July 1 payment between interest and principal.

13. W. C. Olcott has obtained a $31,500 mortgage on his home at 10-1/2% interest. Mr. Olcott's monthly payment has been figured at $474.74, which includes interest and principal *plus* tax and insurance premiums. If tax and insurance premiums total $1,920 per year, what will be the principal balance of the mortgage after the first payment is made?

14. T. P. Holloway, who has a house valued at $60,000, obtained a $10,000 mortgage loan to build a room addition. The loan is payable at the rate of $100 per month, plus 14% interest on the decreasing principal balance. The loan was made on March 1, and principal and interest payments are due on the first day of each month. What amount will be due on April 1? On May 1?

15. What is the amount of the last payment in problem number 14?

TYPES OF AMORTIZATION

So far, the calculations have involved loans having equal payments made up of unequal and changing amounts of principal and interest. Now consider a type of loan where the principal is divided into equal payments, to each of which interest on the unpaid balance is added.

EXAMPLE: Two loans, each for $50,000, bear 13% annual interest, have a 5-year term with annual payments, and are fully amortized (no "balloon" or "bumper" note due at the end of the term). However, one loan has constant and equal payments of principal *and* interest, but the other has constant and equal payments of *principal,* plus interest on the unpaid declining balance. Which loan will earn the most interest?

Loan 1

$50,000 at 13% for 5 years requires an annual payment of $14,215.73. (This figure is from a mortgage payment chart or from a financial calculator. See Table 9.1.

Year	Payment	Interest	Principal	Balance
new				$50,000.00
1	$14,215.73	$ 6,500.00	$ 7,715.73	42,284.27
2	14,215.73	5,496.96	8,718.77	33,565.50
3	14,215.73	4,363.51	9,852.22	23,713.28
4	14,215.73	3,082.73	11,133.00	12,580.28
5	14,215.73	1,635.44	12,580.28	-0-
		$21,078.64 Total Interest Paid		

Loan 2

$50,000 in 5 equal annual payments of principal requires a $10,000 payment plus decreasing and unequal interest payments.

Year	Payment	Interest	Principal	Balance
new				$50,000.00
1	$16,500.00	$ 6,500.00	$10,000.00	40,000.00
2	15,200.00	5,200.00	10,000.00	30,000.00
3	13,900.00	3,900.00	10,000.00	20,000.00
4	12,600.00	2,600.00	10,000.00	10,000.00
5	11,300.00	1,300.00	10,000.00	-0-
		$19,500.00 Total Interest Paid		

An example of this type of loan involving fixed principal payments plus interest on the unpaid balance is one where the interest may change, such as a bank requiring interest at "X% above the prime rate."

Lenders and borrowers have different viewpoints. Some lenders would prefer Loan 1 because it earns $1,578.64 more interest, even though the interest in Loan 2 is repaid much sooner, which actually increases the overall yield or rate of return to the lender. However, many borrowers might prefer Loan 2 because of less interest and a simpler amortization schedule. A disadvantage of Loan 2 to the borrower, however, might be the larger annual payments for the first 2 years. Now, compare both of these loans on graphs shown in Figures 9.2 and 9.3

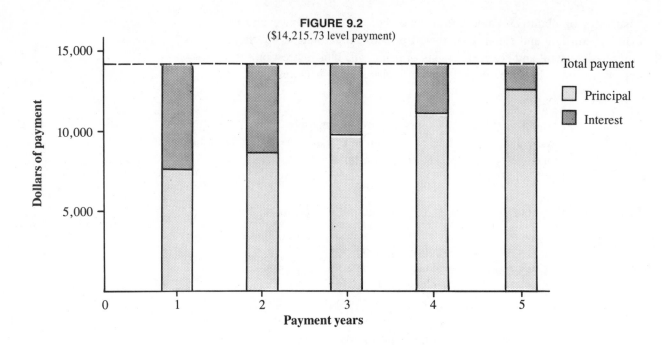

FIGURE 9.2
($14,215.73 level payment)

In Figure 9.2, if the amounts paid each year as principal and interest are added, they always total the fixed constant payment.

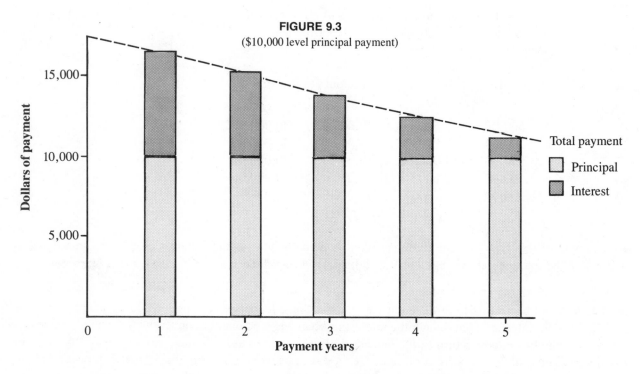

FIGURE 9.3
($10,000 level principal payment)

In Figure 9.3, if you add the amounts of principal and interest paid at each interval, they add up to a total payment that decreases annually.

A "balloon" loan, on the other hand, is one in which the payments are not sufficient to amortize, or completely pay off, the loan during its term. Generally, a balloon loan will have payments based upon a long term, say 10 years, but the entire balance remaining must be paid off at the end of a much shorter term, say 2 years.

EXAMPLE: A $10,000 loan at 14% may have annual payments based upon a 10-year payout, resulting in a $1,917.14 annual payment. To determine how much is owed on the loan after 2 payments have been made, you would follow these steps.

Step 1. $10,000.00 × .14 = $1,400.00 first-year interest
Step 2. $1,917.14 − $1,400.00 = $517.14 first-year principal
Step 3. $10,000.00 − $517.14 = $9,482.86 start of second year
Step 4. $9,482.86 × .14 = $1,327.60 = second-year interest
Step 5. $1,917.14 − $1,327.60 = $589.54 second-year principal
Step 6. $9,482.86 − $589.54 = $8,893.32 start of third year, which is also the end of the second year and is the remaining balance on the loan (the amount of the "balloon" payment).

Chapter 15 presents a much quicker way to calculate remaining balances on loans.

Deferred Interest or "Negative Amortization"

Sometimes, a nonstandard payment schedule for the first few years of a loan is agreed upon by the lender and the buyer to allow the buyer to obtain a loan. Some of these payments are not even sufficient to pay the interest on the loan, and the deficiency is added to the loan balance at each payment period. Because the loan balance increases with each succeeding payment, this is called "negative amortization." Obviously, there must be a point at which the borrower begins making larger payments to reduce this increasing loan balance.

EXAMPLE: Consider a $60,000 loan for 30 years at 13-1/2% which *should have* monthly payments of $687.25. If the borrower's payment schedule calls for him to pay $600.00 monthly for the first year, the loan balance at the end of that year has actually <u>increased</u>.

Look at what happens for the first month of the loan. In each of the first 12 months of the loan, the $600.00 payments will be $75.00 short of paying even the $675.00 interest due on the original loan ($60,000 × .135 × 1/12 = $675.00). Therefore, there is no principal reduction at all and the borrower *owes* more each month than was originally borrowed.

$75.00 unpaid interest
+ 12.25 unpaid principal
$87.25 amount deferred and added to principal

$87.25 amount added to principal
× .135 annual interest rate as a decimal
$11.78 annual interest on amount deferred

$11.78 annual interest
÷ 12 months
$ .98 monthly interest on amount deferred

Now, the $.98 deferred interest must be added to the $87.25 deferred amount. At the end of the first month, the borrower owes $60,000 + $.98 + $87.25, or a total of $60.088.23. This is the new loan balance at the beginning of the second month, and the procedure just outlined will be repeated for each successive month of the first year of the loan.

In recent years, a variety of loan payment arrangements have been made with borrowers. Some of the calculations involved are quite complex and are, therefore, beyond the scope of this text. Furthermore, in some states there still may be some prohibitions against the lender charging interest on unpaid interest. This may not appear as a direct prohibition but, rather, one used in the calculation of interest for usury (illegal rate of interest) purposes.

ACHIEVEMENT EXERCISE

When you have finished both parts of this exercise, check your answers against those on page 204. If you miss any of the questions, review this chapter before going on to Chapter 10.

Part I—Open Response   Complete the following problems.

1. The Pasulkas have obtained a VA mortgage loan at 9-3/4% for $41,500. The bank, however, required a discount in order to extend this loan. The current market interest rate is 10-1/2%. What was the amount of discount required and who paid it? The bank also charged an origination fee of 2.5 points. What was the amount of this fee, and who paid it?

2. The Weill family have obtained a VA mortgage loan at 9-1/2% interest. The loan was for $50,000. The current market interest rate is 10-3/4%. What amount of discount did the lending institution charge? The origination fee was 2 points. How much was the origination fee, and who paid it?

3. Carl Sanderson sold his home to a buyer who was able to get a VA loan for $30,600. Mr. Sanderson had to pay a $765 mortgage discount. How many points did he pay?

4. Mrs. Lang borrowed $75,000 at 11% interest. The mortgage was amortized over a 20-year period at $774.14 per month plus $64.13 for taxes and insurance. How much of the first payment will go to interest? How much will go to principal?

5. What was Mrs. Lang's principal balance after the first payment? After the second payment?

6. Mr. Young has obtained a 25-year mortgage on his home for $30,000 at 11% interest. The monthly payments are $469.04. Each payment includes interest on the declining balance and a tax and insurance reserve of $2,100 per annum, with the remainder applied to the principal. What will the balance of the principal be after the first payment is made?

Part II—Multiple Choice   Select the correct response from the choices supplied.

7. By selecting from a, b, c or d, indicate which of the following statements is (are) true.

 I. When financing the purchase of real estate by a new mortgage loan, the buyer is always the borrower.
 II. Origination fee points charged by the lender cannot be paid by the buyer when the charge is quoted in points.
 III. Discount points, when required in connection with a new VA loan, must be paid to the lender in order for the VA loan to be made.

   a. I only
   b. I and II
   c. I and III
   d. I, II and III

8. When the current market rate of mortgage interest (for conventional loans) is 10%, and the maximum rate set by the VA is 9-1/2%, the discount points required by the lender are estimated as:

   a. 2 points.   c. 4 points.
   b. 3 points.   d. 5 points.

9. Compute the amount of discount that would be required to obtain a VA residential mortgage loan of $40,000 at the maximum VA rate of 9-1/4% when the conventional or market interest rate is 9-5/8%.

   a. $2,000   c. $1,500
   b. $1,200   d. $800

10. A seller paid $1,650 in discount points for the buyer to obtain a $33,000 VA loan with 8-7/8% interest. What is the market rate of interest?

   a. 9%   c. 9-1/2%
   b. 9-1/4%   d. 9-3/4%

11. Both origination fee and loan discount points are paid to the lender in a VA residential mortgage. By selecting from a, b, c or d, indicate which of the following statements is (are) true in regard to a VA mortgage loan.

 I. An origination fee is the lender's charge for originating a mortgage loan and may be paid by the borrower.
 II. Discount points are really prepaid mortgage interest and must be paid by the seller on a VA loan.

   a. I only
   b. II only
   c. both I and II
   d. neither I nor II

12. Which of the following is (are) instruments that generally create a lien against real property?

 I. mortgage
 II. leasehold estate
 III. vendor's lien
 IV. deed of trust
   a. I only
   b. III and IV only
   c. I, III and IV
   d. all of the above

13. If interest is paid after it has been earned by a lender, it:

 I. is paid in advance.
 II. is paid in arrears.
 III. is amortized.
 IV. is said to have accrued.

   a. I only
   b. I and III
   c. I and II
   d. II and IV

14. A homeowner pays $513.83 each month on a 9-1/4%, 25-year mortgage loan. If the amount to be credited to interest next month is $462.50, what is the present principal balance of the loan? (Interest paid in arrears.)

    a. $80,000   c. $62,500
    b. $66,659   d. $60,000

15. The purchaser of a home appraised at $75,000 was granted a 75% mortgage for 29 years at 9-3/4% interest. The first month's interest will be:

    a. $457.03.   c. $579.26.
    b. $609.38.   d. $476.31.

16. Mickey Lee, the buyer, was charged $410 interest for the first month of his mortgage loan. The loan is for 80% of appraised value, and the interest rate is 10-1/4%. What is the appraised value of the property?

    a. $48,000   c. $52,000
    b. $60,000   d. $68,000

17. A borrower pays $335.68 each month on a 25-year, 9% mortgage loan. For the month in which the interest charge is $299.46, what will the approximate unpaid principal balance be after the monthly payment is credited?

    a. $44,757   c. $38,726
    b. $39,928   d. $39,892

18. An owner, Don Jernigan, makes monthly loan payments to his bank of $399.54, to cover principal, 9-1/2% interest, taxes and insurance. The estimated tax bill is $780.00, and the annual insurance premium is $240.00. What amount will be credited to reduce the principal of this loan, if the current unpaid balance is $34,729.26?

    a. $35.99   c. $37.64
    b. $39.60   d. $38.89

19. The monthly amortization payment on a $30,000 mortgage loan at 10% interest for 29 years is $264.75. How much would the balance of the mortgage be at the end of 2 months? Round your answer to the nearest dollar.

    a. $29,471   c. $29,970
    b. $29,985   d. $29,500

20. Jane Froem has a mortgage loan of $40,000. If monthly payments are $350, and interest for the first month is $325, what is the interest rate?

    a. 9-3/4%   c. 9%
    b. 10-1/2%   d. 8-3/4%

21. You make payments of $158.59 a month to pay off a loan of $12,000.00 at 10% interest. By selecting from a, b, c or d, indicate which of the following statements is (are) true.

    I. In an amortized mortgage where equal payments include principal and interest, the amount of principal paid in each installment increases, while the amount of interest paid decreases.
    II. Of the $158.59 payment, $59.08 will be applied to the principal the second month.

    a. I only
    b. II only
    c. both I and II
    d. neither I nor II

22. Interest on most real estate loans is paid:

    I. in advance.
    II. in arrears.

    a. I only
    b. II only
    c. both I and II
    d. neither I nor II

23. If the monthly payments on a $90,000 loan bearing interest at 12% should be $995.58, but for the first year the buyer only pays $800 per month, what is the loan balance at the end of the first month?

    a. $90,000.00
    b. $90,100.00
    c. $89,802.46
    d. $89,004.42

24. If a lender agrees to make a loan based upon an 80% loan-to-value ratio, what will be the amount of the loan if the property appraises for $114,500 and the sales price is $116,900?

    a. $93,200   c. $91,600
    b. $23,300   d. $22,900

25. Bob and Charlotte Hart have an opportunity to buy the property next door to their motor home business. If they obtain a $500,000 loan, which plan offers the smaller monthly payments: a 12% loan for 20 years with a loan constant of 11.01 or a 11% loan for 15 years with a loan constant of 11.37? What are the payments?

    a. the 12% loan, payments are $5,505
    b. the 11% loan, payments are $5,505
    c. the 12% loan, payments are $5,055
    d. the 11% loan, payments are $5,055

26. Donna and David Long have decided to finance the FHA mortgage insurance premium (MIP) on their new house. If the loan amount is $87,500 and the sales price is $92,000, what is the amount of the financed MIP?

    a. $3,203.38   c. $3,496.00
    b. $3,368.12   d. $3,325.00

27. Billie and Ron Jones have a house under contract at $95,000 with a 90% conventional loan at 11% for 30 years. Using a loan constant of 9.52, what monthly income must they have if the lender qualifies at 28/36 and taxes and insurance will be $175?

    a. $3,230.00   c. $2,747.11
    b. $3,532.00   d. $2,907.00

28. Shirley and Lewis Wood want to obtain the maximum FHA insurable loan on the $90,000 house they have under contract. If the FHA allowable buyer's closing costs are $1,550, calculate the maximum loan.

    a. $2,550   c. $3,450
    b. $4,100   d. $2,900

29. Odest and Sam McMillan's new lake house cost $94,000, including the lot but excluding the fishing pier, which the lender will not finance. If the monthly payment on the $75,200 loan at 11.5% for 20 years will be $801.96 principal and interest plus $130 taxes and $46 insurance, what monthly income must they have in order to qualify at 28/36 for a conventional loan if their only other payment is $125 for a boat?

    a. $3,063.78   c. $2,716.56
    b. $3,939.14   d. $3,492.71

ANSWER KEY

Entry Evaluation

- $41,979.35 principal balance after first payment

- $41,958.53 principal balance after second payment

- 6 points $900 discount

Pages 172–196

1. $90,000   sale price (value)
$\underline{\times\quad .80}$ loan-to-value ratio
$72,000   loan amount

2. $72,000   loan amount
$\underline{\times\quad .12}$ annual interest rate
$ 8,640   annual interest amount
$ 8,640   ÷ 12 months = $720 monthly interest amount

3. 4 points equal 4% of the total amount of the loan.
4% × $72,000 = $2,880 discount

1.5 points = 1.5% = .015
$72,000 × .015 = $1,080 origination fee

4. Compute the difference in interest rates.

current market rate − government-regulated rate = difference
12-3/4% − 12% = 3/4%

Convert difference to eighths.

3/4% = 6/8%

Determine the number of points.

6/8% = 6 points

Compute discount rate.

6 points = 6%

Compute discount amount.

discount rate × total loan amount = amount of discount
6% × $88,000 = $5,280 discount to be paid by the seller
1% × $88,000 = $880 origination fee paid by the buyer

Pages 172–196   continued

5. 1/4% difference = 2/8% = 2 points = 2% of the total loan amount
   2% × $50,000 = $1,000 discount paid by the seller

6. 4 points = 4% of the total loan amount   4% × $76,000 = $3,040

   4 points = 4/8 = 1/2% difference   13-1/4% − 1/2% = 12-3/4% interest on this VA loan

   The lending institution received the discount. This means the investor, not the mortgage company. The lending institution typically works through loan originating and servicing agents, such as mortgage companies, who make and pool loans for sale to investors.

7. 13-3/4% − 13-1/4% = 1/2% = 4/8 = 4 points = 4% of the total loan amount

   4% × $68,000 = $2,720 the Bradburys will pay the lending institution

   Mortgage discounts are also called points, and are really prepaid mortgage interest.

8. What percent of $72,000 is $2,160? $\text{percent} = \dfrac{\text{part}}{\text{total}} = \dfrac{2,160}{72,000} = .03 = 3\%$

   3% = 3 points = 3/8 = 3/8% difference in interest rates

   14% + 3/8% = 14-3/8% open market interest rate

   total loan amount × points = origination fee

   $\text{points} = \dfrac{\text{origination fee}}{\text{total loan amount}}$

   $\dfrac{\$720}{\$72,000} = .01 = 1\% = 1 \text{ point}$

9. What is 75% of $77,000?

   percent × total = part

$77,000	value of house
× .75	ratio of loan to value
$57,750	loan

   What is 12-1/2% of the loan?

$57,750	loan
× .125	interest rate
$7,218.75	annual interest

   $7,218.75 ÷ 12 = $601.562 = $601.56 monthly interest (first month only)

10. $57,735.22 × .125 = $7,216.90 $7,216.90 ÷ 12 = $601.41

$616.34	total payment
− 601.41	monthly interest
$ 14.93	Amount to Reduce Principal
$57,735.22	old principal balance
−14.93	amount to reduce principal
$57,720.29	New Principal Balance

11. $45,000 $\times$ .11 = $4,950 $4,950 $\div$ 12 = $412.50 monthly interest

$464.48   monthly payment due June 1
$\underline{- \ 412.50}$ 11% interest on $45,000 outstanding during May
$ 51.98   Applied to Reduce the Principal

12. $45,000.00   loan
$\underline{- \ \ \ \ \ 51.98}$ credited to principal June 1
$44,948.02   Balance of Principal during June
$44,948.02 $\times$ .11 = $4,944.282 = $4,944.28 annual interest
$4,944.28 $\div$ 12 = $412.024 = $412.02

$464.48   monthly payment due July 1
$\underline{- \ 412.02}$ interest on balance of principal during June
$ 52.46   Applied to Reduce Principal

13. $31,500 $\times$ .105 = $3,307.500 = $3,307.50 annual interest
$3,307.50 $\div$ 12 = $275.625 = $275.63 monthly interest
$1,920 $\div$ 12 = $160 tax and insurance reserve for one month
$275.63 + $160 = $435.63 interest plus reserve

$474.74   monthly payment
$\underline{- \ 435.63}$ interest and reserve
$ 39.11   Credited to Principal

$31,500.00   beginning principal
$\underline{- \ \ \ \ \ 39.11}$ credited to principal
$31,460.89   New Principal Balance

14. $10,000 $\times$ .14 = $1,400 annual interest $1,400 $\div$ 12 = $116.67 monthly interest

$$or \quad \frac{\overset{100}{\cancel{\$10,000}}}{1} \times \frac{14}{\underset{1}{\cancel{100}}} \times \frac{1}{12} = \frac{\$1,400}{12} = \$116.67 \text{ monthly interest}$$

$100.00   payment on principal
$\underline{+ \ 116.67}$ interest on $10,000 for one month
$216.67   Total Payment Due April 1

To compute the interest charge for the month of April (which will be payable on May 1), you must first determine the amount of the mortgage balance outstanding during April.

$10,000   loan proceeds received March 1
$\underline{- \ \ \ \ 100}$ payment April 1
$ 9,900   balance outstanding after April 1
$\underline{\times \ \ \ .14}$ interest rate
$1,386.00   Annual Interest

$1,386 $\div$ 12 = $115.50 monthly interest on $9,900 outstanding during April

$100.00   payment on principal
$\underline{+ \ 115.50}$ interest
$215.50   Total Payment Due May 1

15. $100   outstanding loan balance
$\underline{\times \ .14}$
$14.00   annual interest $\div$ 12 = $1.17 monthly interest

$100.00   monthly principal payment
$\underline{+ \ \ \ 1.17}$ monthly interest payment on remaining balance
$101.17   amount of last monthly payment

Achievement Exercise

1. 10-1/2% − 9-3/4% = 6/8% = 6 points
   6% × $41,500 = $2,490 discount paid by the seller
   2.5% × $41,500 = $1,037.50 origination fee paid by the buyer

2. 10-3/4% − 9-1/2% = 1-1/4% = 10/8% = 10 points
   10% × $50,000 = $5,000 discount paid by the seller
   2% × $50,000 = $1,000 origination fee paid by the buyer

3. $\dfrac{\$765}{\$30,600} = .025 = 2.5\% = 2.5$ points

4. $75,000 × 11% = $8,250 (Disregard taxes and insurance)
   $8,250 annual interest ÷ 12 = $687.500 = $687.50 monthly interest
   $774.14 payment − $687.50 applied to interest = $86.64 applied to principal

5. $25,000 − $37.44 = $24,962.56 principal balance after first payment
   $24,962.56 × 9% = $2,246.63 $2,246.63 ÷ 12 = $187.219 = $187.22 applied to interest
   $224.94 − $187.22 = $37.72 applied to principal
   $24,962.56 − $37.72 = $24,924.84 principal balance after second payment

6. $30,000 × 11% = $3,300 $3,300 ÷ 12 = $275.00 monthly interest
   $2,100 ÷ 12 = $175.00 monthly tax and insurance reserve payment
   $275.00 + $175.00 = $450.00
   $469.04 − $450 interest plus reserve payment = $19.04 applied to principal
   $30,000 − $19.04 = $29,980.96 principal balance after first payment

7. c.

8. c. 10% − 9-1/2% = 1/2% = 4/8%
      1 point = 1/8%; 4 × 1 = 4 points

9. b. 9-5/8% − 9-2/8% = 3/8% = 3 points
      $40,000 × 3% = $1,200 discount paid

10. c. $1,650 ÷ $33,000 = .05 = 5% = 5 points
       8-7/8% + 5/8% = 9-1/2% market interest rate

11. c.

12. c.

13. d.

14. b. $513.83 × 12 ÷ 9.25% = $66,659.03 loan balance

15. a. $75,000 × 75% = $56,250 loan amount
       $56,250 × 9.75% ÷ 12 = $457.03 1st month's interest

16. b. $410 × 12 = $4,920 annual interest
       $4,920 ÷ 10.25% = $48,000 loan
       $48,000 ÷ 80% = $60,000 appraised value

17. d. $299.46 × 12 = $3,593.52 annual interest
$3,593.52 ÷ 9% = $39,928
$335.68 − $299.46 = $36.22 principal portion of payment
$39,928 − $36.22 = $39,891.78 loan balance

18. b. $34,729.26 × 9.5% ÷ 12 = $274.94 monthly interest
$780 + $240 ÷ 12 = $85.00 monthly tax and insurance
$399.54 − $274.94 − $85.00 = $39.60 principal reduction

19. c. $30,000 × 10% ÷ 12 = $250 interest, 1st month
$264.75 − $250 = $14.75 principal 1st month
$30,000 − $14.75 = $29,985.25 1st month's balance
$29,985.25 × 10% ÷ 12 = $249.88 interest, 2nd month
$264.75 − $249.88 = $14.87 principal, 2nd month
$29,985.25 − $14.87 = $29,970.38 2nd month's balance

20. a. $325 × 12 = $3,900 annual interest
$3,900 ÷ $40,000 = 9.75% interest rate

21. c. $12,000 × 10% ÷ 12 = $100 1st month's interest
$158.59 − $100 = $58.59 1st month's principal
$12,000 − $58.59 = $11,941.41 1st month's balance
$11,941.41 × 10% ÷ 12 = $99.51 2nd month's interest
$158.59 − $99.51 = $59.08 2nd month's principal

22. b.

23. b. $90,000 × 12% ÷ 12 = $900 1st month's interest
$900 − $800 = $100 shortage in interest alone
$90,000 + $100 = $90,100 balance, 1st month

24. c. $114,500 × 80% = $91,600 loan based on 80% LTV

25. a. $500,000 ÷ 1,000 = $500 × 11.01 = $5,505.00
$500,000 ÷ 1,000 = $500 × 11.37 = $5,685.00
The 12% loan for 20 years has a smaller payment.

26. d. $87,500 × 3.8% (for financed MIP) = $3,325.00

27. b. $95,000 × 90% = $85,500 loan amount
$85,500 ÷ 1,000 = $85.5
$85.5 × 9.52 = $813.96 monthly P & I
$813.96 P & I + $175 T & I = $988.96 PITI
$988.96 ÷ .28 = $3,532.00 required minimum monthly income

28. a. $90,000 sales price + $1,550 buyer's closing costs =
$91,550 FHA acquisition cost
$91,550 − $25,000 = $66,550
$25,000 × 97% = $24,250
$66,550 × 95% = $63,222.50
$24,250 + $63,222.50 = $87,472.50 (round down to next $50)
$87,450 maximum FHA insurable loan
$90,000 − $87,450 = $2,550 minimum FHA down payment

29. a. $801.96 P&I + $130 taxes + $46 insurance + $125 boat =
$1,102.96 PITI + debts
$1,102.96 ÷ .36 = $3,063.78 required minimum monthly income

Ad Valorem Taxes

INTRODUCTION

It often will be necessary for you as a real estate salesperson or broker to be able to calculate real estate taxes, in addition to having a basic understanding of how taxes are levied.

In this chapter, you will compute annual real estate taxes based on the assessed value of property and a tax rate or the market value of property and an assessment ratio. You also will compute taxes given in mills, taxes which use an equalization factor, and tax penalties for delinquent real estate taxes. Each state has different ways of treating this topic, and the concepts presented here may not be applicable in your state. Learn the arithmetic anyway. It's good practice.

ENTRY EVALUATION

Since readers will have varying amounts of knowledge and experience, the short test that follows will allow you to determine your familiarity with the material to be covered. Try the problem before looking at the answer, which is on page 213.

- A property is valued at $67,000. The assessment ratio used in the area is 82% of market value. The tax rate is $2.50 per $100 of assessed value. What are the taxes for this property for one year?

TAXES BASED ON ASSESSED VALUE

Taxes levied against real estate so that each taxpayer will share the cost of various government activities in proportion to the value of his or her property are known as ad valorem taxes. *Ad valorem* means according to value, so, an ad valorem tax is a real estate tax based on the value of the property.

Valuing and assessing real estate for tax purposes is usually the responsibility of the tax assessor or, in some states, the tax appraisal district, but you will find it helpful to have a basic understanding of how the amount of tax is derived. To figure the amount of tax that will be imposed on a parcel of real estate, you must know two things: the percentage or ratio of assessment to market value used in your area, and the tax rate, usually expressed as dollars or cents per hundred or per thousand dollars of assessment.

Suppose, for example, that the assessed value of a particular property is 70% of full market value, which is estimated at $50,000, and the official tax rate in the city or town is $4 per $100 of assessment. The amount of city tax on the property is computed as follows.

Step 1. Compute the assessed value.

$$\boxed{\text{market value} \times \text{assessment ratio} = \text{assessed value}}$$

$$\$50,000 \times .70 = \$35,000$$

Step 2. Compute the tax (tax rate expressed in dollars per hundred).

$$\boxed{\text{assessed value} \times \text{tax rate} = \text{tax}}$$
$$\text{tax} = \$35,000 \times \frac{\$4}{\$100}$$

$$\text{tax} = \$1,400$$

Caution: Taxes on real estate are determined by state and local laws. The material presented here is in general form. Be sure to inquire about tax procedures in your own locality.

1. A house has a market value of $80,000. The assessment ratio is 70%. What is the assessed value?

2. If property is assessed at 40% of its market value, what would be the assessed value of a parcel worth $47,500?

3. If property is valued at $65,000 and assessed for 60% of its value, what is the tax if the rate is $5.30 per $100 of assessed value?

4. If the annual tax on a property comes to $1,467.00, what is the assessed value of that property, given a tax rate of $1.63 per $100 of assessed value, and assuming that this property is assessed at 100% of its market value?

5. A house has a market value of $44,200. The assessment ratio is 50% of market value and the tax rate is $35 per $1,000 of assessed value. What is the annual tax on the property?

Notice that tax rates may be expressed in any of 4 ways. The following rates are equivalent:

$3 per $100
$30 per $1,000
3% (.03)
30 mills

TAXES GIVEN IN MILLS

The tax rate can be expressed as so many *mills* on each dollar of assessed value. A mill is 1/10 of one cent. In decimal form, one mill is written as $.001.

6. Complete the table below.

$$1 \text{ mill } = 1/10 = \$.001$$
$$10 \text{ mills } = 1\cent = \$ .01$$
$$100 \text{ mills } = 10\cent = \underline{\hspace{1cm}}$$

7. Write 54 mills in decimal form.

8. A property is assessed at $75,500. The tax rate is 23 mills. Compute the amount of tax on the property.

9. Property taxes on a parcel of real estate were $1,641.60. The property was assessed at 45% of market value and the tax rate was 57 mills per $1.00 of assessed value. What was the market value of the real estate?

10. In a town in which the tax rate is $7.50 per $100 of assessed value, a house with a yearly tax bill of $1,500 just sold for $50,000.

    a. What is the assessed value?

    b. The assessed value is what percent of the market value?

11. What is the amount of tax on a $100,000 property if it is assessed at 100% of market value and the tax rate is $3.51 per $100?

TAXES USING AN EQUALIZATION FACTOR

In some taxing districts, assessed values are adjusted in order to make them comparable to those of surrounding areas. The assessed value of a property is multiplied by an *equalization factor* determined by the assessor's office.

> assessed value × equalization factor = equalized assessment

The equalized assessment value is then multiplied by the tax rate to compute the amount of the tax bill.

> equalized assessment × tax rate = tax

12. If real estate is assessed at $82,500, to be adjusted by an equalization factor of 1.30, and the tax rate is $4.35 per $100 of assessed equalized value, how much tax will have to be paid?

PENALTIES FOR DELINQUENT TAXES

Unpaid taxes are subject to penalty charges; for example, 1% per month during the delinquency period.

EXAMPLE: Assume that an owner's annual real estate tax of $780 is payable in two equal installments. The due dates are May 1 and September 1. What is the amount of the penalty that will accrue if no tax payments are made until October 30, at which time the full tax will be paid? Assume that delinquent taxes are subject to a penalty of 1% a month.

Step 1. Calculate installment payments.

$780 ÷ 2 = $390 per installment

Step 2. Determine first penalty charge.

$390 × .06 penalty May 1 to October 30 = $23.40

Step 3. Determine second penalty charge.

$390 × .02 penalty September 1 to October 30 = $7.80

Step 4. Add both penalties to arrive at total.

$23.40 + 7.80 = $31.20 total penalty

Delinquent real estate taxes are normally collected by the sale of the property at a tax sale or when the property is sold at a private sale. If the delinquent owner is allowed a redemption period by local law, extra penalties are usually added until the time the property is redeemed or a tax deed is issued to the purchaser at the tax or private sale.

13. Real estate taxes in the amount of $927 were not paid by a July 1 due date. The property was sold at a tax sale on October 1. Find the cost to redeem the property on November 1. The penalty *before* the tax sale was 1% interest per month. The penalty *after* the tax sale was 12% for each 6-month period after the sale, without proration. The redemption fee was $5.

14. The current value of property is $90,000 and the assessed value is 40% of its current value. An equalization factor of 1.5 is applied to the assessed value. The tax rate is $4.50 per $100. What will the first tax bill be, if taxes are paid in two equal semiannual payments?

EXEMPTIONS

Some states permit certain "exemptions" on property taxes and, in some cases, this option to grant exemptions extends to lesser taxing entities such as counties, cities, and school districts. The taxing authority subtracts or "exempts" a prescribed amount of value from the assessed value before applying the other factors.

For example, a state might "exempt" $10,000 for homestead purposes. If the property comprising the homestead was assessed at $60,000, the $10,000 exemption is subtracted and usual factors are applied to the $50,000 valuation.

Or, an exemption might be granted to senior citizens, and, again the amount of the exemption would be subtracted from the assessed value. In some cases, exemptions on land used for agricultural purposes are allowed, and the assessed value is based upon the productivity value and not the market value of the land. Generally, property owners must make a written application for any type of property tax exemption.

ACHIEVEMENT EXERCISE

When you have finished both parts of this exercise, check your answers against those on page 214. If you miss any of the questions, review this chapter before going on to Chapter 11.

Part I—Open Response   Complete the following problems.

1. A property has a market value of $76,000. The taxes in the area are levied on 66% of market value at a rate of $2.50 per $100 of assessed value. What tax will be charged in one year?

2. Mr. and Mrs. Billings own a house which is valued at $45,000. The assessed value is 55% of market value and the equalization factor is 1.3. The tax rate is 53.5 mills. What will the tax bill for one year be?

3. A property is valued at $46,000. The taxes are levied upon 45% of market value and an equalization factor of 1.4 is used. The tax rate is $30 per $1,000 of assessed value. The family owning this property was delinquent in paying the second installment of their tax bill this year, by 2 months plus 2 days. What will the total amount of their second installment be (tax plus penalty), if the penalty is 1% per month? Consider the installments to be equal. Remember that tax penalties are the seller's responsibility; they are not prorated.

Part II—Multiple Choice   Select the correct response from the choices supplied.

4. A residential property was sold for $75,000.00. The assessed value for tax purposes is 22% of market value. What will be the amount of the tax bill, if the tax rate is $6.25 per $100.00 of assessed value?

    a. $937.50   c. $1,031.25
    b. $975.00   d. $1,072.50

5. Julio Martinez, a property owner, received his tax bill for $1,232.50. The published tax rate is $2.25 per $100.00 of assessed value. What is the assessed value of this property?

    a. $8,936.63   c. $54,777.77
    b. $17,000.00   d. $18,390.00

6. Your current real estate tax bill is $1,944.00. The tax rate is $4.50 per $100.00 of the equalized assessed value. When the equalization factor is .80, what is the assessed valuation?

    a. $50,000   c. $54,000
    b. $52,000   d. $56,000

7. What is the market value of property on which the real estate tax is $1,595.54, when the assessment is 45% of market value, all assessments are equalized by a factor of .67, and the tax rate is 63 mills per dollar?

    a. $30,306   c. $70,467
    b. $56,417   d. $84,000

8. Find the tax rate per $100.00 of assessed value when the tax bill is $901.31, and the assessed value is 33% of the market value of $47,500.00

    a. $5.75   c. $57.50
    b. $6.00   d. $.575

9. The Clarks received a tax bill for $870.54, half of which is payable on June 1, and the other half on October 1. A penalty of 1% a month is provided for delinquent taxes. If the Clarks make payment in full on October 15, how much will they pay?

    a. $892.30   c. $887.95
    b. $896.65   d. $883.60

10. A house was assessed for taxes at 50% of market value. The tax rate was $3.75 per $100.00 of assessed value. Five years later, taxes had increased by $300.00. How much did the market value of the house increase?

    a. $8,000   c. $2,250
    b. $16,000   d. $60,000

11. A house is valued at $75,000 and assessed for 60% of its value. If the tax bill is $1,350 what is the rate per $100?

    a. $1.80   c. $4.00
    b. $13.50   d. $3.00

12. The tax rate can be expressed as so many mills on each dollar of assessed value. Indicate which of the following decimal equivalents is (are) correct.

    I. 19 mills = .19
    II. 23 mills = .023
    III. 2-1/4 mills = .225
    IV. 2-1/2 mills = .0025

    a. I only   c. II and IV
    b. III only   d. I and III

ANSWER KEY

Entry Evaluation

■ $1,373.50

Pages 207–210

1. $80,000 × .70 = $56,000 assessed value

2. $47,500 × .40 = $19,000 assessed value

3. $65,000 × .60 = $39,000 assessed value
$39,000 ÷ 100 = $390 $390 × $5.30 = $2,067 tax

4. $1,467 tax ÷ $1.63 tax rate/$100 = $900
$900 × 100 = $90,000 assessed (market) value

5. $44,200 × .50 = $22,100 assessed value
$22,100 ÷ $1,000 = 22.10   22.10 × $35 = $773.50 tax

6. $.10

7. $.054

8. 23 mills = $.023
$75,500 × $.023 = $1,736.50 tax

9. 57 mills = $.057

assessed value × $.057 = $1,641.60 $\dfrac{\$1,641.60}{\$.057}$ = $28,800 assessed value

$\dfrac{part}{percent}$ = total $\dfrac{\$28,800}{.45}$ = $64,000 market value

10. a. tax = $\dfrac{\text{assessed value}}{\$100}$ × tax amount per $100

$1,500 = $\dfrac{\text{assessed value}}{\$100}$ × $7.50

assessed value = $\dfrac{\$1,500}{\$7.50}$ × $100 = $20,000

b. $\dfrac{part}{total}$ = percent $\dfrac{\$20,000}{\$50,000}$ = 40%

Pages 207–210 continued

11. $100,000 market value $\times$ 100%
    assessment = $100,000

    $100,000 $\times$ $\dfrac{\$3.51}{\$100}$ = $3,510 tax

12. $82,500 $\times$ 1.30 = $107,250 equalized assessment
    $107,250 $\div$ $100 = 1,072.50   1,072.50 $\times$ $4.35 = $4,665.38 tax

13. $927 $\times$ .03 pre-tax sale penalty = $27.81
    $927 $\times$ .12 minimum after-tax penalty = $111.24
    $927 + $27.81 + $111.24 + $5 = $1,071.05 cost to redeem property

14. $90,000 $\times$ .40 = $36,000 assessed value
    $36,000 $\times$ 1.5 equalization factor = $54,000 equalized assessment
    $54,000 $\div$ $100 = 540   540 $\times$ $4.50 = $2,430 total tax
    $2,430 $\div$ 2 = $1,215 first tax bill

Achievement Exercise

1. $76,000 $\times$ .66 = $50,160 $50,160 $\div$ $100 = 501.6   501.6 $\times$ $2.50 = $1,254

2. $45,000 $\times$ .55 = $24,750 $24,750 $\times$ 1.3 = $32,175 $32,175 $\times$ .0535 = $1,721.36

3. $46,000 $\times$ .45 = $20,700 $20,700 $\times$ 1.4 = $28,980
   $28,980 $\div$ $1,000 = 28.98   28.98 $\times$ $30 = $869.40 total tax
   $869.40 $\div$ 2 = $434.70 tax installment   3% $\times$ $434.70 = $13.04 penalty
   $434.70 + $13.04 = $447.74 total amount of second installment

4. $75,000 $\times$ 22% = $16,500 assessed value
   $16,500 $\div$ $100 = 165
   165 $\times$ $6.25 = $1,031.25 tax

5. b. $1,232.50 $\div$ $2.25 = 547.77
      547.77 $\times$ $100 = $54,777.77 assessed value

6. c. $1,944 $\div$ $4.50 = 432
      432 $\times$ $100 = $43,200
      $43,200 $\div$ .80 = $54,000 assessed value

7. d. $1,595.54 $\div$ .063 = $25,326.03
      $25,326.03 $\div$ .45 = $56,280.07
      $56,280.07 $\div$ .67 = $84,000.11 market value

8. a. $47,500 $\times$ 33% = $15,675 assessed value
      $15,675 $\div$ $100 = 156.75
      $901.31 $\div$ 156.75 = $5.75 tax rate/$100

9. b. $870.54 ÷ 2 = $435.27
$435.27 × 1% = $4.35
$4.35 × 5 = $21.76
$435.27 + $21.76 = $457.03
$435.27 + $4.35 = $439.62
$457.03 + $439.62 = $896.65 tax and penalties due

10. b. $300 ÷ $3.75 = 80.00
80 × $100 = $8,000
$8,000 ÷ .50 = $16,000

11. d. $75,000 × 60% = $45,000
$45,000 ÷ $100 = 450
$1,350 ÷ 450 = $3.00

12. c.

Property Transfer Taxes

INTRODUCTION

The transfer of real estate is taxed in most states, but some states have no such tax. The amount of tax and the considerations which are exempt from this tax differ from state to state. You should look up the amount of transfer tax charged in your state and the current exemptions from the tax. Some states exempt a transfer in which the total consideration is less than some statutory amount or an existing mortgage is assumed by the purchaser. This does not refer to the amount stated in the deed, but to the actual sale price. Many states require a written declaration to be made and signed by one or both parties to a sale in which the selling price is disclosed together with other facts.

In this chapter, you will compute the transfer tax for various real estate transactions, using different tax ratios and various types of exemption rules.

ENTRY EVALUATION

Since readers will have varying amounts of knowledge and experience, the short test that follows will allow you to determine your familiarity with the material to be covered. Try the problem before looking at the answer, which is on page 222.

- A parcel of real estate sold for $64,000 and the buyer assumed a mortgage balance of $23,600. The state in which the transaction took place levies a transfer tax of $.65 per each $500 or fraction thereof paid in cash at the time of transfer. What is the amount of transfer tax due?

TRANSFER TAX RATES

Many states require that a transfer tax be paid when an interest in real estate is sold and conveyed by a deed. Payment of the tax is usually made by purchasing stamps from a state or local official, affixing them to the deed, and having them canceled. Many state transfer taxes were adopted on January 1, 1968, when the federal revenue stamp tax was repealed.

Details of the transfer tax differ among states. For example, many states exempt sales in which the consideration is less than $100. Other states tax only the net consideration if the buyer is assuming the seller's existing mortgage.

A tax rate of $.50 or $.55 for each $500 or fractional part of $500 of the net taxable consideration is common. A percentage of the taxable consideration is another method used.

EXAMPLE: What value in state transfer stamps must be affixed to a deed when property is sold for $10,600, and the tax rate is $.50 per $500 or fraction thereof of the selling price? "Fraction thereof" means that $501 is treated the same way that $599 is treated.

$$\$10,600 \div \$500 = 21.2 \text{ or } 22 \text{ taxable parts}$$
$$22 \times \$.50 = \$11 \text{ tax}$$

Since the tax is $.50 per $500 or fraction thereof, any fractional part will incur $.50 tax. Therefore, 21 and a fractional part (.2) are, for this tax, the same as 22 parts.

1. A piece of property was sold in a state in which the stamp tax rate is $.55 for each $500 paid in cash at the time of the transfer. A mortgage balance, if assumed by the buyer, is not a taxable consideration. If the total price of the property was $54,000, and the buyer assumed a $24,000 mortgage, compute the amount of transfer tax paid. The assumed mortgage is exempt.

2. Real estate that sold for $57,750 was subject to a transfer tax of $.50 for each $500 or fraction thereof of the selling price. What amount of tax stamps must be purchased, affixed to the deed and canceled?

3. Real estate was sold for $64,750 and a state transfer tax was required at the rate of $.26 per $100 or fraction thereof of consideration. How much tax was paid?

4. Real estate was sold for $40,500, with the buyer assuming the seller's mortgage balance of $20,394. The tax rate was .005 of the consideration paid in cash at the sale closing. What was the amount of tax if the assumed mortgage was exempt?

Approximate Sale Price

EXAMPLE: In certain states, tax stamps are based on the amount of cash paid at the time of transfer. Calculate the *approximate sale price* of the real estate involved in a transaction in which the tax rate was $.50 for each $500 or fraction thereof, a total of $20.50 in stamps was affixed to the deed and the buyer assumed the seller's mortgage of $19,812.

Step 1.   Calculate the parts.

$20.50 ÷ $.50 = 41 parts

Step 2.   Determine the cash paid.

41 × $500 = $20,500 cash paid

Step 3.   Total the cash paid and the mortgage amount.

$20,500 + $19,812 = $40,312 sale price

Usually, only assumed mortgages are deductible in computing stamp taxes. Notes signed by purchasers would not be deducted whether the note were to the seller or a third-party lender. Both of these are called "purchase money" notes.

5. Mr. Toper sold his house to Ms. Reilly for $12,000 cash, a $40,000 first mortgage assumed by the buyer, and a purchase-money mortgage note signed by Ms. Reilly for $13,000. The transaction took place in a state which has a tax rate of $1.75 per $100 or fraction thereof, and exempts assumed mortgages. What was the amount of transfer tax on the sale?

6. Mr. Blair is buying a $40,000 house. He assumed the mortgage, which was for 25% of the sale price, and negotiated a second mortgage for 50% of the balance, paying the rest in cash. If the transfer tax rate is $.55 per $500 or fraction thereof, and assumed mortgages are exempt, what amount of transfer tax stamps must be affixed to the deed?

7. Mr. and Mrs. Finnelli have listed their house with Wagner Realty for $60,000. The best offer that they've received is from Mr. and Mrs. Jackson, who are willing to assume the present mortgage of $20,000, pay $25,000 cash and give a purchase-money mortgage note of $10,000. The transfer tax rate is $.75 per $500 or fraction thereof, and assumed mortgages are exempt. What amount of transfer tax will be charged if the Finnellis accept this offer?

8. Mr. and Mrs. Hanes are purchasing Mr. and Mrs. Ebert's house for $74,000, less the mortgage they will assume, which has a principal balance of $30,000 as of October 2. The interest rate on this amortized mortgage is 8% and payments of $250 are due on the first day of each month, to be applied first on the interest for the previous month, and the balance to be applied to the principal. The last mortgage payment was made November 1. The closing of the transaction has been set for November 13. What amount of transfer tax stamps will have to be affixed to the deed, if the state requires $.50 per $500 or fraction thereof, and exempts assumed mortgages?

ACHIEVEMENT EXERCISE

When you have finished both parts of this exercise, check your answers against those on page 223. If you miss any of the questions, review this chapter before going on to Chapter 12.

Part I—Open Response   Complete the following problems.

1. Real estate was sold for $84,000, with the buyer assuming a mortgage of $52,000. What amount of transfer tax is due if the tax is based on the cash exchanged at closing at the rate of $.45 per $500 or fraction thereof?

2. The Doyles are selling their house to the George family. The total sale price of the house is $54,000. The Georges will assume the present mortgage of $14,000, and the Doyles will take back a purchase-money mortgage note of $20,000. What will be the amount of transfer tax if the state requires $.50 per $500 or fraction thereof and exempts transactions under $100 and assumed mortgages?

Part II—Multiple Choice   Select the correct response from the choices supplied.

3. Real estate is being sold for $85,000, with the purchaser assuming the $56,500 unpaid balance of the sellers' existing mortgage. What is the state transfer tax when the rate of tax is $.50 for each $500 or fractional part of the actual consideration less the amount of any assumed mortgage?

    a. $28.50   c. $56.50
    b. $85.00   d. $29.00

4. The sale price of a house is $112,000. The buyer is assuming the seller's $61,000 mortgage balance and is giving the seller a purchase-money mortgage note for $25,000. What amount of state transfer tax stamps is required if the state transfer tax is 2% of the value of the property?

    a. $520   c. $1,720
    b. $1,020   d. $2,240

5. The state transfer tax is $.30 for each $100 or fraction of the full sale price. The county tax is $.50 for each $500 or fraction of sale price less the amount of any assumed mortgage. Compute the total transfer taxes required for a sale at $95,000 with a $68,000 assumed mortgage.

    a. $81.00   c. $123.50
    b. $108.00   d. $312.00

6. The state transfer tax is 50 cents for each $500.00 or fraction of the sale price less the amount of any assumed mortgage. A report of properties sold lists the addresses, names of grantor and grantee, and amount of transfer tax paid. When an item of the report lists $89.50 transfer tax the sale price of the property is probably:

    a. $89,500.
    b. less than $89,000.
    c. greater than $89,500 if the buyer assumed the seller's mortgage.
    d. a or c

7. The state transfer tax on deeds is $.12 per $100 of sale price; the county tax is $.30 per $100 of sale price. The sale price of the residence is $84,000 and is financed by a mortgage loan for 80% of the sale price. By selecting from a, b, c or d, indicate which of the following statements is (are) true.

  I. The state tax is $180.00.
  II. The state and county taxes total $352.80.

    a. I only
    b. II only
    c. both I and II
    d. neither I nor II

ANSWER KEY

Entry Evaluation

- $52.65

Pages 217–219

1. $54,000 total price − $24,000 mortgage = $30,000 taxable consideration
$30,000 ÷ $500 = 60 taxable parts
60 × $.55 = $33.00 tax

2. $57,750 ÷ $500 = 115.5 or 116 parts   116 × $.50 = $58 tax

3. $64,750 ÷ $100 = 647.5 or 648 parts   648 × $.26 = $168.48 tax

4. $40,500 − $20,394 = $20,106 $20,106 × .005 = $100.53 tax

5. $12,000 cash + $13,000 note + $40,000 assumed mortgage = $65,000 sale price
$65,000 − $40,000 = $25,000 taxable consideration

   or $12,000 + $13,000 = $25,000 taxable consideration

   $25,000 ÷ $100 = 250 parts   250 × $1.75 = $437.50 tax

6. $40,000 × 25% = $40,000 × .25 = $10,000 assumed mortgage
$40,000 − $10,000 = $30,000 taxable consideration
$30,000 ÷ $500 = 60 parts   60 × $.55 = $33 tax

7. $20,000 + $25,000 + $10,000 = $55,000 sale price
$55,000 − $20,000 = $35,000 taxable consideration
$35,000 ÷ $500 = 70 parts   70 × $.75 = $52.50 tax

8. $30,000 × 8% = $30,000 × .08 = $2,400 annual interest
$2,400 ÷ 12 = $200 1 month's interest
$250 total payment − $200 interest = $50 principal reduction
$30,000 − $50 = $29,950 principal remaining to be assumed

   $74,000 − $29,950 = $44,050 taxable consideration
   $44,050 ÷ $500 = 88.1 or 89 parts   89 × $.50 = $44.50 tax

Achievement Exercise

1. $84,000 − $52,000 = $32,000 $32,000 ÷ $500 = 64   64 × $.45 = $28.80

2. $54,000 − $14,000 = $40,000 $40,000 ÷ $500 = 80   80 × $.50 = $40

3. a. $85,000 − $56,500 = $28,500
$28,500 ÷ $500 = $57
$57 × $.50 = $28.50 tax due

4. d. $112,000 × 2% = $2,240 tax due

5. d. $95,000 ÷ $100 = 950
950 × $.30 = $285 state tax
$95,000 − $68,000 = $27,000
$27,000 ÷ $500 = $54
$54 × $.50 = $27.00 county tax
$285 + $27 = $312 total tax

6. d. $89.50 ÷ .50 = $179
$179 × $500 = $89,500

7. b. $84,000 ÷ $100 = $840
$840 × $.12 = $100.80 state tax
$840 × $.30 = $252 county tax

Legal Descriptions

INTRODUCTION

Property must be legally described and identified before a correct transfer can be made. Legal descriptions in many states are based upon the rectangular survey system. In this chapter, we will cover the mathematical computations involved in property descriptions using the rectangular survey system. Subdivisions of larger tracts of undeveloped land generally have lot and block property descriptions, such as "Lot 12, Block 34, Green Garden Subdivision to the city of Able, County of Baker, State of Charlie." This form of legal description will not be discussed since no mathematical computations are involved. Occasionally you may encounter a "metes and bounds" description. This chapter will introduce you to this method because it is important to be able to convert such a description into a sketch (which may be drawn exactly to scale) of the shape of the subject property.

ENTRY EVALUATION

Since readers will have varying amounts of knowledge and experience, the short test that follows will allow you to determine your familiarity with the material to be covered. Try the problem before looking at the answer, which is on page 235.

- Henry Williams owned the SW quarter of a section of land. He sold the W half of the NW quarter of the SW quarter at $275 an acre, and he sold the SW quarter of the SW quarter at $250 an acre. How much money did Mr. Williams receive from the land? How many acres does he still own?

RECTANGULAR SURVEY SYSTEM

The basic unit of measurement in the *rectangular survey system method is the township*—an area 6 miles square (36 square miles).

A township is divided into 36 *sections*, each 1 mile square (1 square mile), and identified by numbers, always in the sequence shown at the right. Section 1 is always at the northeast corner of the township.

Each section, in turn, can be divided into halves, quarters and smaller subdivisions.

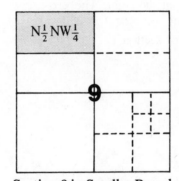

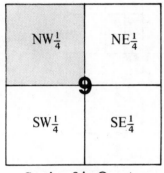

Section 9 in Quarters

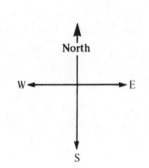

Section 9 in Smaller Parcels

A section of land contains 640 acres and is 1 mile square, or 5,280 feet by 5,280 feet. The diagram at the left, above, shows a section divided into quarters. The shaded part is described as the NW 1/4 (*northwest quarter*) of section 9. To find the number of acres in the shaded quarter, you would multiply 640 acres by 1/4.

$$640 \times 1/4 = \frac{640}{4} = 160 \text{ acres}$$

$$or \ 1/4 = .25 \qquad 640 \times .25 = 160 \text{ acres}$$

The shaded area in the middle diagram above is described as the N 1/2 of the NW 1/4 of section 9. (The location described is found by reading the parts of the description backwards. In this case, the NW 1/4 of section 9 is found, then the N 1/2 of that NW 1/4.) The area can be computed by either of the methods that follow:

$$1/2 \times 1/4 \times 640 = \frac{640}{8} = 80 \text{ acres}$$

$$or \ (1/2 \times 1/4) = 1/8 \qquad 1/8 = .125 \qquad 640 \times .125 = 80 \text{ acres}$$

You can find the acreage of any part of a section by multiplying 640 (acres) by the fraction(s) in the description. Converting the fraction(s) to a decimal, then multiplying, is time consuming. Throughout this chapter, therefore, only the multiplying-by-the-fraction(s) method will be used. An easy way to accomplish this is to pay careful attention to the words "of" and "and." Each time you read "of" (such as SW 1/4 *of* Section 3), remember to multiply by the fraction shown. However, each time you read "and," remember to start a new calculation and add the result to prior results.

1. Determine the number of acres contained in the shaded area of this diagram. The description of the parcel is: SE 1/4 of the SE 1/4 of section 10.

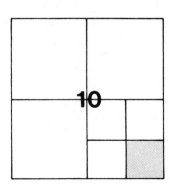

2. Find the number of acres contained in the shaded area of the section at the right. The property is described as follows: NW 1/4 of the SW 1/4 of the NE 1/4 of section 12.

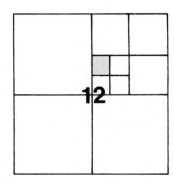

3. The diagram at right shows a section of land. Determine the number of acres in each of the lettered areas.

   A. SE 1/4
   B. W 1/2 of the N 1/2 of the NW 1/4 (or, NW 1/4 of the NW 1/4)
   C. S 1/2 of the NW 1/4
   D. NW 1/4 of the NE 1/4
   E. W 1/2 of the NE 1/4 of the NE 1/4
   F. N 1/2 of the S 1/2 of the NE 1/4
   G. E 1/2 of the S 1/2 of the S 1/2 of the NE 1/4 (or, S 1/2 of the SE 1/4 of the NE 1/4)
   H. SE 1/4 of the SW 1/4 of the SW 1/4
   I. N 1/2 of the NW 1/4 of the SW 1/4 of the SW 1/4

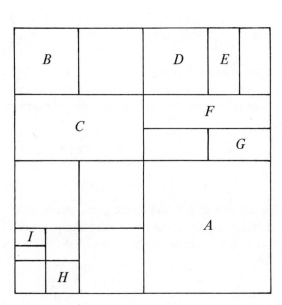

4. Describe the parcel shaded in section 2. How many acres does it contain?

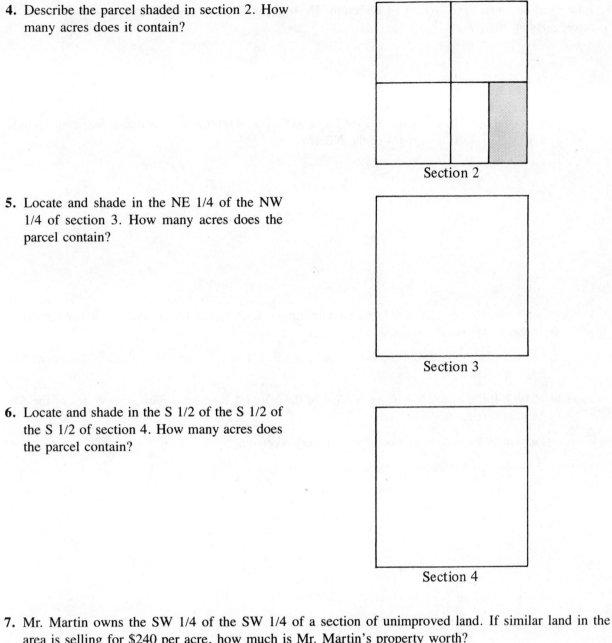

Section 2

Section 3

Section 4

5. Locate and shade in the NE 1/4 of the NW 1/4 of section 3. How many acres does the parcel contain?

6. Locate and shade in the S 1/2 of the S 1/2 of the S 1/2 of section 4. How many acres does the parcel contain?

7. Mr. Martin owns the SW 1/4 of the SW 1/4 of a section of unimproved land. If similar land in the area is selling for $240 per acre, how much is Mr. Martin's property worth?

8. The Valley Development Corporation bought a piece of land described as the W 1/2 of the S 1/2 of the S 1/2 of the NE 1/4 of section 24. If a total of $12,000 was paid for the land, how much did it cost per acre?

9. John Cordova owned the NE 1/4 of a section. He sold the S 1/2 of the NE 1/4. How much land, in acres, does he still own?

10. Mr. Cordova sold the NW 1/4 of the NE 1/4 for $9,000. Based on this price per acre, how much would you pay for the E 1/2 of the NE 1/4 of the NE 1/4?

11. Horace Tucker and William Lawson formed a corporation. Each conveyed real estate in return for shares of stock in the company, as indicated:

Tucker: N 1/2 of the NW 1/4 of the SW 1/4 of the SW 1/4 *and* the SE 1/4 of the SW 1/4 of the SW 1/4 of section 2.

Lawson: SW 1/4 of the NW 1/4 of the SE 1/4 of the NW 1/4 of section 3 *and* the W 1/2 of the SW 1/4 of section 4.

The corporation issued 500 shares of stock for each acre received.

a. How many shares did Tucker receive?

b. How many shares did Lawson receive?

METES AND BOUNDS DESCRIPTIONS

Another system of describing real estate is known as "metes and bounds." This system relies upon the metes (measures of distances) and bounds (directions or courses) as described by the surveyor in his field notes. Surveying is an exacting profession requiring licensure by most states. Real estate licensees should never attempt to prepare a metes and bounds legal description. For example, if the survey does not "close" (the point of ending is not the same as the point of beginning), the survey is defective. If the legal description is defective, then the sales contract cannot be enforced, or the deed can be set aside.

Most real estate licensees will rarely ever need to construct a plat or scaled sketch from a set of field notes. However, if the need does arise, it is important to know how to do it.

First, we need to recognize that the directions stated in a metes and bounds description are the compass directions for each boundary line. We might say that something lies northwest of a certain place or we might say that it lies "westnorth." Although both words point us in the same direction, through accepted convention, we say "northwest," "southeast," etc. We recite the north or south direction *first* and then we recite the direction of declination from north or south. So it is with metes and bounds descriptions. For example, the surveyor's call "N30°E" means that the direction of the subject line is 30 degrees east of due north. Or, we look due north and then we pivot 30 degrees to the right and look again. Now, if we look due east and then we pivot 60 degrees to the left, we are looking in the same direction as before. This is because the compass is divided into 360 degrees and then it is further subdivided into "minutes" and "seconds." Each degree is divided into 60 minutes (written ') and each minute is divided into 60 seconds (written ").

Referring to Figure 12.1, we see that by convention due north is toward the top of the page, east is to the right, south toward the bottom and west toward the left. The compass circle is divided into 4 quadrants as shown so that our example of the call "N30°E" lies in the northeast or upper right quadrant. In like manner, the call "S45°W" lies in the southwest or lower left quadrant.

FIGURE 12.1

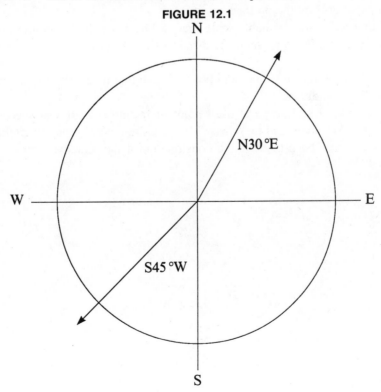

In the preparation of a metes and bounds description, we must now add the *distances* to our call which so far only contains directions. In surveyor's "shorthand," this is done by adding the distance or length of the line after the direction so that a boundary line 1,000 feet long running in a northeasterly direction might appear as "N30°E 1,000 ft." Or "N30°30′30″E 1,000 ft." if the line was not exactly 30 degrees east of north. Such a line would lie in a direction 30 degrees, 30 minutes and 30 seconds east of north.

Let us examine a simple set of metes and bounds field notes. If the subject property is described as:

Beginning at the southwest corner of the Robert B. Hart Survey, Tarrant County, Texas,

> THENCE N0°E 2,640 feet;
> THENCE N90°E 5,280 feet;
> THENCE S0°W 2,640 feet;
> THENCE S90°W 5,280 feet to the point of beginning

we have described a rectangular tract of land whose dimensions are 2,640 feet in the north-south direction and 5,280 feet in the east-west direction. This amounts to 320 acres or one-half of a section. (2,640 × 5,280 = 13,939,200 square feet divided by 43,560 square feet per acre = 320 acres.)

In order to convert the metes and bounds description to a sketch or scaled drawing, we must employ a protractor for measuring the directions or angles and a scale or ruler for measuring the distances. To utilize these tools, simply:

1. Place the center of the protractor (most protractors have a small hole at this point) directly over the point on the paper from which the indicated direction is to be measured.
2. Then carefully align the protractor so that its straight bottom is exactly horizontal with respect to the paper. This will mean that the straight portion is lined up in the east-west direction on your paper.
3. Next, notice the direction from north of the metes and bounds call.
4. Now, on the curved outer scale of the protractor, locate the number of degrees from north indicated by the call (in our example, it was 0 degrees).
5. Place a dot on the paper at 0 on the protractor.
6. Remove the protractor and with a suitable scale draw a line from the beginning point through the dot just made. The length of this line represents the distance shown in the call (in our example, it was 2,640 feet).
7. Move the protractor to the end of this line, and position it so that its center (or the small hole) is directly over the end of the line just drawn.
8. Repeat the above steps until you arrive at the "point of beginning." If you successfully arrive at the point of beginning, your survey is said to "close." If it does not close, either the field notes are defective or (more likely) an error has been made in the construction of the scaled sketch.

Draw your sketch here:

Your sketch should look like this:

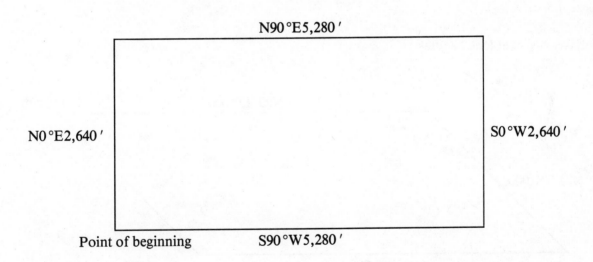

N90°E5,280′

N0°E2,640′   S0°W2,640′

Point of beginning   S90°W5,280′

Let's try another one.
Beginning at the northeast corner of the William H. Long Survey, Coleman County, Texas,

THENCE S45°W 1,000 feet;
THENCE S90°W 2,000 feet;
THENCE N45°E 1,000 feet;
THENCE N90°E 2,000 feet to the point of beginning.

Your sketch should be in the shape of a parallelogram 2,000 feet in the east-west direction and 1,000 feet in the diagonal direction which should be inclined below and to the left of the starting point. Draw your sketch here:

Your sketch should look like this:

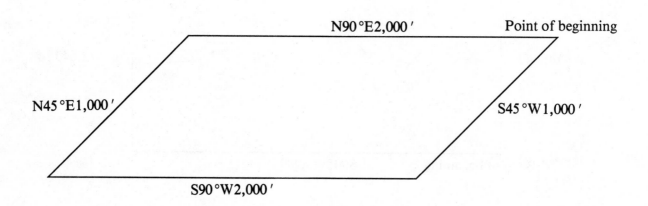

ACHIEVEMENT EXERCISE

When you have finished both parts of this exercise, check your answers against those on page 237. If you miss any of the questions, review this chapter before going on to Chapter 13.

Part I—Open Response   Complete the following problems.

1. The S 1/2 of the SW 1/4 of the NW 1/4 of section 4 was sold for $150 per acre. How much did the parcel sell for?

2. If the S 1/2 of the NW 1/4 of the NE 1/4 of the SW 1/4 of section 24 sold for $325 per acre, what was the total price?

3. The Rand family owned the entire SW 1/4 of section 5. They sold the S 1/2 of the SW 1/4 of the SW 1/4 of section 5 at $450 per acre. They also sold the SW 1/4 of the SE 1/4 of the SW 1/4 of section 5, but at $525 per acre. How much money did the Rands receive? How much land do they own now?

Part II—Multiple Choice   Select the correct response from the choices supplied.

4. Hannah Schwartz owned acreage decribed as the NW 1/4 of section 7. She sold half of her property for $500 an acre and a quarter of the balance for $350 an acre. By selecting from a, b, c or d, indicate which of the following statements is (are) true.

   I. Hannah received $47,000 for the land she sold.
   II. After the sales, Hannah's land totals 40 acres.

   a. I only
   b. II only
   c. both I and II
   d. neither I nor II

5. Emil and Emett Emory owned section 17. They sold the following three tracts of land: W 1/2 of the SW 1/4; NE 1/4 of the SW 1/4; and the N 1/2 of the SE 1/4. Their remaining acreage totals:

   a. 400.   c. 440.
   b. 320.   d. 460.

6. Compare the acreage in the following described tracts of land, and indicate your conclusions by selecting from a, b, c or d. Tract I is the NW 1/4 of the NW 1/4 of the SE 1/4 of section 1.

   Tract II is the S 1/2 of the SE 1/4 of the SE 1/4 of the NW 1/4 of section 3.

   Tract III is the SE 1/4 of the SE 1/4 of the NW 1/4 *and* the SW 1/4 of the NE 1/4 of section 7.

   a. Tract I is twice the size of tract II.
   b. Tract III is four times the size of tract II.
   c. Tract I is one-half the size of tract III.
   d. all of the above

7. By selecting from a, b, c or d, indicate which of the following tracts total(s) 20 acres.

   I. Tract I is the E 1/2 of the S 1/2 of the S 1/2 of the NE 1/4 of section 4.
   II. Tract II is the SE 1/4 of section 18 *and* SW 1/4 of the SW 1/4 of the SW 1/4 of section 18.

   a. I only
   b. II only
   c. both I and II
   d. neither I nor II

8. Indicate the price per acre received for the sale of land described as the W 1/2 of the NE 1/4 of the NE 1/4 of section 1 *and* SE 1/4 of the NE 1/4 of the NE 1/4 of section 1 when the sale price was $18,000.

   a. $300   c. $600
   b. $30   d. $45

9. A legal description of real property may be based on:

   a. the rectangular survey system.
   b. metes and bounds.
   c. lot and block property descriptions.
   d. all of the above

ANSWER KEY

Entry Evaluation

- $15,500   100 acres

Pages 226–228

1. $\dfrac{1}{4} \times \dfrac{1}{4} \times 640 = \dfrac{640}{16} = 40$ acres

2. $\dfrac{1}{4} \times \dfrac{1}{4} \times \dfrac{1}{4} \times 640 = \dfrac{640}{64} = 10$ acres

3. *A.* $\dfrac{1}{4} \times 640 = \dfrac{640}{4} = 160$ acres

  B. $\dfrac{1}{2} \times \dfrac{1}{2} \times \dfrac{1}{4} \times 640 = \dfrac{640}{16} = 40$ acres

  C. $\dfrac{1}{2} \times \dfrac{1}{4} \times 640 = \dfrac{640}{8} = 80$ acres

  D. $\dfrac{1}{4} \times \dfrac{1}{4} \times 640 = \dfrac{640}{16} = 40$ acres

  E. $\dfrac{1}{2} \times \dfrac{1}{4} \times \dfrac{1}{4} \times 640 = \dfrac{640}{32} = 20$ acres

  F. $\dfrac{1}{2} \times \dfrac{1}{2} \times \dfrac{1}{4} \times 640 = \dfrac{640}{16} = 40$ acres

  G. $\dfrac{1}{2} \times \dfrac{1}{2} \times \dfrac{1}{2} \times \dfrac{1}{4} \times 640 = \dfrac{640}{32} = 20$ acres

  H. $\dfrac{1}{4} \times \dfrac{1}{4} \times \dfrac{1}{4} \times 640 = \dfrac{640}{64} = 10$ acres

  I. $\dfrac{1}{2} \times \dfrac{1}{4} \times \dfrac{1}{4} \times \dfrac{1}{4} \times 640 = \dfrac{640}{128} = 5$ acres

4. E $\dfrac{1}{2}$ of the SE $\dfrac{1}{4}$ of section 2 $\dfrac{1}{2} \times \dfrac{1}{4} \times 640 = \dfrac{640}{8} = 80$ acres

5. $\dfrac{1}{4} \times \dfrac{1}{4} \times 640 = \dfrac{640}{16} = 40$ acres

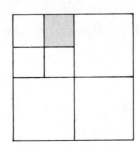

Pages 226–228 continued

6. $\frac{1}{2} \times \frac{1}{2} \times \frac{1}{2} \times 640 = \frac{640}{8} = 80$ acres

7. $\frac{1}{4} \times \frac{1}{4} \times 640 = \frac{640}{16} = 40$ acres

$240 per acre $\times$ 40 acres = $9,600 property value

8. $\frac{1}{2} \times \frac{1}{2} \times \frac{1}{2} \times \frac{1}{4} \times 640 = \frac{640}{32} = 20$ acres

$12,000 $\div$ 20 acres = $600 per acre

9. $\frac{1}{2} \times \frac{1}{4} \times \frac{1}{4} \times 640 = \frac{640}{32} = 20$ acres sold

$\frac{1}{4} \times 640 = 160$ owned − 20 sold = 140 acres still owned

10. $\frac{1}{4} \times \frac{1}{4} \times 640 = \frac{640}{16} = 40$ acres

$9,000 $\div$ 40 = $225 per acre

$\frac{1}{2} \times \frac{1}{4} \times \frac{1}{4} \times 640 = \frac{640}{32} = 20$ acres

$225 $\times$ 20 = $4,500 total price

11. a. *Tucker:* $\frac{1}{2} \times \frac{1}{4} \times \frac{1}{4} \times \frac{1}{4} \times 640 = \frac{640}{128} = 5$ acres, first piece of land

$\frac{1}{4} \times \frac{1}{4} \times \frac{1}{4} \times 640 = \frac{640}{64} = 10$ acres, second piece of land

5 + 10 = 15 acres   15 $\times$ 500 = 7,500 shares of stock

b. *Lawson:* $\frac{1}{4} \times \frac{1}{4} \times \frac{1}{4} \times \frac{1}{4} \times 640 = \frac{640}{256} = 2.5$ acres, first piece of land

$\frac{1}{2} \times \frac{1}{4} \times 640 = \frac{640}{8} = 80$ acres, second piece of land

2.5 + 80 = 82.5 acres   82.5 $\times$ 500 = 41,250 shares of stock

Achievement Exercise

1. $\frac{1}{2} \times \frac{1}{4} \times \frac{1}{4} \times 640 = \frac{640}{32} = 20$ acres $20 \times \$150 = \$3,000$

2. $\frac{1}{2} \times \frac{1}{4} \times \frac{1}{4} \times \frac{1}{4} \times 640 = \frac{640}{128} = 5$ acres $5 \times \$325 = \$1,625$

3. $\frac{1}{2} \times \frac{1}{4} \times \frac{1}{4} \times 640 = \frac{640}{32} = 20$ acres $20 \times \$450 = \$9,000$

$\frac{1}{4} \times \frac{1}{4} \times \frac{1}{4} \times 640 = \frac{640}{64} = 10$ acres $10 \times \$525 = \$5,250$

$\$9,000 + \$5,250 = \$14,250$ total money received

$\frac{1}{4} \times 640 = \frac{640}{4} = 160$ acres

160 acres $-$ (20 acres $+$ 10 acres) $=$ 130 acres still owned

4. a. $1/4 \times 640$ acres $= 160$ acres
$160 \div 2 \times \$500 = \$40,000$
$80 \div 4 \times \$350 = \$7,000$

5. c. $640 \times 1/2 \times 1/4 = 80$ acres
$640 \times 1/4 \times 1/4 = 40$ acres
$640 \times 1/2 \times 1/4 = 80$ acres
$80 + 40 + 80 = 200$ acres
$640 - 200 = 440$ acres

6. a. Tract I $= 640 \times 1/4 \times 1/4 \times 1/4 = 10$ acres
Tract II $= 640 \times 1/2 \times 1/4 \times 1/4 \times 1/4 = 5$ acres
Tract III $= 640 \times 1/4 \times 1/4 \times 1/4 = 10$ acres
$\ 640 \times 1/4 \times 1/4 = 40$ acres
$\ 10 + 40 = 50$ acres

7. a. Tract I $= 640 \times 1/2 \times 1/2 \times 1/2 \times 1/4 = 20$ acres
Tract II $= 640 \times 1/4 = 160$ acres
$\ 640 \times 1/4 \times 1/4 \times 1/4 = 10$ acres
$\ 160 + 10 = 170$ acres

8. c. $640 \times 1/2 \times 1/4 \times 1/4 = 20$ acres
$640 \times 1/4 \times 1/4 \times 1/4 = 10$ acres
$20 + 10 = 30$ acres
$\$18,000 \div 30 = \$600/\text{acre}$

9. d.

Prorations

INTRODUCTION

To *prorate* certain expenses of a real estate closing transaction means to divide the income or expenses of a property between the seller and buyer. This is related to the time of year and the day of the month in which the closing occurs. The seller is charged for the period of ownership so that the buyer's financial responsibility starts at closing. In closing a real estate transaction, the common prorated expenses are: insurance premiums, mortgage interest, real estate taxes, water bills, fuel, and rents.

In this chapter, you will work problems in prorating each of these kinds of expenses, by computing the number of months, days and years for which the buyer or seller is responsible and converting this time period to dollars and cents for the expenses involved.

The key to whether the seller receives a credit for or will be charged for any expense to be prorated is whether the particular expense was paid in advance or in arrears by the seller. The following chart indicates the most common methods of payment.

Interest	In arrears
Taxes*	In arrears
Water	In arrears
Gas	In arrears
Electricity	In arrears
Insurance	In advance
Fuel oil, coal, etc.	In advance
Rent	In advance

*Even though taxes are prorated, a penalty for delinquent taxes is *not* a part of the proration calculations. Penalties for delinquencies are charged to the seller. In a similar manner, security deposits for rental property are not prorated but are transferred to the buyer.

Note: Unless stated otherwise, all problems in this chapter will involve interest paid in arrears and interest paid in advance.

ENTRY EVALUATION

Since readers will have varying amounts of knowledge and experience, the short test that follows will allow you to determine your familiarity with the material to be covered. Try all the problems before looking at the answers, which begin on page 254.

For all proration problems, you should determine:

1. the cost per year, per month and per day
2. the amount of time for the proration
3. the amount to be credited or debited and
4. the party to receive the credit or debit.

■ Mr. Dean is selling his home. He made a monthly mortgage payment on July 1, 1989, which paid interest through June 30. His principal is now $22,450.40; the interest rate is 11%. The closing is set for July 21, 1989, and the buyer will assume the mortgage. What amount of accrued interest will be credited the buyer? Prorate through date of closing.

■ Mr. Dean also has a 3-year insurance policy which expires January 1, 1989. The policy has been paid in full at a cost of $959. Figure the premium proration that the buyer will owe the seller at the closing. Prorate through date of closing.

■ Taxes for 1987 amounted to $1,180, and they were paid in full. The 1988 tax bill will be due in September, 1989. How much will the seller owe the buyer for prorated taxes, if there is no reason to believe that the tax amount will change? Prorate through date of closing.

AN ILLUSTRATION OF PRORATING

For clarity, a number of the prorated items have been placed on time lines. Remember that the date of closing is compared to the date each expense to be prorated is paid.

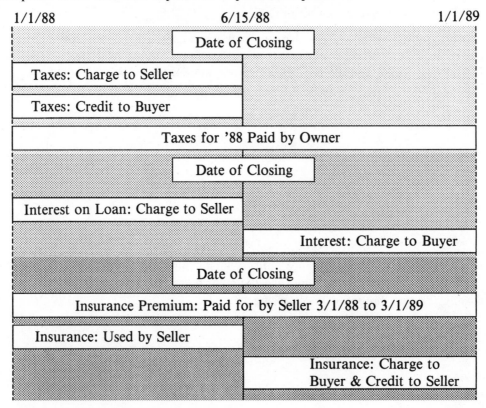

PRORATING INSURANCE

Usually, insurance policies are written for periods of 1, 3 or 5 years; the premiums are payable in advance for periods of 1 or more years; and the policy is transferred to the new owner after a sale. However, if the sale involves a new loan, the lender may require a new policy to be issued. The premium per day is generally computed on a 360-day year (30-day month). The number of years, months, and days (using the exact number of days in the month of closing) that the buyer will pay for at the closing must be calculated. The insurance policy is thus *prorated* (divided between buyer and seller).

Although, in general practice, insurance premiums are computed on a 360-day year and a 30-day month, in some areas the calendar number of days in the year and month are used. The 360-day year and 30-day month with the exact number of days in the month in which closing occurs will be used exclusively in this chapter for computing premiums. A more detailed explanation of the different methods of computing prorations can be found in Chapter 23 of *Modern Real Estate Practice,* 11th Edition, by Fillmore W. Galaty, Wellington J. Allaway and Robert C. Kyle (Real Estate Education Company, Chicago, 1988).

EXAMPLE: A house was covered by a 3-year fire insurance policy which expires May 13, 1989. The total premium for this policy, $604.80, was paid in full in 1986. The house was sold and the closing date set for July 23, 1987. How much money was credited to the seller (paid by the buyer) at the closing to transfer the unexpired (remaining) term of this insurance policy to the buyer?

Step 1. Compute the amount the policy cost per year, per month and per day.

$604.80 ÷ 3 years = $201.600 per year
$201.60 ÷ 12 months = $16.800 per month
$16.80 ÷ 30 days = $.560 per day

Carry all dollars and cents calculations with remainders to 3 decimal places, if necessary. Round off to 2 decimal places *only* after you complete the steps needed to compute the proration. Otherwise, do not clear the calculator between steps.

Step 2. Compute the number of days, months and years of insurance coverage that the buyer assumed. Now you will consider the actual number of days in the month of closing.

years	months	days	
1989	5	13	May 13, 1989 expiration date
− 1987	7	23	July 23, 1987 closing date

If any month or day figure in the expiration date is less than the month or day in the closing date, you must borrow from the column to the left. The *month* you borrow must be the exact number of days in the month of closing. In this example, since 13 days are less than 23 days, borrowing a month means borrowing the 31 days in the month of July. Borrowing a year always means borrowing 12 months.

First, subtract the days.

years	months	days
	4	44
1989	5̶	1̶3̶
− 1987	7	23
		21

Then, subtract the months.

years	months	days
	16	
1988	4̶	44
1989	5̶	1̶3̶
− 1987	7	23
	9	21

Finally, subtract the years.

years	months	days
	16	
1988	4̶	44
1989	5̶	1̶3̶
− 1987	7	23
1	9	21 unexpired term

The buyer owed the seller for 1 year, 9 months and 21 days of this policy.

Warning: Calculate the amount of time remaining *very carefully.* If your figures are inaccurate, your entire proration will be wrong.

Step 3. Knowing the rate per year, month and day, and the number of years, months and days of the unexpired term, you can now calculate what the buyer owed.

$201.60 per year × 1 year = $201.60
$16.80 per month × 9 months = $151.20
$.56 per day × 21 days = $11.76
$201.60 + $151.20 + $11.76 = $364.56 insurance proration
credited to the seller

The insurance proration of $364.56 was credited to the seller, because the buyer paid the seller for it. Therefore, it was debited to the buyer.

These events are shown on the time line that follows, so you can graphically examine them.

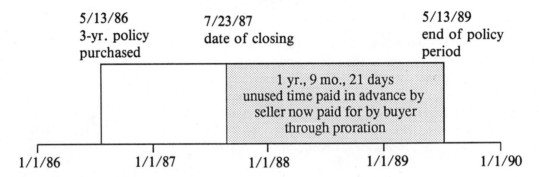

Now, you try prorating.

1. On June 18, 1987, John Schwartz purchased a 3-year fire insurance policy on his home. The total prepaid premium was $540. He sold the house, closing on October 21, 1988. How much money should he receive from the buyer at closing?

a. Compute the yearly, monthly and daily premiums.

b. Compute the unexpired time period.

c. Convert the time period into dollars and cents.

2. A seller has a 5-year fire insurance policy with the premium payable annually, in advance. The last premium paid was $208.50 for the 1-year period ending August 18, 1989. The sale is to be closed on November 3, 1988. What premium proration will the buyer owe the seller at the closing? To whom will this be credited?

PRORATING MORTGAGE INTEREST

Interest on mortgage payments can be paid either *in arrears* or *in advance*. Practices vary, so check those of the lending institution in your area. Arrears interest is most common and means that a May 1 payment includes the interest for April. Advance interest means that the May 1 payment includes the interest for May. Note that interest is charged in arrears in the examples in this text unless otherwise stated. This distinction is very important because it will make a difference in the way in which you compute the proration.

Proration of Interest Paid in Arrears

Arrears interest payments can include interest for the calendar month, for a period up to but not including the date of payment, or for a period up to and including the date of payment. Unless otherwise specified, assume that the payment includes interest for the calendar month.

In *prorating* arrears interest, you need to compute the number of days of *earned* or *accrued* interest to be charged to the seller. This is the period starting after the last interest payment date, to and including the date of closing. This proration is a credit to the buyer and a debit to the seller if the buyer does not obtain a new loan but assumes the existing loan.

EXAMPLE: On May 8, 1989, a home was purchased and the buyer assumed the balance of the seller's $43,300 mortgage with 10.5% interest paid to and including April 15, 1989. How much credit was the buyer given at closing?

Step 1.   Find the annual interest on the unpaid balance of the mortgage.

$43,300 × 10.5% = $4,546.50 annual interest

Step 2.   Find the interest charge per day. Since you do not need to know the monthly charge, you can find the daily charge by dividing by the number of days in the year (using a 360-day year).

$4,546.50 ÷ 360 = $12.629 daily interest

Step 3.   Find the *exact* number of days of earned or accrued interest. Use the actual number of days in the month of closing.

   30   total days in April
 −15   date of last interest payment (April 15)
   15   days of accrued interest in April
 + 8   days of accrued interest in May (closing date)
   23   Total Days of Accrued Interest

Step 4.   Compute the total amount of accrued interest.

  $12.629 daily interest
   × 23 number of days to and including day of closing
   37887
   25258
$290.467   = $290.47 Seller Owes Buyer   This amount would be credited to the buyer.

Try the next problem.

3. After the monthly payment due on June 20, 1989 was made (including the day of payment), the unpaid balance of a seller's 10% mortgage was $38,600. The house was sold, and the purchaser assumed the seller's mortgage. The closing was set for July 6, 1989. Find the amount of accrued interest. Follow the steps described in the example. Carry divisions to three decimal places, if necessary, rounding to two decimal places only in the last step. Remember to leave the numbers in the calculator until the problem is solved.

Step 1.

Step 2.

Step 3.

Step 4.

4. A buyer is assuming a seller's outstanding mortgage balance of $105,865 after the March 5th payment has been applied. Mortgage payments of $924.94 are due monthly, on the fifth day of the month (which includes payment for that day), to be applied first to 9-1/2% interest on the unpaid principal outstanding, and the remainder to the principal. The last mortgage payment was due and paid on March 5. The sale is to be closed on March 29. What allowance will the seller owe the buyer for accrued interest?

Proration of Interest Paid in Advance

Prorating mortgage interest paid in advance is similar to prorating interest paid in arrears, except that it is a prepaid expense that the *buyer owes the seller*. It will, therefore, be a credit to the seller. Study the following example.

EXAMPLE: Mr. Amundsen is purchasing a house from Mrs. Reed and assuming her $38,000 mortgage. The mortgage has an interest rate of 13%, and payments are due the first day of each month. Interest is paid in advance. The last mortgage payment was made April 1, and the closing date is set for April 20. What is the proration that will appear on the closing statement?

Step 1. Find the daily interest charge.

$38,000 × 13% = $4,940 annual interest
$4,940 ÷ 360 = $13.722 daily interest

Step 2. Find the number of days of prepaid or *unearned* interest.

30 number of days in month of closing
− 20 date of closing
10 days of unearned interest

Step 3. Compute the total amount of unearned interest.

10 days × $13.722 = $137.22 total credit to seller for
prepaid mortgage interest

Now, you complete the next problem.

5. Mr. Monroe is purchasing the Johnsons' house and will assume the existing $25,000 mortgage. The mortgage carries an interest rate of 12%, and payments are due on the first of each month in the amount of $295.60. The last mortgage payment was made August 1. Mortgage payments include interest in advance for the month of payment. The closing has been set for August 16. Complete this proration. To whom will the proration be a credit?

PRORATING REAL ESTATE TAXES

Real estate taxes are assessed or levied for definite periods, generally a calendar year or a fiscal year. Payments are due on definite dates. Some due dates are within the tax year (the year for which the tax was assessed); others are after the close of the tax year.

The first problem is to determine the total unpaid taxes as of the day of closing. This may include the tax bill for a full year and/or part of another year. When the current year's tax bill hasn't yet been prepared, it is customary to use the amount of the "most recent ascertainable tax," which means the most recent tax bill available.

In prorating taxes, you will follow basically the same steps you learned in prorating interest in arrears. And, as for interest prorations, the seller must pay the accrued portion of the tax to and including the day of closing. This proration is a credit to the buyer. Late payment penalties are not prorated but are charged to the seller.

EXAMPLE: Assume that the closing date on a home purchased by Mr. Sawyer was April 12, 1989. The taxes of $1,020 for the calendar year of 1988 had been paid. Taxes for 1989 started accruing January 1. Prorate the taxes.

Step 1. Find both the monthly and daily tax charges.

$1,020 ÷ 12 = $85 monthly tax
$85 ÷ 30 = $2.883 daily tax

Step 2. Find the exact number of years, months and days of accrued taxes from the beginning of the tax period (January 1, 1989) up to and including the date of closing (April 12, 1989).

3 months   January, February, March
12 days   12 days in April

Step 3. Compute prorated tax amount.

$85 × 3 months = $255
$2.833 × 12 days = $33.996 rounded to $34.00
$255 + $34 = $289 seller's share of year's taxes, credit to buyer

6. Assume that a sale is to be closed on March 23, 1989. The 1987 tax on the property amounted to $1,080 and was paid in 1988. How much must the seller pay the buyer for prorated taxes? To whom will the proration be a credit?

Step 1.

Step 2.

Step 3.

7. Mr. Wyeth has sold his house and the closing is to be on December 4. The real estate tax in this case is levied for the fiscal year from July 1 to the following June 30. It is payable in 2 installments, on November 1 and May 1. Mr. Wyeth has paid $480 as the first installment of his current tax. Compute the proration and state who will receive the credit.

8. Mr. and Mrs. Biggs are purchasing the Joyce house. The closing has been set for March 20, 1989. The 1987 real estate taxes amounted to $950 and were paid in full. Calculate the real estate tax proration. Who will be credited with this amount?

PRORATING WATER BILLS

Water bills sometimes are prorated. They are calculated in exactly the same manner as real estate taxes. The last available bill is used as the basis of the proration.

9. Mr. and Mrs. Biggs, in Exercise 8, also need to prorate the water bill for the closing of the sale. The last water bill, for 1988, was $120 and was paid in full. Compute the proration and state to whom this amount will be credited.

PRORATING FUEL

10. The Donegans are purchasing the Blys' house. The closing has been set for January 2, 1989. The Donegans have agreed to pay the Blys for the fuel oil remaining in the tank on the day of closing. On the day of closing, the oil supplier measured 240 gallons left in the tank, at a cost of $.80 per gallon. Compute the amount of this proration. Who will receive this credit?

PRORATING RENTS

Rents are prorated only for amounts that have already been collected. Go through the next problem carefully.

EXAMPLE: Mr. and Mrs. Jones are selling their apartment building to Ms. Hanes. Each of the five apartments rents for $315 per month. The transaction is to be closed on September 15, and the September rents have already been collected. Each tenant has also placed a security deposit of a month's rent with the Joneses. What is the rent proration for this transaction and to whom will the amount be credited?

Step 1.   Calculate the total rent for 1 month.

$315 × 5 apartments = $1,575 monthly rent

Step 2.   Calculate 1 day's rent.

$1,575 ÷ 30 days = $52.50 daily rent

Step 3.   Find the *unearned* portion of the month—the amount of
time that the purchaser will own the building in the month
of closing.

   30 days in the month
 − 15 date of closing
   15 days of unearned rent

Step 4.   Multiply the daily rent by the number of days the seller
owes rent payments to the purchaser.

$52.50 × 15 = $787.50 rent
$787.50 + $1,575 security deposits = $2,362.50

The $787.50 will be a credit to the purchaser. The security
deposits will also appear as a credit to the buyer, they are never
prorated.

11. Mr. and Mrs. Barber are purchasing the Ungers' apartment building. The building has eight apartments,
half of which rent for $250 each per month, and the other half for $300 each per month. The Ungers
have a one-month security deposit from each of the tenants. The June rent has been paid, and the sale
is to be closed on June 25. Calculate the proration. What amount will appear for security deposits?

12. Mr. and Mrs. Turner sold their house to the Herbert family. Complete the following prorations for the
closing of this sale, which was on July 15, 1988.

The last real estate tax bill was paid in full and amounted to $1,500. It covered the 1986 real estate
taxes.

The Herberts assumed the Turners' mortgage, which had a principal balance of $54,000 on June 1,
1988, after the June 1 monthly mortgage payment of $475.44 was made. The mortgage had an interest
rate of 8-3/4% per annum. The Turners also made the July 1 payment of $475.44 on the mortgage to
cover interest and principal. The mortgage payment included an interest payment *to and including* the
day of payment.

The annual water bill for 1987 was $144, which was paid September 1, 1987.

The Turners had a 5-year insurance policy, which was to expire August 1, 1991. The full premium of
$1,500 has been paid in full.

The Herberts agreed to pay for the 250 gallons of fuel oil left in the tank on the day of closing. The fuel oil cost $.90 per gallon.

PRORATING *TO* VERSUS PRORATING *THROUGH*

In proration calculations, it is crucial to know whether the sales contract specifies that the prorations be "to date of closing" or "through date of closing." Proration *to* date of closing results in the buyer being charged for the day of closing itself, whereas proration *through* date of closing results in the seller being charged for that day. For example, consider that the daily interest on a $200,000 loan bearing 14% per annum is $77.78, and the daily taxes are $10.00 if the annual taxes are $3,600 (both based upon a 360-day year). In this example, the difference between "to" and "through" date of closing means a difference of $87.78. Now, which party is to receive the benefit of that, and which party is to be charged? The earnest money contract (sales contract) should state how proration is to be done.

For another illustration of the difference, look again at Exercise 12 on page 249, which shows proration *through* date of closing. If you prorated as between the Turners and the Herberts *to* date of closing, you would "back up" one calendar day. This results in an increase in charges made to the Turners (the buyers) and a decrease in charges made to the Herberts (the sellers), as shown in Table 13.1.

| Item | Through date of closing | | To date of closing | |
	Credit seller	Credit buyer	Credit seller	Credit buyer
Taxes		$2,312.49		$2,308.32
Interest		196.58		183.47
Water		78.00		77.60
Insurance	$ 914.16		$ 914.99	
Fuel	225.00		225.00	
Totals	**$1,139.16**	**$2,587.07**	**$1,139.99**	**$2,569.39**

Remember that credits offset charges to each party respectively. This means that if a seller is *charged* for the date of closing for those items paid in arrears, then the seller is also *credited* with the date of closing for those items paid for in advance.

ACHIEVEMENT EXERCISE

When you have finished both parts of this exercise, check your answers against those on pages 257–258. If you miss any of the questions, review this chapter before going on to Chapter 14.

Part I—Open Response   Complete the following problems.

Dr. and Mrs. Barlow sold their home to the Guy family. The closing date was April 25, 1989. The Guys assumed the mortgage, which had a principal balance of $65,500 after the April 1, 1989 payment was made. The sale price of the house was $90,500. The mortgage has an interest rate of 8% per annum, payable in arrears. The monthly payments are $554.96. The Barlows had begun payments on a 5-year fire insurance policy, due to expire July 1, 1992. The $1,200 premium had been paid in full. Real estate taxes had been paid in full for 1988. The tax bill was $1,500. The 1988 water bill of $180 had also been paid in full. The second floor of the house was rented, with the rent of $260 payable on or before the first day of each month. The Barlows also held one month's rent as security deposit. The Guys agreed to pay for the fuel oil remaining in the tank on the day of closing. This amounted to 35 gallons at $.80 per gallon.

Using the foregoing information, complete the prorations necessary and indicate whether they should have been credited to the seller or buyer. Show *all* calculations.

1. Mortgage interest proration:

2. Insurance proration:

3. Real estate tax proration:

4. Water bill proration:

5. Rent proration:

6. Fuel oil proration:

Part II—Multiple Choice   Select the correct response from the choices supplied.

7. Which of the following statements best describes the process of proration?

    a. Determine the time period involved.

    b. Compute the amount per unit of time period.

    c. Multiply the unit amount by the time period.

    d. all of the above

8. Bill Guilbeault paid $297 for fire insurance policies, which cover his store building for a year and expire July 17, 1989. When he sells his building on November 7, 1988, he will be entitled to receive a proration of:

    a. $206.25.   c. $234.75.

    b. $282.50.   d. $197.30.

9. The seller's mortgage loan balance of $17,213.63 at 8-1/2% interest will be assumed by the buyer when the sale is closed on March 18. The monthly payment of $201.31 was made on March 1, and paid interest in advance. Compute the interest proration through the closing date, and by your selection of a, b, c or d, indicate which of the following statements is (are) true.

  I. The buyer will receive a credit of $52.83.
  II. The seller will receive a credit of $73.15.

    a. I only
    b. II only
    c. both I and II
    d. neither I nor II

10. The buyer is assuming the seller's mortgage loan balance of $24,569.20 with 9% interest per annum, payable in arrears. The sale is to be closed on June 3, and the June 1 monthly payment of $265.42 has been made. The interest proration is:

    a. $26.54.   c. $20.45.
    b. $24.57.   d. $18.43.

11. Prorate the annual tax bill of $1,638 levied for the calendar year 1989, when the sale is closed on April 17, 1989.

    a. $623.35   c. $486.85
    b. $409.50   d. $441.35

12. The selling landlord has collected the June rent from all five tenants: two at $345 and three at $425. Compute the proration to be allowed the buyer when the sale is closed on June 19.

    a. $1,244.50   c. $1,425.40
    b. $720.50   d. $872.45

13. Compute the proration that will be due the seller for fuel oil when the sale is closed on Monday. On the previous Friday, the tank holds 110 gallons which cost $.75 a gallon, and the buyer and seller have agreed that 12 gallons a day will be burned on Friday, Saturday and Sunday.

    a. $55.50   c. $82.50
    b. $73.50   d. $69.25

14. Mr. and Mrs. Herndon are selling their apartment building. Each of the six apartments rents for $275 per month. The transaction is to be closed on September 15, and the September rents have already been collected. Compute the rent proration, and by selecting from a, b, c or d, indicate which of the following statements is (are) true.

  I. The rent proration is $825.
  II. The seller will receive a credit of $825.

    a. I only
    b. II only
    c. both I and II
    d. neither I nor II

15. Which of the following is (are) usually prorated in arrears?

  I. interest
  II. taxes
  III. insurance
  IV. rent

    a. I only
    b. II only
    c. both I and II
    d. both III and IV

ANSWER KEY

Entry Evaluation

- $144.06 accrued interest

- $462.63 insurance proration

- $1,838.82 tax proration

Pages 242–249

1. a. $540 ÷ 3 years = $180 per year
$180 ÷ 12 months = $15 per month
$15 ÷ 30 days = $.50 per day

b.

	years	months	days	
		17		
	1989	$\cancel{8}$	48	
	1990	$\cancel{6}$	$\cancel{17}$	June 17, 1990 expiration date
	−1988	10	21	October 21, 1988 closing date
	1	7	27	unexpired period

c. $180 per year × 1 year = $180
$15 per month × 7 months = $105
$.50 per day × 27 days = $13.50
$180 + $105 + $13.50 = $298.50 insurance proration buyer owes seller

2. $208.50 ÷ 12 = $17.375 per month
$17.375 ÷ 30 = $.579 per day

years	months	days	
1988	20		
$\cancel{1989}$	$\cancel{8}$	18	date premium paid to
−1988	11	3	closing date
0	9	15	unexpired period

$17.375 × 9 = $156.375 premium for 9 months
$.579 × 15 = $8.685 premium for 15 days
$156.375 + $8.685 = $165.060 = $165.06 insurance proration buyer owes seller, a credit to the seller

3. Step 1. Find the annual interest.

$38,600 × 10% = $3,860 annual interest

Step 2. Find the number of days of accrued interest.

30	total days in June
− 20	date of last interest payment
10	number of days of accrued interest in June
+ 6	number of days of accrued interest in July
16	total days of accrued interest

Step 3. Find the interest charge per day.

$3,860 ÷ 360 = $10.722 daily interest

Step 4.   Compute the amount of accrued interest.

$10.722 × 16 days = $171.552 rounded to $171.55 accrued interest

4. Annual interest on the unpaid balance of the mortgage:

$105,865 × 9.5% = $10,057.18 annual interest

Interest charge per day:

$10,057.18 ÷ 360 = $27.937 daily interest

Exact number of days of accrued interest:

```
 29  closing date (March 29)
−  5  last interest payment date (March 5)
 24  days of accrued interest
```

Total amount of accrued interest:
$27.937 × 24 days = $670.48

5. Step 1.   Find the daily interest charge.

$25,000 × 12% = $3,000 annual interest
$3,000 ÷ 360 = $8.333 daily interest

Step 2.   Find the number of days of unearned interest.

```
 31  days in August
−16  date of closing
 15  days of unearned interest
```

Step 3.   Compute the total amount of unearned interest.

$8.333 × 15 = $125.00 unearned interest, a credit to the seller

6. Step 1.   Tax charges per month and day:

$1,080 ÷ 12 = $90 monthly tax
$90 ÷ 30 = $3 daily tax

Step 2.   Accrued tax period:

1 year   all of 1984
2 months January, February (1985)
23 days   23 days in March

Step 3.   Accrued tax:

$1,080 × 1 year = $1,080
$90 × 2 months = $180
$3 × 23 days = $69

$1,080 + $180 + $69 = $1,329 seller must pay buyer, a credit to the buyer

7. Mr. Wyeth has paid the first half of the tax, which covers the period from July 1 to December 31. Since the sale will close on December 4, he has prepaid the tax from December 4 to December 31.

Tax charges per year, month and day:

$480 × 2 = $960 annual tax
$960 ÷ 12 = $80 monthly tax
$80 ÷ 30 = $2.666 daily tax

Pages 242–249 continued

Accrued tax:

$2.666 × 27 days = $71.982 rounded to $71.98 accrued tax, a credit to the seller

8. Seller owes buyer for all of 1988, and the period from January 1 to March 20, 1989.

   1 year   all of 1988
   2 months   January, February (1989)
   20 days   20 days in March

   $950 ÷ 12 = $79.166 $79.166 ÷ 30 = $2.638
   $950 × 1 = $950 $79.166 × 2 = $158.332 $2.638 × 20 = $52.76
   $950 + $158.332 + $52.76 = $1,161.092 rounded to $1,161.09

   Accrued tax of $1,161.09 is a credit to the buyer.

9. The seller owes the buyer for 2 months and 20 days.

   $120 ÷ 12 = $10 $10 ÷ 30 = $.333
   $10 × 2 months = $20 $.333 × 20 days = $6.66
   $20 + $6.66 = $26.66 credit to the buyer

10. 240 × $.80 = $192

    Since the buyer must pay this amount, it will be a credit to the seller.

11. $250 × 4 = $1,000 $300 × 4 = $1,200
    $1,000 + $1,200 = $2,200 monthly rent $2,200 ÷ 30 = $73.333 daily rent

       30 total days in June
     − 25 date of closing
        5 days of unearned rent

    $73.333 × 5 = $366.665 rounded to $366.67 seller owes buyer, a credit to the buyer

    Security deposits are 1 month's rent, $2,200, which is also a credit to the buyer.

12. Tax bill proration:

    $1,500 ÷ 12 = $125 monthly $125 ÷ 30 = $4.166 daily

    1 year   all of 1982
    6 months   January through June, 1983
    15 days   15 days in July

    $1,500 × 1 year = $1,500
    $125 × 6 months = $750
    $4.166 × 15 days = $62.49
    $1,500 + $750 + $62.49 = $2,312.49 tax proration, a credit to the buyer

    Mortgage interest proration:

    $54,000 × 8-3/4% = $4,725 $4,725 ÷ 12 = $393.75 interest June 2 through July 1
    $475.44 July 1 payment − $393.75 interest = $81.69 toward principal
    $54,000 − $81.69 = $53,918.31 principal after July 1 payment

    $53,918.31 × 8-3/4% = $4,717.852 $4,717.852 ÷ 360 = $13.105 daily interest
    $13.105 × 15 days = $196.58 mortgage interest proration, a credit to the buyer

Water bill proration:

$144 ÷ 12 = $12 monthly $12 ÷ 30 = $.40 daily

The seller owes the buyer for 6 months and 15 days of the bill due September 1.
$12 × 6 months = $72
$.40 × 15 days = $6
$72 + $6 = $78 water bill proration, a credit to the buyer

Insurance policy proration:

$1,500 ÷ 5 = $300 yearly $300 ÷ 12 = $25 monthly $25 ÷ 30 = $.833 daily

	years	months	days
		7	32
	1991	~~8~~	~~1~~
−1988		7	15
	3	0	17

$300 × 3 years = $900 $.833 × 17 days = $14.161
$900 + $14.161 = $914.16 insurance proration, a credit to the seller

Fuel proration:

$250 × $.90 = $225 fuel proration, a credit to the seller

Achievement Exercise

1. Mortgage interest proration:
   $65,500 × 8% = $5,240 annual interest $5,240 ÷ 360 = $14.555 daily interest
   $14.555 × 25 days from April 1 to April 25 = $363.875 rounded to $363.88 credited to buyer

2. Insurance proration:
   $1,200 ÷ 5 = $240 annually
   $240 ÷ 12 = $20 monthly $20 ÷ 30 = $.666 daily

		6	31
	1992	~~7~~	~~1~~
−1989		4	25
	3	2	6

   $240 × 3 years = $720
   $20 × 2 months = $40
   $.666 × 6 days = $3,996
   $720 + $40 + $3.996 = $763.996 rounded to $764 credited to seller

3. Real estate tax proration:
   $1,500 ÷ 12 = $125 monthly tax $125 ÷ 30 = $4.166 daily tax

   3 months   January through March, 1989
   25 days   25 days of April

   $125 × 3 months = $375
   $4.166 × 25 days = $104.15
   $375 + $104.15 = $479.15 credited to buyer

4. Water bill proration:
   The seller owes the buyer for 3 months and 25 days of the bill for 1989.
   $180 ÷ 12 = $15 monthly $15 ÷ 30 = $.50 daily

Achievement Exercise continued

15×3 months $= \$45$ $\$.50 \times 25$ days $= \$12.50$
$\$45 + \$12.50 = \$57.50$ credited to buyer

5. Rent proration:
   $\$260 \div 30 = \$8.666$ daily

      30 total days in April
   -25 date of closing
        5 days of unearned rent

   $\$8.666 \times 5$ days $= \$43.33$
   $\$43.33 + \$260$ security deposit $= \$303.33$ credited to buyer

6. Fuel oil proration:
   35 gallons $\times \$.80 = \$28$

7. d.

8. a. $\$297 \div 12 = \$24.75$ monthly insurance premium
   $\$24.75 \div 30 = \$.825$ daily insurance premium
   $\$24.75 \times 8 = \$198$
   $\$.825 \times 10 = \$8.25$
   $\$198.00 + \$8.25 = \$206.25$ refund

9. d. $\$17,213.63 \times 8.5\% = \$1,463.159$ annual interest
   $\$1,463.159 \div 12 = \$121.93$ monthly interest
   $\$121.93 \div 30 = \$4.064$ daily interest
   $\$4.064 \times 18 = \$73.158$
   $\$121.93 - \$73.16 = \$48.77$ interest credit to seller

10. d. $\$24,569.20 \times 9\% = \$2,211.228$ annual interest
    $\$2,211.228 \div 12 = \$184.269$ monthly interest
    $\$184.269 \div 30 = \$6.142$ daily interest
    $\$6.142 \times 3 = \$18.43$ interest proration debit to seller

11. c. $\$1,638 \div 12 = \$136.50$ monthly tax
    $\$136.50 \div 30 = \$4.55$ daily tax
    $\$136.50 \times 3 = \$409.50$
    $\$4.55 \times 17 = \$77.35$
    $\$409.50 + \$77.35 = \$486.85$

12. b. $\$345 \times 2 = \$690$
    $\$425 \times 3 = \$1,275$
    $\$690 + \$1,275 = \$1,965$ total rent
    $\$1,965 \div 30 = \$65.50$ daily rent
    $\$65.50 \times 11 = \$720.50$ rent credit to buyer

13. a. $12 \times 3 = 36$ gallons burned
    $110 - 36 = 74$ gallons on Monday
    $74 \times \$.75 = \$55.50$ fuel credit to seller

14. d. $\$275 \times 6 = \$1,650$ total rent
    $\$1,650 \div 30 = \$55.00$ daily rent
    $\$55 \times 15 = \$825$ rent credit to buyer

15. c.

Closing Statements

INTRODUCTION

Note: Before deciding that this chapter has no practical application for you, since closing statements are usually prepared by those who actually close the real estate transactions, consider that real estate licensees routinely use something called "net sheets" in every listing appointment, preparation of an offer from a buyer and presentation of an offer to a seller. This is because prospective sellers are obviously very interested in the amount they will *net* from the proposed sale, and prospective buyers likewise are interested in their *net* due at closing. The generation of these figures involves the preparation of a document similar to a closing statement.

A closing statement is used in closing a real estate transaction. This is the document on which you will record the prorations that you learned to calculate in Chapter 13. It is, basically, a balance sheet on which debits and credits to the buyer and seller are recorded, and from the totals, the amount owed by the buyer is determined as well as the net amount that the seller will receive.

In this chapter, you will calculate prorations and learn to enter them on a closing statement. The examples used are generalities since many of the expenses are negotiable and can be paid by either the buyer or the seller. Also, the methods of closing a real estate transaction vary greatly across the nation and even within states. For example, depending on the area, brokers, attorneys, title insurance companies or "escrow companies" may routinely close real estate transactions. In this text, brokers will be considered to be the closers, and the examples and problems are treated accordingly, even though this may not be the practice in your area.

The closing statement is the most important financial computation of a real estate transaction, and there is no short way to determine whether or not you know how to complete one. Therefore, there is no entry evaluation for this material, and all students are advised to work through the entire chapter.

CLOSING STATEMENT FORMS

Every real estate transaction involving the transfer of property requires the preparation of a written form called a *closing statement*.

The closing statement is a device used to "balance the books." It is a way of calculating how much money is owed or due, taking all factors into account. Usually the buyer owes the seller, but on rare occasions, the seller may owe the buyer. Instead of exchanging money for each part of the transaction, the amounts are entered separately on the closing statement. The entire statement is then balanced to determine the total amount owed. In this way, there is only one exchange of money, and the closing statement serves as the one financial document for the transaction. For instance, if the sellers have 40 gallons of fuel left in their tank on the day of closing, they could siphon it out or ask the buyer for its value in cash. Instead, the value is entered on the closing statement as a *credit* to the *seller* and as a *debit,* or *charge,* to the *buyer,* who owes the seller that amount.

The amounts charged to the buyer are actually added to the purchase price of the house. Amounts that the seller owes the buyer are entered as credits to the buyer and are actually subtracted from the sale price of the house. The overall equations for closing statements are:

Buyer's charges − Buyer's credits = Cash buyer owes at closing
Seller's credits − Seller's charges = Cash seller will receive at closing

CREDITS

Let us consider who receives credit for certain items. Items credited to the *buyer* usually include:

- earnest money deposit (treated as a partial payment)
- existing mortgage balance, when assumed by the buyer
- accrued items — such as real estate taxes — that have accrued or are accruing but are not yet due or paid and for which the seller is debited, or charged, at the closing
- unearned revenues (revenues — such as rent — collected in advance but not yet earned)
- proceeds of a new loan to be taken out by the buyer

Items credited to the *seller* usually include:

- sale price
- prepaid items (items paid in advance — such as a fire insurance policy premium paid for a term that has not fully expired, advance interest on an assumed mortgage, or fuel on hand)
- prepaid insurance and tax reserves (if any) on an outstanding assumed mortgage

Notice that *accrued* items are credits to the buyer, and *prepaid* items are credits to the seller.

1. On the following chart, check the items that would normally be credited to the buyer and those that would normally be credited to the seller.

	Credit to buyer	Credit to seller
a. Selling price of property ($100,000)		
b. Balance of existing mortgage loan, assumed by the buyer ($40,500)		
c. Mortgage interest accrued but not yet due ($300)		
d. Property tax reserve account ($600)		
e. Premium for unexpired portion of insurance policy ($320)		
f. Accrued portion of real estate tax ($450)		
g. Prepaid security service ($175)		
h. Fuel oil in tank on closing day ($150)		
i. Water bill proration earned but not yet due ($100)		
j. Rents collected but unearned ($805)		
k. Tenants' security deposits ($2,000)		

The chart that follows lists the credits that you used in Exercise 1. For each of these credits there must be a debit, or charge, to the other party, who must pay for the items. For example, the selling price is a credit to the seller and must be a debit to the buyer.

> In this chapter, the term *debit* will be used to mean a charge, expense or cost to either the seller or the buyer.

2. Complete the following chart by entering the amount of each debit in the debit column of the buyer or seller.

	Buyer Debit	Buyer Credit	Seller Debit	Seller Credit
a. Selling price				100,000
b. Assumed mortgage loan balance		40,500		
c. Accrued interest on assumed loan		300		
d. Tax reserve account				600
e. Insurance premium proration				320
f. Accrued portion of real estate tax		450		
g. Prepaid watch service				175
h. Fuel oil in tank				150
i. Prorated accrued water bill		100		
j. Unearned rents collected		805		
k. Tenants' security deposits		2,000		

ENTRY OF FIGURES

There are definite rules governing the entry of the figures in a four-column closing statement. In Exercise 2, which you have just completed, you followed Rule 1, which is:

> **Rule 1.** The sale price and all the prorations of accrued and prepaid items between buyer and seller are each entered as a *debit* to one party and a *credit* to the other party.

There are three kinds of items that are *entered only once*. These are a debit or a credit to one party without an offsetting second entry. Such items are covered by Rule 2:

> **Rule 2.** ■ *Earnest money*—a credit to the buyer. This money is deposited by the buyer and is usually held by the broker until the closing, when it is applied toward the purchase price. This money is not directly credited to the seller but becomes a part of the "balance due seller at closing."
>
> ■ *Seller's expenses*—debits to the seller. These are personal expenses of the seller, such as broker's commission, transfer tax stamps, etc., that do not involve the buyer.
>
> ■ *Buyer's expenses*—debits to the buyer. These are personal expenses of the buyer that do not affect the seller, such as the fee for recording the seller's deed and the lender's fee for the buyer's assumption of the seller's mortgage balance.

3. Using the following form, indicate which items are (1) prorated between buyer and seller as a debit to one and a credit to the other, and (2) personal to either the buyer or seller and therefore are entered only once.

	Entered twice	Entered once			
	Debit and credit	Credit seller	Debit seller	Credit buyer	Debit buyer
Sale price					
Earnest money deposit					
Assumed mortgage principal					
Interest on assumed mortgage					
Real estate tax proration					
Fuel oil in tank					
Recording fee for seller's deed					
Seller's commission to broker					
Buyer's title examination cost					

Types of Entries

The following list shows all the entries that are included in the preparation of a four-column closing statement, grouped by type of entry and how each is typically debited or credited. Local practices may differ.

1. *Purchase price*—entered as a debit to the buyer and as a credit to the seller.
2. *Earnest money*—credited only to the buyer. (It is offset by a part of the figure titled ''due to seller at closing.'')
3. *Balance of assumed mortgage and accrued interest*—debited to the seller and credited to the buyer. (The proceeds of a *new mortgage* obtained by the buyer, however, is a credit to the buyer *without* a corresponding debit to the seller, because the buyer receives this money from the lender. The seller's existing mortgage must then be paid off by a debit to the seller.)
4. *Purchase-money mortgage*—credited to the buyer, who assumes an obligation for future payments; also debited to the seller, who accepts the note as cash.
5. *Prorations*—debited to one party *and* credited to the other:

Items debited to buyer and credited to seller

- prepaid insurance premiums
- prepaid real estate taxes
- insurance and tax reserves
- coal or fuel oil on hand
- prepaid utilities
- personal property purchased by buyer
- overdue rent from tenants (local custom may govern this)

Items debited to seller and credited to buyer

- principal of mortgage assumed by buyer
- accrued interest on existing assumed mortgage not yet payable
- accrued portion of real estate tax not yet due
- unearned portion of rent collected in advance
- accrued salaries of personnel (such as janitor or manager)
- tenants' security deposits

Other items may be included, depending on the customs of your area.

6. *Expenses charged (debited) to seller or buyer*—to be paid by the broker or whoever is closing the sale:

Debits to seller

- broker's commission
- legal fee for drawing the deed
- cost of termite inspection
- title expenses required by the sale agreement
- loan discount points
- repairs
- filing fee: assignment of lien
- loan payoff fees
- filing fee: release of lien
- structural certificates
- loan discount fees (if required by contract or lender)

Debits to buyer

- assumption or transfer fee (when buyer assumes an existing mortgage)
- survey (if required by lender)
- new mortgage loan fee (service fee charged by lending institution)
- recording fees: deed and mortgage
- loan origination fee
- copies of restrictions
- credit report
- photos of property
- prepaid taxes, insurance and interest
- mortgage insurance premium
- flood insurance premium
- appraisal fee

Debits to party responsible or shared by seller and buyer

- transfer tax
- cost of title insurance or title examination
- legal fees
- escrow fee
- inspection fees

Other items may be included, depending on the customs of your area and the provisions of the sales contract.

The preparation of a four-column closing statement is similar to the preparation of separate closing statements for the seller and buyer. These statements consist of debits and credits. *A debit is a charge*—a debt or amount that the party being debited owes and must pay out of the closing proceeds. *A credit is an amount entered in a party's favor,* which the party being credited has already paid or promises to pay, in the form of a note for a loan, or for which the party must be reimbursed. When the buyer's debits have been entered and totaled, then the buyer's credits are totaled and subtracted from the debits. This will determine the net amount of cash that the buyer must pay to close the purchase. The difference between the seller's total credits and debits represents the amount due to the seller at the closing.

4. Examine the following situation; then enter the items on the form provided and determine (1) the amount the buyer will owe at closing and (2) the amount the seller will receive at closing.

A house has been sold for $40,000, and the buyer has placed an earnest money deposit of $4,000 with the seller's real estate broker. The seller has agreed to pay the broker a 6% commission on the sale price.

	Buyer		Seller	
	Debit	Credit	Debit	Credit
Sale price				
Earnest money				
Broker's commission				
Subtotals				
Due from buyer at closing				
Due to seller at closing				
Totals				

5. Now prepare a complete closing statement by computing the prorations and entering the other necessary figures for the real estate transaction itemized below. Use the blank form on page 266. Then, compare your statement to the one on page 286.

Sellers are Lester N. Smith and Mary B. Smith, 216 West Park, Pleasantown. They are selling the property located at that address.

Sellers' broker is Homestead Realty.

Buyers are Mark T. Haney and Liza A. Haney, 1313 Grove Avenue, Pleasantown.

Contract of sale is dated June 28, 1989.

Closing date is July 14, 1989.

Sale price is $62,500.

Earnest money is $6,000.

The buyers are to assume the sellers' mortgage, including the 9% interest. The principal balance of the mortgage after the June 20 monthly payment is $47,500.

Real estate taxes of $1,648 for the calendar year 1988 have been paid.

A tax reserve account of $824 is held by the mortgage lender.

The sellers paid $129.60 for a one-year fire insurance policy, which expires April 8, 1990, and which the buyers will assume.

The buyers will be charged $75 by the mortgage lender—the cost of changing records to show their assumption of the sellers' mortgage loan.

Buyers must pay the county recorder $7.50 to record the sellers' deed.

Sales commission is 6% of gross sale price.

$150 fee for sellers' title search.

Sellers' state transfer tax stamps. (The transfer tax in this example is based on a tax rate of $.50 for each $500 or fraction thereof of the sale price in excess of the assumed mortgage.)

Remember that the two "buyer's" columns must always balance, as must the two "seller's" columns. There is no need to compare the totals of both statements.

Important: For these exercises, compute prorations on a 360-day year and 30-day month when calculating dollar amounts. When calculating the number of days, use the actual number of days in the month of closing. However, local custom may vary.

Use the following space for your computations.

SETTLEMENT STATEMENT WORKSHEET

	Buyer's statement		Seller's statement	
	Debit	Credit	Debit	Credit
Purchase price				
Earnest money				
Mortgage—assumed				
Interest on mortgage				
General taxes to date				
Tax reserve				
Insurance premiums				
Buyer's expenses:				
Assumption fee				
Recording fee				
Seller's expenses:				
Title search				
Broker's commission				
Transfer tax				
Subtotal				
Due from buyer				
Due to seller				
Totals				

RECONCILIATION

The use of the four-column statement presents complete and accurate figures of the net amounts that the buyer must pay after deducting the buyer's expenses and that the seller will receive after payment of the broker's commission and all other seller's expenses.

This form of statement presupposes that the broker will handle all the funds at the closing. In order for the closer to be sure that all entries on the statement are properly handled and that more funds are not being paid out than are being received, a cash reconciliation or recapitulation should always be prepared.

6. Using information from Exercise 5, fill in the figures in the following chart for (1) the balance due from buyer, (2) the paid amount due seller, and (3) the totals.

Broker's Reconciliation

	Receipts	Disbursements
Earnest money	6,000.00	
Due from buyer at closing		
Paid seller's expenses:		
Broker's commission		3,750.00
Title and transfer tax		165.00
Paid buyer's expenses		82.50
Paid amount due seller at closing		
Totals		

7. Work the following closing statement problem, and enter the figures on the form on page 269. The broker will close the transaction.

John P. Smith and Helen A. Smith, husband and wife, of 2419 Monroe Street, Rockford, told their broker that they wanted to net $90,500 on the sale of their building after paying the broker's commission of 6-1/2%. ABC Realtors agreed to take the listing of the two-family apartment building. The present mortgage had a principal balance of $37,000 after the May 1, 1989, monthly payment was credited. The monthly mortgage payment, due the first day of each month, is $396, which includes the 9-1/2% interest for the previous month.

Frank P. Jones and Linda K. Jones, of 1010 Lincoln Drive, Rockford, signed a purchase contract for this building on May 15, 1989, which the sellers accepted and signed. This will net the Smiths $89,760 after the broker's commission is deducted. The buyers will assume the sellers' mortgage, and the sellers agree to take back a $10,000 purchase-money mortgage note to be paid on or before 5 years from closing, with 10% monthly interest.

On the closing date, which has been set for June 16, 1989, the sellers will be considered the owners of the property, which means that you are to prorate through date of closing. The buyers have already given the broker a 10% earnest money deposit and have yet to pay a $50 title insurance charge. The sellers' title charge is $100. The real estate tax bill for the calendar year 1988 of $1,420 has been paid in full. The buyers have also agreed to pay for 56 gallons of fuel oil remaining in the tank at closing, at a cost of $.75 per gallon.

The sellers have two insurance policies which are paid in full. The buyers have agreed to assume both policies since they are transferable. One, a 4-year policy that cost $800, expires August 9, 1991. The other, a 3-year policy that cost $330, expires June 30, 1990.

On June 1, 1989, the sellers made their last regular monthly payment on the mortgage. The upper apartment is rented at $300 per month; the sellers occupy the lower apartment. The sellers have collected the June 1, 1989, rent and hold a security deposit equivalent to a month's rent. The sellers agree to pay the transfer tax stamps on their deed, which is $.50 per $500 or any fraction thereof of the next taxable consideration after the deduction of the assumed mortgage. The buyers agree to pay the recording fee of $15, the survey fee of $150, and the cost of preparing the purchase-money mortgage, which is $50. The sellers' expenses include preparing the deed, at a cost of $30, and termite inspection, which also costs $30. The broker is to disburse all of these expenses on the day of closing.

Compute the necessary prorations and prepare the four-column closing statement for this sale. Use the 30-day month for calculating the dollar amount and 30 for the number of days in the month of closing. Figure decimals to three places within the problem, but round to two places when writing in your figures on the statement. Also, prepare a broker's reconciliation using the form on page 270.

Read the following instructions before you begin.

To use the worksheet most efficiently, follow these steps:

1. As you read through the information given for the problem, list the types of expenses included in the transaction in the left-hand column of the worksheet.

2. Go through the list of expenses and consider those expenses related to the buyer; make any necessary proration computations, and record each buyer-related expense as either a debit or a credit to the buyer.

   Debits to the buyer have the effect of *increasing the amount the buyer owes* at closing. They include the purchase price of the property, all prorations of prepaid items and personal expenses of the buyer, such as the fee for recording the seller's deed. Credits to the buyer, on the other hand, have the effect of *decreasing the amount the buyer owes*. They include the earnest money deposit, balance of assumed mortgage and all prorations of accrued items.

3. Next, go through the list of expenses and consider those expenses related to the seller; make necessary proration computations and record each seller-related expense as either a debit or a credit to the seller.

   Debits to the seller have the effect of *decreasing the amount due* the seller at closing. They include the balance of assumed mortgage, all prorations of accrued items and personal expenses of the seller, such as broker's commission and transfer tax stamps, etc., that do not involve the buyer. Credits to the seller have the effect of *increasing the amount due* the seller. They include the selling price of the property and all prorations of prepaid items.

4. Total the buyer's debit and credit columns, and subtract the lesser from the greater total to determine what amount the buyer must pay at the closing (if debits exceed credits).

5. Total the seller's debit and credit columns, and subtract the lesser from the greater total to determine what amount the seller will pay at the closing (if debits exceed credits) or what amount the seller will be paid at the closing (if credits exceed debits).

6. Prepare the broker's reconciliation to verify that all items are entered in the proper columns.

   Use the space below for your computations.

SETTLEMENT STATEMENT WORKSHEET

Property _____

Seller _____

Buyer _____

Settlement Date _____

	Buyer's Statement		Seller's Statement	
	Debit	Credit	Debit	Credit

Broker's Reconciliation

Items	Receipts	Disbursements

8. The following questions are to be answered from the completed closing statement in Exercise 7.

a. The earnest money deposit is a:

    I. credit to sellers.
    II. debit to buyers.

      a. I only
      b. II only
      c. both I and II
      d. neither I nor II

b. The amount of prorated taxes is:

    I. $654.77 debit to sellers.
    II. $654.77 credit to buyers.

      a. I only
      b. II only
      c. both I and II
      d. neither I nor II

c. The amount of the prorated insurance premiums is a:

    I. debit to buyers.
    II. credit to sellers.

      a. I only
      b. II only
      c. both I and II
      d. neither I nor II

d. The purchase-money mortgage is a:

    I. credit to buyers.
    II. credit to sellers.

      a. I only
      b. II only
      c. both I and II
      d. neither I nor II

e. The total of the buyer's debits is:

    I. $41,978.73.
    II. $96,850.70.

      a. I only
      b. II only
      c. both I and II
      d. neither I nor II

f. The tenant's security deposit is a:

    I. credit to sellers.
    II. debit to buyers.

      a. I only
      b. II only
      c. both I and II
      d. neither I nor II

g. The balance due seller at closing is:

    I. $39,103.23.
    II. $41,978.73.

      a. I only
      b. II only
      c. both I and II
      d. neither I nor II

h. The total of the seller's expenses is:

      a. $219.50.
      b. $6,240.00.
      c. $6,359.50.
      d. $6,459.50.

i. The total due from buyer at closing is:

      a. $41,978.73.
      b. $39,103.23.
      c. $2,875.50.
      d. $48,703.23.

j. The listing price is:

      a. $96,000.
      b. $90,500.
      c. $96,800 rounded off.
      d. $89,800 rounded off.

9. Thomas J. Morra and Helen T. Morra of 316 Washburn Street, Pleasantown, have listed their house with Quincy Realty for $89,000 and have agreed to pay the broker a 7% commission on the actual sale price. The present mortgage had a principal balance of $42,000 after the August 31, 1988, monthly payment was credited. Monthly mortgage payments are $405, due the last day of each month, and each pays the interest to and including that date, calculated on the declining balance at 8.5%. James P. Trent and Sara K. Trent of 808 Lake, Pleasantown, signed a contract on September 2, 1988, agreeing to purchase the house for $86,500. They will assume the present mortgage and make the October payment.

The closing date has been set for October 15, 1988. The buyers have given a 10% earnest money deposit to the broker, and the buyers have agreed to pay half of the title insurance policy cost of $150. The sellers have given the broker the authority to pay the full amount in advance. The real estate tax bill for the calendar year 1986 was $1,200 and was paid in full. The water bill for 1987 was $96, and was also paid in full. The Morras have an insurance policy that expires August 9, 1990. The original cost of this 4-year policy was $1,000, and it was paid in full. The buyers will take over this policy since it is transferable. The sellers will pay for the transfer tax, which is $.55 per $500 or any fraction thereof of the net taxable consideration (assumed mortgages exempt) and have authorized the broker to advance the money necessary.

The following additional expenses were incurred in settling the transaction:

Sellers

- title examination fee, $200
- preparation of deed, $75

Buyers

- mortgage assumption fee, 1% of assumed mortgage
- fee to record deed, $.20 per $100 of purchase price

Compute the necessary prorations and prepare the closing statement for this sale. Use the blank form on the next page. Also, prepare a broker's reconciliation using the form on page 274.

Use the following space for your computations.

SETTLEMENT STATEMENT WORKSHEET

Property _____

Seller _____

Buyer _____

Settlement Date _____

	Buyer's Statement		Seller's Statement	
	Debit	Credit	Debit	Credit

Broker's Reconciliation

Items	Receipts	Disbursements

For instructional purposes, we have used simple forms in this chapter, but in actual practice, each person or company performing a closing may use his or her own printed forms. An exception to this practice occurs any time a buyer obtains a new loan that is connected to the U.S. Government in any way. In such a case, a specific Department of Housing and Urban Development form is required, as a result of legislation known as the Real Estate Settlement Procedures Act, or RESPA. A copy of this 2-page form is shown in Figure 14.1. Page 2 of the HUD form must be completed first because page 1 is a summary of the detailed items there. Also, the term *debit* is not used; the RESPA form merely says ''paid from borrower's/seller's funds.'' In this chapter, you learned that in real estate settlement language, *debit* means ''charged to'' or a ''cost to'' the buyer or the seller.

Figure 14.1 is an actual disbursement sheet from a closing office, and this sheet is identical to the Broker's Reconciliation that you have worked with in this chapter. Both show that money received equals money disbursed, or paid out.

FIGURE 14.1

STEWART TITLE

TEXAS   OMB No. 2502.

A.	U.S. DEPARTMENT OF HOUSING AND URBAN DEVELOPMENT	B. TYPE OF LOAN:
		1. ☐ FHA 2. ☐ FMHA 3. ☐ CONV. UNINS
		4. ☐ VA 5. ☐ CONV. INS.
		6. FILE NUMBER 7. LOAN NUMBER
	SETTLEMENT STATEMENT	8. MORTG. INS. CASE NO.

C. NOTE: This form is furnished to give you a statement of actual settlement costs. Amounts paid to and by the settlement agent are shown. Items marked "(p.o.c.)" were paid outside the closing: they are shown here for informational purposes and are not included in the totals.

D. NAME AND ADDRESS OF BORROWER	E. NAME AND ADDRESS OF SELLER	F. NAME AND ADDRESS OF LENDER

G. PROPERTY LOCATION	H. SETTLEMENT AGENT	I. SETTLEMENT DATE:
	PLACE OF SETTLEMENT	

J. SUMMARY OF BORROWER'S TRANSACTION		K. SUMMARY OF SELLER'S TRANSACTION	
100. GROSS AMOUNT DUE FROM BORROWER:		**400. GROSS AMOUNT DUE TO SELLER:**	
101. Contract sales price		401. Contract sales price	
102. Personal property		402. Personal property	
103. Settlement charges to borrow (line 1400)		403.	
104.		404.	
105.		405.	
Adjustments for items paid by seller in advance:		Adjustments for items paid by seller in advance:	
106. City/town taxes to		406. City/town taxes to	
107. County taxes to		407. County taxes to	
108. Assessments to		408. Assessments to	
109. Maintenance to		409. Maintenance to	
110. School/Taxes to		410. School/Taxes to	
111.		411.	
112.		412.	
120. GROSS AMOUNT DUE FROM BORROWER:		**420. GROSS AMOUNT DUE TO SELLER:**	
200. AMOUNTS PAID BY OR IN BEHALF OF BORROWER:		**500. REDUCTIONS IN AMOUNT DUE TO SELLER:**	
201. Deposit or earnest money		501. Excess deposit (see instructions)	
202. Principal amount of new loan(s)		502. Settlement charges to seller (line 1400)	
203. Existing loan(s) taken subject to		503. Existing loan(s) taken subject to	
204. Commitment Fee		504. Payoff of first mortgage loan	
205.		505. Payoff of second mortgage loan	
206.		506.	
207.		507.	
208.		508.	
209.		509.	
Adjustments for items unpaid by seller:		Adjustments for items unpaid by seller:	
210. City/town taxes to		510. City/town taxes to	
211. County taxes to		511. County taxes to	
212. Assessments to		512. Assessments to	
213. School/Taxes to		513. School/Taxes to	
214.		514. Maintenance to	
215.		515.	
216.		516.	
217.		517.	
218.		518.	
219.		519.	
220. TOTAL PAID BY/FOR BORROWER:		**520. TOTAL REDUCTION AMOUNT DUE SELLER:**	
300. CASH AT SETTLMENT FROM/TO BORROWER:		**600. CASH AT SETTLEMENT TO/FROM SELLER:**	
301. Gross amount due from borrower (line 120)		601. Gross amount due to seller (line 420)	
302. Less amounts paid by/for borrower (line 220)		602. Less total reductions in amount due seller (line 520)	
303. CASH (☐ FROM) (☐ TO) BORROWER:		603. CASH (☐ TO) (☐ FROM) SELLER:	

HUD—1
RESPA. HB 430

TEXAS/LDI

PAGE 2 OF OMB No. 2502-0265

L. SETTLEMENT CHARGES	PAID FROM BORROWER'S FUNDS AT SETTLEMENT	PAID FROM SELLER'S FUNDS AT SETTLEMENT
700. TOTAL SALES/BROKER'S COMMISSION Based on price $ @ %=		
Division of commission (line 700) as follows:		
701. $ to		
702. $ to		
703. Commission paid at settlement		
704.		
800. ITEMS PAYABLE IN CONNECTION WITH LOAN.		
801. Loan Origination fee %		
802. Loan Discount %		
803. Appraisal Fee to		
804. Credit Report to		
805. Lender's inspection fee		
806. Mortgage Insurance application fee to		
807. Assumption Fee		
808. Commitment Fee		
809. FNMA Processing Fee		
810. Pictures		
811.		
900. ITEMS REQUIRED BY LENDER TO BE PAID IN ADVANCE.		
901. Interest from to @ $ /day		
902. Mortgage insurance premium for mo. to		
903. Hazard insurance premium for yrs. to		
904. Flood Insurance yrs. to		
905.		
1000. RESERVES DEPOSITED WITH LENDER		
1001. Hazard insurance mo. @ $ per mo.		
1002. Mortgage insurance mo. @ $ per mo.		
1003. City property taxes mo. @ $ per mo.		
1004. County property taxes mo. @ $ per mo.		
1005. Annual assessments (Maint.) mo. @ $ per mo.		
1006. School Property Taxes mo. @ $ per mo.		
1007. Water Dist. Prop. Tax mo. @ $ per mo.		
1008. Flood Insurance mo. @ $ per mo.		
1100. TITLE CHARGES:		
1101. Settlement or closing fee to		
1102. Abstract or title search to		
1103. Title examination to		
1104. Title insurance binder to		
1105. Document preparation to		
1106. Notary fees to		
1107. Attorney's fees to to		
(includes above items No.:		
1108. Title insurance to		
(includes above items No.:		
1109. Lender's coverage $		
1110. Owner's coverage $		
1111. Escrow Fee		
1112. Restrictions		
1113. Messenger Service		
1114. State of Texas Policy Guaranty Fee		
1200. GOVERNMENT RECORDING AND TRANSFER CHARGES		
1201. Recording fees: Deed $ Mortgage $ Releases $		
1202. City/county tax/stamps: Deed $ Mortgage $		
1203. State tax/stamps: Deed $ Mortgage $		
1204. Tax Certificates		
1205.		
1206. IRS Reporting Fee		
1300. ADDITIONAL SETTLEMENT CHARGES		
1301. Survey to		
1302. Pest inspection to		
1303.		
1304.		
1305.		
1400. TOTAL SETTLEMENT CHARGES (entered on lines 103, Section J and 502, Section K)		

CERTIFICATION: I have carefully reviewed the HUD-1 Settlement Statement and to the best of my knowledge and belief, it is a true and accurate statement of all receipts and disbursements made on my account or by me in this transaction. I further certify that I have received a copy of HUD-1 Settlement Statement.

Borrowers _____ Sellers _____

To the best of my knowledge, the HUD-1 Settlement Statement which I have prepared is a true and accurate account of the funds which were received and have been or will be disbursed by the undersigned as part of the settlement of this transaction.

STEWART TITLE COMPANY

Settlement Agent _____ Date _____

SELLER'S AND/OR PURCHASER'S STATEMENT Seller's and Purchaser's signature hereon acknowledges his/their approval of tax prorations and signifies their understanding that prorations were based on taxes for the preceding year, or estimates for the current year, and in the event of any change for the current year, all necessary adjustments must be made between Seller and Purchaser; likewise any default in delinquent taxes will be reimbursed to Title Company by the Seller. Title Company, in its capacity as Escrow Agent, is and has been authorized to deposit all funds it receives in this transaction in any financial institution, whether affiliated or not. Such financial institution may provide Title Company computer accounting and audit services directly or through a separate entity which, if affiliated with Title Company, may charge the financial institution reasonable and proper compensation therefore and retain any profits therefrom. Any escrow fees paid by any party involved in this transaction shall only be for checkwriting and input to the computers, but not for aforesaid accounting and audit services. Title Company shall not be liable for any interest or other charges on the earnest money and shall be under no duty to invest or reinvest funds held by it at any time. Sellers and Purchasers hereby acknowledge and consent to the deposit of the escrow money in financial institutions with which Title Company has or may have other banking relationships and further consent to the retention by Title Company and/or its affiliates of any and all benefits (including advantageous interest rates on loans) Title Company and/or its affiliates may receive from such financial institutions by reason of their maintenance of said escrow accounts.

The parties have read the above sentences, recognize that the recitations herein are material, agree to same, and recognize Title Company is relying on the same.

Purchasers/Borrowers _____ Sellers _____

WARNING: It is a crime to knowingly make false statements to the United States on this or any other similar form. Penalties upon conviction can include a fine and imprisonment. For details see: Title 18: U.S. Code Section 1001 and Section 1010.

FIGURE 14.2

GF#_____

BUYER/BORROWER	SELLER	PROPERTY

RECEIPTS

DATE	RECEIPT NO.	FROM	AMOUNT
			$
		TOTAL	$

DISBURSEMENTS

DATE	CHECK NO.	CHECK TO	AMOUNT
		STEWART TITLE GUARANTY COMPANY	

MESSENGER	RESTRICTIONS
OWNER'S POLICY	RECORDING
MORTGAGEE'S POLICY	TAX CERTIFICATES
ESCROW	

DATE	CHECK NO.	CHECK TO	AMOUNT
		TOTAL	$

_____
ESCROW OFFICER

ACHIEVEMENT EXERCISE

Work the following closing statement problem and enter the figures on the form on page 281. Also, prepare a broker's reconciliation using the form on page 282, and answer the multiple-choice questions that begin on that page. Check your answers against those on pages 294–295.

The Stanicks are purchasing the Rooneys' house. The sale price is $45,000. A 10% earnest money deposit is being held by the broker. The Stanicks will assume the present mortgage, which had a principal balance of $27,800 after the July 1, 1988 monthly payment was credited. The closing date has been set for August 3, 1988. The mortgage has an interest rate of 7.5%, and payments of $220.50 are due on the first day of each month, including interest to, but not including, the day of payment. The last payment was made on August 1, 1988. The Rooneys have a 3-year insurance policy which will expire on September 20, 1990. The $900 insurance premium has been paid in full. The real estate taxes for the calendar year 1987, $1,200, were paid in full. The 1987 water bill of $56 has also been paid in full. The Stanicks will pay for the 60 gallons of fuel remaining in the tank, at $.90 per gallon. The second floor rent is $250 per month, payable on or before the first day of the month. August rent has been paid. The Rooneys hold a month's rent as a security deposit. The Stanicks have agreed to pay half of the $300 title expense. The broker's commission will be 6.5%. Transfer tax in this case is charged at $.50 per $500 or fractional part thereof of the taxable consideration; assumed mortgages are deductible in computing the tax. Prorate through the date of closing.

The following additional expenses were incurred in settling the transaction:

- mortgage assumption fee, $100
- preparation of deed, $50
- fee to record deed, $15
- survey fee, $75

1. Earnest money deposit:

2. Mortgage interest proration:

3. Real estate tax proration:

4. Insurance proration:

5. Rent proration:

6. Fuel proration:

7. Water bill proration:

8. Title expense:

9. Commission:

10. Transfer tax:

SETTLEMENT STATEMENT WORKSHEET

Property _____

Seller _____

Buyer _____

Settlement Date _____

	Buyer's Statement		Seller's Statement	
	Debit	Credit	Debit	Credit

Broker's Reconciliation

Items	Receipts	Disbursements

Questions 11–13 refer to the closing statement you just completed.

11. The earnest money deposit is shown as a:

    I. credit to the seller.
    II. debit to the purchaser.

      a. I only
      b. II only
      c. both I and II
      d. neither I nor II

12. The amount due from the purchaser at closing is:

    I. $12,536.12.
    II. a credit to the purchaser.

      a. I only
      b. II only
      c. both I and II
      d. neither I nor II

13. The amount due the seller at closing is:

    I. $13,553.62.
    II. a credit to the seller.

      a. I only
      b. II only
      c. both I and II
      d. neither I nor II

14. A purchase-money mortgage is:

    I. credited to the buyer.
    II. credited to the seller.
    III. prorated and divided between the buyer and seller.
    IV. debited to the seller.

      a. II only
      b. III only
      c. I and IV
      d. I, III and IV

15. A federal government settlement form is required, when the real estate purchase is connected to the U.S. Government in any way. This rule applies:

    I. as a result of the Real Estate Settlement Procedures Act.
    II. in the state of Idaho.
    III. for FHA-insured loans.
    IV. for HUD housing loans.

        a. I only
        b. none of the above
        c. I, III and IV
        d. all of the above

ANSWER KEY

Pages 261–272

1. a. The *seller* receives credit for the total selling price of the property, which the buyer has agreed to pay.

    b. The *buyer* receives credit for assuming the seller's existing mortgage loan. The balance due on the mortgage note is an offset to the selling price.

    c. The *buyer* receives credit for the interest incurred to date by the seller, which the buyer must pay at the next mortgage payment date.

    d. When the buyer is assuming the seller's mortgage, the *seller* receives credit for any money held in a tax reserve account with the mortgage lender that will be transferred to the buyer.

    e. The *seller* receives credit for the "unused" amount of a prepaid insurance premium he or she is selling to the buyer.

    f. The *buyer* receives a credit for the seller's share of the accrued real estate tax up to the closing date, since the buyer must pay the *total* tax when it becomes due.

    g. The *seller* receives credit for money he or she has paid in advance for services that will benefit the buyer after the closing.

    h. The *seller* receives credit for fuel on hand which has already been paid for but which the buyer will use.

    i. The *buyer* receives credit for the water that the seller has used prior to closing, since the buyer will have to pay for the total billing period when the bill becomes due.

    j. The *buyer* receives credit for rent collected in advance by the seller, which represents rent for that part of the month during which the buyer will own the building.

    k. The *buyer* receives credit for each security deposit held by the seller but which the buyer, as the new landlord, must return if a tenant decides not to renew his or her lease.

Pages 261–272 continued

2.

	Buyer		Seller	
	Debit	Credit	Debit	Credit
a. Selling price	100,000			100,00
b. Assumed mortgage loan balance		40,500	40,500	
c. Accrued interest on assumed loan		300	300	
d. Tax reserve account	600			600
e. Insurance premium proration	320			320
f. Accrued portion of real estate tax		450	450	
g. Prepaid watch service	175			175
h. Fuel oil in tank	150			150
i. Prorated accrued water bill		100	100	
j. Unearned rents collected		805	805	
k. Tenants' security deposits		2,000	2,000	

3.

	Entered twice		Entered once	
	Debit and credit	Debit seller	Credit buyer	Debit buyer
Sale price	x			
Earnest money deposit			x	
Assumed mortgage principal	x			
Interest on assumed mortgage	x			
Real estate tax proration	x			
Fuel oil in tank	x			
Recording fee for seller's deed				x
Seller's commission to broker		x		
Buyer's title examination cost				x

4.

	Buyer		Seller	
	Debit	Credit	Debit	Credit
Sale price	40,000			40,000
Earnest money		4,000		
Broker's commission			2,400	
Subtotals	40,000	4,000	2,400	40,000
Due from buyer at closing		36,000		
Due to seller at closing			37,600	
Totals	40,000	40,000	40,000	40,000

5. Interest:

$47,500 $\times$ 9% = $4,275 annual interest

$4,275 $\div$ 360 = $11.875 daily interest

$$
\begin{array}{rl}
30 & \text{total days in June} \\
-20 & \text{date of last interest payment (June 20)} \\
\hline
10 & \text{number of days of accrued interest in June} \\
+14 & \text{number of days of accrued interest in July} \\
\hline
24 & \text{total days of accrued interest}
\end{array}
$$

$11.875 $\times$ 24 days = $285 accrued interest

General taxes:

$1,648 $\div$ 12 = $137.333 monthly tax

$137.333 $\div$ 30 = $4.577 daily tax

accrued tax period = January 1 through July 14 = 6 months and 14 days

$137.333 $\times$ 6 months = $823.998

$4.577 $\times$ 14 days = $64.078

$823.998 + $64.078 = $888.076 rounded to $888.08 accrued tax

Insurance:

$129.60 $\div$ 12 = $10.80 monthly insurance premium

$10.80 $\div$ 30 = $.36 daily insurance premium

years	months	days
	15	
1989	~~3~~	39
~~1990~~	~~4~~	~~8~~
1989	7	14
0	8	25

$10.80 $\times$ 8 months = $86.40 $.36 $\times$ 25 days = $9.00

$86.40 + $9.00 = $95.40 unexpired insurance premium

Broker's commission:

$62,500 $\times$ .06 = $3,750

Transfer tax stamps:

sale price = $62,500   assumed mortgage = $47,500

$62,500 − $47,500 = $15,000 taxable consideration

$15,000 $\div$ $500 = $30 $\times$ $.50 = $15 transfer tax

Pages 261–272 continued

SETTLEMENT STATEMENT WORKSHEET

Closing date: July 14, 1989	Buyer's statement		Seller's statement	
	Debit	Credit	Debit	Credit
Purchase price	62,500.00			62,500.00
Earnest money		6,000.00		
Mortgage—assumed		47,500.00	47,500.00	
Interest on mortgage		285.00	285.00	
General taxes to date		888.08	888.08	
Tax reserve	824.00			824.00
Insurance premiums	95.40			95.40
Buyer's expenses:				
Assumption fee	75.00			
Recording fee	7.50			
Seller's expenses:				
Title search			150.00	
Broker's commission			3,750.00	
Transfer tax			15.00	
Subtotal	63,501.90	54,673.08	52,588.08	63,419.40
Due from buyer		8,828.82		
Due to seller			10,831.32	
Totals	63,501.90	63,501.90	63,419.40	63,419.40

6.   **Broker's Reconciliation**

	Receipts	Disbursements
Earnest money	6,000.00	
Due from buyer at closing	8,828.82	
Paid seller's expenses		
Broker's commission		3,750.00
Title and transfer tax		165.00
Paid buyer's expenses		82.50
Paid amount due seller at closing		10,831.32
Totals	14,828.82	14,828.82

7. $89,760 ÷ (100% − 6-1/2%) = $96,000 purchase price
$96,000 × 10% = $9,600 earnest money deposit

Mortgage principal and interest proration:
$37,000 × 9-1/2% = $3,515 annual interest $3,515 ÷ 12 = $292.916 monthly interest for May
$396 June 1 payment − $292.916 = $103.084 applied to principal
$37,000 − $103.084 = $36,896.916 June 1 balance
$36,896.916 × 9-1/2% = $3,505.207 $3,505.207 ÷ 360 days = $9.736 daily interest
$9.736 × 16 days = $155.776 rounded to $155.78 accrued interest

Real estate tax proration:
$1,420 ÷ 12 = $118.333 monthly tax $118.333 ÷ 30 = $3.944 daily tax
$118.333 × 5 months = $591.665
$3.944 × 16 days = $63.104
$591.665 + $63.104 = $654.769 rounded to $654.77 tax proration

Oil:
56 gallons @ $.75 per gallon = $42

4-year insurance policy proration:

years	months	days
	7	39
1991	8̶	9̶
1989	6	16
2	1	23

$800 ÷ 4 years = $200 per year $200 ÷ 12 months = $16.666 per month
$16.666 ÷ 30 days = $0.555 per day
2 years × $200 = $400
1 month × $16.666 = $16.666
23 days × $0.555 = $12.765
$400 + $16.666 + $12.765 = $429.431 rounded to $429.43 proration

3-year insurance policy proration:

years	months	days	
1990	6	30	expiration
1989	6	16	closing
1	0	14	

$330 ÷ 3 years = $110 per year
$110 ÷ 12 months = $9.166 per month $9.166 ÷ 30 days = $0.305 per day
$110 × 1 year = $110
$0.305 × 14 days = $4.27
$110 + $4.27 = $114.27 proration

Rent:
$300 ÷ 30 days = $10 per day
June: 30 days − 16 days = 14 days   14 days × $10 = $140 proration

Broker's commission:
$96,000 × 6-1/2% = $6,240

Transfer tax on deed:
$96,000 − $36,896.92 = $59,103.08 taxable
$59,103.08 ÷ 500 = $118.206 rounded to $119 $119 × $.50 = $59.50 tax

Pages 261–272 continued

SETTLEMENT STATEMENT WORKSHEET

Property _____ 2419 Monroe Street, Rockford
Seller _____ John P. Smith and Helen A. Smith
Buyer _____ Frank P. Jones and Linda K. Jones
Settlement Date _____ June 16, 1989

	Buyer's statement		Seller's statement	
	Debit	Credit	Debit	Credit
Purchase price	96,000.00			96,000.00
Earnest money		9,600.00		
Mortgage — assumed		36,896.92	36,896.92	
Interest on mortgage		155.78	155.78	
Purchase-money mortgage		10,000.00	10,000.00	
Real estate taxes		654.77	654.77	
Oil in tank	42.00			42.00
Insurance proration (4-year policy)	429.43			429.43
Insurance proration (3-year policy)	114.27			114.27
Rent proration		140.00	140.00	
Security damage deposit		300.00	300.00	
Broker's commission			6,240.00	
Transfer tax			59.50	
Title insurance	50.00		100.00	
Recording fees	15.00			
Survey	150.00			
Preparation of purchase-money mortgage	50.00			
Preparation of deed			30.00	
Termite inspection			30.00	
Total debits and credits	96,850.70	57,747.47	54,606.97	96,585.70
Due from buyer at closing		39,103.23		
Due to seller at closing			41,978.72	
Totals	96,850.70	96,850.70	96,585.70	96,585.70

Broker's Reconciliation

Items	Receipts	Disbursements
Earnest money	9,600.00	
Due from buyer at closing	39,103.23	
Paid seller's expenses		
Broker's commission		6,240.00
Other expenses		219.50
Paid buyer's expenses		265.00
Paid amount due seller at closing		41,978.73
Totals	48,703.23	48,703.23

8. a. d It is a credit to buyers.

   b. c

   c. c

   d. a

   e. b

   f. d It is a credit to buyers and a debit to sellers.

   g. b

   h. d

   i. b

   j. c $\$90,500 \div 93\frac{1}{2}\% = \$96,791.44$ rounded to \$96,800.

9. Earnest money deposit:
$\$86,500 \times 10\% = \$8,650$ earnest money

Mortgage principal and interest proration:
$\$42,000 \times 8.5\% = \$3,570$ annual interest
$\$3,570 \div 12 = \$297.50$ monthly interest for September
$\$405 - \$297.50 = \$107.50$ applied to principal
$\$42,000 - \$107.50 = \$41,892.50$ principal balance October 1, 1988, to be assumed by buyer

$\$41,892.50 \times 8.5\% = \$3,560.862$ annual interest
$\$3,560.862 \div 360 = \$9.891$ daily interest
Interest has accrued on the 15 days from October 1 through October 15.
$\$9.891 \times 15 = \$148.365$ rounded to \$148.37 accrued interest

Real estate tax proration:
$\$1,200 \div 12 = \$100$ monthly tax $\$100 \div 30 = \$3.333$ daily tax

1 year   1987
9 months   January through September 1988
15 days   15 days of October

Pages 261–272 continued

$1,200 × 1 year = $1,200 accrued tax for 1987
$100 × 9 months = $900 $3.333 × 15 days = $49.995
$900 + $49.995 = $949.995 rounded to $950 accrued tax for 1988
$1,200 + $950 = $2,150 total

Title insurance:
$150 ÷ 2 = $75 title insurance for both buyer and seller

4-year insurance policy proration:
$1,000 ÷ 4 = $250 annual insurance premium
$250 ÷ 12 = $20.833 monthly insurance premium
$20.833 ÷ 30 = $.694 daily insurance premium

years	months	days
	19	
1989	7̸	40
1990	8̸	9̸
− 1988	10	15
1	9	25

$250 × 1 year = $250 $20.833 × 9 months = $187.497 $.694 × 25 days = $17.35
$250 + $187.497 + $17.35 = $454.847 rounded to $454.85 unexpired insurance premium

Water:
Seller pays for 9 months and 15 days of water bill (January 1 through October 15, 1988).
$96 ÷ 12 = $8 monthly $8 ÷ 30 = $.266 daily
$8 × 9 months = $72 $.266 × 15 days = $3.99
$72 + $3.99 = $75.99 water proration

Broker's commission:
$86,500 × 7% = $6,055 broker's commission

Transfer tax:
$86,500 total price − $41,892.50 mortgage = $44,607.50 taxable consideration
$44,607.50 ÷ $500 = 89.215, rounded to 90 parts $.55 × 90 = $49.50 transfer tax

Mortgage assumption fee:
$41,892.50 × 1% = $418.925 rounded to $418.93 mortgage assumption fee

Recording fee:
$86,500 ÷ 100 = $865 $865 × $.20 = $173 recording fee

SETTLEMENT STATEMENT WORKSHEET

Property _____ 316 Washburn Street, Pleasantown _____

Seller _____ Thomas J. Morra and Helen T. Morra _____

Buyer _____ James P. Trent and Sara K. Trent _____

Settlement Date _____ October 15, 1988 _____

	Buyer's statement		Seller's statement	
	Debit	Credit	Debit	Credit
Purchase price	86,500.00			86,500.00
Earnest money		8,650.00		
Mortgage — assumed		41,892.50	41,892.50	
Interest on mortgage		148.37	148.37	
Real estate taxes		2,150.00	2,150.00	
Insurance proration (4-year policy)	454.85			454.85
Water bill proration		75.99	75.99	
Broker's commission			6,055.00	
Transfer tax			49.50	
Title insurance	75.00		75.00	
Mortgage assumption fee	418.93			
Recording fee	173.00			
Preparation of deed			75.00	
Title examination			200.00	
Total debits and credits	87,621.78	52,916.86	50,721.36	86,954.85
Due from buyer at closing		34,704.92		
Due to seller closing			36,233.49	
Totals	87,621.78	87,621.78	86,954.85	86,954.85

Pages 261–272 continued

Broker's Reconciliation

Items	Receipts	Disbursements
Earnest money	8,650.00	
Due from buyer at closing	34,704.92	

Paid seller's expenses:
  Broker's commission
  Other expenses
		6,055.00
		399.50

Paid buyer's expenses		666.93
Paid amount due seller at closing		36,233.49
Totals	43,354.92	43,354.92

Achievement Exercise

1. Earnest money deposit:
   $45,000 × 10% = $4,500

2. Mortgage interest proration:
   $27,800 × 7.5% = $2,085 annual interest
   $2,085 ÷ 12 = $173.75 monthly interest for July
   $220.50 − $173.75 = $46.75 applied to principal
   $27,800 − $46.75 = $27,753.25 principal balance August 1, 1988
   $27,753.25 × 7.5% = $2,081.493 annual interest
   $2,081.493 ÷ 360 = $5.781 daily interest
   Interest has accrued on the 3 days from August 1 through August 3.
   $5.781 × 3 = $17.343 rounded to $17.34

3. Real estate tax proration:
   $1,200 ÷ 12 = $100 monthly tax $100 ÷ 30 = $3.333 daily tax
   7 months   January through July, 1988
   3 days   3 days of August
   $100 × 7 months = $700 $3.333 × 3 days = $9.999
   $700 + $9.999 = $709.999 rounded to $710 tax for 1988

4. Insurance proration:
   $900 ÷ 3 = $300 annually $300 ÷ 12 = $25 monthly $25 ÷ 30 = $.833 daily

years	months	days
1986	9	20
− 1984	8	3
2	1	17

   $300 × 2 years = $600 $25 × 1 month = $25 $.833 × 17 days = $14.161
   $600 + $25 + $14.161 = $639.161 rounded to $639.16

5. Rent proration:
$250 ÷ 30 = $8.333 daily rent

  31 total days in August
−3 date of closing
  28 days of unearned rent

$8.333 × 28 = $233.324 rounded to $233.32

6. Fuel proration:
$.90 × 60 = $54.00

7. Water bill proration:
Seller pays for 7 months and 3 days of water bill (January 1 through August 3, 1988).
$56 ÷ 12 = $4.666 monthly $4.666 ÷ 30 = $.155 daily
$4.666 × 7 months = $32.662 $.155 × 3 = $.465
$32.662 + $.465 = $33.127 rounded to $33.13

8. Title expense:

$300 × $\frac{1}{2}$ = $150 (charged to both buyer and seller)

9. Commission:
$45,000 × 6.5% = $2,925

10. Transfer tax:
$45,000 total price − $27,753.25 mortgage = $17,246.75 taxable consideration
$17,246.75 ÷ $500 = 34.49 rounded to 35   35 × $.50 = $17.50

See the following pages for answers for the settlement statement worksheet and the broker's reconciliation.

11. d

12. c

13. a

14. c

15. d

Achievement Exercise continued

SETTLEMENT STATEMENT WORKSHEET

Property _____

Seller _____

Buyer _____

Settlement Date _____ August 3, 1988 _____

	Buyer's statement		Seller's statement	
	Debit	Credit	Debit	Credit
Purchase price	45,000.00			45,000.00
Earnest money		4,500.00		
Mortgage — assumed		27,753.25	27,753.25	
Mortgage interest proration		17.34	17.34	
Real estate tax proration		710.00	710.00	
Insurance proration	639.16			639.16
Rent proration		233.32	233.32	
Fuel proration	54.00			54.00
Water bill proration		33.13	33.13	
Title expense	150.00		150.00	
Broker's commission			2,925.00	
Transfer tax			17.50	
Preparation of deed			50.00	
Mortgage assumption fee	100.00			
Recording fees	15.00			
Survey fee	75.00			
Security damage deposit		250.00	250.00	
Total debits and credits	46,033.16	33,497.04	32,139.54	45,693.16
Due from buyer at closing		12,536.12		
Due to seller at closing			13,553.62	
Totals	46,033.16	46,033.16	45,693.16	45,693.16

Broker's Reconciliation

Items	Receipts	Disbursements
Earnest money	4,500.00	
Due from buyer at closing	12,536.12	
Paid seller's expenses:		
Broker's commission		2,925.00
Other expenses		217.50
Paid buyer's expenses		340.00
Paid amount due seller at closing		13,553.62
Totals	17,036.12	17,036.12

Time Value of Money

INTRODUCTION

You have heard the expression, ''Time is money.'' This chapter deals with the growth of money in relationship to time and introduces calculations involving *financing* and *interest charges* that are rooted in the time value of money. Both of these concepts can help you with your personal finances, as well as in real estate transactions.

ENTRY EVALUATION

Since readers will have varying amounts of knowledge and experience, the short test that follows will allow you to determine your familiarity with the material to be covered. Try all the problems before looking at the answers, which begin on page 318.

- What are the monthly payments on a $100,000 loan bearing 12% interest and amortized over 20 years?

- If you expect new carpet for the house to cost $5,000, how much must you deposit each month in an account bearing 11% interest compounded monthly in order to accumulate $5,000 in 24 months?

■ Charlie obtains a $90,000 loan at 12% interest payable monthly over 25 years. What is his loan balance after 10 years?

■ Suppose that a generous benefactor offered you a choice of 3 investments at absolutely no cost to you. However, a few strings are attached, and a few assumptions must be made:

1. All investments are risk-free.
2. You cannot reinvest any of the money you receive; you must spend it.
3. The inflation rate is zero.
4. You expect to make 12% compounded annually on the investment.

Your investment choices are:

End of year	Note due in 3 years	Annuity of annual payments	Guaranteed land sale in 5 years
1	0	$5,548.19	0
2	0	5,548.19	0
3	$28,098.56	5,548.19	0
4	0	5,548.19	0
5	0	5,548.19	$35,246.83

Which one do you prefer? Why?

COMPOUND INTEREST AND COMPOUND DISCOUNT

Given a choice, would you prefer to have $1,000 cash today or the promise of $1,000 one year from today? Consider the following points:

1. If you receive it today, you know you have it. (When you think along these lines, you are considering the *risk factor*.)
2. If you have the money today, you can use it to earn more money. (This is the *investment factor*.)
3. If you receive the money a year from now, inflation will have eroded its value. (This consideration is the *present value factor*.)
4. If you receive the money a year from now, you will have lost the interest or other yield that it could have earned. (This is the *opportunity cost factor*.)

As another example, would you prefer receiving $5,000 per year for the next five years or $18,000 in cash today? Why? Some considerations are:

1. The $18,000 cash is risk-free.
2. The total of annual payments over five years is $25,000.
3. You could invest $18,000 today.
4. You could invest $5,000 yearly as you receive it.
5. The $18,000 today will require payment of a larger amount of income tax.
6. The annual income might offset some expected expenses such as a child's college cost.

From these general statements, you could conclude that either choice would depend only upon personal needs and must be made upon a guess at this point. Fortunately, however, compound interest and compound discount tables are a way of arriving at answers to these questions. A simplified comparison of simple and compound interest was discussed in Chapter 8, and a new calculation for each year was computed for compound interest.

An easier way to calculate compound interest is to use the equation:

$$S = (1 + i)^n (P)$$

where:

S = final balance at the end of compounding periods;
i = interest rate per compounding period;
n = total number of compounding periods;
P = amount originally invested.

EXAMPLES: The example used in Chapter 8 was $1,000 ($P$) placed in a savings account earning 12% per year (i). To determine how much will be in the account at the end of the 2 years (n), you could use the equation, $S = (1 + i)^n (P)$, and substitute the numbers you know:

$S = (1 + .12)^2 ($1,000)$
$S = (1.12)^2 ($1,000)$
$S = (1.12) (1.12) ($1,000)$
$S = (1.2544) ($1,000)$
$S = $1,254.40$

This is exactly the amount calculated in Chapter 8. (Refer back to page 164.)

The 12% rate was both the annual interest rate and the rate per compounding period. (Interest was paid to the account once per year.) Therefore, the total compounding periods were the same as the term of the investment, or 2 years.

The procedure for calculating interest compounded monthly is similar. For comparison, assume again an investment of $1,000 (P) placed in a savings account for 2 years. This time, however, the interest paid on savings in the account is compounded monthly. This means that the compounding period is one month.There are 24 one-month periods in two years, so the number of compounding periods (n) is 24. You must adjust the interest rate, too. If the interest rate for *one year* is 12%, the *monthly* interest rate (the rate per compounding period) is 12% ÷ 12 months, or 1% per month. Now, substitute these numbers into the equation used in the first example:

$$S = (1 + i)^n(P)$$
$$S = (1 + .01)^{24}(\$1,000)$$
$$S = (1.01)^{24}(\$1,000)$$

A major computational problem exists here because 1.01 must be multiplied by itself 24 times! Unless you have a calculator with an exponent key, you need some other device to save you tedious computation time. Compound interest tables are such devices. An example of a compound interest table is Figure 15.1.

FIGURE 15.1
12% Annual Compound Interest Table

Effective rate = 12%   Base = 1.1200

Years	Factor
1	1.120000
2	1.254400
3	1.404928
4	1.573519
5	1.762342
6	1.973823
7	2.210681
8	2.475963
9	2.773079
10	3.105848
15	5.473566
20	9.646293
25	17.000064
30	29.959922

Compound interest tables save you work by calculating part of the compound interest equation for you, specifically the $(1 + i)^n$ portion. Once you know that factor of the equation, you simply multiply it by P to get S, the final balance including interest. Look back at the first example. You saw that $(1 + .12)^2 = 1.2544$. This factor can also be found in Figure 15.1, which is for the payment of 12% interest compounded annually. Look down the left column for the row for 2 years (because this is a 2-year investment). The factor next to 2 is 1.254400. Thus, you could have found the factor by looking in the table rather than by multiplying 1.12×1.12.

The factor you need in order to solve the monthly example is not in Figure 15.1, because this table shows only *annually* compounded interest. You need to look at a table such as the one in Figure 15.2, which shows interest compounded *monthly*. In this example, *n* is 24 months, or 2 years, so look down the left column to the row labeled 2 years. The factor there is 1.269734. Multiply that times the original investment:

$$1.269734 \times \$1,000 = \$1,269.73 \text{ in the account after 2 years}$$

Compare this to the previous example. Because it was compounded more frequently, the second investment earned about $15 more.

Now, try a problem yourself.

1. If Charley placed $5,000 in a savings account earning 12% interest compounded monthly, how much will he have at the end of 10 years, provided he neither added to it nor withdrew from it?

FIGURE 15.2
12% Monthly Compound Interest Table

Effective rate = 1%   Base = 1.0100

Months	Factor
1	1.010000
2	1.020099
3	1.030300
4	1.040604
5	1.051010
6	1.061520
7	1.072135
8	1.082856
9	1.093685
10	1.104622
11	1.115668

Years	
1	1.126825
2	1.269734
3	1.430768
4	1.612226
5	1.816696
10	3.300386
15	5.995801
20	10.892553
25	19.788466
30	35.949641

ELLWOOD TABLES

The tables you used in the foregoing examples are a portion of the "Ellwood Tables." These bear the name of their compiler, L.W. Ellwood, who took the traditional compound interest and discount tables and rearranged them into a format well-suited to real estate applications. The remainder of this chapter examines some of these applications.

Ellwood arranged the interest rate factors into six columns, each of which is called a *table*. The first three of these are compound *interest* tables, like the ones you have just used, and the last three columns are compound *discount* tables. Some Ellwood tables are reproduced at the end of this chapter, beginning on page 315. As you learn to use them, you may find the following chart to be a helpful reference:

Table	Title	Memory Aid
1	Amount of 1 at Compound Interest	Savings account
2	Accumulation of 1 per Period	Christmas Club
3	Sinking Fund Factor	Sinking fund
4	Present Value of Reversion of 1	Reversion
5	Present Value of Ordinary Annuity of 1 per Period	Annuity
6	Installment to Amortize 1	Amortization

Here's a breakdown:

- *Table 1* (Savings account) includes figures to help you calculate compound interest over a definite period of time. By using this table, you can answer the question, "If I put a single sum in an interest-bearing account today and do not disturb it, how much will I have in a certain length of time?"

- *Table 2* (Christmas Club) deals with the total accumulation of a series of deposits over a specified period of time with interest at the effective rate. For example, "If I put a certain amount in an interest-bearing Christmas Club account at the same intervals and do not disturb it, how much will I have in a certain length of time?"

- *Table 3* (Sinking fund) can be used to calculate how much money must be placed in an interest-bearing account on a regular basis to accumulate a certain amount in that account in a certain length of time.

- *Table 4* (Reversion) shows discount rates, which can be applied to determine present values, and answers the question, "How much is a future single sum worth to me today?"

- *Table 5* (Annuity) can help you calculate the value today of the receipt of a series of equal payments in the future.

- *Table 6* (Amortization) provides figures to compute the payment that is required to pay off (amortize) a loan amount in a particular length of time.

Of course, these simplified explanations merely show *some* of the uses for these tables. As you proceed, other examples and further discussion will be provided.

Each Ellwood table has a formula, or equation, for use. The formulas are expressed as follows:

Table	Equation
1	$FV = PV \times f$
2	$FV = Pmt \times f$
3	$Pmt = FV \times f$
4	$PV = FV \times f$
5	$PV = Pmt \times f$
6	$Pmt = PV \times f$

where:

$$PV = \text{present value}$$
$$FV = \text{future value}$$
$$Pmt = \text{payment}$$
$$f = \text{factor in the proper table}$$

In earlier chapters, you learned how to re-arrange terms in an equation to separate the knowns from the unknowns. You can also do that with these equations.

EXAMPLE: If you know *PV* and *FV* in a Table 1 problem, you can solve for the unknown, *f*. This *f* corresponds to the interest rate per compounding period and at a particular point in time. The original formula is:

$$FV = PV \times f$$

Solving for *f*, you have:

$$f = FV/PV$$

An abbreviated form of the Ellwood Tables is shown in Figure 15.5 on page 315. Use it to work through some simple problems.

Table 1—Compound Interest

EXAMPLE: First, consider this problem: A house sold for $70,000 2 years ago. If the annual appreciation in the house's area has been 12% per year each year, what is the indicated value today by the compound interest method? (Note—this is *not* designed to replace appraisals.)

Recall the definitions of the Ellwood tables. Table 1 had to do with a single sum left undisturbed for a period of time. Thus, the formula for Table 1 should be used here.

$$FV = PV \times f$$

For clarity, write the *f* as:

$$f^{T1}_{.12a}$$

The T1 indicates that it is a Table 1 factor, and the .12*a* means that the interest rate is 12% compounded annually. Now the formula looks like:

$$FV = PV \times f^{T1}_{.12a}$$

PV in this exercise refers to the *original value* of $70,000, and *FV* refers to the *appreciated value* of today. To find *f*, go to Table 1 (of Figure 15.5) and look down the column until you find 2 years. Then read the factor opposite this. Now you have,

$$FV = \$70,000 \times 1.254400$$
$$FV = \$87,808, \text{ today's indicated value}$$

2. Weldon receives a check for $30,000 from his profit-sharing fund upon retirement. If he invests this in a 3-year certificate of deposit paying 12% compounded annually, what will be the value of the certificate at maturity?

EXAMPLE: If you put a sum of money in an account bearing 12% compounded annually, how long will it take to double itself?

Even though no amount of money to be deposited is given, you should not have difficulty in solving the problem. This is another Table 1 problem, and the formula is:

$$FV = PV \times f$$

What now? No matter what *PV* (present value) is, *FV* (future value) will be twice that amount in our problem. Doesn't this mean that *f*, the factor in Table 1, must equal 2? This is because:

$$FV = 2 \times PV$$

Therefore, all you need to do is go down the Table 1 column (Figure 15.5) and find a factor equal to 2. As you can see, 1.973823 is opposite 6 years, and 2.210681 is opposite 7 years. So the money in the account will take a little over 6 years to double.

3. How long will the money take to triple?

Table 2—Accumulation of Interest

EXAMPLE: Jim and Jane are saving toward the down payment on a house of their own. Both work outside the home, and they plan to deposit $300 per month in a plan that earns 12% compounded monthly. If they do this diligently, how much will they have saved up in four years?

Jim and Jane's savings plan is like a ''Christmas Club,'' in which a commitment is made to add savings on a regular basis. That is a Table 2 problem, and the formula is:

$$FV = Pmt \times f^{T2}_{.12m}$$

Notice that this 12% rate is compounded *monthly*, which corresponds to the frequency of their deposits. Therefore, use Figure 15.6, on page 315. Locate the Table 2 factor from the second column for four years.

$$FV = \$300 \times 61.222607$$
$$FV = \$18,366.78$$

4. Shirley decides that she will place $300 of every commission check she receives in an account paying 12%, compounded monthly. If Shirley's commission check is paid monthly and she does this for 5 years, how much will be in her account?

Table 3—Sinking Fund

EXAMPLE: Suppose that Jim and Jane are now in their newly acquired house, and they want to install a new central heating and air-conditioning unit in three years, at which time they estimate the cost will be $5,000. How much must they deposit each month in an account earning 12% compounded monthly in order to pay cash for the system? This time you know the final amount but not the monthly payments. The formula for such a Table 3 (sinking fund) problem is:

$$PMT = FV \times f^{T3}_{.12m}$$

Locate the proper factor in Table 3 (Figure 15.6 on page 315) at three years.

$$Pmt = \$5,000 \times .023214$$
$$Pmt = \$116.07$$

At this point, notice the relationship between Tables 2 and 3. The formulas look similar, don't they?

$$\text{Table 2: } FV = PV \times f$$
$$\text{Table 3: } FV = Pmt \times f$$

Now, suppose that Jim and Jane did in fact deposit $116.07 each month for three years in a 12% account compounded monthly. What will be the account balance in three years? This is another "Christmas Club," or Table 2, problem (using Figure 15.6).

$$FV = Pmt \times f^{T2}_{.12m}$$
$$FV = \$116.07 \times 43.076878$$
$$FV = \$4,999.93$$

The reason you did not get exactly $5,000 is the effect of rounding errors that limit the accuracy of the calculations.

Tables 2 and 3 are said to be "reciprocals" of each other. That means that if you divide the Table 2 factor into 1, you get the Table 3 factor, and vice versa. For example, if you divide the Table 2 factor of 43.076878 into 1, you get .023214, which is the Table 3 factor used previously. Furthermore, Tables 1 and 4 are reciprocals, and so are Tables 5 and 6.

5. Joan has decided to buy a new car every 3 years for use in her real estate business. She expects the next one to cost $14,000. If she can earn 12% compounded monthly, how much must she deposit each month in order to be able to write a check for the car?

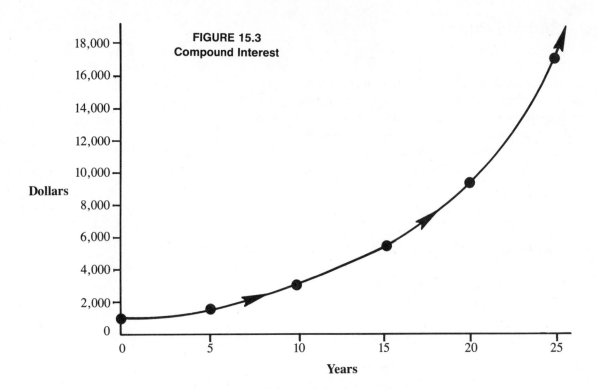

FIGURE 15.3
Compound Interest

Remember that these first three tables are compound *interest* tables, and the last three tables are compound *discount* tables. To illustrate, consider the graph in Figure 15.3. This compound interest curve is derived from Table 1 for $1,000 invested at 12% compounded annually for 25 years. The amounts on the graph, shown in tabular form, are:

End of year	Amount
0	$1,000.00 invested
5	1,762.34 balance
10	3,105.85 balance
15	5,473.57 balance
20	9,646.29 balance
25	17,000.06 balance

Table 4—Reversion

Table 4 indicates the *present value* of a single future sum. That is, it tells you the amount by which the future sum is diminished because it was not available for you to invest today.

EXAMPLE: What is the present value of $17,000.06 due in 25 years if the discount rate (our demanded yield) is 12% annually? Our formula for Table 4 (in Figure 15.5) is:

$$PV = FV \times f_{.12a}^{T4}$$
$$PV = \$17,000.06 \times .058823$$
$$PV = \$1,000.00$$

In like manner, what is the present value of $9,646.29 due in 20 years?

$$PV = \$9,646.29 \times .103667$$
$$PV = \$1,000.00$$

6. What is the present value of $5,473.57 due in 15 years? Use a 12% discount rate.

These examples illustrate the operation of a compound *discounting* function. A plot of this function, shown in Figure 15.4, is the reverse of Figure 15.3.

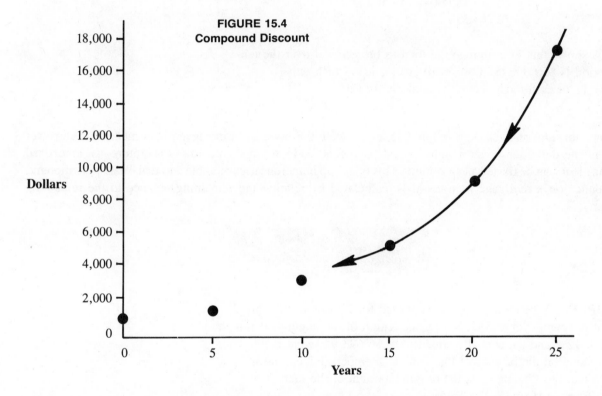

FIGURE 15.4
Compound Discount

7. Jim sold his house and carried back a $25,000 note bearing 12% interest compounded annually, due 1 year from today. What can Jim sell the note for if the investor is satisfied with the 12% interest?

Table 5—Annuities

Perhaps your insurance agent has mentioned an *annuity* to you as one of your investment options. An ordinary annuity is a series of equal payments made at equal intervals.

EXAMPLE: If your policy is paid up, and you have the option of accepting a lump sum payment of $25,000 or an annuity of $5,000 per year for 10 years, what would be the value to you of the annuity if your rate was 12% annually? This is a Table 5 (Figure 15.5) problem, and the formula is:

$$PV = Pmt \times f^{T5}_{.12a}$$
$$PV = \$5,000 \times 5.650223$$
$$PV = \$28,251.12$$

This shows that even though the total to be received over the ten-year period is $50,000 ($5,000 × 10 years), it is worth only $28,251.12 in cash today if your annual rate is 12%.

Now, consider another use for Table 5. If you were the investor, a mortgage loan made to a borrower would fit the definition of an annuity (equal payments made at equal intervals). Therefore, an amortized mortgage loan can be treated as an annuity. This opens up numerous uses of Table 5 to real estate practitioners. The balance on a mortgage loan could be calculated by relating the remaining balance to the remaining term, or:

> How many payments are *yet to be received* on the mortgage loan?

EXAMPLE: When a new loan is approved for 20 years, there are 20 years of payments yet to be received; the length of the annuity. If this loan is at 12% and the annual payments are $6,693.94, what is the present value on the balance of the loan? Remember, this is a new loan, so that the "balance" is the original amount of the loan. The Table 5 formula (from Figure 15.5) is:

$$PV = Pmt \times f^{T5}_{.12a}$$
$$PV = \$6,693.94 \times 7.469444$$
$$PV = \$50,000$$

Now, what is the balance on this loan after five annual payments have been made? First, determine the length of the *remaining* annuity:

20 years	original term of loan
− 5 years	number of annual payments made
15 years	number of annual payments remaining (the length of the annuity)

Next, look up the 15-year factor in Table 5 (Figure 15.5).

$$PV = Pmt \times f_{.12a}^{T5}$$
$$PV = \$6,693.94 \times 6.810864$$
$$PV = \$45,591.51$$

PV is the remaining balance of the loan, but it is *also* the *present value* of a 15-year annuity at 12% annually with annual payments of $6,693.94.

8. Darlene owns a warehouse building leased to a large, stable international company that has signed a 20-year lease at $25,000 per year. Five years later, Darlene decides to sell the lease. The investor wants to discount it at 12% annually. How much should Darlene expect from the sale of this lease?

Table 6—Amortization

EXAMPLE: Jim and Jane have done quite well during their eight years of marriage. Their third child is on the way, and they need a larger house. The real estate agent told them the house they like can be bought with an $85,000 loan and $15,000 cash. If the interest rate is 12%, what are the monthly payments on a 30-year loan?

Be careful to notice the *monthly* payments. This means you must use the *monthly* 12% table (Figure 15.6). All interest rates are quoted on an annual basis, but if the payments on the note are monthly, then the interest rate used is the *interest per compounding period*. The formula for Table 6 is:

$$Pmt = PV \times f_{.12m}^{T6}$$
$$Pmt = \$85,000 \times .010286$$
$$Pmt = \$874.31 \text{ principal and interest}$$

How much more will the payments be if Jim and Jane take out a 25-year loan?

$$Pmt = \$85,000 \times .010532$$
$$Pmt = \$895.22 \text{ principal and interest}$$

9. Janet is working with buyers who are undecided between a 30-year loan at 12% monthly and a 20-year loan at 11% monthly. They want a house that is priced at $80,000, and they plan to pay $10,000 down. Which loan will have the smaller monthly payments?

Loan Discount Points

The final examples of using the Ellwood Tables will involve the discounting of a loan. Chapter 9 discussed loan discount points and the rule of thumb that an 8% discount increases the yield by 1%, or a 1% discount equals 1/8% yield increase. Now, let's examine the reason for this.

Suppose a lender could not charge more than 11% on a 30-year residential loan of $80,000 with monthly payments, but that lender could obtain 12% on a similar commercial loan. Would the lender make the residential loan? No; why should he, if he can earn more interest elsewhere? However, loan discounting is a way of adjusting loan yields. The following examples illustrate how it works.

EXAMPLES: First, compute the loan payments on the 30-year residential loan, based upon the interest rate of 11% stated on the note. Use Table 6, Figure 15.7.

$$Pmt = PV \times f^{T6}_{.11m}$$
$$Pmt = \$80,000 \times .009523$$
$$Pmt = \$761.84$$

The lender will not make the loan at an 11% yield, but rather wants the equivalent of 12%. The next calculations must lead to a determination of how much to charge as "points" to make the loan's yield equivalent to that of a 12% loan.

Remember that mortgage loans can be treated as annuities. The payments on the residential loan "annuity" would be $761.84 if that annuity bears 11% interest, or, conversely, the present value of the annuity at an 11% discount rate is $80,000, or the face value of the loan. What would the present value be if an annuity of the same amount ($761.84) earned a yield of 12%? This is a Table 5 (annuity) problem. Therefore, from Figure 15.6.

$$PV = Pmt \times f^{T5}_{.12m}$$

Again, remember to use the 12% *monthly* table, so that:

$$PV = \$761.84 \times 97.218330$$
$$PV = \$74{,}064.81$$

Thus, to earn the desired 12% return on 30 years' payments of $761.84, the lender would want to loan only $74,064.81.

Knowing that the face amount of the note (the loan) is $80,000, you can find the dollar difference between these two amounts:

```
 $80,000.00  face amount of note
-74,064.81   discounted value of note
 $ 5,935.19  Note (Loan) Discount or Total of Discount Paid
```

This difference of $5,935.19 is the amount paid as a loan discount.

"Points," or the loan discount, are always calculated on the amount of the loan. So, what percent of $80,000 is $5,935.19? (Or, how many points should the lender charge in order to boost an 11% yield to 12%?)

$$\text{percent} = \frac{\text{part}}{\text{total}}$$

$$\text{percent} = \frac{\$5{,}935.19}{\$80{,}000.00}$$

$$\text{percent} = .0742, \text{ or}$$

7.42 loan discount points

In this example, it took 7.42 points to increase the investor's yield by 1%, from 11% to 12%. This is fairly close to the rule of thumb that 8 points equals 1% increased yield. However, if you use larger interest rates and a shorter loan payout, you will quickly discover that the rule of thumb should be used carefully, for it has limitations.

Try another example: Charlotte got a call from a lender who will accept loans for 20 years at 11% monthly if the yield is 12% monthly. (Please remember that the "monthly" only has to do with the compounding period. This does not mean that the investor is earning 12% per month.) One of Charlotte's real estate salespersons has an offer from a prospective buyer for a $115,000 house. If the buyer pays $15,000 down and applies for the 20-year loan, how many discount points will be charged on that loan?

This is a 4-part problem. In order for you to discount an annuity, you must first calculate the payments on that annuity. In this case, these are the payments on the loan, and remember that the note is to bear interest at 11%.

Part 1. Find the monthly payments on a $100,000 loan at 11% for 20 years. This is a Table 6 (Figure 15.7) problem, and the formula is:

$$Pmt = PV \times f^{T6}_{.11m}$$

Substituting values gives:

$$Pmt = \$100,000 \times .010321$$
$$Pmt = \$1,032.10$$

Part 2. But, remember that the investor-lender wants a 12% yield or return on investment. So, calculate the present value of the "annuity" at both 11% and 12%; the difference in these present values will be the dollar amount of the discount. This is a Table 5 (Figure 15.7) problem. The formula is:

$$PV = Pmt \times f^{T5}_{.11m}$$

Therefore:

$$PV = \$1,032.10 \times 96.881538$$
$$PV = \$99,991.43$$

What is the significance of this answer? First, it contains a small error; it should have been $100,000. The reason for the error is that the $1,032.10 payment that you previously calculated was 8.8392¢ too small. The reason for that error is that the Table 6 factor at 11% monthly for 20 years is *truncated* and not rounded. The factor shown is .010321, and the correct factor is .01032188392. (Now, you see that such a small difference as $\dfrac{88,392}{1,000,000}$ or roughly $\dfrac{9}{100}$ makes an $8.57 error in the answer. The second and primary significance of the answer is that it brings us back to our original starting point; the $100,000 loan. This is so because the present value of the annuity exactly equals (except for the error in the table) the beginning amount of the note.

Part 3. Now, you must discount the same income stream from the annuity at the investor's desired yield, 12%. This is still a Table 5 (Figure 15.6) problem. The formula is:

$$PV = Pmt \times f^{T5}_{.12m}$$

Now you have:

$$PV = \$1,032.10 \times 90.819416$$
$$PV = \$93,734.72$$

This is the present value of that same annuity when discounted at 12%.

Part 4. You now have:

$100,000.00 *PV* of annuity at 11% (correct answer)
− 93,734.72 *PV* of annuity at 12%
$ 6,265.28 dollar amount of loan discount to be collected at closing

Finally, you must express this $6,265.28 as a percent of the original $100,000 loan:

$$\$6,265.28 \div \$100,000.00 = .0627 \text{ or } 6.27\%$$

This 6.27% is the number of discount points to be paid at closing. Please notice that the "1% difference in yield = 8 discount points" rule of thumb is not valid. In the example you just worked through, the 1% difference in yield equals 6.27 discount points. Please refer back to the discussion at the end of Chapter 9 and the comment previously made in this chapter in this regard.

After covering the material in this chapter, you now know that "present value" is very important, for it allows you to compare investments mathematically, as in the last question in the Entry Evaluation for this chapter. Here's how to solve that problem: First, consider the $28,098.56 note due in three years. Using Table 4 (Figure 15.5), you find that:

$$PV = FV \times .711780$$
$$PV = \$28,098.56 \times .711780$$
$$PV = \$20,000 \text{ (rounded)}$$

Next, determine the present value of the 5-year annuity, which is a Table 5 problem.

$$PV = Pmt \times 3.604776$$
$$PV = \$5,548.19 \times 3.604776$$
$$PV = \$20,000 \text{ (rounded)}$$

By now, you may suspect that the present value of the guaranteed land sale at the end of 5 years is $20,000; if so, you're right! Here's why, using Table 4:

$$PV = FV \times .567427$$
$$PV = \$35,246.83 \times .567427$$
$$PV = \$20,000$$

As you see, numerically, it would not have made any difference which investment you chose. Personal reasons, however, might make the choice easy. For example, you might have an opportunity for spending money in 3 years, and the opportunity might not be there in 5 years. Nevertheless, you now have ways of mathematically comparing simple investments. Other methods of analysis are available, such as the internal rate of return (IRR), but they are beyond the scope of this text.

USING A FINANCIAL CALCULATOR

If your calculator has the financial functions, you may have noticed the relevant keys. They are:

| n | | i | | PMT | | PV | | FV |

If you have these, you need not use the Ellwood Tables because they are built right into your calculator! You can do all types of these problems without the tables, but you need to remember the basics you have learned so as to understand better the use and capacity of your calculator.

To demonstrate the simplicity of using a financial calculator, look at the keystrokes if the last example is worked on a Hewlett-Packard 12-C calculator. Other brands may work somewhat differently, so check the instructions for your calculator.

Press:	Display:	Means:
1 0 0 0 0 0 PV	100000	loan amount
1 1 g i	9167	interest/month
2 0 g n	240	number of months
Pmt	1032.19	monthly payment
STO 1	1032.19	monthly payment
g reset CLX	0000000	clear register
rcl 1 Pmt	1032.19	monthly payment
rcl n n	240	number of months
1 2 g i	1.00	interest/month
PV	93742.72	present value
1 0 0 0 0 0	100000	loan amount
y x −	6265.28	loan discount
1 0 0 0 0 0	100000	loan amount
÷	.062528	discount points in decimal form

Now, isn't that much simpler?

FIGURE 15.5
12% Annual Compound Interest Table

Effective Rate = 12%   Base = 1.1200

	1	2	3	4	5	6
Years	Future Value of $1 at Compound Interest	Future Value of $1 Annuity	Sinking Fund Factor	Present Value of Reversion of $1	Present Value of Annuity of $1	Installment to Amortize $1
1	1.120000	1.000000	1.000000	.892857	.892857	1.120000
2	1.254400	2.120000	.471698	.797194	1.690051	.591698
3	1.404928	3.374400	.296349	.711780	2.401831	.416349
4	1.573519	4.779328	.209234	.635518	3.037349	.329234
5	1.762342	6.352847	.157410	.567427	3.604776	.277410
6	1.973823	8.115189	.123226	.506631	4.111407	.243226
7	2.210681	10.089012	.099118	.452349	4.563757	.219118
8	2.475963	12.299693	.081303	.403883	4.967640	.201303
9	2.773079	14.775656	.067679	.360610	5.328250	.187679
10	3.105848	17.548735	.056984	.321973	5.650223	.176984
15	5.473566	37.279715	.026824	.182696	6.810864	.146824
20	9.646293	72.052442	.013879	.103667	7.469444	.133879
25	17.000064	133.333870	.007500	.058823	7.843139	.127500
30	29.959922	241.332684	.004144	.033378	8.055184	.124144

FIGURE 15.6
12% Monthly Compound Interest Table

Effective Rate = 1%   Base = 1.0100

	1	2	3	4	5	6
Years	Future Value of $1 at Compound Interest	Future Value of $1 Annuity	Sinking Fund Factor	Present Value of Reversion of $1	Present Value of Annuity of $1	Installment to Amortize $1
1	1.126825	12.682503	.078848	.887449	11.255077	.088848
2	1.269734	26.973464	.037073	.787566	21.243387	.047073
3	1.430768	43.076878	.023214	.698924	30.107505	.033214
4	1.612226	61.222607	.016333	.620260	37.973959	.026333
5	1.816696	81.669669	.012244	.550449	44.955038	.022244
6	2.047099	104.709931	.009550	.488496	51.150391	.019550
7	2.306722	130.672274	.007652	.433515	56.648452	.017652
8	2.599272	159.927292	.006252	.384722	61.527703	.016252
9	2.928925	192.892579	.005184	.341422	65.857789	.015184
10	3.300386	230.038689	.004347	.302994	69.700522	.014347
15	5.995801	499.580197	.002001	.166783	83.321664	.012001
20	10.892553	989.255364	.001010	.091805	90.819416	.011010
25	19.788466	1878.846624	.000532	.050534	94.946551	.010532
30	35.949641	3494.964129	.000286	.027816	97.218330	.010286

FIGURE 15.7
11% Monthly Compound Interest Table

Effective Rate = 11/12%   Base = 1.00916667

	1	2	3	4	5	6
Years	Future Value of $1 at Compound Interest	Future Value of $1 Annuity	Sinking Fund Factor	Present Value of Reversion of $1	Present Value of Annuity of $1	Installment to Amortize $1
1	1.115718	12.623873	.079214	.896283	11.314564	.088381
2	1.244828	26.708565	.037441	.803323	21.455618	.046607
3	1.388878	42.423123	.023572	.720005	30.544874	.032738
4	1.549598	59.956150	.016678	.645328	38.691421	.025845
5	1.728915	79.518079	.012575	.578397	45.993033	.021742
6	1.928983	101.343692	.009867	.518407	52.537346	.019034
7	2.152203	125.694939	.007955	.464640	58.402903	.017122
8	2.401254	152.864084	.006541	.416449	63.660103	.015708
9	2.679124	183.177212	.005459	.373256	68.372043	.014625
10	2.989149	216.998138	.004608	.334543	72.595274	.013775
15	5.167987	454.689576	.002199	.193498	87.981936	.011365
20	8.935015	865.638042	.001155	.111919	96.881538	.010321
25	15.447888	1576.133312	.000634	.064733	102.029043	.009801
30	26.708097	2804.519759	.000356	.037441	105.006345	.009523

ACHIEVEMENT EXERCISE

When you have finished both parts of this exercise, check your answers against those on pages 320–321. If you miss any of the questions, review this chapter before going on to Chapter 16.

Part I—Open Response   Complete the following problems.

1. Write the memory-aid names of all 6 Ellwood Tables.

2. Write the formulas for all 6 tables.

3. Which of the tables are reciprocal?

4. Which tables are compound interest?

5. Which tables are compound discount?

Part II—Multiple Choice Select the correct response from the choices supplied.

6. A business netted $80,000 last year. If each of the 5 preceding years showed an average of 12% annual growth, what is the projected annual net 3 years from now?

    a. $97,418   c. $115,649
    b. $112,394   d. $119,222

7. If Jack places $2,000 in an Individual Retirement Account each year for 20 years and if that account draws 12% compounded annually, how much will be in the IRA in 20 years?

    a. $144,104   c. $200,563
    b. $187,341   d. $288,208

8. Jill's apartment house will need a new roof in 10 years. If she can earn 12% compounded monthly and if the new roof is estimated to cost $75,000 at that time, how much must Jill deposit *each month* in order to accumulate the amount needed?

    a. $4,273.81   c. $3,912.36
    b. $356.15   d. $326.03

9. You have a $20,000 bond due in 5 years and you want to convert it to cash today. How much should I pay you for it if I want to earn 12% annually on my investment?

    a. $11,008.99   c. $11,348.54
    b. $14,915.22   d. $16,329.39

10. A few years ago, I took back a second lien note on which the balance at that time was $16,502.31. The monthly payments are $227.32. Now I want to sell the note. If you want to make 12% on these monthly payments, what should you pay for the note if there are 10 years remaining on it?

    a. $15,844.32   c. $10,219.18
    b. $16,502.31   d. $12,304.28

11. How much are the monthly payments on a $90,000 loan at 12% interest for 25 years?

    a. $910.23   c. $882.10
    b. $925.75   d. $947.88

12. If we know the monthly payment, we can multiply that by 12 to obtain a single annual payment on the same loan.

    I. True, because there are 12 monthly payments per year.

    II. False, because the amortization factors in the table are based upon compound interest.

    III. False, because each time a monthly payment is made, there is a little less principal left to earn interest for the next month.

    IV. True, because real estate loans bear simple interest.

        a. both I and IV
        b. both II and III
        c. I only
        d. II only

13. If a loan was in the original amount of $70,000 with monthly payments of $720.03 for 30 years at 12%, what is the remaining balance after 10 years?

        a. $50,186.38   c. $60,543.21
        b. $55,003.96   d. $65,392.70

ANSWER KEY

Entry Evaluation

- $1,101.09 (use Table 6)

- $187.21 (use Table 3)

- $78,980.75 (use Table 6, then Table 5)

- The present value of each investment is $20,000.

Pages 300–310

1. This problem involves the compound interest table shown in Figure 15.2. Opposite 10 years, locate the factor 3.300386. Multiply this factor by the initial deposit of $5,000:

$$\begin{array}{r} 3.300386 \\ \times\ \$5,000 \\ \hline \$16,501.93 \text{ in the account after 10 years} \end{array}$$

2. This is a Table 1 problem. The basic formula is:

$$FV = PV \times f_{.12a}^{T1}$$

You know that $PV = \$30,000$. From the 12% Table 1 (column 1), go down 3 years and find the factor 1.404928 opposite the number of years. This is the f in the formula. Now, you have:

$$FV = \$30,000 \times 1.404928$$
$$FV = \$42,147.84$$

which is the *future value;* the amount in that account, or the value of that certificate in 3 years.

3. Between 9 and 10 years. (The factor next to 9 years in Table 1 of Figure 15.5 is 2.773079, and the factor next to 10 years is 3.105848.)

4. This is a Table 2 problem. The formula is:

$$FV = Pmt \times f^{T2}_{.12m}$$

Here, you know that the payment *(Pmt)* is $300. Now, go to the 12% monthly Table 2 (column 2), look down the left-hand scale, find 5 years, go straight across, and read the factor 81.669669. Then,

$$FV = \$300 \times 81.669669$$
$$FV = \$24,500.90$$

5. This is a Table 3 problem. The formula is:

$$Pmt = FV \times f^{T3}_{.12m}$$

You now have:

$$Pmt = \$14,000 \times .023214$$
$$Pmt = \$324.996 \text{ or } \$325.00$$

Joan is now her own banker. Instead of *paying* interest, she *receives* interest.

6. $PV = FV \times f$
$PV = \$5,473.57 \times .182696$
$PV = \$1,000.00$

7. This is a single sum due in the future, and you want to know the present value, which makes this a Table 4 problem. The formula is:

$$PV = FV \times f^{T4}_{.12a}$$

Be sure to use the *annual* compounding table. It gives you:

$$PV = \$25,000 \times .892857$$
$$PV = \$22,321.43$$

In essence, Jim lost $2,678.57 in interest on this note sale, and that amount of interest will now be earned by the investor who bought the note. In other words, $25,000 available 1 year from now is worth only $22,321.43 today if money is worth (or working at) 12%.

8. Remember, the lease payments form an annuity since they are of equal amounts and are made at equal intervals. Therefore, you can use Table 5 (Figure 15.5) for this problem. But first, visualize this on a time line:

Year 0	Year 5	Year 20
original term of lease payments		
	remaining term of payments	

Darlene has 15 years left (20 − 5) on the payment schedule at $25,000 annually. The formula is:

$$PV = Pmt \times f^{T5}_{.12a}$$

Pages 300–310 continued

You now have:

$$PV = \$25,000 \times 6.810864$$
$$PV = \$170,271.60$$

Had she not sold the lease, Darlene would have had 15 payments left at $25,000 each, or a total of $375,000 due.

9. This is an amortization problem, which requires Table 6 (Figure 15.6). The formula is:

$$Pmt = PV \times f^{T6}_{.12m}$$

You have:

$$Pmt = \$70,000 \times .010286$$
$$Pmt = \$720.02 \text{ (30 years)}$$

Now, compute the payments at 11% monthly for 20 years (Figure 15.7):

$$Pmt = \$70,000 \times f^{T6}_{.11m}$$
$$Pmt = \$70,000 \times .010321$$
$$Pmt = \$722.47 \text{ (20 years)}$$

Which loan do you suppose the buyers will take?

Achievement Exercise

1. Table 1   Savings account
   Table 2   Christmas Club
   Table 3   Sinking fund
   Table 4   Reversion
   Table 5   Annuity
   Table 6   Amortization

2. Table 1 $FV = PV \times f$
   Table 2 $FV = Pmt \times f$
   Table 3 $Pmt = FV \times f$
   Table 4 $PV = FV \times f$
   Table 5 $PV = Pmt \times f$
   Table 6 $Pmt = PV \times f$

3. 1 and 4, 2 and 3, 5 and 6.

4. 1, 2 and 3 are compound interest.

5. 4, 5 and 6 are compound discount.

6. b. $80,000 \times 1.404928 = \$112,394$ future net

7. a. $\$2,000 \times 72.052442 = \$144,104$ accumulated amount

8. d. $\$75,000 \times .004347 = \$326.03$ monthly deposit

9. c. $20,000 × .567427 = $11,348.54 present value

10. a. $227.32 × 69.700522 = $15,844.32 present value

11. d. $90,000 × .010532 = $947.88 monthly payment

12. b.

13. d. $720.03 × 90.819416 = $65,392.70 remaining balance

16

Lease Calculations

INTRODUCTION

A rented shopping center, store or business office often has a *percentage lease*. Under such a lease, the tenant is required to pay a percentage of the volume of sales or gross income, often in addition to a base rent. In many other types of leases, the rent is adjusted annually, based upon the U.S. Government Consumer Price Index (CPI), as a means of dealing with inflation. In this chapter, you will calculate rents for both types of leased properties.

ENTRY EVALUATION

Since readers will have varying amounts of knowledge and experience, the short test that follows will allow you to determine your familiarity with the material to be covered. Try both problems before looking at the answers, which begin on page 330.

- Hosby's Salon has a lease which provides for the tenant to pay $375 minimum rent per month plus 4.5% of gross sales in excess of $100,000 per year. The gross sales last year were $250,000. What was Hosby's rent?

- Two years ago, Hosby's rent came to $8,100. What were the gross sales for that year?

PERCENTAGE LEASE

Under a percentage lease, the annual rent is a percentage of the volume of sales, usually subject to a minimum monthly payment. The tenant generally pays a minimum monthly rent *plus* a percentage of gross sales income if it exceeds the stipulated minimum amount. Or, some leases may provide for a minimum (base) rent plus a percentage of all sales income.

EXAMPLE: A percentage lease calls for a minimum monthly rental fee of $500, plus 6% of gross annual sales in excess of $100,000 per year. Based on gross annual sales of $250,000, compute the total rent for the year.

First, find the minimum annual rent:

$500 per month $\times$ 12 months = $6,000 minimum annual rent

Then find the percentage of gross sales to add to the minimum:

$250,000 actual gross sales
$-$ 100,000 sales covered by minimum rent
$150,000 Sales Subject to Percentage Rent

$150,000 $\times$ .06 = $9,000 percentage rent

The total rent is the minimum plus the percentage:

$6,000 + $9,000 = $15,000 total annual rent

Minimum or Base Rental

EXAMPLE: Mr. Muncie pays 2% of total gross sales for rent, with a minimum base rental of $1,000 per month. In the past year his sales volume was $400,000. How much rent did he pay? At what sales volume will Mr. Muncie effectively begin to pay percentage rent?

$1,000 $\times$ 12 = $12,000 minimum rent

$400,000 $\times$ .02 = $8,000 percentage rent

Mr. Muncie paid the minimum rent, $12,000, since it was greater than the percentage rent.

$$\text{total} = \frac{\text{part}}{\text{percent}} = \frac{\$12,000}{.02} =$$

$600,000 total gross sales to reach minimum rent.

When Mr. Muncie exceeds $600,000 in total gross sales, his percentage rent will be greater than the minimum rent, and he will pay that rather than the minimum rent.

1. If a percentage lease requires a tenant to pay $400 monthly minimum rent plus 4% of gross annual sales in excess of $120,000, what was the total rent paid for a year in which gross sales amounted to $360,000?

2. A lease provides for the tenant to pay $450 minimum rent per month plus 4% of gross sales in excess of $135,000 per year. What were gross sales last year, if the lessee paid a total rent of $12,420?

3. Flowerland, Inc., has operated a flower shop for several years in a highly desirable, active shopping center. The company has a lease requiring a $500 per month base rental plus a percentage of gross sales in excess of $75,000 per year. If gross sales for the year totaled $141,250 and rent paid amounted to $11,300, what percentage rate was contained in the lease?

4. Burrow's Delicatessen pays a monthly rental of $330 plus 4% of annual gross sales over $99,000. Last year the gross sales were $300,000. What was one month's rent for the delicatessen?

5. The Ski and See Shop had a 3-year lease which required a $600 per month rental guarantee plus an escalating percentage of annual gross sales in excess of $180,000. Complete the schedule that follows by determining how much rent was paid each year.

Year	Percent of gross sales	Actual gross sales	Annual rent
1	4	$200,000	
2	4.5	160,000	
3	5	250,000	

6. Mrs. Young collects rent from four stores in the Yardley shopping center. Last year, she collected $12,500 from Mr. Tompson, $14,000 from Mr. Berry and $9,000 from Miss Huerta. She also collected rent from Mr. Miller, who was to pay 5% of all gross sales, with a minimum payment of $375 per month. His gross sales last year were $75,000. On the average, how much rent did Mrs. Young collect for one month last year?

INDEX LEASE CALCULATIONS

Every month, the U.S. Government, through the Bureau of Labor Statistics, publishes data that reflect the costs of goods and services. These costs are shown as percentages of changes over the past year and the past month. The percentages are then used to adjust the Consumer Price Index (CPI). In general, *index numbers* indicate the change in the size of something over time, by comparison to its size at some specified time. Specifically, the CPI compares the number of dollars needed to buy a certain bundle of goods each year to the number of dollars needed to buy those goods in 1967. Thus, 1967 is the *base year* for the CPI. The CPI for 1967 is 100, and for 1983 it is 299. Thus, a bundle of goods that would have cost a consumer $100 in 1967 would have cost a consumer $299 in 1983.

A landlord can use the CPI to help him or her decide on the size of annual rent adjustments. By tying the adjustments to this index, the landlord is better able to offset the effects of inflation on property management expenses. A number of other indexes are used for lease adjustments. For simplicity of illustration, only the CPI will be used in this book. The math for using another index is the same as the math involved in using the CPI.

EXAMPLE: Dr. Craig leased a small office space to a tenant for $600 per month in July 1983, when the CPI was 299. The lease called for an annual rent adjustment based upon the CPI. If the CPI was 308 in July 1989, what was the new rent?

First, find the amount of change in the index:

$$
\begin{array}{r}
308 \ \text{July 1984 index} \\
-299 \ \text{July 1983 index} \\
\hline
9 \ \text{Change in Index from 1983 to 1989}
\end{array}
$$

Then, divide part by total to find percent of change:

$$9 \div 299 = .0301 = 3.01\%$$

Now find 3.01% of the original rent by multiplying:

$$
\begin{array}{r}
\$600 \ \text{original rent} \\
\times .0301 \ \text{percent of change} \\
\hline
\$18.06 \ \text{Additional Rent}
\end{array}
$$

Finally, calculate the total adjusted rent:

$$
\begin{array}{r}
\$600.00 \ \text{original rent} \\
+ \ 18.06 \ \text{additional rent} \\
\hline
\$618.06 \ \text{Adjusted Rent}
\end{array}
$$

Another way of solving this problem is to divide the original (1983) rent by the original index, to find the amount of rent charged per CPI index point:

$$\$600 \div 299 \ \text{index points} = \$2.0067 \ \text{per index point}$$

The amount charged per index point, $2.0067, is the *adjustment factor*.
Multiply it by the new (1989) index to find the total adjusted rent.

$2.0067 adjustment factor
× 308 new index
$618.06 Adjusted Rent

As you see, the methods produce identical results. Which is
better? The method you find easiest to understand.

Now, it's your turn.

7. If a new warehouse is leasing for $4,000 per month and the CPI is 300, what will the adjusted rent be
in each of the next 3 years if the indexes at each adjustment time are 305, 309, and 315, respectively?

RENT PER SQUARE FOOT

Rent can also be quoted as being so many dollars per square foot on an annual basis.

EXAMPLES: If the rental rate in a new office building is $12.10
per square foot, what is the *monthly* rent on a space having 1,800
square feet?

First, find the total annual rent:

1,800 sq. ft. × $12.10/sq. ft. = $21,780 annual rent

Then, convert annual rent to monthly rent:

$21,780 annual rent ÷ 12 months = $1,815 monthly rent

Or, the rent might be stated on a monthly basis, and then
converted to an annual rate per square foot for comparison. If the
monthly rent is $2,000 for a 2,220-square-foot space, what is the
annual rate per square foot?

First, find the total rent:

$$\$2,000 \times 12 = \$24,000 \text{ annual rent}$$

Then, find the rent per square foot:

$$\$24,000 \text{ annual rent} \div 2,200 \text{ square feet} = \$10.91 \text{ per sq. ft.}$$

ACHIEVEMENT EXERCISE

When you have finished both parts of this exercise, check your answers against those on pages 331–332. If you miss any of the questions, review this chapter before going on to the special credit problem.

Part I—Open Response   Complete the following problems.

1. Ms. Harper pays $300 minimum rent per month plus 4.5% of gross sales in excess of $80,000 per year. If gross sales last year were $125,000, how much rent did Ms. Harper pay?

2. Mr. Jones's lease requires that he pay $250 minimum rent per month plus 5% of gross sales exceeding $60,000. Mr. Jones paid $10,500 rent last year. What were his gross sales?

3. The Yard Goods Shop pays $600 per month minimum rent plus a percentage of gross sales in excess of $144,000 per year. Last year gross sales totaled $350,000 and the rent paid amounted to $17,500. What percentage of gross sales is required by this lease?

Part II—Multiple Choice   Select the correct response from the choices supplied.

4. A store lease provides for the tenant to pay a minimum monthly rental of $416.67, plus 6% of gross annual sales over $100,000. What were gross annual sales last year if the tenant paid $7,820 total rent?

    a. $130,334   c. $147,000
    b. $100,000   d. $136,725

5. A tenant's store lease requires a minimum monthly rental of $600, plus a percentage of gross annual sales in excess of $180,000. If gross sales for last year were $264,000 and the tenant's rent was $13,080, what is the percentage rate stated in the lease?

    a. 6%   c. 7%
    b. 6.5%   d. 7.5%

6. A store lease provides for minimum monthly rental payments of $425, plus a percentage rent of 8% of gross annual sales exceeding $160,000. Last year, when gross annual sales were $229,500, what was the tenant's gross rent bill for the year?

    a. $27,100.00
    b. $10,660.00
    c. $13,787.50
    d. $28,686.25

7. A store tenant's lease called for $600 a month guaranteed rental, plus 4.5% of gross annual sales in excess of $180,000. When gross annual sales were $164,000, what was the amount of the tenant's gross annual rent?

    a. $8,100   c. $7,380
    b. $7,200   d. $7,500

8. A store lease required a tenant to pay a minimum monthly rent, plus 6% of gross annual sales in excess of $80,000. When total gross annual sales were $120,000 and gross annual rent was $6,400, what was the monthly minimum rent?

    a. $400.00   c. $333.33
    b. $350.00   d. $325.00

9. Ms. Chandler pays 3% of total gross sales for rent, with a minimum base rental of $1,500 per month. In the past year, her sales volume was $500,000. By selecting from a, b, c or d, indicate which of the following statements is (are) true.

   I. Ms. Chandler paid $15,000 in rent.
  II. It would take $600,000 total gross sales, to reach minimum rent.

    a. I only
    b. II only
    c. both I and II
    d. neither I nor II

10. The tenant's lease now requires a payment of $2,000 per month. If the lease provides for an adjustment based upon the CPI, which was 300 a year ago and is now 306, what will the new payment be?

    a. $2,040   c. $2,200
    b. $2,120   d. $2,250

11. If the rent on a 1,750-square-foot office is $14.50 per square foot, what is the monthly rent?

    a. $3,192.51
    b. $23,375.00
    c. $2,114.58
    d. $2,022.44

ANSWER KEY

Entry Evaluation

- $11,250 rent
- $180,000 gross sales

Pages 324–327

1. $400 × 12 = $4,800 minimum annual rent

$360,000 actual gross sales
− 120,000 sales covered by minimum rent
$240,000 Sales Subject to Percentage Rent

$240,000 × .04 = $9,600 percentage rent

$4,800 + $9,600 = $14,400 total annual rent

2. $450 × 12 = $5,400 minimum annual rent $12,420 − $5,400 = $7,020 percentage rent

$$\text{total} = \frac{\text{part}}{\text{percent}} = \frac{\$7,020}{.04} = \$175,500 \text{ gross sales subject to percentage rent}$$

$175,500 + $135,000 = $310,500 total gross sales for year

3. $141,250 total gross sales $11,300 total rent
− 75,000 gross sales not subject to percentage   − 6,000 base rent
$66,250 Gross Sales Subject to Percentage $ 5,300 Percentage Rent

$$\text{percent} = \frac{\text{part}}{\text{total}} = \frac{\$5,300}{\$66,250} = 8\% \text{ percentage rate}$$

4. $300,000 − $99,000 = $201,000 annual gross sales over $99,000
$201,000 × .04 = $8,040 $8,040 ÷ 12 = $670
$670 + $330 = $1,000 one month's rent

5. $600 × 12 = $7,200 yearly base

$200,000 − $180,000 = $20,000 $20,000 × .04 = $800
$7,200 + $800 = $8,000 rent for first year

Since the second year's gross sales did not exceed $180,000, the minimum yearly rent of $7,200 was paid for that year.

$250,000 − $180,000 = $70,000 $70,000 × .05 = $3,500
$7,200 + $3,500 = $10,700 rent for third year

6. $12,500 ÷ 12 = $1,041.67 average monthly rent from Mr. Tompson
$14,000 ÷ 12 = $1,166.67 average monthly rent from Mr. Berry
$9,000 ÷ 12 = $750 average monthly rent from Miss Huerta

$75,000 × .05 = $3,750 $3,750 ÷ 12 = $312.50
Mr. Miller paid the minimum monthly rent of $375.

$1,041.67 + $1,166.67 + $750 + $375 = $3,333.34 total average monthly rent

7. $\dfrac{\$4,000 \text{ original rent first year}}{300 \text{ original index}} = \$13.33$ adjustment factor

$13.33 adjustment factor
×305 second year's index
$4,065.65 Adjusted Rent, second year

$13.33 adjustment factor
×309 third year's index
$4,118.97 Adjusted Rent, third year

$13.33 adjustment factor
×315 fourth year's index
$4,198.95 Adjusted Rent, fourth year

Achievement Exercise

1. $300 × 12 = $3,600
$125,000 − $80,000 = $45,000 $45,000 × 4.5% = $2,025
$2,025 + $3,600 = $5,625 rent

2. $250 × 12 = $3,000 rent paid as monthly minimum
$10,500 − $3,000 = $7,500 rent paid as a percentage of gross sales

$\dfrac{\text{part}}{\text{percent}} = \text{total}$ $\dfrac{\$7,500}{5\%} = \$150,000$ $150,000 + $60,000 = $210,000 gross sales

3. $600 × 12 = $7,200 rent paid as monthly minimum
$17,500 − $7,200 = $10,300 rent paid as percentage of gross sales
$350,000 − $144,000 = $206,000 sales on which percentage rent was paid

$\dfrac{\text{part}}{\text{total}} = \text{percent}$ $\dfrac{\$10,300}{\$206,000} = .05 = 5\%$

Achievement Exercise continued

4. c. $416.67 $\times$ 12 = $5,000.04 annual minimum rent
$7,820 − $5,000.04 = $2,819.96 percentage rent
$2,819.96 ÷ 6% = $46,999.33
$100,000 + $46,999 = $146,999.33

5. c. $600 $\times$ 12 = $7,200 annual minimum rent
$264,000 − $180,000 = $84,000
$13,080 − $7,200 = $5,880
$5,880 ÷ $84,000 = 7% lease percentage

6. b. $425 $\times$ 12 = $5,100 annual minimum rent
$229,500 − $160,000 = $69,500
$69,500 $\times$ 8% = $5,560 percentage rent
$5,100 + $5,560 = $10,660 total rent

7. b. $600 $\times$ 12 = $7,200 annual minimum rent = annual rent

8. c. $120,000 − $80,000 = $40,000
$40,000 $\times$ 6% = $2,400 percentage rent
$6,400 − $2,400 = $4,000 annual minimum rent
$4,000 ÷ 12 = $333.33

9. b. $1,500 $\times$ 12 = $18,000 annual minimum rent
$500,000 $\times$ 3% = $15,000 percentage rent

10. a. $2,000 $\times$ 306 ÷ 300 = $2,040 new monthly rent

11. c. 1,750 $\times$ $14.50 = $25,375 annual rent
$25,375 ÷ 12 = $2,114.58 monthly rent

Special Credit Problem

The owner of a square 160 acres of land lost a strip running diagonally across it due to the construction of a new highway a few years ago. The 160 acres were situated in 2 counties but wholly within 1 school district. Now the owner has sold the portion of his land lying east of the highway. From the data given and the sketch shown, prorate the taxes to the seller for the portion sold. The taxes shown are for all of the owner's property before the sale. Try this problem before looking at the solution. This will reinforce what you have learned.

Denton County Tax	$ 51.20
Tarrant County tax	$108.57
Northwest School District tax	$265.96
Closing date	October 1
Acres highway took in Denton County	14.93
Acres highway took in Tarrant County	42.85
Acres highway took in Northwest School District	57.78

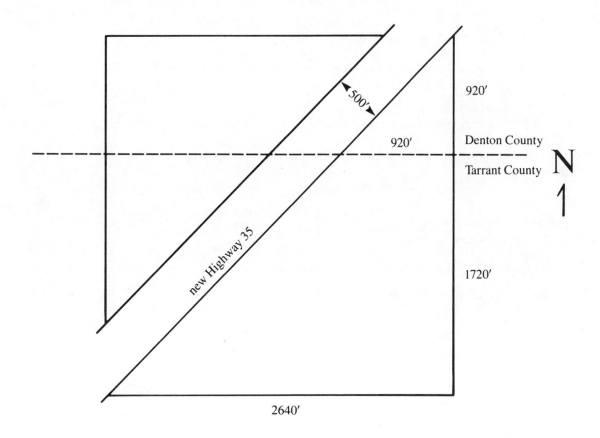

ANSWER KEY

This problem requires 14 major parts, some with several steps, in order to arrive at a solution. The problem is derived directly from a real-world closing with some of the numbers changed. It involves several topics covered in this text. To solve, break the problem into its major parts.

Part 1. Calculate the number of net acres taxed in Denton County (Ch. 5).

Step 1. 920 ft. $\times$ 2,640 ft. = 2,428,800 sq. ft.

Step 2. $\dfrac{2,428,800 \text{ sq. ft.}}{43,560 \text{ sq. ft./ac.}} = 55.76$ ac. total

Step 3.
$$\begin{array}{r} 55.76 \text{ ac. total} \\ -14.93 \text{ ac. in highway} \\ \hline 40.83 \text{ ac. net in Denton County} \end{array}$$

Part 2. Calculate the number of net acres taxed in Tarrant County (Ch. 5).

Step 1. 1,720 ft. $\times$ 2,640 ft. = 4,540,800 sq. ft.

Step 2. $\dfrac{4,540,800 \text{ sq. ft.}}{43,560 \text{ sq. ft./ac.}} = 104.24$ ac. total

Step 3.
$$\begin{array}{r} 104.24 \text{ ac. total} \\ -42.85 \text{ ac. in highway} \\ \hline 61.39 \text{ ac. net in Tarrant County} \end{array}$$

Note: At this point, check your calculations to be sure that the sum of the parts is equal to the whole.

$$\begin{array}{r} 55.76 \text{ total ac. in Denton County} \\ +104.24 \text{ total ac. in Tarrant County} \\ \hline 160.00 \text{ total ac. in property} \end{array}$$

This does agree with the data given, so you may proceed.

Part 3. Calculate the number of net acres in Northwest School Tax District (Ch. 1).

$$\begin{array}{r} 160.00 \text{ ac. total} \\ -57.78 \text{ ac. in highway} \\ \hline 102.22 \text{ ac. net in Northwest School District} \end{array}$$

Part 4. Calculate the number of acres sold in Denton County (Ch. 5).

Step 1. $\dfrac{920 \text{ ft.} \times 920 \text{ ft.}}{2} = 423,200$ sq. ft.

Step 2. $\dfrac{423,200 \text{ sq. ft.}}{43,560 \text{ sq. ft./ac.}} = 9.72$ ac.

Part 5. Calculate the number of acres sold in Tarrant County (Ch. 5).

Step 1. $\dfrac{920 \text{ ft.} + 2,640 \text{ ft.}}{2} \times 1,720 \text{ ft.} = 3,061,600$ sq. ft.

Step 2. $\dfrac{3,061,600 \text{ sq. ft.}}{43,560 \text{ sq. ft./ac.}} = 70.28$ ac.

Part 6. Calculate the number of acres sold in Northwest School District (Ch. 5).

Step 1. $\dfrac{2{,}640 \times 2{,}640}{2} = 3{,}484{,}800$ sq. ft.

Step 2. $\dfrac{3{,}484{,}800 \text{ sq. ft.}}{43{,}560 \text{ sq. ft./ac.}} = 80.0$ ac.

Note: It is time to check your progress again to be sure that the sum of the parts is equal to the whole.

$$
\begin{array}{r}
9.72 \text{ acres sold in Denton County} \\
+\,70.28 \text{ acres sold in Tarrant County} \\
\hline
80.00 \text{ Total Acres Sold}
\end{array}
$$

Again, this agrees with Part 6, so you may proceed.

Part 7. Calculate the total Denton County tax per net acre (Ch. 1).

$\dfrac{\$51.20}{40.83 \text{ ac. net}} = \$1.25/\text{ac.}$

Part 8. Calculate the total Tarrant County tax per net acre (Ch. 1).

$\dfrac{\$108.57}{61.39 \text{ ac. net}} = \$1.77/\text{ac.}$

Part 9. Calculate the total Northwest School District tax per net acre.

$\dfrac{\$265.96}{102.22 \text{ ac. net}} = \$2.60/\text{ac.}$

Part 10. Calculate the Denton County tax on the number of acres sold.

$\$1.25/\text{ac.} \times 9.72 \text{ ac.} = \$12.15$

Part 11. Calculate the Tarrant County tax on the number of acres sold.

$\$1.77/\text{ac.} \times 70.28 \text{ ac.} = \$124.40$

Part 12. Calculate the Northwest School District tax on the number of acres sold.

$\$2.60/\text{ac} \times 80 \text{ ac.} = \$208.00$

Part 13. Obtain the sum of the taxes on the number of acres sold.

$$
\begin{array}{rl}
\$\ 12.15 & \text{Denton County} \\
124.40 & \text{Tarrant County} \\
+\,208.00 & \text{Northwest School District} \\
\hline
\$344.55 & \text{Total Taxes on Acres Sold}
\end{array}
$$

Part 14. Prorate the taxes charged to seller to date of closing (Ch. 13 & 14).

Step 1. $\$344.55 \div 12$ mo. $= \$28.71/\text{mo.}$

Step 2. $\$28.71/\text{mo.} \times 9$ mo. $= \$258.41$ charged to seller

Final Examination I

Complete the following problems. If you would like to review any part of this book, you may do so. When you are finished with Examination I, check your answers against those on pages 346–350.

1. Ms. Burden was one of four equal owners of a debt-free office building, which was sold for $640,000. The following expenses were deducted from the sale price: 5.5% commission, $2,500 for a title insurance policy, and $2,300 for advertising expenses. What was Ms. Burden's share of the net sales proceeds? What percentage of the net sales proceeds did she receive?

   If Ms. Burden originally paid $135,000 for her share in this building, what was her percent of profit or return?

   If Ms. Burden has been one of eight equal partners, what percentage of the net profit would she have received?

2. Mr. Gardner would like to net $40,000 for his residence. The broker will receive a 6.5% commission. What must the sale price be? Round off your answer to the nearest hundred dollars.

3. The Overton family sold their house and received $46,900 after the broker had deducted a 6% commission and $100 for title insurance. What was the sale price of the house?

The salesperson received 3/5 of the commission amount; the broker received the remainder. What amount did the salesperson receive? What amount did the broker receive?

4. A house sold for $45,000, which was 90% of the list price. What price did the house list for? The broker received a commission of $3,150. What was the broker's commission rate? The house originally cost $40,000. What was the seller's percent of profit on the *net* sale price?

5. In the figure below, there are four lots. Lot A sells for $1.25 per square foot, lot B sells for $8.10 per square yard, lot C sells for $.95 per square foot, and lot D sells for $1.05 per square foot.

Mr. Tompson, the broker, sold lots A and C to Mr. Victor. He received a 6% commission on the sale. How much money did Mr. Tompson receive?

Ms. Sloan purchased lots B and D. She also paid Mr. Tompson a 6% commission. How much money did the broker receive on this transaction?

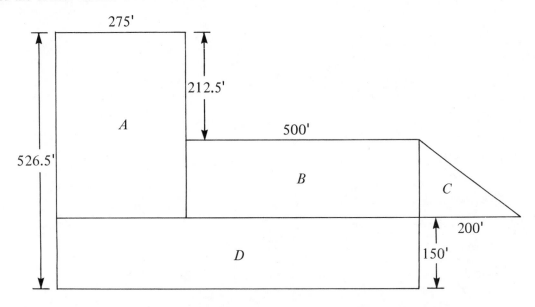

6. The warehouse shown below rents for $.06 per cubic foot. What would it cost to rent the entire warehouse?

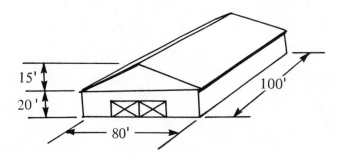

7. A building with an estimated useful life of 40 years is now 15 years old. Its replacement cost has been estimated at $125,000. The land that it is on is valued at $42,000. What is the value of this parcel of real estate via the cost approach to value?

8. An office building earns a net income of $25,000 per year. If the property lists for $150,000, what is the percentage income (rate) for this property?

Mr. Gordon is looking for a property to yield a 20% income rate and is interested in the foregoing property. What must the purchase price of the building be, if he is to make this rate?

9. An apartment building earns a net income of $13,000 per year. What is the value of this property, if the net income represents a 10% investment return?

10. How much income would an apartment complex have to earn to give a 14.5% return on a value of $200,000?

11. Fairport National Bank issued a $3,500 loan at 10.5% simple interest for 5 years. If the loan was paid in full at the end of the 5-year period, what was the total amount of money paid to the bank? If the bank had wished to earn $1,968.75 interest on the above loan over the same period of time, what interest rate would have been charged?

12. Jan Murphy is selling a home to a buyer who has obtained a VA loan for $35,000 at 9.5% interest. The current market rate of interest is 9.75%. How many points will the lending institution require in order to extend this loan? What is the amount of discount required? Who will pay it?

13. Quince Flower Mart has a lease that provides that the tenant pay $375 minimum rent per month, plus 4.5% of gross sales in excess of $100,000 per year. Last year the gross sales amounted to $350,000. What was the rent for the year? What was the average rent for one month? Two years ago, the rent totaled $10,800. What were the gross sales for that year?

14. A piece of property valued at $55,000 is in an area in which the assessment ratio is 68% of market value. The tax rate is $3 per $100 of assessed value. What are the taxes on this property for one year? If an equalization factor of 1.2 is used, what will the taxes be?

15. Mr. Stanton is planning to buy the SW 1/4 of the NW 1/4 of section 5, and the S 1/2 of the SE 1/4 of the NW 1/4 of section 5. The first parcel of land costs $575 per acre and the second, $625 per acre. How much will both parcels cost Mr. Stanton?

16. Miss Weberly is purchasing an apartment building from Mr. Burns for $260,000. She placed a 12% earnest money deposit with the broker, and the closing date has been set for April 25, 1989. Miss Weberly will assume the present mortgage, which had a principal balance of $100,000 on March 1, 1989. The mortgage payments of $800 are due the first day of each month. The interest rate is 8.5%; payments include interest to, but not including, the day of payment. The April 1 payment has been made. The 1987 tax bill, amounting to $2,700, was paid in full. The insurance policy that Mr. Burns holds is a 5-year policy, due to expire February 1, 1983. The $2,875 premium has been paid in full. Mr. Burns has a tax reserve amounting to $1,925. The 1987 water bill for $720 was paid in full. The 1988 water bill for $936 was also paid in full.

Rents are due the first day of each month. The April rent has been collected. There are six apartments, each renting for $380 per month.

The seller agrees to pay the transfer tax stamps on his deed, which cost $.50 per $500, or any fraction thereof of the net taxable consideration after the deduction of the assumed mortgage. The buyer must pay a recording fee of $9.50 to record the seller's deed, a mortgage assumption fee of $80 and a $75 title insurance charge. The seller's expenses include preparing the deed at a cost of $50 and a title charge of $100.

The broker will receive a 6.5% commission on the transaction and is to disburse all expenses on the day of closing.

Compute the necessary prorations and prepare the closing statement for this sale, using the blank form on page 344. Also, prepare a broker's reconciliation, using the form on page 345.

Earnest money:

Mortgage:

Taxes:

Tax and insurance reserve:

Insurance:

Rents:

Water:

Commission:

Transfer tax:

SETTLEMENT STATEMENT WORKSHEET

Property _____

Seller _____

Buyer _____

Settlement Date _____

	Buyer's statement		Seller's statement	
	Debit	Credit	Debit	Credit

Broker's Reconciliation

Items	Receipts	Disbursements

ANSWER KEY

1. $5.5\% \times \$640,000 = \$35,200$
   $\$640,000 - (\$35,200 + \$2,500 + \$2,300) = \$600,000$ net sale price
   $\$600,000 \div 4 = \$150,000$ Ms. Burden's share of net sale price
   $\$150,000 \div \$600,000 = 25\% =$ Ms. Burden's percentage

   $\$150,000 - \$135,000 = \$15,000 \qquad \dfrac{\$15,000}{\$135,000} = .111 = 11.1\%$ of the profit

   $\dfrac{1}{8} = .125 = 12.5\%$ of the net profit as one of eight equal partners

2. $100\% - 6.5\% = 93.5\%$

   $\dfrac{\$40,000}{93.5\%} = \$42,780.748$ rounded to \$42,800

3. $\$46,900 + \$100 = \$47,000$

   $100\% - 6\% = 94\% \qquad \dfrac{\$47,000}{94\%} = \$50,000$ sale price

   $6\% \times \$50,000 = \$3,000$ total commission

   $\dfrac{3}{5} = .6 \qquad .6 \times \$3,000 = \$1,800$ salesman's commission

   $\$3,000 - \$1,800 = \$1,200$ broker's commission

4. $\dfrac{\$45,000}{90\%} = \$50,000$ list price $\qquad \dfrac{\$3,150}{\$45,000} = .07 = 7\%$ commission rate

   $\$45,000 - \$3,150 = \$41,850$ net sale price

   $\$41,850 - \$40,000 = \$1,850$ profit $\qquad \dfrac{\$1,850}{\$40,000} = .046 = 4.6\%$ profit.

5. $A = 275' \times (526.5' - 150') = 275' \times 376.5' = 103,537.5$ sq. ft.
   $103,537.5$ sq. ft. $\times \$1.25 = \$129,421.87$
   To find C: $212.5' + 150' = 362.5' \qquad 526.5' - 362.5' = 164'$

   $\dfrac{1}{2} (200' \times 164') = 16,400$ sq. ft.

   $16,400$ sq. ft. $\times \$.95 = \$15,580$
   $\$129,421.87 + \$15,580 = \$145,001.87$
   $6\% \times \$145,001.87 = \$8,700.112$ rounded to \$8,700.11 commission

   $B = 500' \times 164' = 82,000$ sq. ft. $\qquad 82,000$ sq. ft. $\div 9 = 9,111.111$ sq. yd.
   $9,111.111$ sq. yd. $\times \$8.10 = \$73,799.999$ rounded to \$73,800
   $D = (275' + 500') \times 150' = 775' \times 150' = 116,250$ sq. ft.
   $116,250$ sq. ft. $\times \$1.05 = \$122,062.50$
   $\$73,800 + \$122,062.50 = \$195,862.50$
   $6\% \times \$195,862.50 = \$11,751.75$ commission

6. $\dfrac{1}{2} (15' \times 80' \times 100') + (80' \times 100' \times 20') = 60,000$ cu. ft. $+ 160,000$ cu. ft. $= 220,000$ cu. ft.

   $220,000$ cu. ft. $\times \$.06/\text{cu ft.} = \$13,200$

7. $\dfrac{\$125,000}{40} = \$3,125$ annual depreciation charge

$\$3,125 \times 15$ years $= \$46,875$ depreciation

or $\dfrac{100\%}{40} = 2.5\%$ $2.5\% \times 15$ years $= 37.5\%$ $37.5\% \times \$125,000 = \$46,875$

$\$42,000 + \$125,000 - \$46,875 = \$120,125$

8. $\dfrac{\$25,000}{\$150,000} = 16.6\%$ income $\dfrac{\$25,000}{20\%} = \$125,000$ purchase price

9. $\dfrac{\$13,000}{10\%} = \$130,000$

10. $\$200,000 \times 14.5\% = \$29,000$

11. $\$3,500 \times 10.5\% \times 5$ years $= \$1,837.50$ interest
$\$3,500 + \$1,837.50 = \$5,337.50$ total paid to bank

$\$1,968.75 \div 5$ years $= \$393.75$ annual interest

$\dfrac{\$393.75}{\$3,500} = .1125 = 11\dfrac{1}{4}\%$

12. $9.75\% - 9.5\% = .25\% = \dfrac{1}{4} = \dfrac{2}{8} = 2$ points

$2\% \times \$35,000 = \$700$ discount to be paid by the seller

13. $\$375 \times 12 = \$4,500$
$\$350,000 - \$100,000 = \$250,000$ $\$250,000 \times 4.5\% = \$11,250$
$\$4,500 + \$11,250 = \$15,750$ yearly rent

$\$15,750 \div 12 = \$1,312.50$ monthly rent

$\$10,800 - \$4,500 = \$6,300$ percentage rent $\dfrac{\$6,300}{4.5\%} = \$140,000$

$\$140,000 + \$100,000 = \$240,000$ gross sales

14. $\$55,000 \times 68\% = \$37,400$ $\$37,400 \div \$100 = 374$ $374 \times \$3 = \$1,122$ tax

$\$37,400 \times 1.2 = \$44,880$ $\$44,800 \div \$100 = 448.8$
$448.8 \times \$3 = \$1,346.40$ tax

15. $\dfrac{1}{4} \times \dfrac{1}{4} \times 640 = \dfrac{640}{16} = 40$ acres $40 \times \$575 = \$23,000$

$\dfrac{1}{2} \times \dfrac{1}{4} \times \dfrac{1}{4} \times 640 = \dfrac{640}{32} = 20$ acres $20 \times \$625 = \$12,500$

$\$23,000 + \$12,500 = \$35,500$

16. Earnest money:
$260,000 × 12% = $31,200

Mortgage:
$100,000 × 8.5% = $8,500 $8,500 ÷ 12 = $708.333
$800 − $708.333 = $91.667
$100,000 − $91,667 = $99,908.33
$99,908.33 × 8.5% = $8,492.208 $8,492.208 ÷ 360 = $23.589
Interest has accrued on the 25 days from April 1 through April 25.
$23.589 × 25 = $589.725 or $589.73 accrued interest

Taxes:
$2,700 ÷ 12 = $225 monthly tax $225 ÷ 30 = $7.50 daily tax

1 year   1988
3 months January through March, 1989
25 days   25 days of April

$2,700 × 1 year = $2,700 tax for 1988
$225 × 3 months = $675 $7.50 × 25 days = $187.50
$2,700 + $675 + $187.50 = $3,562.50

Tax reserve:
$1,925 credited to seller

Insurance:
$2,875 ÷ 5 = $575 annual insurance premium $575 ÷ 12 = $47.916 monthly
$47.916 ÷ 30 = $1.597 daily

```
            13
  1992    ✗     31
  1993    2̶     ✗
− 1989    4      25
  ───────────────
    3     9      6
```

$575 × 3 years = $1,725 $47.916 × 9 months = $431.244 $1.597 × 6 days = $9.582
$1,725 + $431.244 + $9.582 = $2,165.826, rounded to $2,165.83

Rents:
$380 × 6 = $2,280 monthly rent
$2,280 ÷ 30 = $76 daily rent

```
  30 total days in April
− 25 date of closing
  ─────────────────────
   5 days of unearned rent      $76 × 5 = $380 accrued rent
```

Water:
Seller pays for 3 months and 25 days of water bill (April 1 through April 25, 1989).
$936 ÷ 12 = $78 monthly $78 ÷ 30 = $2.60 daily
$78 × 3 months = $234 $2.60 × 25 days = $65 $234 + $65 = $299

Commission:
$260,000 × 6.5% = $16,900

Transfer tax:
$260,000 total price − $99,908.33 mortgage = $160,091.67 taxable consideration
$160,091.67 ÷ $500 = $320.183 rounded to 321   321 × $.50 = $160.50

SETTLEMENT STATEMENT WORKSHEET

Property _____

Seller _____

Buyer _____

Settlement Date ____April 25, 1989____

	Buyer's statement		Seller's statement	
	Debit	Credit	Debit	Credit
Purchase price	260,000.00			260,000.00
Earnest money		31,200.00		
Mortgage — assumed		99,908.33	99,908.33	
Interest on mortgage		589.73	589.73	
Real estate taxes		3,562.50	3,562.50	
Tax reserve	1,925.00			1,925.00
Insurance proration	2,165.83			2,165.83
Rent proration		380.00	380.00	
Water proration		299.00	299.00	
Broker's commission			16,900.00	
Transfer tax			160.50	
Title insurance	75.00		100.00	
Recording fees	9.50			
Mortgage assumption fee	80.00			
Preparation of deed			50.00	
Total debits and credits	264,255.33	135,939.56	121,950.06	264,090.83
Due from buyer at closing		128,315.77		
Due to seller at closing			142,140.77	
Totals	**264,255.33**	**264,255.33**	**264,090.83**	**264,090.83**

Broker's Reconciliation

Items	Receipts	Disbursements
Earnest money	31,200.00	
Due from buyer at closing	128,315.77	
Paid seller's expenses		
Broker's commission		16,900.00
Other expenses		310.50
Paid buyer's expenses		164.50
Paid amount due seller at closing		142,140.77
Totals	159,515.77	159,515.77

Final Examination II

SAMPLE REAL ESTATE MATH EXAMINATION

This sample real estate math examination consists of 52 multiple-choice questions, each offering four possible answers. These are the kinds of problems that will probably appear on your state real estate examination.

Read each question carefully so that you understand it fully, then work it out on scratch paper. In working these problems, *carry all figures to three decimal places and round off to two decimal places* (except when working with mills and percentages). Correct answers begin on page 356.

Many people who are preparing for examinations pamper themselves too much. If answers to the sample problems are available, they will peek at them and excuse themselves, while rationalizing that if they were really taking the test, they would be more careful and would give the correct answers. Don't let yourself get away with that! Mark yourself rigidly. Be honest in appraising your weaknesses, and try to strengthen them before you have to take the real test.

If you successfully complete this examination, you should have no trouble passing the mathematics section of your real estate examination.

1. A house is assessed at 30% of its value of $50,000.00. Taxes for the calendar year were levied at the rate of 9 mills for city, 10 mills for county, and 12 mills for schools. Taxes will be due October 1. What is the seller's share of the proration on the settlement date of May 31?

   a. $465.00   c. $271.25
   b. $38.75   d. $193.75

2. The value of a frame house at the end of six years is $35,000.00, not including the lot. What was the original cost of the house if the yearly rate of depreciation is 2-1/2%?

   a. $41,176.47
   b. $40,250.00
   c. $35,897.44
   d. $23,333.33

3. The annual rate of interest on a mortgage loan is 8-1/2%. The monthly interest payment is $201.46. What is the principal amount of the loan?

   a. $2,417.52
   b. $28,441.41
   c. $2,844.14
   d. $14,270.00

4. If concrete costs $150.95 per cubic yard, and labor costs are $5.95 per square foot, what would be the cost of a driveway 28′ × 8′ × 6″?

   a. $1,958.96
   b. $1,877.82
   c. $3,210.62
   d. $1,332.80

5. A salesperson sells a property for $58,500. The contract he has with the employing broker gives him 40% of the total commission earned. The commission due to the broker from the seller is 6%. What is the salesperson's share of the commission?

    a. $2,106   c. $3,510

    b. $1,404   d. $2,340

6. A 64,000-square-foot hillside lot is to be subdivided and sold. One-fourth of the lot is too steep to be useful and 3/16 of the lot is taken up by a stream. The remaining area is flat. If 1/8 of the usable area is reserved for roads, how many square feet of usable area will be left?

    a. 36,000   c. 24,500

    b. 31,500   d. 28,000

7. What would a business be worth if it showed a profit of $585 monthly and earned 13% per year on the total investment?

    a. $7,020   c. $54,000

    b. $91,351   d. $540,000

8. A broker received half of the first month's rent as commission for leasing an apartment and 5% of each month's rent thereafter for collecting the monthly rent of $275.00. What would the broker's total fee be after 18 months?

    a. $247.50   c. $371.25

    b. $2,475.00   d. $385.00

9. An $89,500 investment shows annual net earnings of 10-1/2%. What is the monthly return?

    a. $9,397.50   c. $7,458.33

    b. $986.74   d. $783.13

10. The value of a house without the grounds was estimated to be $48,500 at the end of 8 years. What was the value of the house when new, if the yearly rate of depreciation was 2-1/2%?

    a. $80,833.33   c. $38,800.00

    b. $58,200.00   d. $60,625.00

11. A 60-acre tract listed for sale at $650 per acre was sold for $34,500 on the condition that the purchaser pay the broker's 10% commission on the sale price. How much did the buyer actually save on the deal?

    a. $600   c. $1,050

    b. $3,450   d. $4,500

12. A builder is subdividing a 4-1/2-acre tract into 50′ × 100′ lots. After allowing 71,020 square feet for the necessary streets, into how many lots can the tract be divided?

    a. 25   c. 39

    b. 53   d. 24

13. The mortgage loan on a property is 65% of its appraised valuation. If the interest rate is 9%, and the first semiannual interest payment is $270.00, what is the appraised value of the property?

    a. $4,615.38   c. $3,900.00

    b. $9,230.77   d. $1,950.00

14. How many square feet of concrete would be needed to build a sidewalk 6 feet wide around the two street sides of a 60′ × 100′ corner lot, if the walk were built on the city's easement?

    a. 960   c. 996

    b. 36,000   d. 166

15. $395.00 is 2-1/2% of what amount?

    a. $9.88

    b. $15,800.00

    c. $405.13

    d. $15,405.00

16. After deducting operating expenses, a property earns a net income of $4,500. What percentage of the purchase price is this income of $50,000?

  a. 9   c. 9.9
  b. 8.3   d. 8

17. A lot costs $15,000. It was sold for $19,000 at the end of 3 years. The owner paid taxes of $375 per year. How much profit was made on the sale, counting taxes and lost interest of 5% on the investment each year?

  a. $625   c. $2,875
  b. $3,375   d. $1,750

18. What is the interest on $1,900 for 8 months, 15 days at 10-1/4% per annum?

  a. $140.96   c. $16.23
  b. $194.75   d. $137.96

19. A mortgage company agrees to lend an owner of a property an amount equal to 66% of its appraised valuation at an interest rate of 9% per annum. The first year's interest is $1,800.00. What is the appraised valuation, rounded to the nearest $100.00?

  a. $20,000   c. $13,200
  b. $58,800   d. $30,300

20. The owner of a block of 14 building lots, each with a frontage of 75 feet and a depth of 145 feet, wants to realize $174,600.00 from the sale. However, he wants to withhold 2 lots for himself. What must be the sale price per front foot of the lots sold?

  a. $100.34   c. $194.00
  b. $166.29   d. $86.01

21. A lot 75′ × 110′ sold for $23,600.00. What was the price per square foot?

  a. $127.57   c. $314.67
  b. $1.33   d. $2.86

22. A 100-acre farm is divided into house lots. The streets require 1/8 of the whole farm, and there are 140 lots. How many square feet are there in each lot?

  a. 35,004   c. 27,225
  b. 31,114   d. 43,560

23. An owner's tax bill is $980.60. The total tax rate is 42 mills. The property is assessed at 58.25% of its value. What is the actual value of the property?

  a. $40,081.75
  b. $23,347.62
  c. $41,185.20
  d. $23,990.38

24. A broker has 1.87 acres of land listed for sale at 55-1/2¢ per square foot. What is the total asking price?

  a. $45,208.75
  b. $48,351.60
  c. $24,175.80
  d. $44,801.46

25. A property sold for $51,500.00. If the salesperson received $1,802.50, what was the rate of commission?

  a. 2.5%   c. 4%
  b. 3.5%   d. 3%

26. Find the number of square feet in a lot with a frontage of 75 feet, 6 inches and a depth of 140 feet, 9 inches.

  a. 10,626.63 c. 216.25
  b. 10,652.04 d. 25,510.81

27. What would be the cost of blacktopping the lot described in Problem 26 with a 3-inch layer of asphalt paving at a cost of $28.00 per cubic yard?

  a. $8,265.04
  b. $2,755.05
  c. $3,305.96
  d. $11,020.24

28. Find the cost of building a house 29′ × 34′ × 17′ with a gable roof 8 feet high. The cost of construction is $2.25 per cubic foot.

   a. $55,462.50
   b. $46,588.50
   c. $37,714.50
   d. $27,731.25

29. The market value of a house is $56,500.00, and the assessed value is 40% of the market value. Local taxes on this property are as follows: school tax, 19 mills; sewer and water tax, 7-1/2 mills; township tax, 9 mills; special realty tax, 2-1/4 mills. What is the total yearly tax on this property?

   a. $2,132.88   c. $853.15
   b. $466.69   d. $1,279.73

30. A discount of 3-1/2% is allowed on the taxes in Problem 29 if paid before April 1 of each year. What is the amount of the discount when the property owner pays the tax prior to April 1?

   a. $74.65   c. $20.86
   b. $16.33   d. $29.86

31. A house sold for $45,650.00, giving the owner of the property a profit of 10% over its original cost. What was the original cost of the property?

   a. $41,085   c. $40,650
   b. $41,500   d. $39,500

32. A house is sold on August 6 (the settlement date). The insurance premium for the current calendar year on this house is $695.50 and was paid in advance by the sellers earlier in the year. Find the amount due the sellers as a credit for the insurance premium they prepaid through the day of settlement, on a 30-day-per-month basis.

   a. $415.37   c. $278.20
   b. $405.71   d. $695.50

33. Ms. Jenkins earns $30,000 per year and pays $500 rent per month. What percentage of her income is expended for rent?

   a. 20   c. 5
   b. 8.3   d. 15

34. A tract of land containing 2,613,600 square feet sold for $375 per half-acre. What was the sale price?

   a. $45,000   c. $54,000
   b. $49,005   d. $22,500

35. What is the cost of constructing a fence 6 feet, 6 inches high around a rectangular lot with a frontage of 90 feet and a depth of 175 feet, if the cost of erecting the fence is $1.25 per linear foot, and the cost of material is $.825 per square foot?

   a. $2,083.56   c. $1,752.31
   b. $2,053.75   d. $3,504.63

36. A $40,000.00 mortgage with 8% interest has monthly payments of $335.00. After the second monthly payment, what is the principal balance due on the mortgage?

   a. $40,000.00
   b. $39,862.88
   c. $39,931.67
   d. $39,467.12

37. An agent leased a building for 15 years at an annual rent of $24,000. The agent will receive a commission of 10% of the first 5 years' rent, 5% of the rent for each of the next 3 years, and 2% for the remaining years. What is the agent's total commission?

   a. $4,080   c. $18,960
   b. $61,200   d. $19,920

38. A $42,000 loan at 8% interest was repaid in 6 months. What was the total amount repaid?

   a. $45,360   c. $40,320
   b. $43,680   d. $43,360

39. A property is assessed at 25% of value. The assessment is $16,250.00. What is the value of the property?

    a. $21,666.67
    b. $65,000.00
    c. $48,750.00
    d. $37,916.67

40. A broker pays his salespeople 20% of the commission for listing a property and 40% of the commission for selling it. The commission is 5%. A salesperson received $3,600 on a property that she both listed and sold. What was the selling price?

    a. $120,000   c. $72,000
    b. $200,000   d. $100,000

41. A broker pays his salespeople 10% of the commission for listing a property and 50% of the balance of the commission for selling it. If the broker's commission is 6% of the sale price, and the salesperson received $2,640 for both listing and selling a property, what was the sale price?

    a. $80,000.00
    b. $44,000.00
    c. $73,333.32
    d. $88,000.00

42. A seller paid $32,000.00 for a residence. The seller wants to list it at a 20% profit after paying the broker a 5% commission. What is the listing price?

    a. $33,684.21
    b. $36,480.00
    c. $40,421.05
    d. $36,096.00

43. A buyer is assuming the balance of a seller's present mortgage of $18,450.00 bearing 8% interest payable in advance. The last payment was made April 1 and included $123.00 interest in advance for the month of April. Compute the interest proration if the buyer is liable for interest commencing April 18.

    a. $49.20   c. $51.58
    b. $73.80   d. $53.30

44. A seller's 1-year insurance policy costs $175.00 for the term ending July 31. The seller must pay for the insurance through March 17. Compute the amount of money owed by the buyer on a 30-day-per-month basis.

    a. $31.80   c. $64.91
    b. $65.13   d. $58.33

45. The real estate tax for the current calendar year is $1,425.00, which is payable later in the year. The seller is responsible for taxes through April 21. Compute the seller's share on a 30-day basis.

    a. $439.37   c. $436.68
    b. $391.87   d. $356.25

46. On a four-column closing statement, the purchase price of the house is the same as the:

    I. amount due the seller.
    II. total credit to the seller.

    a. I only
    b. II only
    c. both I and II
    d. neither I nor II

47. The earnest money deposit is a:

    I. credit to the buyer.
    II. debit to the seller.

    a. I only
    b. II only
    c. both I and II
    d. neither I nor II

48. The existing mortgage balance, when assumed by the buyer, is a:

    I. credit to the buyer.
    II. credit to the seller.

    a. I only
    b. II only
    c. both I and II
    d. neither I nor II

49. A developer bought 20 acres of land at $5,000 per acre. Twenty-five houses were built on the land at an average cost of $50,000 each. Streets and other expenses amounted to $200,000. If the developer wants to realize a 25% profit on the investment, what must the average house sell for?

    a. $77,500   c. $66,500
    b. $62,500   d. $78,750

The following questions pertain to the four-column closing statement.

50. The amount of the prorated insurance is a:

  I. debit to the seller
  II. debit to the buyer.

    a. I only
    b. II only
    c. both I and II
    d. neither I nor II

51. The loan origination fee, when paid by the buyer, is a:

  I. credit to the buyer.
  II. debit to the buyer.

    a. I only
    b. II only
    c. both I and II
    d. neither I nor II

52. The amount of a purchase-money mortgage is a:

  I. credit to the buyer.
  II. debit to the seller.

    a. I only
    b. II only
    c. both I and II
    d. neither I nor II

ANSWER KEY

1. d. $50,000 $\times$ 30% = $15,000 assessed value
city: 9 mills $\times$ $15,000 = $135
county: 10 mills $\times$ $15,000 = $150
school: 12 mills $\times$ $15,000 = $180
$135 + $150 + $180 = $465 annual taxes
$465 $\div$ 12 = $38.75/month
$38.75 $\div$ 31 days = $1.25/day
4 months $\times$ $38.75 = $155
31 days $\times$ $1.25 = $38.75
$155 + $38.75 = $193.75

2. a. 2-1/2% = .025 $\times$ 6 years = 15% = amount of depreciation taken
100% = original cost $-$ 15% depreciation taken = 85%
present value = 85% of original cost = $35,000
$35,000 $\div$ .85 = $41,176.47 original cost of house

3. b. $201.46 $\times$ 12 = $2,417.52 annual interest
$2,417.52 = 8-1/2% of loan amount
$2,417.52 $\div$ .085 = $28,411.41 loan amount

4. a. concrete: 28′ × 8′ × .5′ = 112 cu. ft. ÷ 27 = 4.15 cu. yds.
4.15 × $150.95 = $626.16
labor: 28′ × 8′ = 224 sq. ft.
224 × $5.95 = $1,332.80
$626.16 + $1,332.80 = $1,958.96

5. b. $58,500 × 6% = $3,510 broker's total commission
$3,510 × 40% = $1,404 agent's share

6. b. 64,000 × 1/4 = 16,000 sq. ft. too steep
64,000 × 3/16 = 12,000 sq. ft. stream bed
16,000 + 12,000 = 28,000
64,000 − 28,000 = 36,000 sq. ft.
8/8 − 1/8 roads = 7/8 × 36,000 = 31,500 sq. ft. useable

7. c. $585 × 12 = $7,020 annual income = 13% return
$7,020 ÷ .13 = $54,000 value of business

8. c. $275 ÷ 2 = $137.50 leasing commission (1st month)
$275 × 17 months × 5% = $233.75
$137.50 + $233.75 = $371.25 total fee

9. d. $89,500 × 10.5% ÷ 12 = $783.13 monthly return

10. d. 8 × .025 = .20
1.00 − .20 = .80 = present value = $48,500
$48,500 ÷ .80 = $60,625 original value

11. c. $650 × 60 = $39,000 list price
$34,500 × 10% = $3,450
$34,500 + $3,450 = $37,950
$39,000 − $37,950 = $1,050 saved by buyer

12. a. 4.5 × 43,560 = 196,020
196,020 − 71,020 = 125,000 net sq. ft.
50 × 100 = 5,000 sq. ft. lot size
125,000 ÷ 5,000 = 25 lots

13. b. $270 × 2 = $540 annual interest
$540 = 9% of loan amount
$540 ÷ .09 = $6,000 loan amount = 65% appraised value
$6,000 ÷ .65 = $9,230.77 appraised value

14. c. 100 × 6 = 600
6 × 6 = 36
60 × 6 = 360
996 sq. ft.

15. b. $395 = .025 of amount
$395 ÷ .025 = $15,800 amount

16. a. $4,500 ÷ $50,000 = 9.0% of purchase price

17. a. $375 × 3 = $1,125 taxes
$15,000 × 5% × 3 years = $2,250 interest lost
$1,125 + $2,250 = $3,375 holding costs
$19,000 − $3,375 − $15,000 = $625 net profit

18. d. $1,900 × 10.25% = $194.75 annual interest
$194.75 ÷ 12 = $16.23 monthly interest
8 × $16.23 = $129.83
$16.23 ÷ 30 = $.54 × 15 = $8.12
$129.83 + $8.12 = $137.96 earned interest

19. d. $1,800 ÷ .09 = $20,000
$20,000 ÷ .66 = $30,303.03
round to $30,300 appraised valuation

20. c. $174,600 ÷ 12 = $14,550 lot price
$14,550 ÷ 75 = $194 price per front foot

21. d. 75 × 110 = 8,250 sq. ft.
$23,600 ÷ 8,250 = $2.86 price per square foot

22. c. 100 × 1/8 = 12.5 acres in streets
100 − 12.5 = 87.5 net acres
87.5 × 43,560 = 3,811,500 net sq. ft.
3,811,500 ÷ 140 = 27,225 sq. ft. per lot

23. a. $980.60 ÷ .042 ÷ .5825 = $40,081.75 property value

24. a. 1.87 × 43,560 × .555 = $45,208.75 asking price

25. b. $1,802.50 ÷ $51,500 = .035 = 3.5% commission

26. a. 75.5 × 140.75 = 10,626.63 sq. ft.

27. b. 10,626.63 × .25 = 2,656.66 cu. ft.
2,656.66 ÷ 27 = 98.39 cu. yds.
98.39 × $28 = $2,755.05 paving cost

28. b. 29 × 34 × 17 = 16,762 cu. ft.
29 × 34 × 8 ÷ 2 = 3,944 cu. ft.
16,762 + 3,944 = 20,706 total cu. ft.
20,706 × $2.25 = $46,588.50 construction cost

29. c. $56,500 × 40% = $22,600 assessed value

school:	$22,600 × .019 =	$429.40
water & sewer:	$22,600 × .0075 =	$169.50
township:	$22,600 × .009 =	$203.40
special:	$22,600 × .00225 =	$ 50.85
		$853.15 annual tax

30. d. $853.15 × 3.5% = $29.86 discount

31. b. $45,650 ÷ (100% + 10%) = $41,500 original cost

32. c. $695.50 ÷ 12 = $57.96 monthly
$57.96 ÷ 30 = $1.93 daily
$57.96 × 7 = $405.72
$1.93 × 6 = $11.58
$405.72 + $11.58 = $417.30
$695.50 − $417.30 = $278.20 refund of insurance premium

33. a. $30,000 ÷ 12 = 2,500
$500 ÷ $2,500 = .20 = 20% of monthly income

34. a. 2,613,600 ÷ 43,560 = 60 acres
$375 × 2 = $750 per acre
60 × $750 = $45,000 sale price

35. d. 90 + 175 × 2 = 530 linear feet
530 × $1.25 = $662.50
530 × 6.5 = 3,445 sq. ft.
3,445 × $.825 = $2,842.13
$662.50 + $2,842.13 = $3,504.63 total cost

36. b. $40,000 × 8% ÷ 12 = $266.67 1st month's interest
$335 − 266.67 = $68.33 1st month's principal payment
$40,000 − $68.33 = $39,931.67 balance after 1st payment
$39,931.67 × 8% ÷ 12 = $266.21 2nd month's interest
$335 − $266.21 = $68.79 2nd month's principal
$39,931.67 − $68.79 = $39,862.88 balance after 2nd payment

37. c. 24,000 × 10% × 5 = $12,000
24,000 × 5% × 3 = $ 3,600
24,000 × 2% × 7 = $ 3,360
$18,960 total commission

38. b. $42,000 × 8% × .5 = $1,680
$42,000 + $1,680 = $43,680 total repaid

39. b. $16,250 ÷ .25 = $65,000 value

40. a. $3,600 ÷ .60 = $6,000
$6,000 ÷ .05 = $120,000 sale price

41. a. $2,640 ÷ [.10 + (1/2 × .90)] = $2,640 ÷ .55 = $4,800
$4,800 ÷ .06 = $80,000 sale price

42. c. $32,000 × 20% = $6,400 net profit
$32,000 + $6,400 = .95% list price
$38,400 ÷ .95 = $40,421.05

43. d. $123 ÷ 30 = $4.10 daily
$4.10 × 13 days = $53.30 interest credit to seller

44. b. $175 ÷ 12 = $14.58 monthly
$14.58 ÷ 30 = $.486 daily
4 × $14.58 = $58.33
14 × $.486 = $6.80
$58.33 + $6.80 = $65.13 insurance credit to seller

45. a. $1,425 ÷ 12 = $118.75 monthly
$118.75 ÷ 30 = $3.96 daily
3 × $118.75 = $356.25
21 × $3.96 = $83.12
$356.25 + $83.12 = $439.37

46. d.

47. a.

48. a.

49. a.

50. b.

51. b.

52. c.

Appendix A: The Two-Column Closing Statement

INTRODUCTION

As you learned in Chapter 14, every real estate transaction involving the transfer of property requires the preparation of a written form called a *closing statement*. There we dealt only with the 4-column type. However, a 2-column format is still used by some brokers, so this appendix will concentrate on the preparation and use of this form.

CLOSING STATEMENT FORMS

The closing statement is a device used to "balance the books." It is a way of calculating how much money is owed, taking all factors into account. Usually the buyer owes the seller, but on rare occasions, the seller owes the buyer. Instead of exchanging money for each small transaction, the amounts owed are entered separately on the closing statement. The entire statement is then balanced to determine the total amount owed. In this way, there is only one exchange of money, and the closing statement serves as the one receipt (document) for a transaction. The overall equations for the 2-column closing statement are:

> total credits to seller − total credits to buyer = cash buyer owes seller
>
> total credits to buyer − total credits to seller = cash seller owes buyer

The formula used is determined by whether the buyer's or seller's credits were greater. If the seller's credits were greater than the buyer's, the first formula would be used; if the buyer's credits were greater than the seller's, the second formula would be used.

In preparing a 2-column closing statement, certain items must be considered. (Refer to the form on page 363 as you read.)

Items credited to the buyer usually include:

- earnest money deposit
- existing mortgage balance, when assumed by the buyer
- accrued items—such as real estate taxes—that have accrued or are accruing but are not yet due or paid
- unearned revenues (revenues—such as rent—collected in advance but not yet earned)

Items credited to the seller usually include:

- sale price
- prepaid items (items paid in advance—such as a fire insurance policy premium paid for a term that has not fully expired, advance interest on an assumed mortgage or fuel on hand)
- prepaid insurance and tax reserves (if any) on an outstanding assumed mortgage

Notice that *accrued* items are credits to the buyer, and *prepaid* items are credits to the seller.

The 2-column statement on the opposite page illustrates the same transaction shown on page 286. In this format, the statement is divided into 2 parts: the division of items between buyer and seller, and the broker's settlement. The upper portion of the 2-column statement accounts for those items given by one party to the other—items that on the 4-column statement would be credited to one party and debited to the other. As you can see, only the credit is entered; there are no debit entries on this portion of the statement. While the format of the 2-column statement is different from the 4-column one discussed in Chapter 14, the results are the same—the buyer must pay the seller a balance of $8,828.82.

BROKER'S SETTLEMENT

Because he or she is the seller's agent, the broker may hold the earnest money deposit under the terms of the sales contract until the sale is closed. The bottom portion of the two-column statement, the broker's settlement with the seller, is similar to the cash reconciliation illustrated on page 286.

The earnest money received by the broker is entered as a credit to the seller. All of the expenses paid by the broker for the seller are entered as debits. These would include the cost of the broker's commission, transfer tax, recording fees, and title examination charges.

Various additional items can be included in the 2-column statement. If, as in the sample transaction, the broker has paid some of the buyer's expenses from the seller's earnest money, the seller must collect from the buyer for these expenses. In the closing statement on page 363, note the "credit seller" entries by which the buyer reimburses the seller for assumption and recording fees. If such items are to be included in this form of closing statement, they are entered in the broker's settlement as debits and then re-entered in the upper portion of the statement as credits to the seller.

At the closing, the broker will have ready for delivery to the seller a signed receipt covering the broker's commission and the reimbursement for the listed expenses. The broker will also bring to the closing a check for $2,002.50 ($6,000.00 − $3,997.50) payable to the seller for the balance due the seller from the broker. The seller has also received the buyer's check for $8,828.82, making a total of $10,831.32. This is the same total due the seller that is shown on the 4-column statement you've already completed.

CLOSING STATEMENT

PROPERTY	BROKER
SELLER	ADDRESS
PURCHASER	ADDRESS
DATE OF CONTRACT	DATE OF CLOSING

	CREDIT PURCHASER	CREDIT SELLER
Purchase Price		6 2 5 0 0 0 0
Earnest Money	6 0 0 0 0 0	
First Mortgage—Assumed by Purchaser	4 7 5 0 0 0 0	
Interest	2 8 5 0 0	
General Taxes 19		
General Taxes 19 prorated from 1/1 to 7/14	8 8 8 0 8	
Tax Reserve		8 2 4 0 0
Special Assessments		
Insurance Premiums, Unearned		9 5 4 0
Rents from to		
Coal tons @ $		
Janitor from to		
Water from to		
Gas & Light from to		
Assumption Fee		7 5 0 0
Recording Fee		7 5 0
Subtotal	5 4 6 7 3 0 8	6 3 5 0 1 9 0
Balance Due Seller	8 8 2 8 8 2	
TOTAL	6 3 5 0 1 9 0	6 3 5 0 1 9 0

SETTLEMENT	DEBIT	CREDIT
Earnest Money		6 0 0 0 0 0
Abstract or Guaranty Policy	1 5 0 0 0	
Recording Fees – Buyer	7 5 0	
Commission	3 7 5 0 0 0	
Assumption Fee – Buyer	7 5 0 0	
Transfer Tax Stamps	1 5 0 0	
Subtotal	3 9 9 7 5 0	6 0 0 0 0 0
Balance Due Seller	2 0 0 2 5 0	
TOTAL	6 0 0 0 0 0	6 0 0 0 0 0

Accepted   Accepted

_____   _____
            Seller   Purchaser

Prepared by

_____
            Broker

CLOSING PROBLEM

1. Work the following closing statement problem and enter the figures on the form on the next page.

Sellers are Randolph P. Gunther and Jane M. Gunther, 41 Lane, Fairport. They are selling the property located at that address.

Sellers' broker is Apollo Realty, David Salin, Broker.

Buyers are Carl W. Link and Ann C. Link, 823 Hill, Fairport.

Contract of sale is dated July 15, 1988.

Closing date is August 18, 1988.

Sale price is $58,000.

Earnest money is $5,800.

The buyer is to assume the seller's mortgage, including the 9% interest. The principal balance of the mortgage after the July 21 payment was $34,600.

Real estate taxes of $1,100 for the fiscal year beginning July 1, 1987, and ending June 30, 1988, will not be paid until October 15, 1988.

A tax reserve account of $1,400 has been held with the mortgage.

The seller paid a $264.80 annual premium on an insurance policy effective to April 15, 1989, which the buyer will assume.

The last water bill the seller paid, for $45, covered the months of April, May and June, 1988. The next bill is due October 1, 1988 and will cover July, August and September.

The broker has been holding the purchaser's earnest money deposit and is to be reimbursed for all payments and purchases made on behalf of the seller.

The broker will pay the recording fee of $65 and the title search fee of $125.

The broker will receive a commission of 6% of the selling price.

The broker is to pay for the seller's transfer tax stamps, which is $.50 per $500 or any fraction thereof of the net taxable consideration (assumed mortgages exempt).

Compute the prorations on a 360-day year and a 30-day month when calculating dollar amounts. When calculating the number of days, use the actual number of days in the month of closing. When you have finished, compare your work against the solutions on pages 366–367.

CLOSING STATEMENT

PROPERTY	BROKER
SELLER	ADDRESS
PURCHASER	ADDRESS
DATE OF CONTRACT	DATE OF CLOSING

	CREDIT PURCHASER	CREDIT SELLER
Purchase Price		
Earnest Money		
First Mortgage		
Interest		
General Taxes 19		
General Taxes 19 prorated from to		
Tax Reserve		
Special Assessments		
Insurance Premiums, Unearned		
Rents from to		
Coal tons @ $		
Janitor from to		
Water from to		
Gas & Light from to		
Subtotal		
Balance Due Seller		
TOTAL		

SETTLEMENT	DEBIT	CREDIT
Earnest Money		
Abstract or Guaranty Policy		
Recording Fees		
Commission		
Transfer Tax Stamps		
Subtotal		
Balance Due Seller		
TOTAL		

Accepted   Accepted

_____   _____
       Seller   Purchaser

Prepared by

_____
       Broker

ANSWER KEY

1. Mortgage interest proration:

$34,600 × 9% = $3,114 annual interest $3,114 ÷ 360 = $8.65 daily interest

```
  31  total days in July
− 21  date of last interest payment (July 21)
  10  number of days of accrued interest in July
+ 18  number of days of accrued interest in August
  28  total days of accrued interest
```

$8.65 × 28 days = $242.20 accrued interest

General taxes:

$1,100 ÷ 12 = $91.666 monthly tax $91.666 ÷ 30 = $3.055 daily tax

```
1 year       June 30, 1983 to June 30, 1988
1 month      July
18 days      18 days in August
```

$1,100 × 1 year = $1,100 accrued tax for 1983–84
$91.666 × 1 month = $91.666 $3.055 × 18 days = $54.99
$91.666 + $54.99 = $146.656 rounded to $146.66 accrued tax for July 1 to August 18, 1988

Insurance premiums:
$264.80 ÷ 12 = $22.066 monthly insurance premium
$22.066 ÷ 30 = $.735 daily insurance premium

years	months	days
	15	
1988	3	46
~~1989~~	~~4~~	~~15~~
−1988	8	18
0	7	28

$22.066 × 7 months = $154.462 $.735 × 28 days = $20.58
$154.462 + $20.58 = $175.042 rounded to $175.04 unexpired insurance premium

Water:
$45 ÷ 3 = $15 monthly water bill $15 ÷ 30 = $.50 daily water bill

```
1 month   July
18 days    18 days in August
```

$15 × 1 month = $15 $.50 × 18 days = $9
$15 + $9 = $24 accrued water bill payment

Broker's commission:
$58,000 × 6% = $3,480 broker's commission

Transfer tax:
$58,000 total price − $34,600 mortgage = $23,400 taxable consideration
$23,400 ÷ $500 = 46.8 = 47 parts   47 × $.50 = $23.50 transfer tax

CLOSING STATEMENT

PROPERTY 41 Lane, Fairport	**BROKER** Apollo Realty
SELLER Randolph P. Gunther and Jane M. Gunther	**ADDRESS** 41 Lane, Fairport
PURCHASER Carl W. Link and Ann C. Link	**ADDRESS** 823 Hill, Fairport
DATE OF CONTRACT July 15, 1988	**DATE OF CLOSING** August 18, 1988

	CREDIT PURCHASER	CREDIT SELLER
Purchase Price		58 000 00
Earnest Money	5 800 00	
First Mortgage—Assumed by Purchaser	34 600 00	
Interest　9%	242 20	
General Taxes 1987 – 1988	1 100 00	
General Taxes 1988　prorated from 7/1 to 8/18	146 66	
Tax Reserve		1 400 00
Special Assessments		
Insurance Premiums, Unearned		175 04
Rents　from　to		
Coal　tons @ $		
Janitor　from　to		
Water　from July 1 to August 18	24 00	
Gas & Light　from　to		
Subtotal	41 912 86	59 575 04
Balance Due Seller	17 662 18	
TOTAL	59 575 04	59 575 04

SETTLEMENT	DEBIT	CREDIT
Earnest Money		5 800 00
Abstract or Guaranty Policy	125 00	
Recording Fees	65 00	
Commission	3 480 00	
Transfer Tax Stamps	23 50	
Subtotal	3 693 50	5 800 00
Balance Due Seller	2 106 50	
TOTAL	5 800 00	5 800 00

Accepted　　　　　　　　　　　　　Accepted

_____　　　　_____
　　　　　　Seller　　　　　　　　　　　　　　　Purchaser

Prepared by

_____
　　　　　　Broker

Appendix B:
The Metric System

INTRODUCTION

The metric system is an international language of measurement. It is named for the basic unit of length, the *meter,* and was first commonly used in France. The meter, equivalent to 39.37 U.S. inches, is a unit of measure just slightly larger than a U.S. yard (36 inches). Many common measuring instruments have the word *meter* in their names: for instance, a speedo*meter* is used to measure speed and a thermo*meter* is used to measure temperature.

The metric system is the most widely used system of measurement in the world today; in fact, the only major country not using the metric system is the United States. However, during past years, a strong movement toward adopting the system has developed in this country, since the United States loses billions of dollars of foreign business annually because its measurements are not compatible with world standards.

This chapter will give you a basic comprehension of the metric system, an understanding of the sizes of the more common metric units and the logical relationship among them, and practice in converting from U.S. to metric units and from metric to U.S. units.

DIMENSIONS AND UNITS

To think clearly about units of measure, you must be able to distinguish between the quantity being measured (for example, *length*) and the units in which it is measured (for example, *feet*).

When measuring length, it is convenient to have units of different sizes. For example, in the U.S. system of measurement we use inches, feet, yards, rods, chains, and miles. The relationship among these different units is not consistent. For example, to go from feet to inches you must multiply by 12, while to go from yards to feet, you must multiply by 3.

The metric system, too, uses units of different sizes to state length, but it has a consistent structure built around the number 10. In the metric system, to change from one unit to the next higher or lower unit of length, you simply multiply or divide by 10.

The following list presents the metric units of length in order from smallest to largest. In the metric system, each unit is exactly 10 times larger than the next smaller unit. Knowing this, you should be able to supply the missing number in the list.

Measures of Length

1. Fill in the following blank.

$$
\left.
\begin{array}{rcl}
0.001 & \text{meter} & = 1 \text{ millimeter} \\
0.01 & \text{meter} & = 1 \text{ centimeter} \\
0.1 & \text{meter} & = 1 \text{ decimeter}
\end{array}
\right\} \quad \text{units smaller than a meter}
$$

$$
\begin{array}{rcl}
1.0 & \text{meter} & = \text{basic unit}
\end{array}
$$

$$
\left.
\begin{array}{rcl}
10.0 & \text{meters} & = 1 \text{ decameter} \\
100.0 & \text{meters} & = 1 \text{ hectometer} \\
\underline{\hspace{2cm}} & \text{meters} & = 1 \text{ kilometer}
\end{array}
\right\} \quad \text{units larger than a meter}
$$

The metric system has another feature that makes it easy to learn. The names of units larger than the basic unit (multiples) and units smaller than the basic unit (submultiples) are made by joining together two names: (1) the name of the multiple or submultiple and (2) the name of the basic unit. For example, in the metric system the prefix *kilo-* means "one thousand," and the basic unit of length is the *meter.* So one *kilometer* means "one thousand meters." The prefix *milli-* means "one thousandth."

2. What does one *millimeter* mean? _____

Whether you know it or not, many aspects of your life have already been touched by the metric system. For example, the electric meter in your home measures in *kilo*watts.

3. The prefix *kilo* should tell you that one kilowatt is how many watts? _____

The numbers on the dial of your AM radio refer to the radio wave frequencies at which the stations operate.

4. For example, a station at 600 *kilo*cycles on your dial is broadcasting at a frequency of how many cycles per second? _____

5. A station broadcasting at a frequency of 890,000 cycles per second would be operating at what kilocycle reading on your dial? _____

The numbers on the dial of your FM radio refer to *mega*cycles per second. *Mega-* is a Greek root meaning "great." In the metric system it means "a million times."

6. Thus, a station located at 98 on your FM radio dial would be broadcasting at a frequency of how many cycles per second? _____

Study this chart:

Submultiples			
Prefix	**Prefix + *Meter***	**Abbreviation**	**Multiply by**
deci-	decimeter	dm	0.1(1/10)
centi-	centimeter	cm	0.01(1/100)
milli-	millimeter	mm	0.001(1/1000)
Multiples			
deca-	decameter	dkm	10
hecto-	hectometer	hm	100
kilo-	kilometer	km	1000

Suppose you want to state 6.921 meters in terms of decimeters. Since the prefix *deci-* means "one tenth," and a decimeter is a unit 0.1 times (1/10) as large as a meter, there will be 10 times as many decimeter units as meter units.

7. Copy the number 6921 and place the decimal point in the proper place to show the number of decimeters equal in length to 6.921 meters. _____

8. Find the number of centimeters equal in length to 6.921 meters. _____

9. Find the number of millimeters in 6.921 meters. _____

10. 8.329 meters is another name for how many:

        a. millimeters? _____

        b. centimeters? _____

        c. decimeters? _____

Dividing a number by 10, 100 or 1,000 is as simple as multiplying a number by 10, 100 or 1,000. Study the examples below.

Multiply	**Divide**
$5.3 \times 10 = 53.0$	$5.3 \div 10 = 0.53$
$5.3 \times 100 = 530.0$	$5.3 \div 100 = 0.053$
$5.3 \times 1000 = 5300.0$	$5.3 \div 1000 = 0.0053$

11. A length of 7,500 meters is equal to how many:

        a. decameters? _____

        b. hectometers? _____

        c. kilometers? _____

12. Supply the appropriate equivalent in meters for each of the following measurements:

    a. 9.6 kilometers   _____ meters

    b. 9.6 hectometers   _____ meters

    c. 9.6 decameters   _____ meters

13. One meter is equal in length to how many:

    a. millimeters?   _____

    b. centimeters?   _____

    c. decimeters?   _____

    d. decameters?   _____

    e. hectometers?   _____

    f. kilometers?   _____

The following exercises are based on the U.S.-to-metric and metric-to-U.S. conversion table that can be found at the end of this appendix. Refer to it when necessary to find the equivalents you need to work the problems.

Even though the metric system is not yet the official system of measurement used in the United States, it is still common practice to use metric measures in manufacturing certain types of American products, such as cameras, film, and optical and other types of instruments. This is true because the various parts of some of these products may be manufactured in several different countries. For example, camera lenses manufactured in Germany are most likely to be measured and labeled in metric units. If the camera bodies into which these lenses were to be fitted were made in the United States and were measured using U.S. units, this would lead to considerable confusion and very expensive conversions from one system of measurement to the other. For this reason, most camera parts, film and other instruments are made using the metric system of measurement.

The United States is a very large manufacturer and exporter of photographic film. Because film made in this country is used in every country in the world, it is measured in metric units. One of the most widely used still cameras is the 35-mm single-lens reflex camera.

14. If the 35-mm film for this camera were measured by the U.S. system, how wide would it be?

    a. about 2 inches wide

    b. just under 1 inch wide

    c. just under 1-1/2 inches wide

15. Assume that you saw this short description in a newspaper: "Never once losing the pace, England's James Rulander set a new Olympic record today for the 1500 m race." How many kilometers long was the race? _____

16. Using the U.S. system of measurement, how long was the race?

    a. just under 2 miles

    b. slightly more than a mile

    c. just under a mile

Metric units are not only used in track meets, but they are also used in international swimming and speed skating, field events and a variety of other sports. A popular international swimming event is the 200-meter freestyle.

17. If the swimming pool is 20 yards long, approximately how many times will the swimmer have to swim the length of the pool to complete the race?

    a. about 7 times
    b. about 9 times
    c. about 11 times
    d. about 13 times

18. Some scientists who study the earth, such as physicists, geologists, astronomers and chemists, think that the inner core of the earth consists of solid iron and nickel and has a radius of about 3,400 km. What is the radius in miles? _____

19. What is the radius in meters of the inner core of the earth? _____

Measures of Area

So far, you have learned how to construct and manipulate units of length. However, in many of the mathematical problems you will encounter in the real estate field, you will need to measure areas. Let us see what happens to metric units when we start squaring them.

Suppose you have a square whose sides each measure 1 meter. The area enclosed is called 1 square meter and is written 1 m^2 ($1 \text{ m} \times 1 \text{ m} = 1 \text{ m}^2$).

20. What is the area of a square whose sides are each 3 meters long?

_____

21. Now look again at the 1m × 1m square and express the length of the sides in millimeters. Then find the area of the square in millimeters.

each side =

area =

22. How many square decimeters are there in a square meter?

23. A rectangle has sides 1.5 m and 0.5 m long. What is the area of the rectangle in cm^2?

If you know the conversion factor for yards to meters, you can obtain the conversion factor for square yards to square meters:

$$1 \text{ yd.} = 0.9144 \text{ m, so}$$
$$1 \text{ yd.} \times 1 \text{ yd.} = 0.9144 \text{ m} \times 0.9144 \text{ m, and}$$
$$1 \text{ sq. yd.} = 0.836127 \text{ m}^2$$

24. In the U.S. system the acre is the unit most commonly used in buying and selling land. One acre is 4,840 square yards, or how many m²?

In the metric system an area of 100^2m is called an *are.* One hundred ares is one *hectare,* which is the unit commonly used in land measurement. Thus,

$$1 \text{ hectare} = 100 \text{ m}^2 \times 100 = 10,000 \text{ m}^2$$

To convert acres to hectares, you can, of course, use the direct conversion factor:

$$1 \text{ acre} = 4,046.85 \text{ m}^2$$
$$1 \text{ acre} = 4,046.85 \div 10,000 = 0.404685 \text{ hectare}$$

For most practical purposes you can round off this awkward number and say that:

$$1 \text{ acre} = 0.4 \text{ hectare.}$$

25. What is one hectare in terms of acres?

26. Express 15 acres in terms of hectares.

27. A parcel of land contains 217,800 square feet.

    a. How many acres does the parcel contain?

    b. How many ares?

   c. How many hectares?

28. The following ad appeared in a newspaper:

For Sale: Spacious 3-bedroom home on a large 0.4 hectare corner lot. Country charm, yet only a 1.6-kilometer walk to town and shopping. Additional vacant land in 1.2-hectare parcels.

Based on the U.S. system:

   a. How many miles from town is the home?

   b. What is the size of the lot in acres?

   c. What is the size of each vacant parcel in acres?

29. Mr. Jones owns a vacant lot that measures 25 m by 100 m. If the land is worth $1,000 per are, what is the value of the lot?

     The following conversion tables include metric equivalents for measures of capacity and weight as well as for length. If you already understand the concepts behind the units of length, you will also easily understand the other metric measures. The same prefixes and division and multiplication processes apply in all three cases. For instance, since one liter equals 1.056 quarts, one decaliter equals 10.56 quarts (2.64 gallons) and one hectoliter equals 105.6 quarts (26.4 gallons), and so on.

Conversion Tables

Metric to U.S.	U.S. to Metric

Common Measures of Length

1 centimeter	= 0.3937 inch	1 inch	= 2.54 centimeters
1 meter	= 39.37 inches	1 yard	= 0.9144 meter
1 meter	= 1.093 yards	1 mile	= 1.609 kilometers
1 kilometer	= 0.621 mile		

Common Measures of Capacity

1 liter	= 1.056 quarts	1 quart	= 0.946 liter
1 liter	= 0.264 gallon	1 gallon	= 3.785 liters

Common Measures of Weight (Mass)

1 gram	= 0.0352 ounce	1 ounce	= 28.35 grams
1 kilogram	= 2.2046 pounds	1 pound	= 0.4536 kilogram
1 metric ton	= 2,204.62 pounds	1 ton	= 0.907 metric ton

Metric Tables

1 millimeter (mm) = .001 meter (m)	1 milligram (mg) = 0.001 gram (g)	1 milliliter (ml) = 0.001 liter (l)
1 centimeter (cm) = .01 meter	1 centigram (cg) = 0.01 gram	1 centiliter (cl) = 0.01 liter
1 decimeter (dm) = 0.1 meter	1 decigram (dg) = 0.1 gram	1 deciliter (dl) = 0.1 liter
meter (basic unit)	gram (basic unit)	liter (basic unit)
1 decameter (dkm) = 10 meters	1 decagram (dkg) = 10.0 grams	1 decaliter (dkl) = 10.0 liters
1 hectometer (hm) = 100 meters	1 hectogram (hg) = 100.0 grams	1 hectoliter (hl) = 100.0 liters
1 kilometer (km) = 1000 meters	1 kilogram (kg) = 1000.0 grams	1 kiloliter (kl) = 1000.0 liters

ANSWER KEY

1. 1,000

2. one thousandth of a meter (0.001 m)

3. 1,000

4. 600,000 (One kilocycle equals 1,000 cycles per second.)

5. 890

6. 98,000,000 or 98 million

7. $6.921 \times 10 = 69.21$
Multiplying by 10 has the same effect of moving the decimal point one place to the right.

8. 692.1
Multiplying by 100 has the effect of moving the decimal point two places to the right.

9. 6,921
Multiplying by 1,000 has the effect of moving the decimal point three places to the right.

10. a. 8,329

    b. 832.9

    c. 83.29

11. a. 750

    b. 75

    c. 7.5

12. a. 9,600

    b. 960

    c. 96

13. a. 1,000.0

    b. 100.00

    c. 10.0

    d. 0.1

    e. 0.01

    f. 0.001

14. c. There are 25.4 mm to the inch.
$35 \text{ mm} \div 25.4 = 1.37 \text{ inches}$

15. 1 kilometer = 1,000 meters
$1,500 \text{ m} \div 1,000 \text{ km/m} = 1.5 \text{ or } 1\text{-}1/2 \text{ km}$

16. c. 1 km = about 0.6 miles, therefore 1-1/2 km = 0.9 miles
To be more exact: 1,500 meters = $1.5 \text{ km} \times 0.621$ or 0.9315 miles

17. c. 1 meter = 1.09 yards
200 meters = 218 yards
$218 \div 20 = 10.9$, or about 11 lengths of the pool

18. $3,400 \text{ km} \times 0.621$, or about 2,111 miles

19. $3,400 \times 1,000 = 3,400,000 \text{ m}$

20. $3 \text{ m} \times 3 \text{ m} = 9 \text{ m}^2$

21. 1 m = 1,000 mm
Therefore: $1 \text{ m} \times 1 \text{ m} = 1,000 \text{ mm} \times 1,000 \text{ mm} = 1,000,000 \text{ mm}^2$

22. 1m = 10 dm
Therefore: $1 \text{ m} \times 1 \text{ m} = 10 \text{ dm} \times 10 \text{ dm} = 100 \text{ dm}^2$

23. $1.5 \text{ m} \times 0.5 \text{ m} = 150 \text{ cm} \times 50 \text{ cm} = 7,500 \text{ cm}^2$

24. $1 \text{ yd.}^2 = 0.836127 \text{ m}^2$
$4,840 \text{ yd.}^2 \times 0.836127 = \text{approximately } 4,046.85 \text{ m}^2$

25. $1 \div 0.4 = 2.5$ acres

26. $15 \times 0.4 = 6$ hectares

27. a. finding acres:
   1 sq. yd. = 9 sq. ft.   4,840 sq. yd. = 1 acre
   Therefore: 217,800 sq. ft. $\div$ 9 = 24,200 sq. yd.   24,200 sq. yd. $\div$ 4,840 = 5 acres

   b. finding ares and hectares:
   1 acre = 40 ares
   Therefore: 5 acres $\times$ 40 = 200 ares

   c. 1 acre = 0.4 hectares
   5 acres $\times$ 0.4 = 2 hectares

28. a. 1 km = 0.621 mile
   1.6 km $\times$ 0.621 = approximately 1 mile

   b. 0.4 hectare = 1 acre

   c. 1.2 hectares $\div$ 0.4 = 3 acres

29. $1 \text{ are} = 100 \text{ m}^2$
$25 \text{ m} \times 100 \text{ m} = 2,500 \text{ m}^2$ $2,500 \text{ m}^2 \div 100 = 25 \text{ ares}$
The lot is worth 25 $\times$ \$1,000 or \$25,000.

TABLES OF MEASURE

Measures of Length

1 foot (ft.) = 12 inches (in.)
1 yard (yd.) = 3 feet (ft.)
1 rod (rd.) = 5-1/2 yards
1 rod = 16-1/2 feet
1 mile (mi.) = 5,280 ft.
1 mile = 320 rods (rd.)
1 chain = 66 feet
1 chain = 4 rods
4 rods = 100 links
1 link = 7.92 inches
1 vara = 33-1/3 inches (Texas)

Measures of Surface (Square Measure)

1 square foot (sq. ft.) = 144 square inches (sq. in.)
1 square yard (sq. yd.) = 9 square feet (sq. ft.)
1 square rod (sq. rd.) = 30-1/4 square yards (sq. yd.)
1 township = 36 sections
1 section = 1 square mile (sq. mi.)
1 square mile = 640 acres
1 acre = 43,560 square feet
1 acre = 10 square chains

Circular Measure

area = 3.14 × radius × radius
360 degrees (°) = 1 circle
90 degrees (°) = 1/4 circle
1 degree (°) = 60 minutes (')
1 minute (') = 60 seconds ('')

FORMULAS

Percentages

$$total = \frac{part}{percent}$$

$$percent = \frac{part}{total}$$

$$part = percent \times total$$

Interest

principal × rate × time = interest

$$PRT = I \qquad \frac{I}{RT} = P$$

$$\frac{I}{PT} = R \qquad \frac{I}{PR} = T$$

Area and Volume

area of a rectangle = length × width
area of a triangle = 1/2 (base × height)
volume of a rectangular prism = length × width × height
volume of a triangular prism = 1/2 (base × height × width)

Income Approach to Appraising

$$\frac{net\ income}{rate\ of\ return} = value$$

$$\frac{I}{R} = V \qquad \frac{I}{V} = R \qquad V \times R = I$$

Cost Approach Method of Appraising

land value + building replacement cost − depreciation = estimated value

Straight-Line Method of Computing Depreciation

$$\frac{replacement\ cost}{years\ of\ useful\ life} = annual\ depreciation\ charge \qquad or \qquad \frac{100\%}{years\ of\ useful\ life} = depreciation\ rate$$

percent of depreciation × building replacement cost = total depreciation

---

ELLWOOD TABLES

Table	"Name"	Formula
1	Savings account	$FV = PV \times f$
2	Christmas Club	$FV = Pmt \times f$
3	Sinking fund	$Pmt = FV \times f$
4	Reversion	$PV = FV \times f$
5	Annuity	$PV = Pmt \times f$
6	Amortization	$Pmt = PV \times f$

PV = Present value
FV = Future value
Pmt = Payment

More Real Estate Books That Help You Get Ahead

15-DAY FREE EXAMINATION ORDER CARD

810060

Please send me the books I have indicated. I'll receive a refund with no further obligation for any books I return within the 15-day period.

Just detach, sign and mail today to:

Real Estate Education Company
a division of
Longman Financial Services Institute, Inc.
520 North Dearborn Street
Chicago, Illinois 60610-4975

☐ Please send me your latest catalog.
☐ Please send me more information on the Longman Investor Bookshelf.

NAME_____

ADDRESS _____

CITY/STATE/ZIP _____

TELEPHONE(   ) _____

TEXTBOOKS

		Order #		Price	Total Amount
☐	1.	1970-04	Questions & Answers to Help You Pass the Real Estate Exam, 3rd ed.	$21.95	_____
☐	2.	1970-02	Guide To Passing the Real Estate Exam (ACT), 3rd ed.	$21.95	_____
☐	3.	1970-01	The Real Estate Education Company Exam Manual, 4th ed. (ETS)	$19.95	_____
☐	4.	1970-06	Real Estate Exam Guide (ASI), 2nd ed.	$21.95	_____
☐	5.	1970-03	How To Prepare for the Texas Real Estate Exam, 3rd ed.	$19.95	_____
☐	6.	1556-10	Fundamentals of Real Estate Appraisal, 4th ed.	$34.95	_____
☐	7.	1557-10	Essentials of Real Estate Finance, 5th ed.	$38.95	_____
☐	8.	1559-01	Essentials of Real Estate Investment, 3rd ed.	$34.95	_____
☐	9.	1513-01	Real Estate Fundamentals, 3rd ed.	$22.95	_____
☐	10.	1551-10	Property Management, 3rd ed.	$34.95	_____
☐	11.	1560-01	Real Estate Law, 2nd ed.	$38.95	_____
☐	12.	1965-01	Real Estate Brokerage: A Success Guide, 2nd ed.	$35.95	_____
☐	13.	1510-01	Modern Real Estate Practice, 11th ed.	$32.95	_____
☐	14.	1510-	Supplements for Modern Real Estate Practice are available for many states. Indicate the state you're interested in _____	$10.95	_____
☐	15.	1510-02	Modern Real Estate Practice Study Guide, 11th ed.	$13.95	_____
☐	16.	1961-01	The Language of Real Estate, 3rd ed.	$26.95	_____
☐	17.	1512-10	Mastering Real Estate Mathematics, 5th ed.	$25.95	_____
☐	18.	1560-08	Agency Relationships in Real Estate	$24.95	_____

PROFESSIONAL BOOKS

				Price	
☐	19.	1913-01	List for Success	$18.95	_____
☐	20.	1913-04	Close for Success	$18.95	_____
☐	21.	1913-03	How to Avoid the 10 Biggest Home-Buying Traps, Revised Ed.	$11.95	_____
☐	22.	1913-02	The Complete Guide to Factory-Made Houses, Revised Ed.	$11.95	_____
☐	23.	1926-01	Classified Secrets, 2nd ed.	$29.95	_____
☐	24.	1907-01	Power Real Estate Listing, 2nd ed.	$16.95	_____
☐	25.	1907-02	Power Real Estate Selling, 2nd ed.	$16.95	_____
☐	26.	5606-24	The Mortgage Kit	$14.95	_____
☐	27.	4105-07	How To Profit from Real Estate	$19.95	_____
☐	28.	4105-06	How To Sell Apartment Buildings	$19.95	_____
☐	29.	4105-08	Landlord's Handbook	$19.95	_____
☐	30.	1913-05	The Complete Homeseller's Kit	$14.95	_____
☐	31.	1909-01	New Home Sales	$24.95	_____
☐	32.	1909-03	New Home Marketing	$34.95	_____
☐	33.	1922-02	Successful Leasing and Selling of Office Property, 3rd. ed.	$34.95	_____
☐	34.	1922-01	Successful Industrial Real Estate Brokerage	$34.95	_____
☐	35.	1978-02	The Recruiting Revolution in Real Estate	$34.95	_____

Book Total _____

PAYMENT MUST ACCOMPANY ALL ORDERS:

(check one)

☐ Check or money order payable to
Real Estate Education Company

☐ Charge to my credit card
(circle one) **VISA** or **MasterCard** or **AMEX**

Account No. _____ Exp. date _____

Signature _____
ALL CHARGE ORDERS MUST BE SIGNED.

Or call toll-free 1-800-621-9621, ext. 650;
In Illinois, 1-800-654-8596, ext. 650 (charge orders only)

Also available at your local bookstore.

Orders shipped to the following states must include applicable sales tax:
AZ, CA, CO, CT, IL, MI, MN, NJ, NY, PA, TX, VA and WI.   _____

Add postage
and handling   _____
(see chart)

Total   _____

TOTAL BOOK PURCHASE	SHIPPING & HANDLING CHARGES
$ 00.00- 24.99	$ 4.00
$ 25.00- 49.99	5.00
$ 50.00- 99.99	6.00
$100.00-249.99	8.00
$250.00 and over	11.00

PRICES SUBJECT TO CHANGE WITHOUT NOTICE

Real Estate Education Company

LONGMAN
WHERE EXPERTS BEGIN

REAL ESTATE EDUCATION COMPANY

PROPERTY MANAGEMENT, 3rd Edition,

by Robert C. Kyle, with Floyd M. Baird, RPA/SMA, Contributing Editor

The revised third edition presents management techniques for apartment buildings, co-ops, condominiums, office buildings, and commerical and industrial properties. Includes steps for creating a management plan and discussions of how to handle owner/tenant relations, leasing procedures, marketing space, and other problems. *Property Management's* popular, practical approach to management is enhanced by numerous sample forms, ads, and charts.

Key features added to the third edition:
• discussion of single family homes—how they differ from apartments, vacation homes, and timeshare properties
• section on trust relationships
• coverage of the "intelligent building," including maintenance of automation systems, tele-communications, and office automation
• discussion of industrial development incentives, including industrial revenue bonds, foreign trade zones, and others

Check box #10 on the order card. $34.95   **Order Number 1551-10**   **copyright 1988**

ESSENTIALS OF REAL ESTATE INVESTMENT, 3rd Edition,

by David Sirota

Completely updated and reorganized, the third edition provides the most timely treatment available of an area of real estate that is constantly changing. Effects of the 1986 Tax Reform Act on the real estate investment process and its applications are fully explained.

Third edition highlights include:
• financing and insurance topics consolidated into one chapter
• additional discussion of defaults and foreclosures
• updated coverage of S Corporations—*vis-a-vis* the Subchapter S Revision Act and 1986 Tax Reform Act
• explanation of how the Uniform Partnership Act controls partnerships

Check box #8 on the order card. $34.95   **Order Number 1559-01**   **copyright 1988**

REAL ESTATE BROKERAGE: A SUCCESS GUIDE, 2nd Edition,

by John E. Cyr and Joan m. Sobeck

Newly published in its second edition, this text sets the industry standard on opening and operating a real estate brokerage office. Revised and updated to reflect today's market, it features coverage of such timely topics as agency and the effects of the 1986 Tax Reform Act. Also included is a new chapter focusing on industry trends.

Key features of the second edition include:
• presentation of agency and the law
• discussion of one-appointment approach to obtaining listings (in addition to two-appointment method)
• changes resulting from the 1986 Tax Reform Act—revised income tax deductions related to brokers' expenses, effects on investor ownership, depreciation, maintenance, refinancing, and installment sales
• glossary

Check box #12 on the order card. $35.95   **Order Number 1965-01**   **copyright 1988**

AGENCY RELATIONSHIPS IN REAL ESTATE

By John W. Reilly

This timely book explains all of the real estate agent's basic relationships with buyers and sellers of real estate—including the hot topic of "dual agency"—in clearly written, nontechnical language. The text also fully discusses kinds of services offered to clients, as opposed to customers, as well as types of agency representation a broker may choose to offer. Practical information on how to avoid misrepresentations is also presented.

Agency Relationships in Real Estate features:
• extensive appendix on all U.S. cases involving agency
• in-text situations and examples that highlight and emphasize key points
• checklists that show the agent's responsibilities and obligations
• quiz and discussion questions that reinforce important concepts

Check box #18 on order card $24.95   **Order Number 1560-08**   **copyright 1987**

 Real Estate Education Co.

LONGMAN
WHERE EXPERTS BEGIN